Books by LEWIS COTLOW

PASSPORT TO ADVENTURE

AMAZON HEAD-HUNTERS

ZANZABUKU

IN SEARCH OF THE PRIMITIVE

IN SEARCH OF
THE PRIMITIVE

LEWIS COTLOW

IN SEARCH OF
THE PRIMITIVE

With Photographs

LITTLE, BROWN AND COMPANY
BOSTON - TORONTO

Portions of this book have been published previously. We are grateful
to Holt, Rinehart and Winston, Inc. for permission to include material
from *Amazon Head-Hunters* by Lewis Cotlow; and to Holt, Rinehart
and Winston, Inc. and Robert Hale Ltd. for permission to include
material from *Zanzabuku* by Lewis Cotlow. Copyright 1953, © 1956
by Lewis N. Cotlow. Reprinted by permission of Holt, Rinehart and
Winston, Inc. and Robert Hale Ltd.

Of the photographs in this book, five appeared previously in *Amazon
Head-Hunters* by Lewis Cotlow, and seven in *Zanzabuku* by Lewis
Cotlow. Copyright 1953, © 1956 by Lewis N. Cotlow. Reproduced
by permission of Holt, Rinehart and Winston, Inc.

The maps on pages 2, 170, 286, and 402 were prepared by Caru
Studios, Inc.

*Published simultaneously in Canada
by Little, Brown & Company (Canada) Limited*

PRINTED IN THE UNITED STATES OF AMERICA

To: Chief Ukumhearik of the Dani tribe in the Baliem Valley of New Guinea, and the late Chiefs Peruche and Utitiaja of the Jivaro headhunting tribes of the upper Amazon—exemplars of the primitive

Acknowledgments

NO explorer can do his work alone, even when he travels alone. Without the help of many people, I could not have made one of my expeditions, but to list all these men and women would take more pages and make duller reading than I want to be responsible for. But most of those who helped, and what they did for me, are mentioned in the course of the book. In addition to these, I want to express my gratitude to:

General Matthew B. Ridgway, former Chief of Staff of the United States Army, for opening many doors and smoothing my path on my third expeditions both to South America and to Africa.

General Sir Dudley Ward, former Deputy Chief of the Imperial Army, and the late Sir Geoffrey de Havilland, whose letters to East Africa unrolled several red carpets on that rough terrain.

The Chrysler Corporation, which contributed the remarkable Dodge trucks on my expedition filming *Zanzabuku*.

RKO Radio Pictures, for permission to reproduce some still pictures from *Savage Splendor*, the film made in the course of the Armand Denis–Lewis Cotlow African expedition; and from *Jungle Head-hunters*, the film of my explorations in South America.

Republic Pictures, for permission to reproduce some still pictures from my African film *Zanzabuku*.

Harry C. Mills, a valued friend who first suggested an association with Republic Pictures in making *Zanzabuku* and then guided me in it.

The staff of the American Museum of Natural History, many of whom are mentioned in this book, but whose unfailing help cannot be overemphasized.

The patrol officers, district commissioners, and other officials of the Department of Native Affairs in New Guinea, whose ever-ready and cheerful help made possible my filming of *Primitive Paradise*.

Brigadier Sir Donald Mackinnon Cleland, Territorial Administrator of Papua – New Guinea.

A. H. L. Lovink, Netherlands Ambassador formerly to Australia, now to Canada.

Sir Percy C. Spender, formerly Australian Ambassador to the United States, now President of the International Court of Justice, The Hague.

Randal Heymanson, C.B.E., President, American-Australian Association.

The corporals and fliers of the Royal Canadian Mounted Police, who made it possible for me to film *The High Arctic*.

Commissioner (now retired) C. W. Harvison, Superintendent W. G. Fraser, and Superintendent J. T. Parsons, all of the Royal Canadian Mounted Police.

James Houston, Canadian Civil Administrator in the Arctic, 1951-1962, for valuable suggestions and increased understanding of the Eskimos.

Edward Weyer, Jr., who was for many years on the staff of the American Museum of Natural History, for reading the first draft of this manuscript and offering many helpful suggestions.

Marshall McClintock, for editorial help in preparing this book.

LEWIS COTLOW

How It All Started

ALL my friends in Kenya had warned me against trying to enter the Congo, and they were not the kind to exaggerate danger. They had lived through the Mau Mau terror, and I had been in Kenya at the peak of its ferocity.

Yet one night in the spring of 1964 I sat in the heart of the Congo's Ituri Forest, facing three Pygmies across a glowing fire, listening to them tell wonderful stories of the most exciting events in their lives — elephant hunts. After turning in for the night, I could not sleep. I heard the eerie sounds of the living forest, but it had no answer for the question that was nagging me — "What on earth am I doing here?"

It struck me as incredible that I should be in this tropical forest in a new African nation that was seething with rebellion, tribal wars, and a consuming hatred of the white man. Despite the advice of people who knew the situation better than I — and despite the shrieking headlines — I went in. Ironically, the Ituri Forest itself was a safe place. Few besides the primitive Pygmies and a handful of missionaries dared penetrate it more than a few yards. But what, I wondered, would I run into when I left the forest sanctuary? The territory around it — the home ground of the murdered Patrice Lumumba — was charged with unrest. Stanleyville was a time bomb.

It helped little to give myself the obvious answer: that I had come to see the Pygmies — which is much like saying that one climbs the mountain because it is there. I had already seen the Pygmies on three journeys into the forest, had learned to admire them, and had seen them adjust to *uhuru* — freedom — and to the chaos of war outside their hunting grounds.

Indeed you may want to know, why had I gone to visit the Pygmies in the first place, back in 1937? For that matter, why had I traveled to Jivaro headhunter country at the headwaters of the Amazon, filmed the newly discovered Stone Age men of the New Guinea highlands, visited the northernmost settlement of the world where Eskimos still lived as their ancestors had?

When World War I ended, I was in Walter Reed Hospital with the flu. Discharged from both hospital and the army, I decided to stay in Washington rather than return to my native New York. I was twenty years old, had almost no money, and wanted to continue my education. So I entered night classes at George Washington University and got a job as secretary and then, within a few weeks, as assistant to a United States Shipping Board supervisor.

The Board was in charge of a fleet of about twelve hundred ships the government had built during the war, many of them fine new freighters. Turning these over to private shipping companies to operate, the government retained ownership and shared with the companies any profits accruing from their operation. To protect its interests, the government put a representative, called a supercargo, aboard most ships. This man was in charge of all business matters concerning cargoes and ship repairs, and also investigated and photographed harbor facilities wherever his ship touched. He occupied the owner's cabin, dined with the captain, and received a good salary, plus expenses when ashore.

I wanted desperately to become a supercargo, but there were few openings, and I was several years younger and much less experienced than the men holding such jobs. But after a few months, my boss recommended me for an opening, and I went aboard the *Saco*, bound for Danzig, as supercargo. The captain, an old Yankee salt, resented sharing any authority with a twenty-one-year-old upstart who had never been to sea. I really couldn't blame him for being angry at having to consult me when he loaded or discharged his cargo, made repairs, or took on fuel, but I had a job to do and I meant to do it. The captain never missed a chance to show contempt and indignation, but the other officers were friendly. And in Danzig I proved my usefulness by cabling a report on the docking facilities that saved the Shipping Board a considerable amount of money.

My next trip as supercargo was on the *West Hampton*, whose captain was affable and helpful. For two and a half months we sailed the

Mediterranean. We anchored at Venice, where, after finishing my business chores, I was able to visit the canals and piazzas of that beautiful city. While the ship waited several weeks for a return cargo, I visited Florence, Rome, and Naples.

Back in the United States, I had a two-week breather before joining the *West Conob* in San Francisco for a trip to the Orient. A violent storm made me wretchedly ill for ten days, but also drove the ship so far off course that we put in at Honolulu, where I recuperated quickly. Although we ran into another bad storm after putting to sea again, I withstood it well enough to catch my first glimpse of Japan from the deck — snow-clad Fujiyama floating above the horizon.

After we had docked at Yokohama and I had performed my duties connected with entering a port, I sent off a letter of introduction from a friend to an American-educated Japanese merchant. The next day he and his kimono-clad wife came to the ship, and were more hospitable than anyone could have expected. They took me to see the great Buddha at Kamakura and to the island of Enoshima in the Inland Sea, where I was introduced to the Japanese custom of mixed bathing in nearly boiling water.

Our next port was Kobe, where we encountered delays in taking on cargo, enabling me to visit Nikko, in a most beautiful forest, Osaka, Tokyo, and Kyoto — the last my favorite Japanese city. In this cultural center of the nation, I began my collection of Oriental works of art and started taking photographs for my own pleasure. By the time we sailed for Shanghai I was deeply and irretrievably enchanted with Japan.

After Shanghai came Hong Kong, where we were laid up for a month for repairs. I became well acquainted with the main streets and back alleys of that amazing crossroads of the world, and spent two exciting days in nearby Canton. We sailed on to Saigon, then back to San Francisco by way of Manila and Honolulu.

The Shipping Board then decided to send the *West Conob* on a pioneering voyage around the world to investigate the possibilities of a regular round-the-world service, with the ship picking up and discharging cargoes at various ports of call as it proceeded around the globe.

Our first port was Yokohama, where delays in unloading our cargo of tin plate made it possible for me to do more traveling and photographing in Japan. Next we sailed to Tientsin, China, where we unloaded grape juice, canned milk, and other foods. Down the coast to Hong Kong we went, picking up tea for the Philippines, where we took on coconut oil for Barcelona, gum opal for Marseilles, automobile parts for Calcutta, embroidery for Port Said, and cigars for Singapore.

In Singapore I missed my ship and caught up with it only after a frightening night trip through the treacherous Malacca Straits in a small boat manned by two Malayans who spoke no English. At Calcutta a strike of longshoremen delayed the loading of four thousand tons of gunny sacks for New York, so I was able to visit the Taj Mahal, sacred Benares, Allahabad, Delhi, and the Vale of Kashmir.

After leaving Calcutta we made short stops at Colombo, Ceylon, and at Bombay, then spent a few weeks in Karachi, in what is now Pakistan, where I investigated and photographed its harbor facilities. We sailed across the Indian Ocean, through the Red Sea and Suez Canal into the Mediterranean. At Piraeus, the port of Athens, we found no cargo. The same discouraging situation greeted us in Naples. We discharged our cargoes at Marseilles and Barcelona, picked up a few thousand barrels of grapes at Malaga, and sailed for home. The pioneer round-the-world freighter service was not successful, but I had seen something of the world.

The postwar depression was affecting business everywhere, and strikes were causing costly delays in many ports visited by our ships. I realized that the Shipping Board's operations would soon stop, but I held on to the bitter end. My last two trips as a supercargo took me to South America, where I visited Rio de Janeiro, Santos, Montevideo and Buenos Aires. The last cargo consisted of hides and wheat, which we took to Rotterdam and Hamburg. There we encountered the usual delays, allowing me to visit Paris and Berlin for the first time.

Then it was all over. The merchant marine went into mothballs. I had no job. But I had a taste for travel and a curiosity about the world that could never be wholly satisfied. I was twenty-four years old, with a specialized training for which there was no demand. I had to start from scratch, but fortunately six thousand dollars in savings let me pick and choose for a while. I hoped to find a career that would, if I worked hard and made good, make it possible for me to do more traveling. Travel demanded two things — time and money. What field might possibly give me both?

After turning down two good fifty-weeks-a-year jobs and weighing the conflicting advice of friends and relatives, I decided on insurance. At first it sounded as prosaic to me as it does to most people, but the more I looked, the more factors I found in its favor, at least for me. I was interested in people, and life insurance concerns human beings as closely as anything, outside of medicine, the law, and social work. And if I worked hard, trained a good staff, and made good, I could eventually take off two or three months a year for travel, without jeopardizing my income or my clients' interests.

I started to work and went back to school, at New York University. I lived frugally, worked diligently, and found the business more and more interesting as I moved ahead. After five years, when I was thirty years old, I was over the hump, with sales of more than a million dollars' worth of insurance.

About this time, a friend asked me to lecture about my travels before her women's club. I was reluctant, but decided that I could put together a talk on Japan with slides from the many photographs I had taken there. But since I had never lectured before, I sought some expert advice from Burton Holmes, whose travelogues had always fascinated and inspired me. He was most helpful, and advised me to have my black-and-white slides hand-colored. (I was able to repay Holmes some years later, when he used some of my motion-picture footage from South America in one of his travelogues.)

Despite my nervousness, the lecture was warmly received — so much so that a visiting guest asked me to lecture before *her* club. After several such talks, rewarded with cups of tea and tiny sandwiches, I wondered if I should be more professional. A lecture agent said I should. He printed a leaflet, and booked me to lecture on "The Soul of Japan" in a number of Eastern cities.

Next I started to travel again. At first I took two months off every year, then gradually increased my travel time. I visited the places I had missed as supercargo — Iceland, the Scandinavian countries, Russia, the British Isles, Germany, France, the Balkan States. In 1935 I went back to Japan for more material for my lecture, and revisited China. In Peiping and other places I added not only to my photographic files — by this time movies as well as stills — but also to my art collection, with some fine jade pieces, porcelains, and bronzes. From China I went to Manchukuo, then by train across Siberia to Russia.

During these travels I met archeologists, anthropologists, and explorers, who talked to me about their work in lands off the beaten track. Their stories of primitive tribes, wild animals, tropical forests, and the ways of living far from civilization fascinated me. I realized that, despite all my extensive travels, I had not even glimpsed more than half of the world, had never met the most unusual people on earth.

So I was ripe for the ringing words of Jan Smuts when he spoke at a luncheon of the Foreign Policy Association in 1936. "Come to Africa!" he urged. "Come to Africa before it is too late!"

He described its rich animal life, its forests, mountains, and plains. He spoke of the many tribes still living as they had since the Stone Age. And he warned that civilization, probing ever more deeply and rapidly, would bring the curtain down on the primitive world within a couple of decades.

I spent hours at the library reading about Africa. I spent more hours in the African Hall of the American Museum of Natural History, and came to know many of the fine staff of that museum, all of whom were encouraging and helpful. I met Martin Johnson, who went over his maps with me, pointing out places of special interest and giving advice on equipment, cameras, and film. I met Attilio Gatti, who had just returned from several years in the Belgian Congo. He showed me his pictures and told me about many primitive tribes, especially the Pygmies of the Ituri Forest. He spoke of the gorillas that lived on the mountains around Lake Kivu, of the rare and once legendary okapi, of elephants and buffalo and hippos and other wild creatures of the continent that is richest in animal life.

His enthusiasm was contagious. Before I left him, I knew that I would go to Africa.

But there were many problems I had not faced in my earlier travels. How much would a trip into equatorial Africa cost? I found little helpful advice from the explorers I consulted. They were scientists who had the financial backing of museums, universities, or foundations. They had trucks, and armies of native bearers when they left their trucks behind. They could tell me what such large-scale operations might cost, but not the expenses of one man setting out with limited equipment and a modest goal. All I could do was to play it by ear, making up new tunes as I went along. If a project cost too much I would have to abandon it. When I ran out of money I would come home.

I made arrangements to have a small truck and native driver, with the necessary equipment, waiting for me at Juba in southern Sudan, a stopover on the Cairo-to-Capetown route of British Imperial Airways' flying boats. From Juba we could drive into the Belgian Congo, then to Uganda, Kenya, and Tanganyika.

Since I wanted to make a photographic record of my trip, I had two 16-millimeter movie cameras and two still cameras. I would have liked to use color film, because everyone who talked to me about Africa spoke of its color. But I had tried color film and had found that in time the color faded badly. Explorers I consulted had had the same experience, especially when the film was used in the tropics. I resigned myself to black-and-white film.

Then, two days before I was to sail, a client with whom I had lunch told me of some remarkable new improvements in Kodachrome, especially regarding its stability against heat and humidity. I telephoned the Eastman company and ordered three thousand feet of the new film, to be packed for the tropics and delivered to me on the *Conti di Savoia*. Eastman said it would do its best.

As the gangplank was being hauled away from the ship, a messenger appeared, running and shouting. The gangplank went back down, the messenger clambered aboard, and I had my film. That's how close I came to missing the distinction of being the first exhibitor of reliable color film from equatorial Africa.

But my good luck did not hold. In Rome, Imperial Airways informed me that I could not land at Juba because the company's new and larger flying boats could not set down there during the low-water season. The nearest landing was at Entebbe, Uganda, on Lake Victoria, about five hundred miles south of Juba.

Here was my first chance to make up new tunes as I went along. I was dismayed, but boarded the plane for Entebbe and flew right over my truck, driver, and supplies at Juba, sight unseen. But I did see my first elephants, as we flew over the Sudd, a vast expanse of papyrus and grass in the Sudan. The pilot dropped down so I could photograph them — a herd of about a hundred that panicked as the plane roared above them.

Next I saw the northern end of Victoria Nyanza. This vast body of blue water extends two hundred fifty miles southward — the largest lake in Africa, second largest in the world. Rolling slopes lead down to its many bays, and it usually looks placid. But some of its shores are papyrus-filled swamps. Some are mountains rising three thousand feet above its water level, which is almost four thousand feet above sea level. Sudden violent storms can toss small boats about as if they were peanut shells. And there are always crocodiles waiting to welcome you if you go overboard.

But as we circled for a landing all was peaceful. I saw villages of beehive huts along the shore and on some islands. And there, on a promontory jutting into the lake, I saw Entebbe, Britain's administrative capital in Uganda (then a protectorate, but since 1962 an independent nation).

Two very young and very British officials took me from the plane to shore in a small rowboat. "You are the explorer we were told about," they said as they welcomed me with tea in their offices. "What can we do to help you?"

It was the first time I had been called an explorer. I had been just a traveler, interested in seeing new places, new people. But if leaving the traveler's track made me an explorer, so be it. I would try to be a good one.

In Search of the Primitive recounts the adventures, perils and rewards of a lifetime of travel and exploration. I would not exchange those experiences for anything in the world. Exciting in themselves, they were also a liberal education — the kind that will soon, alas, no longer be available, for the domain of the truly primitive is shrinking day by day. Some of my explorations were described in three earlier books: *Passport to Adventure, Amazon Head-Hunters,* and *Zanzabuku.* Since the present book is designed to be a comprehensive summation of my entire career as an explorer, I have not hesitated to borrow from my other books, but in doing so I discovered an interesting thing about myself: even where I have not altered the presentation of certain events, I found that my attitude had undergone a subtle change. From my present vantage point I can, in retrospect, discern a pattern that was not apparent to me at the time, and this new awareness has found expression in the present volume. Though it saddens me to admit this to myself, it is unlikely that I will undertake in future the kind of trip it has been my pleasure to record on film and in writing. Such rigors are for younger men. I wish them well. And I hope that, like me, their search for the primitive will lead them to the discovery of uncharted areas within themselves.

Contents

Illustrations

Maps

I
AFRICA

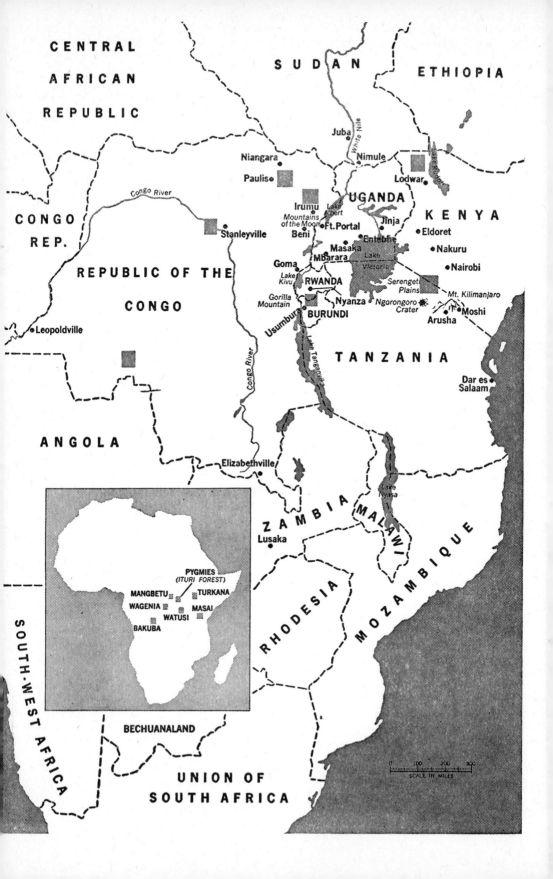

1

Through Africa Unarmed

KAMPALA, the largest city and now the capital of Uganda, was the jumping-off place for my first trip into equatorial Africa, in 1937. It was far from primitive, boasting a comfortable hotel, three banks, a drugstore, hundreds of shops, and crowded traffic — consisting chiefly of shoeless dark-skinned men on bicycles and dignified, graceful women in colorful, toga-like robes or gowns.

In the stores I found all the equipment I needed. But my most important find in Kampala was Cézaire. He was a slender, soft-spoken Belgian in his early thirties who had been placer-mining — unsuccessfully — in Central Africa for several years. He spoke English, French, and several native dialects of the regions through which I wanted to travel. More important, he owned a car, an old Chevrolet sedan with a rack on top, a tent strapped along one side, and room for luggage and several extra five-gallon tins of gasoline. Most important, Cézaire and I hit it off well after only a few minutes' talk. We came to an agreement quickly and spent the next four months together.

We headed west from Kampala on a red dirt road that within two hours turned into a narrow tunnel through green walls; it had been a footpath or animal track not too many years before. I had one of my Bell and Howell movie cameras on the seat beside me, a Leica hanging from my neck. I was ready for the primitive world I was so eager to see. But I was still startled at my first sight of it, in the form of three elephants whose gray-black heads and backs loomed above the tall grass a short distance away from the road. I wanted to record on film

my introduction to the wilderness and wild things, so I signaled Cézaire to stop the car.

He reminded me that we had no guns, as he had advised waiting
until reaching the Congo before buying them. But I saw no evidence
of young elephants about — elephants are most dangerous when they
have young to look out for — and decided to go ahead. I circled a bit
against the wind and managed to get a good shot of the animals with
my telephoto lens from about one hundred fifty yards.

When we drove on, I could see that Cézaire was worried about
being the guide of an overeager amateur who might get two men
killed.

"Don't worry, Cézaire," I said. "I won't take any foolish chances.
But I'm not going to miss any good bets just to make sure I'm a hundred per cent safe, either. We take calculated risks every day back in
the civilized world."

"Sure, because you *know* the civilized world. You don't know this
world — yet. I'd like to see you live to enjoy it and understand it. And,
incidentally, I'd like to keep on living myself. You know, lots of men
have been killed by elephants. Why, even Carl Akeley — the greatest
of them all — missed being killed only by a fluke."

I knew the story. The great naturalist's escape from a charging elephant was a classic of African adventure. As the huge beast lunged at
him, Akeley seized its tusks, one in each hand, and pushed down with
all his might to drive the tusks into the ground. He succeeded, but the
elephant toppled forward in a somersault above him. Akeley flattened
himself, but the weight of the animal drove its tusks deeper. When
its head was just a couple of inches above Akeley's body, the tusks hit
a rock and sank no further. The elephant fell with an earth-shaking
thud, banging the naturalist on the way. Then the beast yanked its
tusks from the ground, got to its feet, and tromped away. Akeley's
helpers ran to revive him.

"But Akeley had been tracking the elephant," I told Cézaire. "The
elephant had doubled back on its tracks and attacked Akeley from the
rear. I'm not going to bother any elephant that much. I just want some
good pictures. Anyway, I heard in Kampala that if a man hugs a tree,
an elephant will probably pass by without noticing him."

Cézaire asked me to look around for trees. There were none.

But I recalled the story about the native cyclist who was coasting down a steep hill, came around a bend, and saw an elephant directly ahead. He couldn't stop, so he just rang his bicycle bell for all he was worth, and the elephant rushed off into the bush. I took most of these tales with considerable salt — although the Akeley story was true — but when I later came to know Commandant Ernest Hubert of the Albert National Park in the Congo, I felt I could believe anything. He had stopped a charging hippo by waving his arms wildly and shouting, "Hey! Hey!" He had chased other wild animals by throwing chunks of mud at them. He once frightened away a lion by holding up his hand imperiously and shouting, "Stop!"

Cézaire and I reached the town of Fort Portal, center of an area of coffee plantations, just as the sun was setting on our first day's travel in Uganda. The small Busirasagama Rest House offered a fair dinner and adequate accommodations, but the colobus monkeys living in the trees surrounding the house chattered and jabbered most of the night. I finally fell asleep shortly before dawn, only to be awakened in about an hour by the innkeeper, who wanted me to see the sun rise over Mt. Margherita, highest peak in the Ruwenzori range. These mountains were so often blanketed with clouds that they were not visible for weeks at a time, so I was glad to see them, even at the cost of a few hours' much desired sleep.

When we arrived the night before, it had been so nearly dark that the mountains had seemed only a huge black mass, and I was not prepared for the majestic sight that greeted me in the morning. And I was even less prepared because I knew that I was just one-half a degree north of the equator — and the equator meant to me what it means to most people, burning sands or dense tropical jungles. But what I saw was like the Alps or the Himalayas — a huge and imposing mass of earth from which peaks of unbelievable grandeur rose to heights of more than fifteen thousand feet. Margherita, one of the twin peaks composing Mt. Stanley (itself one of the six mountains in the range) shot its glistening spire 16,814 feet into the sky, higher than any of its neighbors. The top two thousand feet was covered with snow and glaciers, which were frosty pink in the light of the rising sun.

The ancient astronomer Ptolemy called the Ruwenzori the Mountains of the Moon, without having seen them. Or perhaps he had seen them. People of ancient times knew more than we give them credit for;

much of their knowledge was lost forever and some was not rediscovered for centuries. Ptolemy's maps showed a glacier-covered mountain range in the heart of Africa, whose streams were the sources of the Nile. Even before him the Greeks had written that the Nile rose from snow-fed lakes, and later Arab geographers agreed. But until less than a century ago, all this was considered arrant nonsense. Snow-covered mountains on the equator? Glaciers in the heart of tropical Africa? Nothing but ancient myth and legend. When Africans told the first white explorers about snowy peaks in the center of the continent, their tales were dismissed as fantasy. Stanley even camped for some weeks on Ruwenzori's foothills without knowing the peaks were there, for clouds obscured them completely. He saw them later. They were first scaled in 1906.

The Ruwenzori are not volcanic in origin like Kilimanjaro and Kenya, the only two loftier peaks in Africa, or like the Virunga chain farther south, which we were to visit later. They are instead a gigantic upthrust of earth and stone from the surface of the globe, an upheaval of uncertain origin that also formed the great African rifts. A massive crack in the earth, with branching crevices, runs from deep in Africa northward into Asia Minor. The Red Sea is part of it, and probably also the Gulf of Akaba, the Dead Sea, the Jordan Valley, and the Gulf of Galilee. In Central Africa the rift is split in two — on the east, the Great Rift; on the west, the Albertine Rift. Each is a deep trough, sometimes forty miles wide, between two gigantic escarpments a thousand or more feet in height. In the trough lie fertile lands, beautiful lakes, volcanoes active and extinct, and the great mass that is Ruwenzori.

The rift has given us some of the most spectacular beauty in the world, and it has also presented some almost insuperable problems to the invading forces of civilization. When the first railroad in East Africa reached the escarpment, the tracks ended. A thousand feet down on the floor of the trough other tracks were laid. Passengers and goods had to be lowered on cable cars. In time, of course, engineers solved the problem with a series of hairpin bends, which, later, the builders of auto roads followed.

Even though I was no mountain climber, I was tempted by Ruwenzori, for I knew that its slopes harbored rich animal and vegetable life. Elephants, buffaloes, chimpanzees, wild pigs, many kinds of antelope and monkeys lived there. Leopards ranged as high as thirteen thousand feet. In the tropical forests on the mountainsides there were bamboos, palms, ferns of great size, buttercups, daisies, violets, and giant lobelia twenty feet tall. And — very high — green moss, moss eighteen inches thick on tree trunks, moss that the climber had to cut through, even tunnel through. There were deep caves, rushing mountain torrents from the glaciers leaping over ledges in lovely cascades.

But such a climb would take a large party, much equipment, many weeks. I wanted to see too many different things on this first trip to the primitive world — pygmies, giants, fishermen, hunters, and even more varieties of animals than could be found on Ruwenzori. One of the animals I wanted most to see and photograph did not live there — the gorilla.

So we left Fort Portal, skirted the Ruwenzori by going south, then headed west toward the border of the Belgian Congo. We slowed down for a large group of dark men walking along the road. When I saw that they were all quite short, I said hopefully to Cézaire, "Pygmies?"

"Baamba," he replied. "Part Pygmy, part Bantu."

We stopped and talked to the Baamba awhile, and I was delighted to find that Cézaire could communicate with them easily. Although some eight hundred different languages are spoken in Africa, natives and whites have found a way of communicating in a lingua franca introduced by Arab slave traders and by Stanley. His carriers from the east coast spoke Swahili, and a dialect of this simple tongue, called Kingwana, is used throughout Central Africa.

As we left the Baamba, Cézaire asked if I had noticed that their teeth were all filed to sharp points.

I nodded.

"The story is, and it may be true," Cézaire said, "that this is a holdover from the time when this tribe was cannibalistic, and that was not too long ago. Human meat is rather tough, I hear, especially in old adults, the easiest ones to catch."

We did not pursue the subject, but it was one I would encounter in future expeditions, in different parts of the world.

We crossed the border into the Belgian Congo at the little town of Kasindi, where the customs officer turned out to be an old friend of Cézaire's. He asked us to have lunch with him, and we discussed my plans. When I mentioned gorillas, he told me about the new regulations for their protection. No one was allowed to enter any known gorilla country with a gun of any kind. So we again postponed buying guns.

The officer told us that a large herd of buffalo and another of elephants had gone past the town during the night, heading for the Semliki River. "I could hear them a mile away," he said. "If you want to follow them in your car, you might get some good pictures."

He sent a native boy in the car with us to show us the way through the tall elephant grass leading down to the river. By the time we stopped on a steep bank, I had my cameras ready. There were no buffalo or elephants in sight, but a dozen or more hippopotami were basking in the sun at the edge of the water. Not wanting to miss anything, I clambered down the bank for a few shots of the animals. As I started up again, Cézaire shouted at me from the car. I looked up and saw a huge elephant lumbering toward the car along the top of the embankment.

Apparently he had not yet seen the car, for he was shuffling along unconcernedly, his big ears pumping rhythmically to and fro. But he was less than two hundred yards away, and if he wanted to, he could cover that distance fast. I scurried up the bank to the car and leapt in as Cézaire started the motor. The elephant heard it, stopped, and veered off to one side. I learned later that a loud noise from a racing motor is one of the best elephant deterrents.

We were circling around an acacia thorn on our way back to Kasindi when we spotted four elephants, their backs just showing above the grass. I made Cézaire stop so I could get a picture. The boy warned me that I was in the elephants' wind, and Cézaire warned me not to try it, but I insisted. I planned to lift the camera high on its tripod above the grass, which was so tall they would not see me at all. I walked slowly to about a hundred fifty feet from the feeding animals and was lifting the camera when Cézaire shouted to me. One of the elephants had turned to face me. Its trunk was lifted, its great ears outstretched. It was very obviously annoyed. I took to my heels and Cézaire speeded up the engine. As I reached the running board he let in the clutch and we lurched away from four angry elephants.

"Do you see what I mean?" Cézaire asked.

The boy spoke. "There were young ones, too. I saw the backs of the *totos*."

So that was why they were angry. I told Cézaire I realized I had to be more careful, hold down my enthusiasm. He smiled with relief, but I was not sure how well I would be able to control my eagerness.

An hour later, after we had dropped the boy at Kasindi and were heading south toward Beni, a beautiful waterbuck dashed gracefully across the road in front of the car. If Cézaire had slowed down a bit more, I would have jumped out with my camera and tried to follow it. Later, of course, I became used to this business of animals dashing across the road. Many African humans did it too. And they were always too fast for me to get a picture.

We drove to the foot of Mount Bugalamisa, in the Tshibinda Forest a few miles southwest of Lake Kivu. I had learned from H. C. Raven, of the American Museum of Natural History, that this mountain was one of the last natural homes of gorillas. But he had spent two weeks with native Pygmies before he caught sight of one of the beasts. I did not have that much time, but I decided to wait three or four days, hoping to see a gorilla.

We had already made arrangements to stay at an experimental cinchona plantation at the foot of the mountain, operated by a young Luxemburger named Marcel Ernsterhoff, who lived with a dog and a cat and supervised the hundred-odd workmen on the place. His establishment would serve as our base, and he would find Pygmies to lead us up the mountain eight or nine thousand feet, where the gorillas lived.

Of all animals the gorilla is closest to man in many ways, and some people wonder if he might have been an ancestor of ours. He is possibly the smartest primate other than man, even though his brain is only half as large as man's. But his body is twice as big and ten times as strong. A gorilla has a tremendous reach of eight feet. He could twist off your head as easily as you could pick an apple off a branch.

The gorilla loves his wife and children and takes care of them as dutifully as any human being. He doesn't knowingly bother creatures that do not bother him. His footprint shows a heel, and only two living beings have that — men and gorillas. There is one conspicuous though perhaps unimportant difference. The gorilla has hair all over him — *except* on his chest.

Until about a century ago the gorilla was a legend, like the Mountains of the Moon. And he turned out to be just as real as they. Explorers saw skeletons, skins, and finally live gorillas. They even took some young ones to the world's great zoos, but these are usually of the smaller variety found in the plains of the French Cameroons. The giant gorillas live only in the Eastern Congo.

There was nothing I wanted to do quite so much as see and film the mountain gorilla at home. But Ernsterhoff brought me sharply to reality. If a gorilla charged a man without a gun, the man had no chance. And there could be no guns. It was Carl Akeley who had convinced the authorities, some years before, that the gorilla was in danger of extermination. He persuaded the Belgian king to set aside forever the huge tract of land called the Albert National Park as a refuge for all animals, but above all the gorilla. Despite this, gorillas were still shot. Hunters and scientists returned from expeditions into the gorilla mountains claiming that the beasts had charged them. They shot in self-defense. Sometimes the statement was true, sometimes not.

So there was only one sure way to make the world safe for the gorilla — forbid all firearms. If an explorer objected because it was too dangerous to go near gorillas unarmed, the answer was, "Then don't go."

When Ernsterhoff knew that I understood the regulations and the dangers, he was most helpful. He sent one of his boys into the forest for Kasciula, chief of the Pygmies in that area. The man's name was familiar to me, for he had guided Attilio Gatti on his gorilla-hunting expedition and had helped scientists of the American Museum of Natural History. Kasciula had lived in the forest with gorillas all his life. He knew their ways, and he even claimed to know some of the older male apes individually. He knew how to save his own life — so he could save mine. When Pygmies saw or heard signs of gorillas, they usually made a detour. And they knew that gorillas smelling or hearing men in the vicinity made a similar detour. The two varieties of primates had no wish to tangle with each other.

"But you will be tracking them down," Ernsterhoff said. "You want to take pictures of them. They probably won't understand that you want to do nothing else. If you get close enough to take pictures, they will think you mean to attack."

He reassured me somewhat by saying that leopards were far more of a problem to him than gorillas. The big apes came down the mountain now and then to raid the banana groves, after which they scurried up again. But leopards seemed to kill for the joy of it, not always eating all of their kill. (The leopard was for a long time maligned in this way, but recent studies have proved that he hides his catch and finishes eating it later. He does *not* kill for the sake of killing.)

Gorillas living in a gorilla world are among the most peaceful of nature's creatures. They want to be left alone to live their lives in their own fashion. I would leave them alone if they would just let me take a few pictures of them.

The next morning thirteen Pygmies appeared, led by Kasciula himself. Actually they were not true Pygmies — they were a few inches too tall — but they were all around five feet in height. They were a mixture of Pygmy and Bantu, like those we had met on the road. I knew I would meet pure Pygmies later in the Ituri Forest, so all I was concerned with at this time was that these men knew gorillas.

Kasciula gave me great confidence, although I did not know just why. He was spindly-legged, pot-bellied, had a gray kinky beard and a small, bulbous nose. But his eyes were alive, darting, perceptive. And he was relaxed and alert at the same time, as he palavered with Cézaire in basic Kingwana. The business deal was simple and fair. If he and his men led me to gorillas, they would receive three sacks of salt and two dozen tins of tobacco — both highly prized. If they failed, I would give them what I chose.

I looked at the men with Kasciula, and had some misgivings. One was at least twenty years older than the chief, with white hair, white beard, and a body that looked to be no more than a skeleton covered with skin. And then I saw the two boys — they must have been about fourteen years old — who had been brought along, so Kasciula said, for experience. The entire group was armed with what seemed to be fragile weapons against a gorilla — thin wooden-shafted spears, and something called a *mgoosu,* a long wooden handle with iron chopping blade on one end, sickle on the other. This last was a weapon used only to attack dense foliage.

Kasciula said it would save time if he sent up some scouts to find where the gorillas were feeding. Families moved around a good deal, but stayed in one locality for several days. So six men moved off, and the rest of us sat around and talked and smoked.

The next day the scouts came back and reported that there was a band of gorillas near the summit of the mountain. They would probably be there for a few days. Kasciula announced that we would start early the next morning.

And early it was. The heavy mist was just rising under the first rays of the sun as we walked along an avenue of cinchona trees, crossed a swamp, and plunged into the tangled underbrush. I had brought only my Leica with black-and-white film, because I knew that the thick growth would tear and snag at everything hanging from me. The slope was steep, and Cézaire and I had to crawl on hands and knees occasionally. Most of the Pygmies were ahead of us, cutting through the tangle with their mgoosus, and they were going at about half their normal pace. But a tunnel for a Pygmy is not a fit tunnel for me or you. I had to move bent over, much like the normal walk of the gorilla I was here to see, but my knuckles were not calloused as his are. Nettles and branches covered with thorns snatched at my clothes, while I saw that they just slid off the skin of the almost naked Kasciula in front of me.

It was damp on the jungle-covered mountain slopes, I slipped and slid backwards on the steep muddy path. Whenever this happened, Kasciula stopped and held his spear back to me so I could grab it and haul myself up again. Then my camera banged against my chest and I wondered why I had brought it. The light in the forest was like that of late dusk, not nearly enough to take pictures even with the fastest film of those days.

I looked back and saw that Cézaire was having just as hard a time as I was, and that the Pygmies were helping him. Then Kasciula called a halt and we all sat down to rest. I passed out cigarettes, to the delight of the Pygmies. Cézaire and I panted and sweated. The Pygmies did neither.

After two more hours, my heart was pounding, my head was throbbing, and my knees were buckling. Then we came upon an elephant path, and the going was a little easier. We stopped for a bite of lunch. Near the summit we ran into more elephant paths, but they were not fresh. Then the ground leveled off and I knew that we had reached the ridge along the top of the mountain. There was more light. It was not so humid. The Pygmies slowed down, moving more cautiously and with absolute silence. I tried to walk the way they did, but twigs snapped under my feet, leaves rustled as I passed, and I felt that every wild animal within half a mile would know that a white man was coming.

Kasciula pointed at some big tracks. "Elephants," he said. "Not new." We walked farther, and he became alert. He pointed and I saw another track, with the clear heel and the marks of knuckles. I knew that a gorilla had walked along this path only a few short hours before us.

Then, suddenly, with a blazing gleam in his eye, Kasciula pointed. There was dung — gorilla dung — and still steaming! The old Pygmy smiled at me. He led us along a path that circled an outcropping of rock, and across a little glade not ten feet wide into which bright sunlight streamed. I was glad I had my camera.

Beyond the glade, Kasciula pointed again, and we saw gorilla beds, three of them rather close together. A gorilla makes its bed by sitting down in a thick clump of saplings and bushes, then pulling other saplings and branches down around him, tucking them in, tying them, and arranging them into what looks like a gigantic bird's nest. The beds looked quite comfortable. When there are leopards around, mother and babies go up into a tree and fill a comfortable fork with branches and leaves and moss; papa sleeps at the base of the tree, his back against the trunk. Nothing is likely to get past him.

We crossed the small glade and plunged into thick forest again, but I saw sunlight ahead. Then we came onto a kind of rocky plateau with nothing but low scrub growth on it. Could we spot a gorilla here?

We walked silently to the other end of the open space, and Kasciula pointed. I couldn't see a thing but vegetation. Then, as I stared, I saw some leaves move, I heard a crackling of branches. Kasciula nudged me and pointed. I saw a black head emerge in the midst of the green leaves. A hairy arm reached out and pushed some branches aside. Then the gorilla hunched himself on all fours into the open.

I was prepared for something big, but not that big. Pictures I had seen had never struck me with the massive strength of this gorilla walking freely in his own home. With his knuckles touching the ground at every step, his head wagging from side to side, he looked awkward at first. But there was so much relaxed physical power in every movement that I soon saw it as a special kind of grace. I can still feel the awe and excitement that gripped me as I watched that gorilla amble along the edge of the trees. I had gone in search of the primitive, and here it was — the very essence of it.

I had my camera in my hand, but could not use it yet. The animal was in deep shadow from the trees, and he would have been no more than a dark blur against a dark background in any picture.

Suddenly he stopped and turned toward us. He must have heard something or caught our wind. He looked at us, curious, then stood upright to stare more intently. He saw us clearly, but he did not appear angry or afraid. His fist beat against his chest, and I heard the sound for which gorillas are most famous. There was no cry, no roar, no scream — just a pounding *tom-tom* as from a muffled drum. There was nothing menacing in it, any more than in the sounds from log drums of primitive men all over the world. The gorilla used his big barrel of a chest as a sounding board, and opened his mouth wide so the sound would come out. It was an automatic or instinctive reaction to the sight of something unusual.

Another gorilla head emerged from the green leaves, then disappeared again. We heard more chest-beating, and the same sound repeated farther away. The signal was relayed to all gorillas in the neighborhood.

The first gorilla seemed to be as interested in us as we were in him. He reached up and grabbed an overhead branch to help him stand straight to look at us better. I saw the crest of furry, thickened skin on top of his head, the shiny black leather of his face and upper chest, his flat, wide-flaring nose. If he would just move forward a few feet he would be in sunlight and I could get a good picture.

But he had enough of us, dropped down, and moved slowly back into the shadows. I snapped the shutter, but I knew the film would show little recognizable.

The old graybeard of the Pygmies touched my arm and nodded toward the other side of the ridge. His eyes told me there was something interesting to see over there, so I followed him. Another Pygmy and the two boys came with us, while Kasciula, Cézaire, and the others stayed to see if our first gorilla friends would appear again.

The old man led me to a ledge of rock that rose about three feet above a grassy glade sloping down toward the thick jungle growth. On the edge of the grass in the deep shade cast by the trees stood four gorillas, apparently father, mother, and two youngsters. The mother and children were busy eating, but the father heard us and looked up inquiringly. I could not hear a sound from him, but he must have communicated with the others in some way, for they glanced up without showing any fear. When he saw they were safe, the big gorilla turned to examine us more carefully.

He was magnificent, and I wanted nothing more at that moment than to get a picture of him. But he was still in deep shade. Then he moved forward into the open stretch below us, walking on all fours slowly and without menace. He just seemed to want to get a better look at us. If he kept going he would enter a bright patch of light where the sun's rays cut down across the tops of the trees.

I could not wait calmly while he shuffled toward us. He might stop short and go back into the forest. But if I leapt down from the ledge and met him halfway, I could get close enough to take a good picture the moment he stepped into the patch of light.

I acted as quickly as I thought. I clambered down the rocky ledge and ran across a dozen yards of green grass — breaking the most elementary rule in dealing with all wild animals: *Never run!* And I broke it in the worst possible way, by running *toward* the gorilla's family. I realized later, when I got my senses back, that there was only one interpretation he could put on my actions — that I was charging to attack him, his mate, and his children.

By then he was in the light and I had my camera to my eye. So I did not see at once the sudden change that had come over the gorilla. His curiosity was converted to fury, the strongest imaginable fury, erupting like an explosion. Through my viewfinder I saw him raise himself to his full height, turn toward me, and open his mouth for a cry of rage. As I pressed the shutter, his scream split the air. It was a blood-curdling shriek of such intense, blind fury that I was terrified. I ran.

I caught a glimpse of the gorilla as I turned. He had dropped to all fours and was racing toward me. Such fear seized me as I have never known, but somehow I was not paralyzed. My legs moved, and I raced for the ledge, hoping I could run as fast as the gorilla, which has an amazing speed for a creature of his bulk. Only one thing saved me, I know, and that was a depression in the ground between the gorilla and me, a kind of shallow gulley with fairly steep sides. He had to run down into it and climb up the other side, and that slowed him just a little.

I reached the bottom of the ledge and looked up to see only the wizened old Pygmy standing there. Where were the others? I did not feel too certain that a three-foot ledge and a thin Pygmy spear could stop an angry gorilla, but it was the first step to safety. So I grasped the ledge and started to swing my right leg up, when I felt my shoe slipping off.

Now, I know that it is ridiculous to save one shoe at the possible cost of your life, just as I know that running to get a picture of a gorilla is foolish, but both actions were almost automatic. You want a picture — you run to get it. You feel a shoe coming off — you reach down to slip it back on. And that is what I did.

The old Pygmy veteran reached down one bony arm toward me. I grasped it and vaulted up to the ledge. The gorilla was still coming, only about ten paces from the bottom of the ledge. I knew he could clamber up it easily, and he looked angry enough to do it.

But Kasciula and the others were racing across the ridge toward us, obviously summoned by a call from my old friend. They reached us just as the gorilla came to the ledge, and when the beast saw the number of men confronting him, he stopped. He snarled, and his eyes burned with hatred. But some of the Pygmies lifted their spears high, ready to fling them if he started up the ledge. Others braced the butts of their spears in the ground, making a sharp-pointed fence at the top of the ledge.

The gorilla panted and glared and looked at all of us carefully. Then he turned and ambled slowly toward the forest, looking back occasionally to threaten us with furious snarls, warning us not to follow. When he was a few feet from the trees he stopped and turned. He barked at us. It was a bark halfway between a hound's and a seal's. It did not have the fury of the gorilla's scream, but it was not friendly either. It was a special warning, and his family in the forest took it up at once. I saw that the two young ones had climbed into a tree, while the mother stood at the bottom. They all barked at us, and then their friends and neighbors for miles around took up the cry, and the air was filled with a cacophony of shrill barks.

Kasciula and his Pygmies relaxed. Then the one who had, with the two boys, come along to the ledge with me and graybeard started to scold the youngsters. It seems that they had been so terrified at the gorilla's scream when he charged me that they had taken to their heels, and the man had gone to haul them back and teach them how to act in the face of a gorilla attack. That was when graybeard's thin arm had saved me.

I tried to explain how it was all my fault, and so on. I had come to my senses again and realized what a foolish thing I had done. But there wasn't much talk, because everyone agreed with me — Cézaire particularly. The Pygmies would not have minded a battle very much.

They love gorilla meat, and their chief sport is hunting. Kasciula said to me, "The gorillas may attack if we stay here. But we will do as you say, stay and take the attack or go away. What do you wish?"

It was not my wish to assume responsibility for the death of a gorilla or a Pygmy or me or Cézaire, so I ordered a retreat to the plantation. As we walked down from the summit into the forest, the barking of the gorillas subsided. When Kasciula signaled that he considered everything safe, we stopped for a brief rest. I passed out cigarettes and the Pygmies puffed away happily. They seemed to be saying to me, "Don't worry about what you did. It may have been foolish, yes, but we do the same kind of thing every day." So I felt good. I had seen gorillas. I had taken one picture that I was sure would turn out, even if it was not very good. And I had come to know these wonderful men who sat around me grinning and talking softly.

Never again did I take such a chance with any animal as I took with the gorilla. I know that despite my normal good luck I could not have gotten away with it twice. I have crept close to lions, hippos, rhinos, elephants, buffaloes, and other dangerous animals in order to get good pictures of them, but I have never again actually invited an attack.

I assured Cézaire that I had learned my lesson and then made a suggestion — that we give up the idea of buying guns.

"If we lived through the gorilla hunt without guns," I said, "we can get along without them for the whole trip. I never expect to be in half as much danger from any other animal again, so why carry weapons?"

Cézaire had never heard of such a thing, but had to agree that if I would stop tempting fate we could get along fine. So for the rest of our trip — through the Congo, Tanganyika, and Kenya — we traveled unarmed. And that gave me the title of the lecture film I worked up from this expedition, *Through Africa Unarmed*; it was particularly successful because it was the first color movie to come out of Africa. It was good color, and it lasted.

2

The Watusi

OF THE MANY startling and almost incredible changes that occurred in Africa between my first and last expeditions, none is so drastic as the fate of the handsome, aristocratic Watusi,* whom I visited on three of my four trips.

They never seemed to belong in Central Africa, anyway, and even the experts could not be sure where they had come from four or five centuries ago. In a continent of small and pygmoid peoples, here were giants six and a half to almost eight feet tall, slender and graceful. And their clothing was just right — long flowing robes like a Roman senator's toga, snowy white and with sunbursts of gold or broad red stripes.

It was obvious that they were not primitive Stone Age people, even though they were discovered by Europeans as recently as 1894. They were instead relics of a high civilization from some ancient time. The most widely accepted theory as to their presence in the heart of Africa is that famine, plague, drought, or war drove tens of thousands of Watusi from Egypt — some say Ethiopia — to search for new lands.

---

* Strictly, *Wa*, as in Watusi, and *Ba*, as in Bahutu, are common prefixes meaning "race" or "people," and mean the entire group *as* a race or people. Singulars are formed from such collective plurals by changing prefixes. Thus an individual man or woman of the Watusi is a Mutusi. Moreover, many residents of Africa, when speaking of these groups here and now (rather than as the entire race), drop the *Wa* and *Ba* entirely, referring to the Tusi (or more commonly Tutsi) and the Hutu.

However, to avoid confusion I shall throughout this book follow the nomenclature of most non-technical American publications, and allow one word for each tribe, collectively, singly, without regard to sex.

They took with them their families, their customs, their dress, and their precious cattle.

The Watusi cattle are as different from other cattle in Central Africa as their owners are different from the men of that region. Even such well-known cattle-raising tribes as the Masai, in southern Kenya and in Tanganyika, and the Turkana, in far-northern Kenya, have small scrawny beasts by our standards. But the Watusi cattle are magnificent creatures, stocky and solid, though with surprisingly thin legs for such big bodies. They have straight backs and long dewlaps, and a dignified carriage — made difficult, I am sure, by the huge, gracefully curved white horns that reach a span of ten to twelve feet.

With the ancestors of these unusual cattle, plus some goats and sheep, the ancestors of the Watusi had several hundred years ago migrated perhaps a thousand or more miles to find a new home. They found it in a lovely highland and mountain region east of the Congo and Lake Kivu — perhaps the most beautiful lake in the world. For as long a time as anyone knows, the area was divided into two states, which I first knew as Ruanda and Urundi.

The Watusi must have been warriors at the time of their great migration, for they conquered the inhabitants of the lands they wanted and made them, for the most part, into serfs or slaves. But when the German explorer Count von Götzen discovered Lake Kivu and Ruanda-Urundi in 1894, the Watusi were not fighters. And when I visited them in 1937 and 1946, I searched for legends and ceremonies that recalled some long-forgotten triumphs in war, such as persist in most cultures, even long after their fighting has ended. Only in one of the many exciting Watusi dances did I see what might be described as a poetic triumph of the Watusi over an enemy.

It may be, of course, that the Watusi conquered the inhabitants of their new home by the force of their intelligence, their majestic bearing, their assurance of superiority, their advanced civilization (as compared with that of the native Bahutu), or even the impression created by their magnificent long-horned cattle. The Bahutu may have thought they were gods, just as the Aztecs thought of Cortez and his Spaniards when they first appeared on horseback. It is conceivable that the Watusi did not have to fight a single battle, but I think this is highly unlikely, because primitive man is usually fiercely possessive of his land.

In any event, the more numerous Bahutu accepted the Watusi as overlords, whether through defeat in battle, awe, or respect. In only one important area did the Watusi bow to the Bahutu — they adopted their language. They had to, in order to command and demand. The Bahutu and the handful of Pygmy Batwa of the region obeyed. They did the work that needed to be done. They took care of the Watusi cattle — and solicitous care it was. They also chopped down the trees of half the country to make pasture land for the precious cattle, which contributed nothing to the economy of the country, for they were never slaughtered and even their milk went first to their calves. If any was left over, humans were allowed to drink it.

The result was, until the early part of the century at least, recurrent famine, for the terraced farms did not provide enough food when a bad crop year occurred. The Watusi were not overly concerned, for the Bahutu and Batwa did most of the dying during famines. And there were always enough left to do all the work that needed to be done.

A disease of cattle, rinderpest, kept things in some sort of balance for many years, for it periodically killed off cattle just as famine regularly killed off Bahutu. Both propagated rapidly and made up for any deficiencies within a few years. Then modern veterinary science, introduced by the Belgians and the missionaries, almost eliminated rinderpest. So at the time of my first visit in 1937, there were more cattle than ever before.

And more human beings, too. Ruanda-Urundi, together about the size of Maine, had the densest concentration of people of any area in Africa except Egypt, with two hundred humans per square mile, in comparison with the Congo's eight, for example. It also supported a million cattle, a million goats, and half a million sheep.

The Belgians had been administering the twin kingdoms for about twenty years when I first went there — under a mandate from the League of Nations, and later from the United Nations. They followed, with some reservations, the basic principle of governing which the Germans had established when they controlled Ruanda-Urundi, dealing through the established Watusi kings and their chiefs. But where the Germans had continued the absolute powers of the kings, including unquestioned control over life and death, the Belgians gradually restricted the kings' powers in such essential matters. They even went so far as to remove King Msinga of Ruanda, who was notorious for his cruelties and atrocities, and replace him with his son Rudahigwa. This was the king I met on my first trips to Ruanda.

I passed through the southern kingdom of Urundi, and stayed for a few days in its capital, Usumbura, which was a small city, and not just a town, with a hotel, shops, hospital, and other evidences of European influence. I spent most of my time in Ruanda because I knew, from talking and reading, that it was more colorful, more dramatic than Urundi. The Watusi of Ruanda were taller and more aristocratic, and their cattle had longer horns. The high-jumping was higher and the dancing more beautiful.

At the time I did not question why these slight differences should exist between two small neighboring kingdoms ruled by the Watusi. I just preferred the one that seemed to be "purer" Watusi. Only with the violent events of the past few years has the significance of these differences become apparent to me.

When Cézaire and I drove into Ruanda, we headed first for the town of Kigali, a place of only a few thousand people, although now the capital of the country. At that time, however, the capital was an even smaller town, Nyanza. Near Kigali, however, we knew we would find a mission of the Catholic White Fathers, who knew the country so well they could give us an excellent briefing.

Not far from the mission, just as it was getting dark, I saw my first Watusi, towering almost eight feet tall, with a resplendent robe hanging gracefully from his shoulders to the ground. His small and almost delicate triangular face, with short black goatee, large soft eyes, and high-bridged straight nose, and above it a piled-up hairdo calculated to increase the impression of great height — everything about him was striking, even his satiny bronze skin and his long, tapering fingers. His grave courtesy when Cézaire asked him the way to the mission spoke at the same time of warmth and reserve, friendliness and dignity.

At the mission, the White Fathers, mostly Hollanders, welcomed us and invited us to share an excellent meal with them. Afterwards there was conversation, made a bit more voluble, I think, by the fine cigars I just happened to have with me.

The White Fathers had been working for decades among the Watusi, but for a long time they had made little headway in their missionary work. They had used modern medicines and treatments as a first method of gaining confidence, followed by education of children. Religion, they felt, would follow — and it had done so, though not as rapidly as the Fathers might have wished.

The White Fathers thought the legend of Watusi migration from Egypt was true. They pointed out that, like the Egyptians, the Watusi studied the entrails of chickens for omens of the future. They believed in the transmigration of souls and used animals as clan totems. One claimed the chameleon, another the toad, while the totem of the royal family was the crested crane. The Watusi held the monkey in great reverence. According to legend — all legends were passed down by a special court group called "the makers of intelligence" — an early Watusi king, trapped by enemies in a cave, had been led to safety by a monkey. Another special group appointed by the king, called "the men of the cavern," had the duty of protecting and safeguarding monkeys. Still another had charge of an eternal fire, since fire had been given to an early Watusi "Prometheus" by the gods.

After chapel and breakfast the next morning, Cézaire and I were about to start for Nyanza when we saw four Bahutu carrying on their cushioned heads a *matshela*, a kind of palanquin made of woven fibers in the shape of a long basket. They set it down, a tall woman stepped from it, and I met Kangazi, one of the thirty wives of the deposed king, Msinga, who had been exiled only a few miles away in Kamambe. Although Watusi women are not nearly as tall as the men, their average height is considerably above that of American women.

It was unusual for me to meet a Watusi woman in this way. They commonly lived in almost Moslem seclusion and in public were extremely shy and self-effacing. Being the wife of a deposed king must have made some difference, for Kangazi was at ease, forthright and pleasant. She willingly posed for pictures and then agreed to accompany me the short distance to Nyanza, where Mwami (King) Rudahigwa held court.

Back in the thirties there were few visitors to Ruanda, and they were always welcomed warmly — which usually meant a visit with the king. So when Kangazi and I arrived before the Mwami's palace, he came out to greet us. In 1937 the royal home was a traditional Watusi *inzu*, a domed structure of poles and thatch, circular except for a rounded growth on one side that served as a kind of foyer. The interior was divided into sleeping, eating, and cooking sections by fiber mats that made me think of Japanese screens between rooms.

The Mwami, surrounded by numerous princely attendants, shook my hand warmly when Kangazi introduced me. He seemed to be a pleasant young man, not quite as handsome or tall as some of his courtiers, but with the unmistakable air of ruler and leader. We talked for a while in French, Rudahigwa's command of the language being perfect and mine quite halting, and then I presented him with a black silk umbrella and a small silk American flag. He seemed pleased and fondled the flag gently, almost as a woman might a lovely handkerchief. I did not know if he was just being polite or if he really liked my gifts, for it is not an easy task to choose a present for a king, even an African king. People who were accustomed to give shiny trinkets to Africans learned not to follow the habit when dealing with the Watusi. I had heard of a traveler who visited Nyanza shortly after Rudahigwa ascended the throne. After an interview, the European produced some miserable dime-store jewelry, which he distributed to the king and his royal entourage. Rudahigwa thanked him just as politely as he would have if the baubles had been priceless gems. But after the visitor had left, all the Watusi court tossed the trinkets to their Bahutu servants. At that time the Bahutu were happy to have them.

The Mwami showed me the great ceremonial drums, most sacred possession of the tribe, which were supposed to accompany him wherever he went. Drums were the heartbeat of Africa — big drums, little drums, slit drums made from hollow logs that boomed high when struck at one end and low at the other end, drums that were beaten with sticks, drums that were pounded by hand, drums that were rubbed. They were played for dances, for feasts, to summon the men to council, to announce the arrival of a neighboring chief, to send long messages. In Ruanda the royal drums had three names, Ishakwe, Inyahura, and Inumvu. They were beaten each morning to announce that the king had awakened and all Watusi must awake. They broadcast his retirement at night, even though he had not usually gone to bed when they were struck and nobody else went to bed then, either. What counted was tradition.

The most sacred of all Watusi drums was the Kalinga, symbol of the authority of the king. It was the equivalent of crown, scepter, and seal. When the Belgian authorities had to rid themselves and the country of Rudahigwa's uncooperative father, Msinga, they took from him the Kalinga. Without that drum, Msinga lost all power, prestige, and authority over the Watusi — and he knew it. He gave up without a fight. In a short time, when Rudahigwa was established as king, the Kalinga was produced and given to him. With it, he and his followers knew that he was the true Mwami.

During our talk, King Rudahigwa invited me to attend the great festival of the presentation of the sacred cattle, with dancing, high-jumping, archery contests and other spectacles. Only two or three times a year did this event take place, and once more my good fortune held, for it was scheduled to begin in just three days.

During those days I looked, talked, traveled, and shot pictures. I visited the deposed king Msinga, who lived in an unpretentious but comfortable inzu with numerous wives and children of widely varying ages. The youngsters were the first Watusi children I had seen, and they were all fat. This is all the more striking because one never saw an adult Watusi, male or female, who was really obese. I learned that until puberty Watusi children lived almost exclusively on milk, sweet or curdled. Then fermented honey, bananas, occasionally some meat, and a few vegetables were added to the diet — an excellent one for reducing, according to the evidence I saw.

Msinga greeted me in friendly fashion, but he was obviously an embittered man unable to adjust himself to a lowly position after having ruled as a complete — and cruel — autocrat for thirty-six years, a reign that was still recalled with a shudder by most Watusi and Bahutu alike.

The ex-king was even taller than his son, but less handsome. Cataracts filming his eyes contributed to his distressing expression, and the first question he asked me was, "Do you have any medicine for my eyes?" He looked disappointed when I said no, but immediately launched into a few sentences in German, as if to show off. Or perhaps the language recalled to him his days of glory, when Ruanda had been part of German East Africa and his dictatorial powers had not been restricted in any way.

He was pleased and flattered when I asked him to pose for pictures with members of his household, and he picked up one of the fat babies to hold in his arms during the filming. By the time I left I felt a little sorry for the venomous old man, who must have sensed my changed feelings, for he presented me with a particularly fine example of Watusi basketry.

At last the day came for the big festival, and hundreds of Watusi and Bahutu were streaming into Nyanza from all parts of the country. Mwami Rudahigwa was more resplendent than ever in a magnificent white robe and a beautiful headdress with dangling pearl strands and a crest of feathers and white monkey fur. He stood at one end of a wide field, surrounded by about seventy-five of the chief Watusi nobles. I saw among them a few men who were conspicuous because of their, to me, average height, and I learned that for unusual services in the past some Bahutu and even a few Batwa had been admitted to the fringes of Watusi aristocracy.

Along the sides of the field were hundreds of Bahutu and Batwa tribesmen, some ready to take part in the ceremonies but most as spectators. Even the trees some distance from the field were filled with clusters of Bahutu who had scrambled up for a good view. All eyes were on the king, who would give the signal for the beginning of the show. He held in his hand the small silk flag I had given him. Behind him stood a servant with the black umbrella.

The opening event was the high jump. Two slender straight reeds were stuck in the ground and a thin rod placed horizontally between them. On the ground in front of the jumping standard was the top of a hardened anthill, about six inches high. One Watusi youth took off his headdress of white feathers, tucked his toga up around his waist, and raced about twenty paces — incredibly long strides — toward the standard. On his last stride one foot reached the anthill, from which he sprang up and over the bar, which was set, I guessed, at about five and a half feet. Five or six more jumpers followed, and all cleared the bar by at least a foot. It was raised rapidly, in sizable moves, until it rested at more than eight feet. All the jumpers sailed over the bar as easily as before. I don't know how high they might have gone if they had kept jumping until all but one were eliminated, but apparently this was a spectacle rather than a contest.

Another group of Watusi was just as good at javelin-throwing, which came next, but in the third event, archery, they made a poor showing indeed, even though some Bahutu and Batwa joined with Watusi in this sport. The Batwa, with their tiny bows and arrows, were more accurate than the Watusi with their long, strong bows.

They must have known that they were far from superior in this sport, for all during the contest there was much exhortation on the part of the spectators, including the king, and prayerful self-stimulation on the part of the contestants. They petted their bows, stroked their arrows, talking soothingly to them as a gambler might to his dice before the throw. Near the end of the event, one of the White Fathers was invited to join in. He hit the bull's-eye — to loud cheers of the assembled Watusi, Bahutu, and Batwa.

With these preliminaries over, the most important ceremony of the afternoon, from the Watusi point of view, took place — the presentation of the sacred cattle. The animals were gathered in a clearing not far from the field, but all I could see from a distance was a forest of long white horns. They were led out one by one to be viewed by the king and his court. First came the *inyambo*, cattle belonging to the Mwami himself, followed by the *insanga*, owned by other Watusi chiefs. Since the cattle were judged by quality as well as by numbers as the evidence of wealth and prestige, they were all examined by highly critical eyes.

The beasts were dignified and quiet, lowing gently on occasion. They reminded me of elderly aristocratic ladies or dowager queens, conscious of their importance and of all the proprieties that must be observed on this state occasion. Each cow had its own Bahutu attendant, or groom, who led it in review, talking to it soothingly all the time, waving away flies that might annoy it; the grooms, as special favors for performing such important tasks, were allowed to drink the cows' milk. They had done a magnificent job in preparing the cows for this occasion. The animals' coats glistened silkily in the sun as a result of having been rubbed with butter. Their long curving horns looked like ivory, having been polished with sand, and the tips of most were decorated with long feathery tufts. Each cow's forehead carried a headdress of pearls and fine embroidery. The cattle were of various colors — some red and white, some black and white, others red and light gray.

As each animal was presented before the king, its groom cried out its qualities, gesticulating, jumping up and down, beating the ground with his staff to emphasize the most admirable points of his beast. The Mwami and his assembled nobles discussed each animal thoughtfully and carefully. The vocabulary of the Watusi is rich in words referring to cows, many having subtle meanings.

The presentation of the cattle took a long time, and I began to find it rather tiresome. I was eager to see the final event of the afternoon, the most important from my point of view — the Watusi dancing.

I have watched and filmed dancing in most of the countries I've visited, for dancing is often more revealing of a group's feelings and heritage than any other activity. But I have been disappointed frequently, since many primitive dances are little more than a halfhearted shuffling of the feet, a few steps forward, a few steps back. I had heard and read, however, that the Watusi dancers were perhaps the most exciting in the world. The members of the chief dancing group were selected in childhood and specially trained for years before appearing in public.

I found the most advantageous spots for filming and had my cameras ready. The drums rolled and the orchestra burst into its stirring equivalent of a fanfare, at which fifty or more tall and lithe Watusi dancers rushed onto the field shouting and whooping. They were dressed in rich costumes — crossed bands of embroidery and pearls over the chest, leopardskin bands about the waist, from which dangled thin strands of fur, leather anklets with small bells attached, a collar of more beaded embroidery and a ring of white monkey fur, and a plumed headdress like a lion's mane that tossed gracefully with each movement of the head.

The dancers ranged themselves in rows, each man about ten feet from the next on either side. Then the leader leapt into place before them. He was Butare, son of one of the highest Watusi princes and a minister at the king's court, one of the Biru, council of elders. He was dressed much like the others except that he wore a robe of flaming red cloth of very fine texture. When it swirled about his legs, it looked like leaping flames. Butare's white teeth flashed in a happy smile as he led his dancers, and part of the beauty of the spectacle came from the joy that animated the performers.

All the dancers were graceful and dynamic, but Butare was so amazing that it was hard to take my eyes from him to watch his company. He made leaps of astounding length and grace, leaps in which he floated through the air seemingly in defiance of the law of gravity, as did Nijinsky at his peak. Every muscle of his body contributed to each gesture, each movement. Toes, fingers, the arch of his supple neck, his flashing eyes and teeth all spoke the same message. The skirt, the streaming headdress, the long staff in his hand — all became extensions of the dancer's body as he advanced, swerved, retreated, thrust.

In the final dance of the afternoon, called "the thundering legion," the dancers became an advancing army, proud, irresistible, sweeping all before them. Their feet stamped the earth so hard clouds of dust arose from the field. The ground shook beneath me. They chanted as they danced, and the musicians, as well as Bahutu and Batwa dancers, joined in the chant. No longer was there silence, but the vast crowd shouted and cheered and urged the dancers on to greater and greater efforts. At the end, I was limp and exhausted. The dancers trouped off, panting but smiling with pleasure, and the dust slowly settled back to earth under the hot sun. I looked happily down at my camera, knowing that it contained the first colored motion picture film ever taken of Watusi dancers.

It was 1946 before I returned to Africa to make a film, *Savage Splendor* (with Armand Denis), for RKO Pictures. Denis took one route and I another, so we could film as many different tribes, animals, and events as possible. With a professional cameraman to help me, I headed first for Ruanda, where the ceremonies attending the presentation of the cattle were scheduled.

I was astonished at the many changes that had come in nine years, including five years of world war during which contact with the outside world was drastically reduced and the march of civilizing or Europeanizing influences slowed down. For one thing, I could not arrange a meeting with King Rudahigwa just by dropping in, as I had in 1937. I had to make my appointment through the resident Belgian commissioner. And a few years later I probably would not have been able to see him at all.

The Mwami had moved from his thatched inzu into a brick and concrete house with flush toilets, picture windows, and broadloom carpeting. Some lion and leopardskin rugs lay on top of the carpets, and a few Watusi baskets and other craft objects could be seen, but even those pieces that the king possessed were not as attractive or as expertly made as several things I had brought home with me in 1937. When artistic ability and craftsmanship deteriorate that much in nine years, you can be sure that a culture is dying, even if it does so gracefully — as seemed to be the case in 1946.

Another change that had come about was in the Mwami's name. His full name had been, in 1937, Mutara III Rudahigwa, the Mutara meaning "peacemaker" or "evolutionist." By 1946 he had become a Christian and he was Mwami Mutara III Charles Léon Pierre Rudahigwa; he was the thirty-ninth ruler in a dynasty that could trace its line back clearly for four hundred years.

Still, I found him the same reserved but pleasant person that I had met nine years before. He was just getting over a bout of malaria, but he greeted me warmly and recalled several incidents from my first visit. He and the Belgian resident were most helpful in making arrangements for me and my cameraman to film the ceremonies the following day, but I was worried. With all the other changes I had seen, would the dances and other spectacles of the festival be as striking and beautiful?

Happily, there was no change that I could detect. The cattle were just as well groomed, the costumes of the dancers just as striking — and Butare still led the Watusi dancers. There was only one disappointment. Even with two cameramen, we could film only small segments of the great scenes before us. I wanted to be up higher, where we could get some shots showing the whole assemblage — cattle waiting for the presentation, orchestra, dancers, and so on.

I mentioned this to the territorial administrator after the day's shooting. He consulted with Rudahigwa, had a platform built, and called upon the dancers and cattle-tenders to repeat their performances the following day. They agreed gladly and went through their acts with even more spirit, I thought, than on the first day.

A pleasant surprise then came to me. I had so admired the beauty, grace, and poise of the Watusi women I had seen that I wanted more film of them. Except for my chance meeting with Kangazi and my pictures of the women dancers, I had enjoyed nothing but formal introduction to a Watusi lady. They were reserved, and aloof. But I knew that they occupied important positions in the world of Ruanda. Watusi women were not the beasts of burden and the drudges of all work that the women of other African tribes were. They were never forced to marry against their will, and they had the right of divorce. In the main, husbands treated their wives as companions, as equals, as persons of intelligence to be consulted on all affairs pertaining to the family. They made beautiful basketware, some of it so fine that the baskets could be used to contain liquids. They wove lovely cloth and managed the home and the bringing up of the children. But they performed no menial tasks.

All this was true of the noble or chieftain class of the Watusi. In 1946, on my second visit, I began to learn about Watusi that were not quite so aristocratic and exalted. Since I had spent most of my time filming around the king's residence, it was natural that I should have seen only the very highest caste among the Watusi, the Baganwa — the group from which all rulers, chiefs, and high officials were chosen. Next was a slightly lower caste, families with fewer cattle, fewer Bahutu servants, fewer Batwa slaves. Still, the women and men of this group did little physical and no distasteful work. There were also lower classes among the Watusi, however, and these members of the ruling race actually performed a fair amount of labor. But the lowest Watusi was so far above most Bahutu that they could not really be compared.

The coming of civilization had produced an interesting effect on the relationship between Watusi men and women. One of the most praiseworthy goals of missionaries and European colonial administrators in most of Africa was that of improving the lot of women, who in most tribes were mere chattels. But in Ruanda, where the women already occupied an enviable position, that position was gradually being undermined as an unforeseen sequel to another praiseworthy effort. Many Watusi young men were educated in good schools, were being trained to become leaders of their communities or at least responsible officials under the Belgians. They learned French, many skills, and some knowledge of the world. But the Belgians had started no schools for women, so they could not understand French when it was spoken in their homes. They had less in common with their husbands, who were increasingly interested in things they had learned at school. Now, however, the Watusi men were beginning to complain about the situation, requesting schooling for their daughters.

The Belgian administrator in Ruanda, after consulting with Rudahigwa, arranged for me to visit with several Watusi ladies and take motion pictures of them. Even with his help and Rudahigwa's permission, it was not easy to gain their cooperation. I could not pay them or give them gifts as an incentive. But I asked them to inconvenience themselves in order to help me show the outside world what Watusi women were like and what they did. They finally agreed, reluctantly. As the filming of scenes over a period of several days continued, they became quite friendly. In the end I had films of them being carried in their palanquins by their Bahutu servants, as if on the way to visit friends; then the meeting with friends and gathering together in the compound of one of their houses. For my cameras they wove baskets, played games, ate a light meal brought to them by their servants. Through all this, they understood that I wanted them to re-create everyday scenes, so they behaved quite naturally.

When I was leaving, and trying ineffectually to express my gratitude, they thanked me instead, and one of them presented me with a gift — a low, hand-carved stool that I had admired.

I had a high regard for the Watusi, even though I did not like the idea of a haughtily aristocratic minority ruling a completely subservient majority. Both in 1937 and 1946, moreover, the Bahutu, so far as I could see and learn, were docile people who accepted their position. And the handful of Batwa Pygmies were fiercely devoted to their Watusi masters.

Still, when I returned to Africa again 1954 — after a third expedition to South America — to produce the film *Zanzabuku* for Republic Pictures, I did not visit the Watusi. If I had gone, I might have heard the first rumblings of the violent volcano that was to erupt within a few years, but I doubt it. For once more I would have filmed the high-jumping, the dancing, the king and his court, and would have seen or heard little of the Bahutu discontent that was beginning to grow after centuries of patient docility.

The next time I went was in February and March, 1964, after the volcano had erupted and was still spitting fire and brimstone. Then I did not go into Ruanda itself, on the emphatic advice of everyone I talked to. While it was true that few Europeans or Americans had been hurt in the uprisings, there was always the chance of getting caught in the middle of a Watusi raid across the border and the Bahutu counterattack. So I contented myself with a visit to Usumbura, capital of Burundi — from this point on I shall use the official names of the two newly independent nations, Rwanda and Burundi — where I saw thousands of Watusi refugees and talked with some of them, as well as with missionaries, newsmen, and others who had been in Rwanda during most of the upheaval.

I knew the facts of what had occurred in Rwanda through newspaper reports, and something more of what was behind the facts through letters and talks with friends. But much of this was contradictory, and I wanted to find my way through conflicting reports and opinions to some kind of understanding of the downfall of the Watusi in Rwanda.

The revolutions that were sweeping most of Africa aimed at ridding the continent of white colonial powers and giving independent rule to the native inhabitants of the different countries; but in Rwanda, there was a switch. While considerable resentment was expressed against the Belgian administrators, the revolution of the Bahutu majority was directed against the Watusi minority that ruled the country. The spirit of revolution sweeping Africa — and other parts of the world — was the overthrow of alien "masters," whether they were black or white or bronze. In Rwanda, these were the Watusi. The Bahutu were not, as a matter of fact, strongly anti-Belgian.

I learned that many incidents leading up to the revolution had centered around the Mwami Rudahigwa. After World War II the king traveled a good deal in Europe, first at the behest of the Belgians, who hoped that he would see the advantages of a gradual civilizing of his country under Belgian auspices and control. But apparently his travels had a contrary effect. He wanted Rwanda to achieve the independence he saw in many sovereign nations in Europe. Rudahigwa became a nationalist, leading him to a position of opposition to Belgian colonial authorities.

This point was agreed upon by people who were pro and con Rudahigwa, pro and con Watusi, but everything else elicited strong disagreements. I taped interviews with two men who knew the country well, and they were almost entirely contradictory.

Peter Guilbaird was an English missionary, in charge of missionary schools in Burundi, but before the revolution in Rwanda he had run a school there, with about two hundred boarding pupils divided about equally between Watusi and Bahutu children, all of whom got along well together. Although his heart had gone out to the Watusi in the terrible troubles they had undergone in the revolution, he agreed that before the revolution there had been much injustice. "Much had to be put right, but the *way* it was done was wrong. There was no chance to evolve."

Guilbaird was convinced that Rudahigwa was "liberal" in his political views, and cited his motto, paraphrased from the Bible, about a rope of three strands being stronger than a single strand — meaning that he wished to unite into one people the three tribes of Rwanda. The missionary was convinced that Rudahigwa wanted to become a constitutional monarch, leading *all* of his people gradually to democracy. In any event, the Belgians, seeing his nationalistic leaning, began to encourage the Bahutu to oppose and eventually rise up against him. This was in 1955 and 1956, when two different underground revolutionary movements were formed by the Bahutu, countered by a growing nationalist movement calling for immediate independence, a movement backed by Rudahigwa and the leading Watusi chiefs.

The United Nations had started prodding the Belgians as early as 1946 to reform the entire social and political structure of the twin Watusi kingdoms. By 1956, the Belgians had supervised elections on the local level in both Rwanda and Burundi, all of which had been won by the Bahutu, whose movements were thus greatly strengthened.

Claude Poli, of the French News Agency, whom I also met in Usumbura, disagreed with missionary Guilbaird primarily on the motives and character of Rudahigwa. He scoffed at the idea that the king could be called a liberal. Although the Mwami *talked* approval of democratization, his drive for quick independence was an effort to retain and regain power. If Rwanda could gain independence while the Watusi still controlled everything, and before the Bahutu gained a stronger foothold through more elections, then Rudahigwa would remain ruler and even win back the absolute power that his father had once possessed. So said M. Poli, and to demonstrate Rudahigwa's despotic cruelty, he told me of an incident of recent years.

His story went that when the first rumblings of Bahutu discontent were heard one of the Mwami's counselors went walking with him one day, and they discussed what should be done about the leading Bahutu "troublemakers." Since the power of life and death had been taken away from the Watusi, they had to devise some other deterrent. They came to a hillside covered with stones, and the counselor suggested that they might heat up a lot of stones and make the Bahutu leaders walk across them. Rudahigwa nodded approval, but said it must be tried out first. So he tried it out on the counselor himself!

Concern about Rudahigwa's motives suddenly ended in August, 1959, when he died while staying at a hotel in Usumbura, a death calling forth many conflicting stories. One fantasy was that he committed ritual suicide on the insistence of his mother because he had been unable to have children. Most Africans believed that he was murdered by "whites," which meant Belgians. But everyone agreed that Rudahigwa had gone to Usumbura to consult his doctor, a doctor he had seen many times, that he became quite ill in his hotel, was given injections, and died. There is general agreement that he was *genuinely* ill and that he died in spite of the injections, which had kept him alive for several days.

Rudahigwa's death stimulated Watusi nationalist activities. Two thousand chiefs assembled to choose a new Mwami — a twenty-year-old clerk in a Belgian administrative office whom they named Kigere V. The Watusi then began a series of rallies calling for immediate independence, which the Bahutu countered with their own meetings.

Only an incident was needed to start bloody fighting, and several occurred at about the same time. A Bahutu leader was murdered, and Bahutu "gangs" rose up to avenge him. Some Watusi overlords called for a group of Bahutu to work in the fields; the Bahutu refused; the Watusi descended on their village with their warriors, the Batwa Pygmies, and killed many of the villagers, including women and children. Back home again, they issued another summons for Bahutu workers. The Bahutu came, all right, but with spears, knives, bows and arrows, and clubs. Those Watusi they did not kill fled over the border into Burundi.

So the revolution began, in November, 1959. And it was as violent and vicious and bloodletting as most revolutions, with torture, burning of houses and plantations, and atrocities. I heard of one instance from the lips of a missionary who had witnessed it. He was trying to help a Watusi chief escape across the border. A group of Bahutu stopped his car, ordered the seven-and-a-half-foot Watusi out, and chopped off his legs just below the knees. They had cut him down to their size.

As the revolution spread over the country, the Belgians brought in troops from the Congo. Early in 1960 they stopped the fighting, except for sporadic outbursts and individual killings. An estimated five to six thousand Watusi had been killed, and many Bahutu.

Later that year local and regional elections were held, resulting in sweeping victories for the Bahutu. The leading Watusi who had not already fled began to leave the country, heading for Uganda, Burundi, Tanganyika, and the Congo. Many Watusi remained in Rwanda, but in the main they were people of the lowest rank in the old Watusi hierarchy, scarcely better off than the leading Bahutu. In 1961, the Bahutu took over the government, abolishing the kingdom and establishing a republic, with Grégoire Kayibanda, a Catholic seminarian, as president and prime minister. There were two Watusi in his cabinet. Six Watusi were elected to the legislature but never attended a meeting.

As a result of UN-supervised elections, Rwanda and Burundi became independent nations on July 1, 1962. Meanwhile about one hundred fifty thousand exiled Watusi, most in refugee camps near the borders of their country, were organizing for counterrevolution. I heard accusations of money and arms coming to them from such different powers as Egypt, Morocco, Russia, and China — China was the most frequently mentioned. If this was true, it is ironic indeed to think of Chinese Communists, strongest supporters of the world revolution of the proletariat, giving aid to the aristocratic Watusi against the proletarian serfs of Rwanda.

By late 1963, only a few months before my visit, the exiled Watusi were able to make several daring and occasionally devastating raids across the borders of Rwanda, killing many Bahutu but losing many men themselves. Before the raids died down in 1964, an estimated twenty thousand Watusi had been killed. During this period, the enraged Bahutu vented their anger on the Watusi who had remained in Rwanda, committing many atrocities.

I met one girl who had been a victim of such vengeance. She was Evanys Mukmegema, a twenty-three-year-old Watusi of singular beauty, intelligent and very feminine. Since she was not of the highest Watusi caste, she had been working for European missionaries in the northern part of Burundi, although originally from Rwanda. She was to have been married to a young Watusi schoolmaster attached to a mission station in Rwanda, and went there for the ceremony. The day after the wedding, Bahutu bands came and, before her eyes, killed her father, her brother, and her husband. They then raped the girl repeatedly. For weeks she was barely able to move, but was protected and nursed by her mother, who hid her. She was finally able to make her way to Burundi, where she was cared for at Peter Guilbaird's mission.

At the time of elections in Rwanda there had also been elections in

Burundi, but without any bloodshed. The voters there had decided upon a constitutional monarchy, with Mwami Mwambutsa IV as king. He had already ruled for forty-nine years, longer than any ruler in the world. Some people called him a playboy — and it was well known that he liked to play poker, attend night clubs, enjoy white girl friends, and drive fast cars. But he was immensely popular in his country, with both his Watusi and Bahutu subjects. But the popularity of a ruler cannot explain the strikingly different histories of Burundi and Rwanda, both of which shared the same four-century heritage.

In Burundi, some generations ago there had been a breaking down of caste lines. Watusi and Bahutu intermarried frequently, and qualified Bahutu won places of importance in the government. Many Watusi actually worked, instead of being waited upon, and they did not act like divinely appointed rulers of the world. Whether consciously or unconsciously, the Watusi of Burundi were much more farsighted than their cousins in Rwanda. They had gone a long way toward the unification of their nation before independence came to them.

Both former Watusi nations are desperately poor, and now they distrust each other. Neither one alone — nor both together — can be economically self-sufficient. And there may be more sporadic warfare in Rwanda, making matters worse. In any event, the fantastic Watusi are done for.

Before getting into my little chartered plane at the airport near Usumbura, I looked northward toward Rwanda and waved good-bye to the aristocratic, gracious, and handsome giants who had once been my friends. Why couldn't they have learned in time, like their brothers in Burundi, that the world of master and slave was coming to an end?

3

The Pygmies

FROM giants to midgets in one day's drive — this was perhaps the most striking, although only one of the startling, contrasts Central Africa offered. (The swift Westernizing of the continent brings more amazing contrasts every year.) On three out of four trips to Africa, I arranged to move from Watusi country to Pygmy country in as short a time as possible in order to savor the excitement of meeting opposites so close together.

There were so-called Pygmies, the Batwa, in the Watusi country, of course, but they were actually pygmoids, a mixture of true Pygmy and Bantu or Sudanic Negro, like those who had led me up the gorilla mountain. The Pygmies of the Ituri Forest in the eastern Congo, the Bambuti, are true and pure Pygmies, ranging from something under four feet to a maximum of five feet in height. Two average Ituri Pygmies, one standing on the shoulders of the other, would not quite reach the height of the tallest Watusi.

But the contrasts between the two peoples are far more than physical. Their customs, dress, beliefs, food, ideals, and environments were as different as one could conceive. The Watusi were the representatives of a civilization, even though that civilization had been in an arrested state for many centuries. The Bambuti Pygmies are genuine representatives of the Paleolithic Age, and have picked up a few handy gadgets from modern times only in the last few decades. They are about as primitive as any people on earth. Even the Bambuti's few borrowings from civilization, such as knives, spear points, tobacco, and beer, have not altered their way of life to any appreciable degree.

The most striking and most recent contrast, which I saw only on my 1964 trip, lies in the effect of uhuru, freedom, on Watusi and on Pygmy. The aristocratic Watusi of Rwanda, though still fighting, are done for; their cousins in Burundi survive because of their far-sighted collaboration with their former serfs. The Bambuti of the Ituri, on the other hand, are maintaining and even increasing their independence of the chaotic world around them and their forest homes.

In 1937 our route between Watusi and Pygmy territories crossed the western or Albertine section of the Great Rift, that massive crack in the earth's surface made when the planet was young. In Central Africa the Rift is thirty to forty miles wide, with towering cliffs or mountain ranges on either side for much of its length. And it contains the beautiful lakes of the region, Tanganyika, Kivu, Edward, and Albert.

Cézaire and I drove in his old Chevrolet around 844 sharp turns, climbing an escarpment close to four thousand feet high. Some sections were only a narrow shelf carved out of the precipice, and in such places we often came upon a barrier operated by an African perched on a high rock. He had a shiny, empty gasoline tin suspended from a pole and another by his side on which he could drum. When we came along, he raised the tin to indicate we could proceed and pounded loudly on the other tin to let his counterpart know that a car had entered the narrow stretch. We saw his partner, miles away, in about twenty minutes. He raised his tin for us, pounded the one by his side to let his collaborator know we had passed through, and went back to sleep. And at many turns we looked — or at least I did, for Cézaire didn't dare — down upon the gem of the world, Lake Kivu, with smoking volcanoes at its northern end sending down endless slow-moving avenues of lava to hiss and cool off in the blue water.

Thus the Great Rift told me, no matter which way I crossed it in my several trips, that I was going abruptly from one world to another. The terrain itself emphasized that I was spanning a gulf of ten or twenty thousand years. Border guards and small towns with Belgians and even fairly pleasant rest houses did not really matter. They were nothing but pinpricks along the edge of an expanse of forest of some thousand square miles. Even the villages on the few roads cutting the eastern and northern parts of this great unknown were but tinier pinpricks always in danger of being erased by the voracious tropical forest.

It was from one of the smallest of these dots, a Negro village on the narrow road between Beni and Irumu, that I first went into the Ituri Forest to visit the Pygmies. The Bantu Negroes in this region were of a tribe called the Bandande, and their chief was Kalumé, to whom I had been directed by the Italian explorer Attilio Gatti. Gatti had even written out for me in phonetic Kingwana, the lingua franca of much of the Ituri region, a speech for me to make to Kalumé. After a friendly and courteous greeting from this important man, I launched into the series of strange sounds feeling that I was making a fool of myself and that the chief would understand nothing I said, but Kalumé seemed to get some meaning from the words I spoke and was even friendlier at their conclusion.

I fell back at once on the interpretative resources of Cézaire, who helped me conduct my business with Kalumé. It was not difficult. Of course we could visit and talk with "his" Pygmies. Would we rest in the village while Kalumé summoned some from the forest? No, I would prefer to visit them in their own homes. While the Bantu chief seemed a bit displeased at this, he agreed to take us to the nearest Pygmy camp in the forest. A few gifts for him and his *capitas,* or subchiefs, plus some palm wine, salt, and other gifts for the Pygmies would suffice.

At the time, I did not realize how unusual this arrangement was. In the main, the Negroes of the villages will not penetrate the dense forest, even for a short distance, for they look upon it as evil, threatening, incalculably dangerous. They summon the Pygmies to them or have Pygmies guide and protect them when they must leave their villages. But Kalumé was an unusual man, aside from the fact that the nearest Pygmy camp at that time was only about four miles away, over a well-trod (for the Ituri Forest) path. So the chief sent a man ahead to let "his" Pygmies know that white men were coming with gifts.

The village Negroes and the forest Pygmies have developed — over how many centuries no one knows — an unusual interdependency, which has been widely misunderstood. Every explorer, every government official, every outsider of any kind, has found that he could make contact with the Bambuti Pygmies only through the Bantu of the villages on the edge of the forest. Even missionaries like my friends

Bill Deans and Bill Spees, who have lived with the Pygmies for decades, made their first acquaintance with the small forest people through village Negroes. The fabulous Pat Putnam, for many years the only white settler in the Ituri, talked to the villagers before he could talk to "their" Pygmies.

When I wanted to buy a Pygmy bow and arrow or a spear to bring home, I had to arrange the purchase through the Bantu who "owned" the Pygmy who had these things for sale. When I needed Pygmy guides or hunters on my trips, I negotiated (at least at the beginning) with the Negro village "masters."

None of these terms in quotes is really correct, even though the villagers would have you believe that they are owners and masters. The Bambuti are not slaves, by any means. They are, on the contrary, fiercely independent, jealous of their rights and prerogatives. They also know their great strength — the forest in which they live, the forest they love, the forest that gives them about 98 per cent of what they want from life, the forest that is hated and feared by their so-called masters in the villages.

A villager may say that he "owns" a certain number of Pygmies — the number owned is an important status symbol to him and his fellows — and he always refers to them as "my" Pygmies. But certainly they are not slaves. He could not remove a single Pygmy from his section of the forest if he tried, and he would not dream of trying. He is always aware of the fact that "his" Pygmies may disappear forever into the forest if he is not fair to them. They may miss the beer and palm oil and bananas, but they can get along without them if need be. When the hunting is good, I've heard the village "masters" complain that they cannot get their Pygmies to come when called. And the villagers want the meat and the ivory tusks that the Pygmies bring to them for barter. They have no other way of getting such things.

Still, the Bantu acts contemptuous of the Pygmy, although he is at the same time afraid of him. He laughs at the pygmy, and explains to the white man that he is not really a human being — just an animal, perhaps a cut above the chimpanzee, but still an animal because he lives in the forest. To the villager, only an animal can live in such a terrifying place. The villager knows that, left in the forest alone, he would starve in a few weeks — if the evil spirits didn't get him first.

The Pygmy is as contemptuous of the village Negro as his "master" is of him, although he may act subservient enough when in the village or in the presence of Negroes. One reason for much misinformation about Pygmies is that white observers and writers have seen them only in the villages, where they act quite different from their natural selves in their beloved forest. Colin Turnbull, the brilliant young anthropologist now associated with the American Museum of Natural History, has told me that the Pygmies have just two words they use when referring to the village Negroes — one meaning savage, one meaning animal.

The chief reason for the Pygmies' contempt for the Negro is the latter's fear of the forest. Another stems from the villager's many superstitions, his belief in sorcery and witchcraft, and the mysterious and complicated rites he goes through to ward off supernatural dangers. The Bambuti Pygmies are, in truth, a bewildering contradiction; they are an authentic part of the vanishing Stone Age world, but they have an extraordinary lack of concern about the supernatural. There are no real medicine men among them, just as there are no chiefs. Most primitive tribes that I've come to know believe that death is unnatural, only life is natural. Thus, when someone dies, death has been caused by a curse, sorcery, witchcraft, brought on by an enemy through the medium of some malignant spirit. The Negro villagers on the edges of the Ituri Forest believe this. It is true that if a Pygmy dies there is, first, loud and prolonged grief in the camp of the dead one. And after this mourning, the Pygmies take the body to the village of their "masters" for proper rites and burial, because the Negroes insist upon it. But after burial, when the villagers summon their medicine man and go through their own particular rituals to determine the enemy who caused this particular death, the Pygmies become disinterested, bored, and finally leave. It is obvious that to them this is a lot of nonsense. The forest has given life. It has also given death. They mourn over the death just as they rejoiced over the life. But trying to figure things out beyond that seems nothing but a waste of time to them. They are great realists.

This is not to say that they have no sense of the spiritual, emotional, and super-mundane things of life. If they have a god, it is the forest itself. When things go badly for them, they feel that the forest is unhappy, that they have in some way neglected it. So they hunt and feast and dance and sing to make the forest happy again with their own happiness. And the forest always responds.

But what about this dependency of the Pygmies on the villagers?

Why do they take their dead to the village to go through Negro rites and burial? Why do they allow their boys of ten and twelve to undergo the painful and cruel initiation which they share with Negro youths of the same age? Colin Turnbull, in his excellent book *The Forest People*, gives the answer to the last question, and that answers all others of the same kind. The Negroes believe that any male who has not been circumcised and initiated into manhood through a long and painful process is not really a man. He is a mere boy and will remain a boy all his life, and Negroes will have nothing to do with him. Therefore the Pygmies, who want to continue trading with the villagers, have their sons become men in Negro eyes, although they soften the rigors of the initiation whenever they get a chance.

The Pygmies hunt and bring some of their meat, and the elephant tusks, to their "masters" in the villages. They also work in the villagers' plantations sometimes, but never for long periods. In return they receive from the villagers salt, bananas, palm wine, knives, and iron spear and arrow tips. These are things the forest does not give them. If their trading has not brought them as many bananas as they want, they are likely to raid some of the village plantations at night — but never the plantations of their "masters." If they are caught, their "masters" must pay the owner of the plantation that was raided.

The Pygmies may seem to have mortgaged themselves for the sake of their new appetites, which were introduced and whetted by the villagers. But who gets the better of the bargain? While the villagers no doubt rob the Pygmies frequently in the trading of ivory, the Pygmies make out quite well in every other department. In fact those who have lived with the forest people the longest and come to know them best are certain that the Pygmies in the main get the best of things in their dealings with the villagers.

Even though the villagers look on Pygmies as animals, they will take Pygmy women as wives readily enough, especially if their Negro wives are sterile — an increasingly common condition resulting from that early fruit of civilization, venereal disease. But intermarriage works only one way, for no Negro woman ever marries a Pygmy. She could not possibly stand the nomad hunter's life in the forest, and almost no Pygmy male would completely abandon his natural home for life in the village.

Many Pygmy women after marrying Negro villagers eventually return to the forest. Once when I was living at a Pygmy camp, two young men from the village came to visit their Pygmy mother who had run away from her Negro husband. There was a noisy and joyous reunion, then the sons returned to the village. They were thorough-going villagers, just as their mother was truly a forest Pygmy. The husband did not really mind; he had his sons, the chief object of taking the Pygmy as wife.

On my 1964 trip to the Ituri, I heard from Ella and Bill Spees, missionaries, a legend that shows fairly accurately the relationship between Pygmy and Negro villager. The Spees first came to the forest in 1929, and know the Pygmies about as well as anyone can. They have, of course, heard hundreds of stories from the small people, but I suspect that, even if told by Pygmies, the legend's origin was in the villages. For when it begins, there is no one living in the forest, only in the villages, and that is the reverse of the probable truth.

Anyway, the tale goes that long ago a man — a villager obviously — took his dog and went hunting in the forest. They could find no game, but in time the man looked up and saw a huge beehive high in a tree. Taking his knife to cut into the hive, he climbed the tree, but just as he got to the hive he dropped his knife. It was a long hard climb down and up again, so he called to his dog. "Dog, bring up my knife."

Now, everyone knows that dogs do not climb trees, but this was an exceptional dog in many ways. It said to its master, "No, I won't, because if I do you'll go back to the village and tell everyone about it, and they'll think I'm peculiar, climbing trees and talking." The master swore that he wouldn't tell anyone if the dog brought up his knife.

So the dog took the knife in his mouth, climbed the tree, and gave it to his master. The man cut open the hive and got lots of honey. But when he was down on the ground again, he could hardly wait to get back to the village to tell everyone about his remarkable dog.

When the dog heard his master breaking his word and telling everyone about what had happened, he was furious and told all the other dogs about it. They decided to leave the village. That night each dog took out of the fire a stick with glowing coals at one end and ran off into the forest.

The next day the men in the village wanted to go hunting, but there were no dogs. They called and called, but no dogs came, and they could not figure out what had happened. They had to go hunting anyway, so they went into the forest without dogs. But they could not find their way very well without their animals, and they could not find any game at all. So they went deeper into the forest, although they did not like it, and finally came upon a clearing with small huts like beehives and many little people.

"These must be our dogs turned into little people," the men said. They wanted the dog-people to come home to the village, but the little things were so happy in the forest that they would not go. So the men made an agreement with them.

"When you were our dogs," they said, "you used to hunt for us and we used to feed you. If you will still hunt for us, we will feed you."

The little forest people agreed. A few days later a villager and his Pygmy were hunting when a huge bird with green wings flew overhead. The Pygmy shot a tiny arrow from his small bow and shot it down. When the bird landed, it became a banana tree, with big green leaves and bunches of bananas. The Pygmy and his master decided to divide the catch somehow. The Pygmy said, "I'll take the bananas and have a feast." The villager said, "I'll take the roots so I can plant them."

When the Pygmy finished his feast, he wished he had more bananas. When he went to the village, he found that his master had planted the roots and now had a fine banana plantation, with lots of bananas. So the Pygmy brought some game from the forest, and the villager gave him bananas.

And that's the way it still is today. The Pygmies have no plantations but are great hunters. The villagers are very good gardeners but poor hunters. The Pygmies still don't know how to make fire, but carry burning embers when they move their camps. And the original agreement between villager and Pygmy still holds, because they need each other.

Returning to my first trip, in 1937, we left the village with Kalumé and two of his capitas, skirted a banana plantation, and plunged into the forest. For a few minutes I was almost unable to see, moving so suddenly from the bright sunlight into the dark gloom of the forest, but the path was wide and easy to follow — for a few hundred yards. Then the trees began to close in. The jungle seems to resent the intrusion of strange people and to make every effort to push them back and trip them up.

Except for my gorilla search up Mt. Bulgalamisa, this was my first excursion into a tropical forest, and I shall never forget it. Thorns reached out and snagged my clothes, holding fast until they tore the tough cloth. Nettles stung my face and hands, giant ferns slapped my face wetly, and looping lianas entangled me like the tentacles of an octopus. When we left the path for a few hundred yards to detour around a giant mahogany recently toppled by lightning, the going was even worse.

But the fall of the huge tree had opened up a hole in the forest canopy, so we could see a patch of sky and take a few pictures. Everywhere else there was only a greenish twilight haze in the forest, with dancing bits of sunlight darting around as the leaves moved far overhead.

We came upon a nest of termites, a dome ten or more feet in height, that must have held billions of the tiny creatures. The sickly white, wormlike things live inside, guarding their queen, an immense, bloated egg machine, many times larger than her guards. The workers, unable to endure the light, never emerge, but toil ceaselessly to cultivate the fungus on which they all feed. When I tapped the mound with a long pole, however, the soldiers poured out, searching frantically and pugnaciously for the enemy and squirting streams of viscous liquid from their head-syringes.

In a short time we came upon a stretch of land relatively free of entangling undergrowth, but in its place was swampy, gooey mud that clung to me with the tenacity of glue. Later, as we were splashing across a narrow stream, I saw a long snake slither into the underbrush — incredibly thin but almost eight or nine feet long. I learned later that it was probably a black mamba, one of the deadliest of all African snakes.

I slipped and half fell across a rotting log that lay beside the path, and a parrot screeched overhead, as if making fun of my awkwardness. A score of other parrots joined it, and I heard a whirring of wings above me. But I could see nothing. We rested a few moments in a fairly clear space, and I admired some pink and white orchids. As we started on again, a cloud of big butterflies rose up and circled hysterically toward the high branches. Weaverbirds wheezed, and tiny sunbirds tittered above me.

In another five minutes there was no sound in the forest except for the noise I made as I stepped on dry branches and stumbled over half-hidden roots. I stopped and heard nothing but vacant sound, like that on the other end of a dead telephone line. Not a leaf swished against another, and the forest seemed uninhabited. But in another few minutes there was a bedlam of sound, a turmoil of movement. Birds screeched, black and white colobus monkeys argued and scolded as they swung from branch to branch. A covey of guinea fowl took off like a squadron of bombers. I heard a sudden crash of branches and rustle of leaves only a few feet to my right, and I wondered what creature had suddenly bolted in terror at the approach of man — leopard, elephant, okapi, wart hog? I wanted to see an okapi; I did not want, at the moment, to encounter a leopard or an elephant. I was sure of only one thing — it was not a Pygmy. He would never have made so much noise.

I got my second wind and was going along at a great rate, avoiding roots, thorns and vines like a real woodsman, I thought, but then the mosquitoes and numerous other unidentified insects began to attack in earnest. They had been with us from the beginning, but some kind of telegraphic system, like the Pygmies' drums, had notified the hordes ahead of us to lie in wait. The clouds around our heads, moving with us as we slowly advanced, bit and stung and buzzed and flew into our eyes and ears. When I complained loudly, Cézaire remarked that we were fortunate not to have encountered any safari ants. The Ituri was saving them for later.

But in spite of the hardships, I was excited. How often can you walk only four miles and move ten or twenty thousand years in time?

Suddenly bright sunlight struck my eyes. We had stepped from the half-light of the forest into a clearing, where the sun's rays cut the gloom like a shining sword. I stopped, blinked, and looked at a dozen leafy beehives about four feet high and six feet across — Pygmy homes.

But no Pygmies! I stood beside Kalumé, his two capitas, and Cézaire, waiting for the small men to appear. But nothing stirred. We could hear only our own breathing.

I saw a leaf move on the other side of the clearing. I caught a glimpse of a coppery face. Then the leaves were still again. I realized that dozens of eyes were watching us. If the Pygmies had decided that we were enemies to be done away with, they could have killed us all with their tiny arrows in a few minutes. But they have a protection much stronger than any weapon — the forest. Although in the old days they have been known to kill, they are not an angry, belligerent people. They can at any time disappear into their friendly home, the forest, and no one will find them.

So we stood at the edge of the clearing. Then Kalumé called out, "Aputo! Manzaele! Nzala!" and cried to the unseen Pygmies that the bwana had brought salt and was a friend. A few moments later, the leaves parted at several spots and three small figures appeared, hesitant, watchful, dignified but shy. They stopped fifteen feet in front of us and stared. And I stared.

At first glance Pygmies are caricatures of human beings, miniature imitations fashioned by a clumsy hand. I caught myself looking at them as I might at circus freaks or zoo animals until checked by the thought, "How do I look to them?"

If a Pygmy looks like a wizened ten-year-old in my eyes, I must appear to him as an awkward giant. My figure must seem unalluringly straight and flat, lacking the many curves that appeal to a Pygmy — balloon-like belly, swayback, and outsize, impudent buttocks. His golden-brown skin no doubt seems just right to him, a proper compromise between the brown-black of his Bantu neighbors and the pasty pallor of the occasional white visitor.

Some Pygmies suspected, I knew, that I was not that color all over, but how could they tell when instead of wearing a sensible bark-cloth apron I covered all but my hands and face with layers of cloth and encased my feet in heavy leather boots? On later trips, deep into the forest where I met Pygmies who had never seen white men, some of them rubbed my hand to see if the white would come off.

But Kalumé's Pygmies had seen white men. Nevertheless they stared at me just as I stared at them, with a kind of disbelief. The Bambuti of the Ituri are about four feet tall, and for most of us the only human beings that size are children. But Pygmies are obviously *not* children, in spite of a certain childlike quality, a naive directness, about them. Some have gray kinky hair and chin whiskers, and faces as wrinkled as a butternut. There are three-foot-nine-inch matrons with babies on their hips, suspended in a kind of sling from the shoulder. The shortness of the mothers is accentuated because Pygmy babies are normal in size, as large as ours at the same age. Pygmy children just stop growing when they are nine or ten years old.

Looking at the Pygmy babies, I was struck by the realization that they were the same size as Watusi babies of the same age. And both were just about the same as gorilla babies — as to size *and* appearance. They all start just about even, but something in their genes carries them to obviously different ends.

It is confusing to look at a female the size of your niece in the fourth grade and note that she is a toothless old hag with breasts like empty leather pouches. Or to see a young fellow apparently not old enough for his First Communion and realize that he may have slain fifty elephants. One's preconceived notions about values and relationships collapse in such circumstances, which is one good reason for exploring.

The first three Pygmies Kalumé had called were gradually joined by others, who slipped noiselessly into the clearing until there were at least thirty facing us. We unpacked the salt, palm wine, and cigarettes and passed them around. I took pictures, and Cézaire took pictures of me with my new friends. The Pygmies showed me their leafy homes and laughed when I got on my hands and knees to peer through tiny doors. They showed me their miniature spears, their toylike bows and arrows, their babies.

We sat down cross-legged while some of the great hunters told me tales of the killing of elephants. Cézaire could not get every word, and when they were excited he could not keep up with them in his translation, but gestures and pantomime told me all I needed to know about the excitement, the perils, and the triumphs of the hunt. The narrative was supplemented with displays of old, badly healed scars, accompanied by the moaning and groaning that had occurred when the wounds were inflicted five, ten, or twenty years before.

On the 1946 *Savage Splendor* expedition, perhaps the largest gathering ever to take place in the Ituri Forest occurred, chiefly through the help of Bill Deans, the American missionary who for more than twenty years had given help, friendship, and encouragement to every outsider who came to the Ituri with a serious purpose. I had met him in Stanleyville, where I was waiting for equipment for trips to the Wagenia, Mangbetu, Watusi, Bambuti, and other tribes. Bill had made arrangements with Bantu chiefs in the village to call their Pygmies together, and had assembled the necessary palm wine, salt, dried fish, and other articles for gifts and payments. By the time I arrived at his headquarters in Bunia, Bill had gone on to Irumu, but my supplies were already loaded in his one-ton truck. We followed him in the truck, crossed the Ituri River on a pontoon bridge, then drove about ten kilometers on a narrowing road into the forest until we came to Bill's original mission. It was now run by other missionaries, for Bill had moved even deeper into the forest, to a station called Nyankunde.

Even after reaching Bill Deans's new mission, there were still miles to be covered on foot through that thickest of all jungles. The going was slow because we had with us about thirty Pygmies and their wives to guide us and carry in our supplies. It was incredible to see what big loads those tiny women could haul, bundles supported by lianas across their foreheads in the tumpline style of American Indians and many primitive people all over the world. And many of the wives carried a baby on one hip, babies who were jostled along placidly sleeping or staring wide-eyed at the passing scenery.

After about an hour we came to one small Pygmy clearing, with ten or eleven beehive huts in it. I saw no resident Pygmies, and the ashes looked quite dead. It was an abandoned camp, as the general messiness and smells indicated, aside from the absence of humans. Pygmies are not very tidy, except for their persons, and when a camp becomes too dirty, or when the game is hunted out, they just move on to another location. They have so few personal or household goods that moving is no great chore, and housebuilding takes less than an hour.

In any one camp, all the residents are members of the same family; cousins, brothers-in-law, uncles and aunts are included, but there is always some close relationship. There is no real chief or headman. A fine hunter may be looked up to more than anyone else, and his opinion carries great weight, but he is not a chief. The group settles its problems, disagreements and fights as a group, without formal procedures.

In another camp a few miles away, you will find another family group. Group A may also have some blood ties to Group B, but they live and hunt separately and often keep out of each other's way. While there is no actual association of family groups into what can correctly be termed a clan, a working arrangement exists between neighboring groups. Daughters of one group marry sons in another. Two affiliated groups may "belong" to Bantus of the same village. They do not engage in serious quarrels over hunting territories.

Each large affiliation or pseudo-clan, however, has a very definite territory in which it hunts, roams, and lives. Fifty miles or more into the jungle there may be another such grouping of families in a different cluster of camps. Wars between these so-called clans formerly were quite frequent, and there are still clashes when anyone trespasses. But in recent years "clans" are inclined to stay within their own territories. All Pygmies know just where the boundaries are, although there is no marking of any kind. You cannot persuade or bribe or pay your Pygmies to guide you across that boundary.

This situation has prevented any white man from exploring the whole Ituri Forest. He cannot arrange to have himself passed on from one tribe to another, as many explorers on this continent did with the Indians, and as Mick Leahy did when he discovered the highlands of New Guinea. If you start out from one side of the jungle determined to cross it, your Pygmies will accompany you so far and no farther. There you are in the middle of the jungle, with little men who refuse to go another step, and no other little men on the other side to guide you on another leg of your journey. You are limited to the territory of your original Pygmies, but that may be hundreds of square miles of land — enough to tell you all you want to know about Pygmy life and environment. And if you go first to one group, and then circle the forest and live with a different group, you will find no significant difference in looks, customs or beliefs.

On the long walk to our movie location we passed two more camps. The first was abandoned, but I believe the last one was occupied at the time, although not by anyone I could see. I saw some pottery jars which would have been taken along if the group had moved, and signs of fires that had been burning recently. The inhabitants were probably looking at us as we passed through, and would return to their homes as soon as we disappeared.

In the afternoon I saw some light through the trees ahead, a startling sight after hours in the forest. As we emerged from the trees, blinking and squinting, I saw a clearing such as I had never expected to find in the Ituri. It was fully two hundred feet across, with only a few tall trees standing in it. I smiled happily, knowing that here I could find enough light for filming. (Those were the days before fast film.)

I settled down for a long stay with the Pygmies, except for one short trip outside for supplies and a little respite from the claustrophobic effect of the deep forest. I pitched my tent at one side of the clearing. There were already about twenty Pygmy huts on the other side, and my Pygmies started at once to build their own houses near these.

The women did most of the work but some of the men helped, while others just bossed their wives. From the woods they brought supple saplings about eight feet long, while the man of the family drew a circle on the ground to mark the dimensions of the house. The thick ends of the saplings were driven into the ground along this line, about a foot apart. Then the women bent the saplings over toward each other, interlacing them and tying them together into a rounded arch. With all this bracing of one sapling against another, the framework was quite sturdy.

It was late in the day so I wandered about the clearing, looking for activities that could be filmed when the opportunity arose. I stopped at one house under construction to watch a Pygmy hunter who obviously fancied himself as a first-class architect. He limited his help to suggestions, advice and orders to his wife, but there were plenty of those. As I watched, I was struck once again with the fact that language is often no barrier, especially when one is dealing with such expressive people as the Pygmies. I did not need to understand a word in this case to know exactly what was going on.

No, that sapling should bend over this way, the imperious man gestured, and his wife did as he said.

No, no, these are too close together. She made them farther apart.

That is not tied tightly. It will come loose in the night and a leopard, or at least the rain, will come in. She tied the vine again.

The next step in construction was fitting phrynium leaves into the latticework of the saplings, starting at the bottom and overlapping them as she moved upward, much as we place shingles. In this process, the man found her work abominable. She left openings, didn't overlap properly, and generally did a sloppy job. To his specific corrections, he added a few general denunciations of her as wife, mother, and workhorse. Through all this she kept working steadily, and I thought she was doing a remarkably fast and efficient job. But of course I was not going to sleep in the hut, and he was.

Suddenly he leaned forward and snatched away a big leaf she had just fixed in place. With that, she had enough. She turned on him — all three foot six inches of her — and glared. From her lips there burst a volcano of sound, shrill, rapid-fire and filled with venom. Again I needed no words to understand. She was telling him off as eloquently as ever the job was done, telling him that he was a lazy good-for-nothing, that she did all the work and did it well, that all he did was get in the way and act like a big shot — and he wasn't even a very good hunter! I could tell when that last shot hit him, for he recoiled as if struck. Anger blazed in his eyes and he started to talk back, but she picked up a good-sized stick and waved it at his face. He stepped back, a little bewildered, glanced at me and looked ashamed, then walked away, muttering. The woman proceeded to finish the house in short order.

A couple of smooth logs to sleep on, the family jars or pots, the man's weapons — bow and arrow, spear, perhaps a knife, hunting nets — these were the total furnishings of a Pygmy home. At night the occupants usually started a fire inside to drive away the chill dampness of the ground and keep away insects and leopards. Insects were a constant menace, but leopard raids were relatively rare. I had heard of leopards breaking into Pygmy huts and making off with a child, but I could never obtain firsthand confirmation of such a tragedy. But there is no reason to doubt the truth of the stories. The leopard is clever, more silent and cunning than a Pygmy, and desperate when hungry or cornered.

The next morning I found about seventy-five Pygmies in and around the clearing. During the evening of our arrival I had heard the drums, and knew that the message was going out that the *bwana bukuba*, had arrived, the white man bearing many gifts. The newcomers would have filled up the clearing with their huts, but I needed plenty of clear space for filming. I persuaded them to retire to other clearings nearby or make new ones. On the third day, more Pygmies arrived, and the day after that still more. By the fifth day at least five hundred Pygmies had established themselves in and near the big clearing — far more than I could possibly use, so many that they got in each other's way. Bill Deans, who had hoped to get a hundred together for me, was astonished.

He was delighted, too, for he had never obtained the ears of so many Pygmies at one time. He held meetings and preached the gospel to them, and most of the Pygmies listened attentively. I have grave doubts as to just how much they understood — or cared. But they respected Bill Deans.

Even though too many Pygmies had come, I could not disappoint them in their expectation of delicacies. Some had traveled scores of miles through the forest to reach the clearing, get their gifts, and help in any way they could. So each day I handed out presents to the new arrivals, giving me some good footage but necessitating a trip out of the forest for more supplies.

When the Pygmies lined up for distribution of pay, or gifts, there was never any pushing, arguing, or shoving. They were all quiet and orderly, smiling broadly, talking to each other in low voices, rolling their always-startled eyes, smacking their lips. I poured out a big bag of salt on huge leaves, then gave each person a handful as he stepped forward. Although I tried to make every handful the same, once in a while there was a noticeably small batch. Never did the Pygmy getting it object, but I received searching looks several times.

It rained a good deal during my different trips into the Ituri, but fortunately the downpours came chiefly at night. Many a day I just sat, or paced back and forth, waiting for the small patch of gray sky overhead to turn blue, for the murky light to grow clear and bright. Even when there was no rain the forest dripped almost continually as the moisture in the heavy air condensed on leaves and branches. And when the sun finally did appear, the forest floor exhaled misty clouds that hung in the clearing, coated camera lenses, and penetrated clothing, bedding, shoes, and soul. Much of the time I was wetter than the Pygmies, who wore no "protective" clothing, and when I climbed into my saturated pajamas at night I almost envied the Pygmy, who lay down more or less naked on a couple of smooth logs. The fire he burned in his hut all night made smoke that would have suffocated me, but it dried the air a bit and drove out all but small attack forces of man-eating insects.

In spite of these filming and personal difficulties, we managed on the *Savage Splendor* expedition to take many pictures of routine Pygmy activities and a few more exciting events specially staged. We filmed the making of huts, and women going off into the forest for firewood, greens, and herbs, each with a baby rocking on one hip. A mother never puts her baby down on the ground, even for a moment; there are too many animals nearby waiting to snatch such a succulent morsel. This explains why Pygmy women always kill one of twin babies right after they are born. Mothers cannot handle two babies at a time. With one baby on hip, they can perform any task — house construction, cooking, gathering food, working in the gardens in the villages. With a baby on each hip, they could do little. Pygmy women never eat the tiny double bananas one sometimes gathers because they think they will bring twins — and the only worse thing is sterility.

We filmed the making of bark cloth, in which the men often join their wives. Pygmies use bark from six different trees and nine different vines for cloth — the one selected depending upon what is at hand and in good condition. The bark is stripped off in long pieces, soaked in water, then pounded with a small stone against a larger flat stone. Alternate soaking and pounding produce a broad, soft, and fairly tough cloth rather like felt. But the pounding must be done with care, to prevent holes in the cloth and to make a web of interlacing fibers of about uniform thickness.

Pygmy men wear their bark cloth rather like a diaper, fastened to a liana G-string in front, passed between the legs, and tied in back. When the cloth is large, it looks like a pair of outsize bloomers. The women's dress is much briefer, and often consists of big leaves rather than bark cloth, tucked under G-strings front and back. I once followed some women into the forest when they were searching for food and saw some of them shop for new costumes while there. Coming upon some particularly large and glistening green leaves, one woman plucked them, removed the old leaves, and fitted the new ones in place. Several others followed suit, and some tucked small red flowers in their waistbands.

One vine used for bark cloth is called, in English, the trelliswork fig tree, although it is not a tree at all. One of these vines will start growing up the trunk of a huge ironwood or teak tree — about the hardest woods known. The vine circles and climbs, growing thicker and thicker as the years go by, moving out along the lofty branches of the tree. In time the trunk of the vine is as thick as that of the tree, and later the tree is choked completely. In its place stands a huge trelliswork fig tree, strong and proud as if it had done the job of growing all by itself instead of as a parasite.

During the first week of my stay in the Ituri, I was an object of curiosity, especially to those Pygmies who had never or rarely seen a white man. But they soon grew used to me, accepting me as an unusual but regular fixture of their forest who occasionally asked them to act out things while some black boxes made whirring noises. When filming started, I learned that I had encountered some of the finest natural acting talent in the world, a quality I later found in many other primitive peoples. The Pygmies were real hams who enjoyed nothing quite so much as acting out parts familiar to them. They did not try to steal the show or upstage each other, nor did they posture before the cameras with self-conscious grins. They really acted. I am sure they did not understand the nature of cameras or the purpose of my filming, but they welcomed the idea of acting out scenes from their experiences.

One day after some talk among a few oldsters about fights between Pygmy clans in the bygone days, translated for me by Bill Deans, I asked if the Pygmies would put on a battle for me — as if two enemy groups had come upon each other in the forest, in disputed territory. The forest people, especially the older men who remembered, seized on the idea eagerly and set about planning the "war." The scene had to be shot on the edge of the clearing, rather than in thick woods where most such fighting took place, so I would have enough light. The Pygmies agreed on the two groups, and one old man, crippled with rheumatism and over seventy, insisted on being part of the play because he had fought in many wars in his youth. So vivid was the acting the next day that he seemed to discard both rheumatism and old age in that glorious moment of the charge against an enemy.

The acting of the Pygmies was almost frightening when we shot the sequence. The happy, carefree little folk of the forest suddenly became vicious and savage warriors, bent on spilling blood. With shrieks and whoops that unhinged my spine, they tore at each other, shooting their arrows with what looked like fair accuracy. But not an arrow hit a man; all sailed cleanly over everyone's head — although a couple came rather near me.

On several occasions I had to delay the start of filming because of one huge tree that held back the light for about half an hour. After consulting Bill Deans, I decided to have it cut down. The Pygmies turned out to be poor lumberjacks even with steel axes we supplied, but they finally chopped most of the way through the big trunk. I set myself to get a picture of the toppling giant, calculating the direction of its fall as well as I could, and placing myself in what appeared to be a safe but advantageous spot. The Pygmies had tied a long liana halfway up the tree, extending to the ground at an angle, which a dozen men were going to pull, then hop out of the way as the tree began to fall of its own weight. I was about twenty feet to one side of the calculated line of fall, hoping to catch the tree falling *almost* directly toward the camera.

A final few hacking strokes with the axes, a mighty tug by the men on the ground, and the tree tipped toward me. I had the camera at my eye and started it, watching through the viewer as the tree majestically, as if in slow motion, keeled over. Suddenly I realized that I was getting too good a picture. The tree was falling directly — not almost — toward me. I pulled the camera away from my eye and stared up. Someone was yelling to the Pygmies on the ground to pull hard toward them, but they could have little effect as the heavy tree gained momentum.

It was too late for me to run anywhere. I just ducked and thought fleetingly that this was a hell of a way to die. Amid a roaring and crashing of branches, and a trembling of the earth, I felt one small branch whip across my back. I looked up and breathed again. Another, smaller tree, a dozen paces to my left, had caught the full impact of the big giant and had deflected its fall away from me.

More than anything else, I wanted to film Pygmies hunting, but I soon learned that this was probably impossible. Hunting took place in the dusky forest, with too little light and too rapid movements. And usually I could not go along with the Pygmies on their serious hunts because I could not keep up with them and would make far too much noise.

I went on two or three hunts for okapi, which we never got, and on two elephant hunts. I saw the Pygmies track, stalk, and kill half a dozen different creatures encountered accidentally or by design. I heard them use their wooden whistles to attract game, whistles in three sizes hanging from their necks. And I saw the work of their wonderful if unattractive Bisenji dogs.

The dogs looked like mongrels, with traces of hyena and fox. Their short-haired coats appear moth-eaten and full of badly darned holes. But there are no better hunting dogs in the world, and none that can match them for courage. When they go with their masters on the hunt, they can follow the spoor even more surely and swiftly than the Pygmies unless the prey crosses a good-sized stream, and even then they are good at picking up the trail on the other side. They never get so far ahead of the hunters but that the men can hear the clop-clop of the little wooden bells tied around each dog's neck. Since the Bisenji has no bark, the bell is essential.

No "man's best friend" relationship exists between master and dog, so far as I could see. Never did I witness a pat or other sign of affection, but I did see many a kick. Still, no Pygmy underestimates the value of his dog, and a dog would give his life for his master, as shown by one experience the Pygmies told me about.

Three Pygmy hunters were moving swiftly through the forest on the trail of some animal, and their dog was just a few feet from the first hunter. Suddenly a leopard sprang from a low branch upon the first Pygmy, who evaded the beast's man-killing first blow but suffered a severe slashing of his right shoulder and arm. He flung his spear at the leopard, but his wounded arm did not send it true. Turning, the Pygmy clambered up a small tree safely because the leopard's attention had been diverted by the charge of the second hunter. This hunter's spear missed its mark, too, and broke against a rock.

Luckily for the second hunter, the leopard saw Number Three and went for him, enabling the second hunter to climb a tree to temporary safety. The third hunter kept hold of his spear and tried to plunge it into the leopard as it sprang. The spear just sliced the animal's leg a bit, making him angrier than before. Then the leopard and hunter number three battled it out, the hunter struggling to keep the leopard's claws from his throat and at the same time maneuvering to get in another thrust with his spear.

He would have been slashed to ribbons if it had not been for the dog, which rushed at the leopard from the side and from the rear, snapping at the big cat's legs and flank, then racing away as the leopard turned to rid himself of this pest. The two hunters in the trees could do nothing to help, as they had no weapons. All they could do was watch man and leopard struggle, with the dog snarling, rushing in and out. Once the dog sank his fangs into the leopard's tail and tugged. The leopard whirled, howled, and apparently decided to kill the pesky dog once and for all. That gave the third hunter just the chance he needed. He lunged with his spear, which pierced the leopard's side, cut into its heart, and dropped it. By this time the hunter was bleeding so badly that he could hardly stand, but all three men managed to get back to camp. As their wounds were cleaned and dressed, they all sang the praises of the dog, giving him full credit for saving their lives. But they did not show the animal one sign of affection.

When the men go hunting with nets, the whole camp joins in—women, children, and dogs. The nets are woven of thin vines into lengths of twenty to thirty yards, tough, strong, and durable. With five or six nets tied together end to end, a big, almost invisible semicircle can be made among the trees. The hunters station themselves in hiding along the outside of the net, while the women, children, and dogs start to close in from a point a mile or two away. They make as much clamor as possible, frightening all game toward the net and the hunters. Small or large forest antelope are the most common catches in nets, although occasionally there are some small buffalo, wild pigs, or armadillos.

Pygmies also hunt by digging pits camouflaged with saplings and brush along well-established animal trails that crisscross the forest. Poison-tipped stakes are fitted in the bottom of the pit to kill the prey. But if the Pygmies want the animals alive, they omit the stakes and make the pits deep enough so animals cannot get out. Elephant pits are usually staked; those for the okapi and the bongo antelope are not.

Small creatures are often caught in noose traps. Elephants and buffalo are sometimes caught with spear traps. The spear in this case is really a heavy pointed log, tipped with poison and suspended over an animal trail. A thin but strong vine across the trail triggers the log so that it falls on the animal below.

Just as there is nothing quite so gay and happy as a successful Pygmy hunt, so there is nothing so depressing as the hunt that fails. I went with the Pygmies once when they caught absolutely nothing. On the way back to the camp, the men said not a word, and they even muffled the wooden bells on their dogs so when they raced ahead to the clearing there would be no sound to announce the return of the hunters. As they trooped into the clearing silently, with heads cast down, the faces of the women fell. No one said a word about the hunt.

One thing will divert Pygmies from their hunting — finding a beehive with honey. Once I watched them scramble up a tall tree where there was a hive in a big hole. They used a heavy liana looped around the trunk to help them in their ascent, much as a telephone linesman uses a wide strap. At the hive the first hunter made an opening, with his spear since he did not have his special beehive adze with him. Hundreds of bees swarmed out, but he plunged in his hand, brought it out full of honeycomb dripping with honey, and crammed it into his mouth. Each hunter climbed the tree in turn and ate his fill, and some took along what they could in leaves. But not once did a bee sting a man. I have questioned many people about this apparent immunity to bee-stings, but I could never learn the reason for it. Someone told me that Pygmies often smear their skins with honey first, and the angry bees will not sting through it. But the Pygmies I saw did no smearing.

Being such good tree-climbers, Pygmies often rob parrots' nests of eggs and, also, of baby parrots, which they take to the Bantu villagers as pets. Sometimes Pygmies shoot monkeys high in the trees, and the little creatures are caught in a lower branch as they fall. A Pygmy will scoot up the tree like a squirrel to retrieve it.

Pygmy marksmanship, with their tiny bows and arrows, is amazing. Bill Deans told me about a Pygmy who was guarding a banana grove outside a village as directed by his Bantu "master," who wanted to end the raids of monkeys and baboons. Suddenly a full-grown elephant lumbered from the forest and confronted the lone Pygmy, who had only his twenty-inch bow and a few arrows. The little hunter knew that there was only one way to kill the huge animal—a clean shot through the eye into the brain. And he would have no second chance. He aimed his arrow and shot at the right eye—a tiny target in the massive head. It struck its mark, the elephant stumbled, and dropped.

The forest is full of hazards, and the biggest beasts are not necessarily the most dangerous. Bill Deans told me about some of these unromantic dangers during his visit to New York between my second and third expeditions. This man, who loves the forest almost as much as the Pygmies do and who has lived most of his adult life there, was suffering from bilharzia, which sent him home for treatment. It is a pernicious disease in which a microfilaria is introduced into the bloodstream; eventually the entire intestinal tract is seriously infected. You can get it just by standing in water or washing in it—water that the Pygmies drink every day without serious consequences.

Bill told me, "Then there's the tsetse fly carrying sleeping sickness, the anopheles with malaria and blackwater fever, and the fly that carries *filaria bancrofti*, which caused my brother's death in the Ituri. There are many deadly snakes — pythons fifteen to twenty feet long, and the poisonous viper that almost got me recently. I was sitting in front of my tent and a Pygmy suddenly darted up and crashed his spear down right at my feet. I was startled but I couldn't believe that he meant to attack me. Then he pointed to the viper whose fangs were only inches from my leg, now dead from the quick thrust of his spear. It is a beautiful place, the Ituri, but it is dangerous, too."

Pygmies hate snakes. Some tribes believe in reincarnation and think that the souls of departed Pygmies live in snakes. But even these Pygmies will eat snakes they have killed. One of the worst snakes is the spitting cobra, which can shoot its venom five or six feet with deadly accuracy, always aiming for the eyes. H. A. Hunter tells of a trip in the Ituri during which a spitting viper actually shot its venom into the eyes of the leading Pygmy, who fell to the ground writhing with pain. His companions gave him first-aid treatment by urinating directly into his eyes. This gave some relief, and further treatment of the same kind effected complete cure. Pygmies ordinarily suck snakebites immediately, and they also have several herbs that seem to be good antitoxins.

Another menace of the forest is the safari ant. The ants travel in solid columns a few inches wide and are more dangerous than many large beasts of the forest. Their bite is like the prick of a red-hot needle, and burns for hours afterward. And no matter how many ants you kill, there are always ten times as many ready to take their places.

Dr. Paul Schebesta, one of the first white men to live with the Pygmies, tells of an experience with ants and a monkey. One of his associates caught a colobus monkey and wanted to make a pet of it. The monkey seemed amenable, for the man fed it well and did not bind its arms or legs. A long chain clamped to one leg kept the monkey close to a stump, on which it slept.

One night Dr. Schebesta and his friend heard piercing shrieks from the monkey, roused themselves and rushed to see what was wrong. The monkey was struggling to pull away from the stump, but it could scarcely be recognized as a monkey. It was a writhing mass of ants, the chain was a thick rope of ants, and the stump was alive with them. The monkey's owner put the little creature beyond torture with one merciful shot. By that time there was not much flesh left on the monkey.

Everyone was roused to repel the ant invasion, for within a few hours the horde would have attacked everyone and everything in camp.

Another explorer was awakened in the middle of the night by a persistent clicking sound. Reaching his hand out under the netting to find his flashlight, he felt his forearm burned as with red-hot pincers within a few seconds. Ants had invaded his tent, and the clicking sound was the noise of a million ant mandibles attacking food, shoes, and the net itself.

I've encountered ant armies on the march in the forest many times. When I did not see them in time to step over the long column, a hundred ants were swarming up my clothing in a flash. Only once was our clearing invaded, and then the Pygmies fortunately saw the army just after it had emerged from the forest. Everyone snatched up a burning brand of wood from the fires and ran to the defense. Boiling water is a good weapon, even though its effects are temporary, but there is usually not enough of it in a Pygmy camp to do much good. A line of fire across the path of the ants is best, although it must be extended continually as the ants try to outflank it. Even after the attack was apparently repelled, the Pygmies dug a trench around my tent and kept fires going in it all night in case the vicious army returned.

The next day was devoted to the complete extermination of the invaders. The Pygmies tracked the line of march back into the forest to the ants' nest. When they found the big mound, with rivers of ants pouring down its sides, the Pygmies gathered dry leaves, twigs, and branches and made a bonfire on top of the nest. They had to run quickly to escape the avenging hordes that streamed forth.

Pygmies love the hunt more than any other activity—and the elephant hunt most of all. But not every male Pygmy is an elephant hunter; this most dangerous work is reserved for the most alert, courageous, and cool-headed. When an elephant hunter's reflexes slow down, he reluctantly gives up the chase for the mammoth and confines his activities to antelope, pig, and okapi.

There is hardly a Pygmy family that has not lost at least one of its members to the biggest forest animal. I tried to learn how many elephants an experienced hunter might have killed in his career, but it was difficult to arrive at any clear answer because Pygmies apparently know no numbers beyond ten. Several times, in answer to my question,

"How many?" I got the answer, "Without number." This might mean to a Pygmy twelve or ninety or somewhere in between. From Bantu villagers and missionaries, I gathered that many hunters kill fifty to sixty elephants during their lives.

Pygmies do not embark on an elephant hunt casually, as they might for lesser animals. The elephant calls for preparation. When the Pygmies with whom I lived planned a hunt, they went into the forest the day before in search of kola nuts, large and pink, which their women boiled, pounded, and boiled again. This is the nut from which is extracted the flavoring for all cola drinks. Pygmy men also chew the kola nut for greater virility, then spit the fibers onto their arms to advertise the fact to the girls.

The hunters—usually from three to five hunt together—drink kola water on the morning of the hunt, eat a meal, then set off into the forest. Since it is fairly well populated with elephants, the Pygmies can often locate a small group by noon. They would prefer a solitary elephant, of course, but the big animals are rarely alone. They travel with four or five or even many more companions. The hunters must worry as much about the rest of the herd as about the elephant they plan to hunt down. Elephants are often surprisingly intelligent and show great concern for their fellows. I've seen, for example, two elephants support a wounded brother on either side, leading him to safety as two soldiers might help a wounded comrade from a battlefield.

When the Pygmy hunters have located their elephants, they study the terrain carefully, compare the elephants, and select the one they are after. They prefer the elephant with the largest tusks, but they must choose one that is on the edge of the group, not in the middle. The elephants are not aware of the Pygmies at this time, for the hunters keep out of the wind, and they have also smeared themselves with elephant dung, found in plentiful supply along the trail.

The Pygmies move back into the forest a few hundred yards and smoke hemp, or marijuana, to bolster their courage. They obtain this from the villagers, who have found it one of the most binding ties between the forest folk and their Negro "masters."

With the most experienced hunter in the lead, the Pygmies return to the elephants, which may be asleep in the noonday heat or quietly munching whatever greens are within reach. To anyone except a

Pygmy, the project appears completely ludicrous at this stage. Here are six, eight, or ten elephants, the largest land animals in the world, about to be attacked by three, four, or five of the tiniest humans in the world. But Pygmy spears are razor sharp, and Pygmy strength is greater than their size indicates. Their biggest asset, however, is courage, of which they have plenty even without the aid of marijuana.

If the designated elephant lifts its trunk and turns its head as if it has heard or smelled something, the approaching Pygmies freeze into immobility. The elephant sniffs only what smells like another elephant, sees nothing move — its eyesight is not very good — lowers its head, and goes on eating or dozing.

When the hunters decide upon hamstringing, one of the two common methods of hunting elephants, two of them step cautiously from the rear until they stand beside the huge hind legs. The others place themselves to rout the other animals and then take up pursuit of the hunted one.

At a silent signal, the two leading Pygmies reach out with their sharp spears and slash at the tendons behind the elephant's knees. They dart away at once as the wounded elephant whirls to grab them with its trunk. The other Pygmies shout and jump for all they are worth to frighten the other elephants into a stampede. Usually the beasts are so startled that they rush away. The wounded one tries to follow, but it can barely drag itself along, since its hind legs are useless.

The wounded elephant bellows angrily, pulls itself painfully along the ground with its hind legs dragging. It reaches out and grabs a tree with its trunk and, unless the tree is huge, rips it up by the roots. With the other elephants out of the way, the Pygmy hunters dart in close to thrust their spears into the elephant's belly. The animal lashes out at them with its trunk, but the hunters attack first from one side and then the other. Sometimes the elephant manages to move some distance, with the Pygmies following and harassing it, until the belly wounds bring it to earth.

Sometimes, of course, the plan does not work out. Perhaps the tendons are not completely severed, and the elephant snatches up one of the hunters and tramples or gores him to death. Perhaps the other elephants refuse to stampede and attack the hunters instead. Bill Spees told me of one Pygmy hunter who was separated from his compan-

ions while trailing an elephant that had been wounded but not incapacitated. The elephant circled around to foil his pursuer and attacked
him from the rear, goring him in the side. The hunter dropped to the
ground and, although bleeding badly, retained consciousness and his
quick wit. He lay motionless. The elephant approached, poked the
hunter with his trunk several times, and seemed to conclude that the
Pygmy was dead. Then, like most good elephants, it had to bury its
victim. The elephant dug a hole with its tusks, pushed the hunter into
it with its trunk, then tried to cover the man with dirt, brush, and
leaves. The Pygmy said later that this was his most difficult time —
trying to keep his nose free to breathe without moving enough to
show the elephant that he was still alive.

The elephant did not make things any easier for the Pygmy by going away at once, but stayed nearby awhile to make sure there was no
movement from the man. (Buffalo may do the same thing after they
have killed a man.) At last the elephant went on his way and the
wounded hunter pushed himself up into the air. Within a few minutes, the other Pygmies came and found him. Fortunately they carried
him to the mission rather than to the village witch doctor. Penicillin,
cleanliness and rest healed the Pygmy's wounds, and during the time
he spent at the mission he became converted to Christianity. Spees
thought that in view of this momentous change in his outlook on
things, the Pygmy might give up elephant hunting. But the young
man shook his head and said, "No, once an elephant hunter always an
elephant hunter."

One morning I saw three Pygmies start off on an elephant hunt.
With only three, I knew they would not use the hamstringing method
of killing their prey because with two men at the elephant's hind legs
there would be only one to startle the rest of the herd. It takes more
than one man to raise enough clamor to stampede a herd of elephants.
These three hunters would get their elephant, if they got him, by darting in, one after the other, to plunge a spear into the elephant's belly.
When the animal whirled around to grab the first attacker, another
hunter would spear from the opposite side. And after the first lunge,
all three would shout and yell and raise the greatest hullabaloo possible to rout the other elephants. These three little men would be very
busy for a few minutes — racing in to plunge spears through tough
hide, pulling them out and dodging the trunk that reached for them,

screaming and keeping their eyes on the other elephants, which might attack instead of running away. Even if the elephants stampede, the hunters have much danger and much hard work ahead of them. The wounded elephant follows the rest of the herd and, even though he may have had ten spear thrusts in his belly, he can move along at a good clip. The hunters pursue their prey, using their spears when they get a chance, dodging the trunk that snatches at them. The elephant, wasting its time in counterattacks and somewhat weakened, is far behind its fellows by this time. At one point it decides to ignore its tormentors and run to catch up with the rest of the herd.

The Pygmies now must track and follow their elephant until it is so weakened that they can give the final killing spear-thrusts. An elephant that is not hamstrung may travel many miles before that time comes, but Pygmy hunters would follow it to the end of their hunting grounds if necessary.

During the day, after the departure of the three hunters, the people in camp went about their business as usual. I was discussing the possibilities of filming an elephant dance in case the hunters were successful. As the afternoon wore on, there was an air of expectation throughout the camp. I saw women stop their work and listen for some sound from the forest that would announce the return of the hunters. And I kept thinking of them, too, hoping that this might not be a hunt that meant death to a Pygmy. I knew that the leader of the group was Edodo, generally considered the bravest and most cunning hunter in the entire area, so the outlook should be good.

Toward evening, one of the three hunters raced into the camp shouting joyously and waving an elephant's tail, proof of their triumph. They had killed their elephant, after tracking it for miles, in a clearing not far from the edge of the forest and the Negro village whose chief was Pawanzas, of the Walese tribe. And Edodo, the chief Pygmy hunter, had as his "master" that same Pawanzas.

No elephant is touched by its Pygmy killers without the consent and, if possible, the presence of the Bantu "master." If the animal is deep in the forest, the Bantu may not want to travel that far into such terrifying country, but he must be notified just the same. In this case he would certainly come to the carving ceremony, since his village was so close. Edodo had, after the killing, sat down to contemplate his huge victim, while one hunter ran to the village to inform Pawanzas, and another came to the Pygmy camp with the good news. And this bearer of good news had a special message to me from Edodo, who had worked with me enough to know — even if he didn't understand why — that for pictures I needed a clearing and adequate light. This dead elephant lay in a clearing, with fair light.

So early the next morning I set out with the entire Pygmy camp. Never did I travel through the forest more quickly, for the Pygmies were in no mood to slow down for me. And even with cameras, I was able to keep up with them, for I knew that this was a rare opportunity that might never come again. But it was a long trek, and I was tired when we reached the clearing in the early afternoon. I was appalled at the huge crowd that had already gathered. Several hundred men and women, most equipped with jars, baskets, or vine bags, milled happily about the clearing. They were about equally divided between Bantu villagers and Pygmies, all of them relatives — some rather distant — of the Pygmy hunters or the Negro chief. Obviously several Pygmy camps had heard the good news, as well as some not-too-distant Bantu villages.

I was glad to see that the butchering had not started, since the Bantu chief Pawanzas had not yet arrived. So I had some time to clear a space that would let us get good camera shots of the elephant and the activities centering around it. In spite of the crowd, this was not difficult, as everyone was happily cooperative.

Pawanzas arrived with several attendants, and took center stage. Then he signaled to the three hunters who had made the kill, and they scrambled up the elephant's side to the top. It was obvious that, after lying in the hot sun for several hours, the beast's belly was bloated. It looked to me as if it were about to burst. And in a moment it did, when Edodo plunged his spear into the elephant's side. A geyser of gas and stomach juices spurted into the air seven or eight feet, spreading an odor that made my senses reel, my nostrils close. The Pygmy hunters shouted happily and pushed their faces into the liquid, gulping it, bathing in it.

When the gassy geyser subsided, the hunters returned to the ground. Several dozen Pygmies and villagers then lined up, each with a sharp knife or spear, and behind each man stood his wife, ready and waiting with a container of some kind. At another signal from Pawanzas, the men raced for the elephant and clambered up its sides, slipping, clutching for a firm hold — each one trying to reach the back-bone first. The men yelled, the women shouted encouragement, and the scene looked like a small riot. But there was a plan despite the bedlam. When a man reached the backbone, he gained the right to cut a strip of meat down the side from that point. As I learned later, he did not get to keep all the meat he cut, so there was no contest in which a winner might get more meat than his fellows. The whole thing was a joyous game instead of a laborious butchering.

Shoulder to shoulder, Pygmies and villagers started hacking away at the meat. As one man cut a big chunk of flesh away, he flung it back over his shoulder. He knew that his wife had her eye on him and would snatch whatever he threw. Soon big chunks of meat were fly-ing through the air, women were rushing about to grab the pieces, everyone was shouting or laughing, and only a few were quarreling.

Finally the meat was cut away from the exposed side, and there was a lull in the proceedings while two Pygmies took an axe and chopped a hole through the elephant's ribs into the chest cavity. They then took up their sharp spears and hopped inside the breast. In a moment I saw two spear points sawing their way along the ribs, as the men worked from the inside out, cutting away more meat and flinging it out through the hole, along with heart, liver, and other entrails — prized portions indeed.

I had been wondering if there would be enough meat to give that big crowd more than a bite or two each, but I had not calculated on the amount of flesh that comes from a seven- or eight-ton elephant, especially when every morsel is used. (Even chunks of tough skin were taken home by the Pygmy women for making soup.) Pawanzas was in charge of the distribution, which everyone seemed to accept as equitable. Since he was the "master" of the hunters and also chief of the village, he allotted himself choice and plentiful portions. His *capi-tas* were well taken care of, but no better than Edodo and his two fellow hunters. The other Pygmies from Edodo's camp received con-siderably more than the second or third cousins from other camps. But everyone there, Pygmy and villager alike, received something. Pawan-zas and the Pygmy hunters haggled over the tusks, which had to be specially paid for, and when they came to an agreement, everyone headed for home.

Back at the Pygmy camp, the women got busy cooking the meat, while the men and children stood around uttering anticipatory shouts of pleasure, jabbering delightedly, twittering like birds, in a mounting bedlam that suddenly ended with the serving of food on big green phrynium leaves.

I was amazed at the quantities of meat that disappeared into Pygmy stomachs. I have shopped and cooked and camped enough to judge the weight of meat fairly accurately, and I know that seven or eight pounds of elephant meat went down the throats of most of the men — and not much less down those of the women and children. The skin over their bellies was stretched so tight it looked as if it hurt, and I realized why that portion of Pygmy anatomy is always distended. When Pygmies have a lot of food, they eat all they can possibly hold, as if they might have to go days without more food — which does sometimes happen. They have neither the facilities nor the inclination to keep anything for the next day, except inside themselves.

When they finished eating, they seemed to be drugged, supremely happy but anesthetized. They lay back and fell asleep, one by one. And there was no dancing that night. The next morning all slept late, and no one went hunting. They loafed and napped and talked about the good meal of the night before. But by noon they had summoned enough strength to equal their high spirits, so they danced. Dancing is usually an evening activity, but Pygmies do not care about the time of day when they feel like dancing. On this occasion, they had something good to dance about — the elephant hunt.

Again good fortune was with me, for the sun was shining brightly down into the clearing. We had plenty of time to get cameras set up, for the Pygmies had to build their elephant before they started dancing. And it was interesting to see how in their reconstruction they cut him down to size. Their model of the huge beast was no taller than the Pygmies themselves. Four upright sticks driven into the ground were the legs, a larger log between them the body. For the tail, the dancers used the actual tail of the elephant they had killed the day before.

Huge phrynium leaves at the front end of the log made realistic elephant ears, but the best touch was the slightly curved banana stalk that served as the trunk. This admirable figure stood in the center of the clearing, and the hunters retired to the edge of the forest, armed with frail spears. The hunters had taken time to make up, too, which they did not do for the hunt itself. They all had bright parrot feathers in their hair or wore small headdresses of feathers and flowers.

The drummers began a low, slow beat — so slow, in fact, that I did not realize at first that there was a definite rhythm. I heard one muffled thump and then, several seconds later, another muffled thump. When the hunters, led by Edodo, appeared at the edge of the clearing, I realized what perfect stalking music it was.

The hunters appeared as Pygmies always do when they move through the forest, silently and suddenly. One moment you see nothing but leaves, lianas, and tree trunks forming a wall. The next moment you see a Pygmy standing on this side of the wall, without having disturbed a leaf. They were all wary, cautious, and eager as they searched for the elephant, looking first this way, then that, while they spread out slowly, seeming to cover much greater distances in their movements than they actually did. With a flick of the hand, one hunter signaled to another to follow him. Two notes of a birdsong came from Edodo, and the others turned in his direction. They were following elephant spoor through the forest and had momentarily lost the trail, had spread out to find it again, signaling to each other all the time. Edodo found the trail and gestured to the others, who fell in behind him.

With bodies bent forward, arms raised with ready spears, the hunters moved toward the center of the clearing in tiny steps, turning in a half circle toward the left, then curving back toward the right, trying to show that they had traveled many miles through the forest after their prey. As they came closer to the elephant, the drums increased their tempo ever so slightly, and so did my breathing.

Suddenly there was one loud BOOM! from the drum. Edodo jerked his body erect, threw his arms back, and stared with both fear and elation at the dummy elephant, which somehow became in our eyes a true mammoth quietly eating grass and ferns in the jungle, his back to his small attackers. A long moment of silence followed as the other hunters stared over Edodo's shoulder at the beast. Then came a flurry of movement, jittery and nervous, as the hunters retired seven or eight paces to consult on strategy. The drums took up a soft but rapid beat.

The hunters talked and gesticulated, then separated to form a kind of half circle closing in on the animal from the rear and sides. Edodo was the leader, the hunter chosen to cast the first spear, as he had been on the real hunt the day before. He crept up close behind the dummy elephant, hesitated, looked suddenly terror-stricken as if the elephant might have started to turn, darted back to the edge of the forest in a rapid, shuffling step. Then once more, cautiously, dancingly, he moved toward the make-believe beast, every feature of his face and every muscle of his body showing the excitement of the chase, the danger of his position, the fear that no Pygmy denies.

The drums kept pace with his movements, mounting in tempo as he came closer, slowing down as he retreated. Three times Edodo approached, three times ran back, but on the fourth sally, with a great whoop, he plunged his spear with both hands under the body of the dummy elephant. Then he raced for the woods, and a second hunter attacked from the other side. One after another the dancers speared the motionless dummy, until it almost seemed to twist and turn in its counterattacks. The drums beat loudly and rapidly now, and I thought they had reached their peak. The Pygmy spectators began to shout, cheer, and laugh.

The dancers pantomimed the tracking of the wounded elephant, then fell upon it together, plunging their spears into the dummy ferociously until they knocked it over. The drums boomed and the whole camp cheered, chattered, laughed. With frenzy the hunters danced around the fallen mock elephant, and several little boys dashed from the crowd to join them. The whole camp took up the dance, jumping and cavorting around the clearing in perfect time to the drumbeats. These scenes, later one of the highlights of *Savage Splendor*, may not have been graceful, but the joy of the dancers made them a delight to watch.

4

More Pygmies

NOT every day in the Ituri Forest gave me an elephant carving or a special dance, by any means. Many days I spent wandering about the camp, listening, asking Bill Deans, when he was there, the meaning of animated conversations, shooting some scenes when the light was good, and coming to know the Pygmies better and better.

But in this endeavor I was often frustrated, for I learned that it was almost impossible to know how Pygmies thought and felt. How could I truly understand people who eat roots my stomach cannot digest, or drink water which, unless I boiled it, would make me deathly sick, or devour anything from caterpillar and ant grubs to bats, snakes, and, formerly, snacks of humans? Who else can scoop handfuls of honey from a bees' nest without getting stung? Or swallow handfuls of sand when hunger's pangs are severe and no food is at hand? Who else dines upon and makes belts from the okapi, a beast so rare that until about fifty years ago it was considered only a tall tale of superstitious natives?

If you have a rugged constitution and an iron stomach, and bring in some of your own supplies, you can live for a time *with* the Pygmies and under their protection, but you cannot live *like* a Pygmy. Getting to know them is sometimes like trying to understand a creature of a different species, with the unique advantage that this creature can speak.

Pygmies reveal little of their nature while standing for inspection, even after gifts of salt and palm wine and tobacco. You would not act very natural under the penetrating gaze of a Martian, though he might have passed out ten-dollar bills. But if he stayed around long enough, you would return to your normal life. You'd become accustomed to this more or less permanent fixture observing you and, if he were at all acute, he would begin to see what made you tick — at least enough to go back home to Mars and write a book about you.

I could learn more about the Pygmies after living with them for some time than the Martian could learn about me. After all, we *are* of the same species. We spring from the same stock. A Pygmy could give me a blood transfusion and I'd get along fine. After a time, the startling differences between us dwindled in importance. They were only patterns of behavior dictated largely by the Pygmy's environment. His inner drives were essentially the same as mine. He was stirred by the same emotions that stirred me, even though the stimuli were sometimes different. He was afraid of lightning and the hoot of an owl, which didn't bother me. I was afraid of elephants and getting lost in the forest, which didn't much bother him. But we both felt fear. We both hoped for good hunting, although we hunted different things. He seethed with anger when someone stole a forest antelope from his trap, just as I would boil if someone took a good piece of insurance business away from me by unfair tactics. We both loved, bragged about, and become annoyed with our women, using only slightly different ways of expressing these feelings. The Pygmy usually was a monogamist but had played around considerably before marriage and maybe even a bit after — and that sounded familiar. We both liked music and dancing, but he managed to find much more time for these pleasures than I did.

You might say that you could *never* understand someone who voluntarily smears himself with elephant dung, but "civilized" people sometimes go to even greater lengths to earn a living.

Maybe I can't see things through a Pygmy's eyes, as when he looks at a bat and sees food. Certainly I can't smell things through his nose, as when he sniffs a putrefying elephant dead four days in tropic heat and gleefully hurries to the feast. "I eat the meat, not the smell, *bwana*," he explains. But even if I cannot put myself in his place, I can feel hunger, which lies behind his actions and mine.

Feelings — they are the heart of both of us, the bridge of understanding, the common language. Customs are just the costumes with

Ukumhearik, chief of the Dani tribe in the Baliem Valley, poses with me during my visit to this remote region in West Irian (formerly Netherlands New Guinea). One of the most dynamic leaders I have encountered, Ukumhearik holds the power of life and death over thousands of Stone Age men whose chief occupation and glory are wars, whose greatest triumph comes when they eat a slain enemy in view of his clansmen, and whose chief article of clothing is the penis gourd, without which they would not think of being seen by another person.

A chief dressed for a feast, or sing-sing, at Mt. Hagen in the Wahgi Valley of New Guinea. He has blackened all his body with charcoal except for the tip of his nose, from which hangs a small shell. His ceremonial spear is three-pronged, beautifully carved, and fitted with a band of fur.

Followed by native carriers with my cameras and equipment, I cross the Wahgi River on a swaying vine suspension bridge. This lush and salubrious valley with its hundreds of thousands of inhabitants was discovered in 1933.

Three women, adorned with bird of paradise plumes, shells of various sizes, and layers of brilliant paints, are ready for dancing at a Wahgi Valley sing-sing. Two of them are chanting and thumping their small drums.

Some women of the New Guinea village of Kambaramba, sometimes called "the brothel of the Sepik," prepare *sac-sac*, a nutritious but rather tasteless food made by pounding and running water over the pith of the sago palm.

Kondon Agaundo, one of the paramount chiefs of the Chimbu region in the Wahgi Valley of New Guinea, in full ceremonial regalia, with a fine specimen of the three-pronged spear and with a rare, slender bird of paradise plume circling through the hole in his septum. Kondon was one of the first natives to be elected to the legislative assembly, where he wore "European" clothes and made speeches in *pidgin* pleading for the universal teaching of English.

ABOVE: The smoked and mummified body of a slain Kukukuku warrior, supported by one of his wives, who for months tended the slow fire over which it was suspended. She is about to carry it to its last resting place on a ledge high in the barren mountains of eastern New Guinea. BELOW: Warriors of the Jivaro headhunting Indians, around the headwaters of the Amazon, peer through the dense foliage with their lances ready for attack.

ABOVE: In the upper Xingu River region of Brazil's Mato Grosso, four friendly tribes meet for an annual ceremony for the dead, called a *guarúp*. In addition to mourning, the Indians indulge in dancing and sports, the chief of which is wrestling. Here the men have gathered for a series of bouts that will determine the intertribal championship. BELOW: The Colorado Indians of Ecuador make me a blood brother by coating me with a red paste and striping my face and chest with an almost indelible black dye. I am the fourth seated figure from the right.

ABOVE: Markosie, great hunter of the small Eskimo settlement on Ellesmere Island, files down the sharp fangs of Koyo, one of his best dogs. Like most Eskimo huskies, Koyo is a vicious fighter and has recently injured another dog. This dental treatment will curtail his destructive power if not his belligerence. BELOW: Eskimo women and children await the return of the men to their temporary hunting village on the thick ice of Jones Sound, just south of Ellesmere.

ABOVE: Okoko, brother of Markosie and soon-to-be husband of Ouisa (shown elsewhere listening to my radio) has killed a polar bear and proudly displays its skin, which will be a welcome item in furnishing his new home. BELOW: As the ice begins to break up, a walrus family floats slowly along on its gradually diminishing ice floe. With some Eskimo hunters, I film the scene from a neighboring ice floe. Just after I took this picture, the disturbed walruses slid into the water. The hunters took to their boat and got one of the huge animals with a harpoon.

which emotions clothe themselves to fit environment and heritage. The Pygmy's customs are as well adapted to his world as his dress; and when I recognized this, when I saw the feelings behind them, I was at home in the Ituri, visiting friends who put on an amazing show for me just by being themselves. I witnessed a reasonable facsimile of the lives led by the ancient ancestors of all of us, with only minor changes in height, color, weapons, and species of beasts hunted and roots eaten.

When I think back on the many quiet days I have spent in the Ituri Forest, a kind of composite day emerges. I am awakened by a mild murmur of voices from the Pygmy huts. Then there is a loud shout, an answering shout, both in anger. Others join in, and I know that the usual morning quarrels have begun. Curses and imprecations fly back and forth. I pull on some soggy clothes and step from my tent to feel the splash of a huge drop of water — they seem larger in the Ituri than anywhere else in the world — from a branch above. The smell of the place assails me. During the day my nose will become so numb that it will no longer perceive this odor, but on first awakening, the smell is strong — a combination of sweat, dirt, dung both human and animal, half-spoiled meat, with forest smells of damp rotting wood, swampy ground, and thousands of flowers.

Another smell begins to cover this odor — the pleasant fragrance of woodsmoke and cooking food, which reminds me to look at my own fire, the only one in camp that is cold and dead. Everything is so damp that getting a fire going is quite a task, but we manage it and start to get breakfast. Meanwhile, I listen to the mounting sounds of quarreling, for now the women have joined in with their shrill, strident voices.

The morning is dark and gray, which accounts in part for the excessive quarrelsomeness of the Pygmies, for they are as easily depressed as elated. A rainy or dull day puts them in bad humor, and the entire camp seems to get up on the wrong side of its logs. Since no Pygmy can conceive of repressing even the smallest and most insignificant emotion, he snaps at the first chance. The one snapped at growls back, and by the time the growl has grown to a loud roar, a friend of Pygmy A joins in to say something nasty about Pygmy B, whereupon Pygmy B curses him and Pygmy A tells him to mind his own business.

The wife of the interrupter thereupon feels called upon to add her bit, even though she is supposed to be getting breakfast. Husband tells wife to shut up, so wife yells at husband, calling him mean to the children, a poor hunter, and a philanderer. So we have a second battle going, which overlaps the first. This is going on all over camp.

I can tell without looking when the Pygmy breakfasts are ready, for the noise diminishes and alters its tone. There is talk and chatter all over the clearing, but it is happy, anticipatory. I see two men who have just quarreled sitting side by side on the ground, dipping boiled bananas into a common pot of palm-wine sauce, looking at each other with wide smiles, chewing rapidly and happily. Breakfast is a big meal, for the Pygmies will not eat again until evening.

As breakfast ends there are loud sighs of contentment, cheerful talk of plans for the day, jokes. Three or four young men take up their bows and arrows and start a kind of target practice, shooting at a broad leaf on the other side of the clearing. It is too early for filming, but I persuade them to have another practice later in the day. And I ask them to shoot at bananas thrown into the air. They are delighted, and show remarkable accuracy, one banana being pierced with three arrows almost simultaneously.

The work of the day begins. No big hunt is planned, so I decide to stay in the clearing and get what pictures I can when the light improves. Some hunters go off into the forest for small game, and many women leave to gather food, followed by some of the older children. I wander from hut to hut, watch a group of Pygmies forging iron spearheads (an uncommon skill among the forest people), another group preparing poison for arrows. I come upon two boys, eight or nine years old, wrestling in front of a sizable audience. There are cheers and shouts of encouragement for both battlers, who are sweating and enjoying themselves immensely. When the match ends, several boys decide to go hunting. They get bows and arrows from their huts and disappear into the jungle, talking excitedly. Occasionally they actually return with some small game, although frogs and caterpillars are more likely to be the prey of boys this young.

Behind one hut I see a boy and girl talking. They seem embarrassed when they see me, but I pretend not to be looking at them. I guess that they are about twelve years old, for the girl's breasts have just begun to develop. After a furtive look around, they walk into the forest together. Sexual relations between Pygmy youngsters are common but not flaunted. Some mothers try to keep a watchful eye on their daughters, because the birth of children before marriage can cause difficulties. But in general the fact of free sexual relations among boys and girls is accepted without much thought or concern. This attitude changes drastically at marriage, however, for fidelity stands high in the Pygmy moral code. Husbands and wives guard each other jealously, and the only crime worse than adultery is stealing game from another man's trap. Only these two crimes may lead one Pygmy to kill another — and that is rare. The more common procedure in the case of adultery is for the husband to administer a thorough beating to his wife and perhaps to the offending male, although the latter may make amends by paying over a certain number of arrows or a spear.

I saunter to another cluster of huts just in time to see a boy of about six overturn a pot of water while trying to roll a hoop made from a liana. His mother, busy pounding bark cloth, jumps up in a rage, grabs a piece of firewood, and brandishes it as if she would bash her son's head in. He runs howling toward the forest, and she races after him a few steps, finally flinging the wood at him and missing badly. She returns to her work as if nothing had happened, though she can hear the hyena-like howls of her offspring in the woods. Finally some other women go into the forest after him. The yells turn into sobs, then silence. In a few minutes the boy returns with the women, showing a few startlingly clean areas of face where tears have washed the dirt away. He glances cautiously at his mother, but she pays no attention. So he takes up his hoop again and goes back to his play.

But for every angry outburst against a child, I saw a dozen scenes of love and affection, not just by a child's father and mother but by all adults of the group — secondary fathers and mothers. There is little conscious training of children, and thus no real discipline. Boys play with small bows and arrows and spears, gradually learning to track and hunt as they grow up. Girls learn to gather plants and berries along with their mothers, to cook, to make bark cloth and houses. As the years go by they find themselves doing these things in earnest instead of in play. And what else does a Pygmy child need to learn?

Although there is considerable fondling of children by parents, uncles, aunts, and other relatives, there is no public display of affection between adults. Indeed, physical contact between men and women seemed to be carefully avoided, for to a Pygmy there is only one reason for such contact — lovemaking, which is a private affair. When they have a tug-of-war, for instance — yes, grownups play almost as many games as their children — the teams are always men against women. In this game, Pygmies hold each other around the waist, with the first person in each line grasping a short stick. Because of this physical contact, Pygmies would never consider mixed teams.

The marriage relationship among Pygmies is complicated. In some groups the task of locating a potential wife is a problem for young men, because of the economic value of women. Females may be valued for their individual qualities, but in the main they are looked upon as essential workers and as the producers of more Pygmies. A family group, as tenacious of its collective life as the individual of his own life, will not let a girl go without acquiring another in return. Thus there has arisen the "head-for-head" system, called in Kingwana *kichwa-kichwa*.

A young man of sixteen or seventeen may find in a neighboring group a girl of thirteen or fourteen he would like to marry. The basis for his choice may depend in part on her beauty and figure, but her aptitude for hard work carries more weight. The young man must not only win the consent of the girl's father and pay him a purchase price — which might be six arrows and a spear, or eight arrows and so much bark cloth, or four arrows and a good piece of iron — but he must also become matchmaker and persuade a girl in his own family group to marry a young man in *his* girl's neighboring group. When all this is accomplished, the girl goes home with her husband, without any ceremony. But this is not the end.

When the wife bears a child, the husband makes an additional payment to her father. Even if she has no child, he makes a further payment at the end of six months or a year, when both parties to the marriage decide it will probably work out. If the girl should prove sterile, or if the young couple should decide the marriage is no good, the man can return the girl to her father and get his payment back. But this return is complicated by the other couple involved, who may want to continue their marriage.

Even after many years of happy, successful marriage, a girl's strongest ties remain with her original family group and never with her husband's. She knows that her family will welcome her back happily — and her husband knows it, too, which puts a brake on his dictatorial powers over her. A wife is his property; she is there to work and everyone knows it. It is all right for her husband to beat her once in a while, if only to remind her who is boss. But there are limits beyond which he cannot go. If he beats his wife too hard or too often, if he philanders regularly, if he fails to provide the necessities of life, if he is constantly mean to his children — then the wife will just walk back home to her family. The family will welcome her and protect her, unless she is being too sensitive about an occasional smack on the head, in which case her family tells her to go back to her husband. Usually a wife leaves her husband only for very good cause.

The sun has dipped below the treetops on the western side of the clearing, and in about an hour the hunters come home — one with a monkey, another with a snake, and a group of three with a young antelope. There is laughter through the clearing, and I know that the same scene is being enacted in all the clearings nearby where my five hundred Pygmies are camping. With that number, however, this section of the forest will be cleaned out of game in a few days.

The game is divided according to a rule that has apparently existed for centuries. The first and prize portions go to the hunter who struck the fatal blow. If the hunter used another's bow, the owner of the other bow gets a prize piece. The owner of the hunting dog, if one was involved, gets a special piece. Other members of the hunting party come next, and then all others in the group. No one is left out.

Fires flicker in front of the beehive huts as the women and girls prepare the evening meal, the men watching and talking to each other with animation. Some hungry children are crying for their food, while the older ones stand near the fires, looking, sniffing, and waiting not too patiently.

Dinner is served on leaves on the ground, and the Pygmies eat as long as there is anything in the pot. The women clean up as the men lie back and stretch. Some get up and walk about the clearing, others watch me eat my dinner. A group comes from a neighboring clearing for a chat. This is the happy time of day. No bickering, no screaming now. The only sounds are sounds of happiness and contentment.

The dusk deepens, and someone begins to tap out a rhythm on the drums, while a reedlike flute or whistle makes unmelodious melody. I see some young men tapping their feet, waving their hands in time with the drums. Then one man does a little jig, claps his hands, laughs. The fellow next to him does the same, and the desire to dance spreads around the clearing like an engulfing wave. Soon there are fifteen men and women following one another around in a circle, waving arms, singing, stamping, laughing. The drums are inspired by the dancers, and the pounding rhythm pulses through the forest. Children join the dances, and finally some of the oldsters.

Pygmies can go on dancing for four or five hours when they are enjoying themselves. They can dance all night if the moon is full and no outsiders are there. For the Pygmies have two kinds of dancing. Those I watched were of the first kind; the other is an obscene dance in which the rule against physical contact is broken, and broken resoundingly.

On my quiet day in the forest, however, the dance ends after about two hours. It is completely dark now. Some of the fires are taken inside the huts to drive out insects and keep away marauding beasts. One by one the families disappear through the tiny doors. I sit outside my tent for a while, looking at the spots of flickering red that still glow here and there, listening to the sounds of the forest. There are not many at night, for the birds and most monkeys are still. Occasionally a leopard screams, a hyena laughs its unpleasant laugh, an owl hoots, and peepers try to imitate birds.

Finally I turn in, and fall asleep before I know it. Some time later I am awakened. I hear something like a huge sigh far away. This is a familiar sound to me now, after a few weeks in the forest. A storm is coming. The first signal is a high wind in the distant treetops, and that is the sigh I hear from miles away. I hurry out of my tent to check my stakes and ropes.

Back inside, I listen to the sigh that has grown to a roar. The branches overhead begin to stir, whispering to each other that the big wind is coming. They toss and twist, and then suddenly the big wind comes, like a huge wall of irresistible energy. Branches groan, snap and crash to the ground. My tent tugs at its ropes, trying to take wing and fly. Not far away, a giant tree, writhing under the lashes of the wind, topples over, and the ground shakes beneath me as in an earthquake.

One minute behind the strong wind comes the driving rain. It pelts against my tent like pebbles hurled by a blast of dynamite. Inside, I feel the fine spray on my skin as the drops are vaporized and filter in. It sounds like Victoria Falls outside, as water pours from the leaves and cascades into the clearing.

Far away the deep bass boom of thunder begins, rolling across the universe slowly and majestically. Every half minute I hear it, but there is nothing menacing about it. Then I see the flashes of lightning that precede each thunderclap, and by the time between them I know the peak of the storm is still some distance away. I become fascinated counting the seconds between the flash and the rumble as the storm comes closer and closer, until the lightning is a blinding flash and the thunder a menacing roar that threatens to split the earth open. I peer out through the tent flap and see a lake where the clearing was. The black sky is ripped apart by a jagged bolt of lightning that reaches down to the top of a tall tree. I hear the tree crash, taking a dozen others with it in its fall.

Lightning and thunder, wind and rain, all combine at once to concentrate their forces on our clearing, pounding my tent and the Pygmy huts like fragile things on an anvil. But for all the high voltage around us, the noise as of atomic blasts, the violent wind and lashing rain — for all of that, all we get is wet. And we are used to that.

Now I begin to count the seconds as lightning and thunder are separated in time once more, the storm passing beyond us. One second, two seconds, three seconds. It seems as if the wind is dying slightly, although the rain pours steadily. Bright flash, four seconds, crash-boom-rumble. Five seconds. I never get beyond seven seconds, for I am asleep again.

When I went back to Africa in 1954-1955 to make the film *Zanzabuku* for Republic Pictures, I headed for the Ituri Forest. On this expedition I was really well equipped, with an assistant producer and four other cameramen, a Dodge Power Wagon and truck, and with more time than I had ever taken before. But one cannot take such equipment into the Ituri, so while the other men were busy at other chores, I went back to the forest with two dedicated cameramen, Johnny Coquillon and Dave Mason. Bill Spees was there to help us, and I had a specific project in mind.

In the Ituri I had walked across many bridges made of vines. (I use the word *liana* most of the time because the word *vine* suggests something small, while the tropical forest vine is a thick, strong, flexible piece of vegetation; the Pygmies can weave lianas together to make them long and very strong.) Now I wanted to film Pygmies making a liana bridge. It would not be an easy task. I had to find the right spot, assemble a group of Pygmies, and persuade them to tackle this difficult job. If they had felt the need of a bridge at the spot I selected, they would have built it long before, so my location would seem ridiculous to them. I had to have the right light, the right angles. They could comprehend none of this. I had to convince them, anyway.

After a good deal of searching, we found the right place on the Ituri River. It was about ninety feet wide there, so throwing a liana bridge across it would be spectacular indeed. For a quarter of a mile the river flowed along a straight course. Tall trees lined each bank — a necessity for the Pygmy method of bridge-building. But the undergrowth was sparse, leaving clear spaces from which my cameras could get good shots up and down the river. Most important, this stretch of river flowed from west to east. When the sun rose, its light would not be cut off by two-hundred-foot trees until almost noon. In the afternoon, the sun would set at the western end of the stretch, giving me light until at least four o'clock. Each day I would have three or four more hours of filming time than I had ever enjoyed in the forest.

Pygmies were assembled, given pay, and briefed on the project. They seemed agreeable, but I heard a few of them mutter, "*Bumbafu! Bumbafu!*" while shaking their heads. Bill Spees explained it.

"When someone tries to do something that is difficult and daring and not very sensible, he is *bumbafu*. These Pygmies don't need a bridge here, because their camp and the village of their Negro masters and their hunting ground are all on this side. But you want a bridge, even though it's difficult and dangerous to build one. So you are *bumbafu* — 'a crazy white man.' "

From the Pygmy point of view they were right, of course. But they were willing and eager so long as I gave them food and gifts. We set some of them to work at once clearing out some smaller trees that might get in the way of the cameras. Others went in search of long and strong lianas, and still others made a few platforms on which cameras could be mounted for shots from different angles.

The crux of the problem in bridge-building is the first long liana that must somehow be stretched across the river. After that the work is precarious but comparatively simple for Pygmies. We selected a tree, tall and straight, at the water's edge, from which the first attempt would be launched. Free of low branches, it looked like a double-length telephone pole with another tree on top. Opposite this tree, on the other bank of the river, stood several trees of comparable height with widespreading branches.

Looping stout lianas around the trunk of the first tree, one of the more agile Pygmies worked his way up to the first big branch, taking one end of a hawser-like vine with him. He climbed out on the branch and tied the long liana securely to it, using smaller vines as tough as wire to reinforce it. A second long liana was attached about two feet away, so that two long and supple wooden ropes fell to the ground. These were simply the ropes for a giant swing, to which a small seat was attached. The idea was to place a strong young Pygmy in the seat, set him swinging, and hope that he could swing out far enough to reach a branch of one of the trees on the opposite bank.

None of the Pygmies seemed eager to act as the swinger. As the time approached for the first launching, they looked at the river's width, at the great height of the swing, and were hesitant. They insisted the job could be done, but each one disclaimed any special ability as swinger or bridge builder, and many pointed to other men as experts in the field. We finally settled on a young fellow of about twenty named Meru, who seemed both proud to have been chosen and afraid to get in the swing. But he looked like a brave man, and I heard he was one of the best elephant hunters of the group. When I told Meru about the special gifts of dried fish, nuts, salt and palm wine that would go to the man who carried the first liana across the river, he was more eager for the task.

The Pygmies had cut a clear path through the forest leading straight back from the tall tree, a kind of narrow alley in which the swing could be pulled back to launch Meru on his flying mission. A long liana, tied to the seat of the swing, was led back through this path and passed up to two or three Pygmies perched high in the branches of a tree. The idea was for them to pull Meru back and up as far as possible, then suddenly let him go. He was equipped with a sharply curved piece of hardwood that looked something like a longshoreman's hook. As he swung up close to the branch on the other side of the river, he was supposed to catch his hook over the branch and hold on for dear life. I was afraid that this movement would jerk him right out of the swing seat, but the Pygmies assured me that he would be fastened to it securely and would manage to scramble up on the branch once he caught hold of it.

Meru settled himself in the swing, hooked his arms around the lianas, and grasped his wooden hook; others tied him to the seat. Then the Pygmies in the tree back at the end of the cleared path began hauling on the long liana, pulling Meru back and up, higher and higher. We had one camera on a platform filming this action and another on the river bank to shoot the flight of the swing across the river. I stationed myself near the base of the tree with the swing, where I could see in both directions and give the necessary signals.

Slowly and laboriously the Pygmies in the tree hauled Meru up on the back half of the swing's arc, until he was suspended, almost face down, near the far end of the narrow alleyway. Then I gave the signal, "Cut!" and one of the Pygmies in the tree cut the hauling liana. Meru's tiny body hurtled down and out at increasing speed, barely missing the trees beside the cleared area. In a fraction of a second he reached the bottom of the arc and sped over the water and up toward his goal. But something went wrong! He didn't zoom upward as he should. I looked up to see the branch with the swing bending from the force of the pull that had been exerted on it. Meru's foot touched the top of the water, cut down his speed, and prevented him from coming anywhere near the tree on the opposite bank.

The swing dropped back toward us, and the Pygmies grabbed it to bring it to a stop. Meru was obviously deeply frightened, and I did not blame him. If the branch had broken he would have been a goner. Even if it had bent a little more so that his body struck the water, he probably would have been killed by the force of the impact.

He stepped from the swing rather shakily, and I put my arm around his shoulder to calm him and reassure him. He kept shaking his head and muttering something that sounded like "*Zanzabuku! Zanzabuku!*" I had no idea what it meant, for it was apparently a word or phrase from the original Pygmy language. But as he gestured at the swing, the branch, and the river, shaking his head as if to say "Never again!" I gained a good idea of what he meant. He was telling me that this job was too dangerous. Somehow, in spite of the tenseness of that critical moment, I could not forget the word, and it has come to my mind several times when I suddenly found myself in a hazardous situation. *Zanzabuku* must mean something like "dangerous task" or "perilous mission." Anyway, I had a title for both a book and a motion picture.

I took Meru to one side, got him to sit down, and offered him a cigarette. We smoked quietly for a while. I wanted to give him a chance to collect himself. After this trouble, certainly no other Pygmy would volunteer to swing, and Meru was adamant against trying again.

Strong measures were called for, so I got out a bottle of Holland beer that I'd bought at a *duka* outside the forest. He enjoyed it, as he did the cigarette, and I did not press him for a decision at this time. Instead I called off work for the day. But I went on talking to Meru about other things, about his elephant hunting, dancing, his hunting dog, and other pleasant subjects. I was looking for some basis of appeal that might weigh heavily with him. I *had* to persuade him to try the swing once more, after it was properly fixed.

Persuading a Pygmy is, however, totally different from persuading anyone else. The appeals I might make to almost any civilized person were ineffective to a Pygmy. I could not use his vanity, telling him how movies of his great feat would be shown in theaters all over the world and millions would applaud his bravery and skill. Meru did not know what pictures were and cared not a whit for the opinions of people outside the Ituri Forest. I could not really use the argument that all the Pygmies would look up to him, for Pygmies lack almost all serious competitive spirit and they cannot understand the importance of being better than the next fellow except as hunters. There was not much more I could do for his acquisitive nature, for the rewards already offered seemed like riches to him. Riches at least for a day or two, and beyond that Meru was not concerned.

Finally I hit upon something I might use. When I asked him about his wife and children, he said with a rueful expression that he was not married. There was a girl in a neighboring Pygmy group that he wanted for a wife, but he could not persuade his sister to marry a young man in that group and thus make the head-for-head exchange of women.

There was only one thing for me to do — turn matchmaker. I located the sister and talked to her. She did not have anything against the fellow in the other group. But she was only thirteen and didn't feel like getting married yet. Marriage meant a great deal of hard work, and she was having a good time as it was.

So now I had to do a selling job on Meru's sister. In many other primitive tribes I would have found the task easier, for the appeal of mirrors, beads, scissors, safety pins and such is very strong. Pygmies, however, do not care much for personal adornment, have no idea what a mirror is for, and have nothing to cut up or pin up. I had to rely on things to eat, and on pottery jars with which she could start housekeeping.

In the end I won her over. She agreed to take the young man from the neighboring group right away, and that meant Meru would have the girl he wanted. He was overjoyed, and the next day when the affair was settled by all parties concerned, he agreed to make one more effort to span the river. But first we had to find a branch that would not bend under the force of his swing.

About ten feet above the branch we had used was another, much thicker and stronger. We cut off the lower branch, and found longer lianas for the swing. In another day we were ready.

Meru was lashed to his seat, given his hook, and started on the backward pull. Higher and higher he rose, until I gave the signal for him to be released. Down and out he flashed, and this time Meru arched out over the water and up toward the branch on the opposite shore. At the top of his swing, his arm darted out with the hook — and missed the branch by inches!

The Pygmies groaned — and I did too. Meru swung to a stop, and I walked up to him disconsolately. He had said he would try it just once. But he was not frightened any more. The branch and the swing had held firm, so there was nothing to be afraid of. He was truly a courageous fellow!

Meru explained to the men who hauled him back that they must pull him just a few feet higher. Then he could reach the tree on the other side.

After time out for a cigarette, Meru got in the swing again for the third — and, I felt sure, the last — try. Some of the other Pygmies were no help, for they cried out "*Utanguka!*" (You'll fall!) as Meru was being hauled up in the air. But the young man was determined, and I don't think he even heard them. I waited to give the "Cut!" signal until Meru was several feet higher than before, then watched him speed down and out, looping up gracefully toward the distant branch across the water. At exactly the right moment Meru lunged with his hook and caught the branch. His body jerked so violently that I felt sure he would lose his grip, but he pulled himself up slowly until he lay panting on the long-sought goal, the swing seat still strapped to his body, and the two long lianas stretched across the river.

"*Mukaramisu!*" the Pygmies cried, calling Meru the fearless one.

Everything after that was anticlimax, although there were many fascinating shots for the cameras as the main supporting vines were placed lower down on both trees, arching down over the river like the cables of a suspension bridge. The Pygmies built ladder-like approaches from the ground and set quickly to work enlarging the bridge. More thick lianas passed across the water, a little higher than the first two, so they could serve as handrails. Pygmies worked their way out from the tree making a narrow footpath, and more vines were woven in and out to make a kind of netting on either side, between footpath and handrails. Finally the day came when I stepped onto the bridge and made my way across. The bridge swayed and danced under my feet, and I looked with a good deal of trepidation at the rushing water below. But the bridge was strong and would no doubt last a long time.

It had been an arduous task, but it turned out so well that I felt like celebrating. I gave Meru more than I had promised, and made sure that the marriages would take place, which they did at once. When I left the Ituri Forest the third time I felt happy. And somehow I no longer felt that the Pygmies were strange or unusual human beings. We had been through too much together.

Although the bridge-building was the most exciting incident, there were a dozen others that made me like Pygmies better than ever before — and understand them better, too. I finally learned, for instance, the secret of the Pygmy's uncanny ability to find his way through the forest. What has always baffled outsiders most is not the Pygmy's marvelous tracking of animals, but rather the beeline route he follows, without a path, in going from any one spot in his jungle to another, even five or ten miles away. William Spees showed me that there is no mystery, no sixth sense. The Pygmy is very observant, and above all he is thoroughly familiar with his section of the forest — with every single part of it. There he has lived his entire life. He has lived a month in one spot, a month in another, ranging throughout the whole territory, and has hunted through those woods almost daily.

When he wants to make sure just where he is, he looks up and sees an ironwood or mahogany tree that has stood in its spot for longer than the Pygmy's grandfather can remember. To a forest dweller's eyes, this particular tree is different from any other tree in the forest.

"It's just as if he looked up at the tree," Bill Spees said, "and read it, as you would read a street sign saying Broadway and 42nd Street. It's as simple as that."

A little more than nine years elapsed between my third and fourth trips to Africa, but thousands of years of "history" in the lives and goals of millions of people. Just as I had unrolled history to the Stone Age by stepping into the world of the primitive, many of these African people were trying to leap, in a few years, from pre-history to the age of One World and the United Nations.

During this period I followed the major developments in newspapers and magazines, and through letters from friends in Africa and others who had been there. But there were big gaps in my secondhand knowledge, the biggest concerning the Bambuti Pygmies of the Ituri Forest. I didn't know enough.

So I had to go back to Africa. No ambitious film production this time, with trucks and assistants and cameramen. I went for myself and no one else, to satisfy a need for knowledge of people I knew — not only the Bambuti, but also the Mangbetu, the Wagenia, the Babira, the Bakuba, the Masai, the Kikuyu, the Turkana, and others. I went as unburdened as on my first trip twenty-seven years before, with only my personal cameras and a tape recorder. I looked and I listened. And I found the Pygmies of the Ituri retreating back into the Stone Age, successfully.

After learning the sad tale of the Watusi in Usumbura, Burundi, I found I could not catch the regular airline plane into the Congo. It didn't fly any more. So I arranged passage to Bunia with a bush pilot who was still flying a small plane over the border. I was delayed because the pilot had found a minor Belgian official who decided to go back to his post in the little town of Goma, with his wife, baby, and the baby's pram. It was hard to fit us all into the little Cessna, but we made it, and I did not mind too much for it cut my charter cost down to $150. After an hour's flight we dropped the Belgians off at Goma, where the Congolese officials got very busy and argumentative about my passport until a wise one among them suggested that they leave the decision to the higher officials in Bunia, my destination.

By this time I was wishing I had heeded the advice of my friends in Kenya, all of whom had said emphatically that I should not try to go into the Congo. Colonel Mervyn Cowie, Sir Charles and Lady Betty Markham, and others warned that I was taking a greater chance than any I had encountered on any previous trip. Carr Hartley, the great animal catcher who had been so helpful to me in the filming of *Zanzabuku* and who is one of the most courageous men I have known, backed up his warning with an account of a personal experience. Just a few months before my arrival, he had driven into the Congo to pick up some wild animals that had been caught for him. On his return, he was stopped by Congolese soldiers, forced from his car at gunpoint, and questioned for more than an hour.

"When a truculent and not too bright soldier pokes a rifle in your belly and asks questions that mean he thinks you've been helping the rebels," Carr told me, "you are really scared. It took me over an hour to convince those boys that my trip was not political or subversive. My skin is white, so I had two strikes against me. So is yours, and you may not be as lucky as I was. I'll tell you one thing — I'm not going in there again. And neither should you."

But I had been in touch with Bill Deans and Bill Spees, who were still in the Congo. They had been forced out at one time, but had come back again. There had been turmoil and confusion and danger, but the two Bills thought it would be safe for me to visit the Congo at that time. So I weighed the pros and cons and took my usual calculated risk. You can't live a full or interesting life without taking risks, so you just have to weigh the dangers against the value of your objectives. I decided it was worth some obvious though not inevitable dangers to get a first-hand view of the Pygmies and the situation in a country I knew so well. So I went on to Bunia, flying over beautiful Lake Kivu on the way and wondering about the Belgians who had built the beautiful homes lining the western shore. Where were they now, and what would happen to these small Shangri Las they had made for themselves?

Many things had happened since my last visit, although I found that hard to believe as I sat with Bill Spees and some Pygmy friends around a campfire and listened to their tales of elephant hunting. For one thing, there had been the effort of some Belgian administrators to "do-mesticate" the Pygmies. There was supposed to be a census, but no-body could take a census in the Ituri Forest, for no one but a Pygmy could find his way around in it. Also, it was not the kind of thing a Pygmy could understand. So the Belgians decided to move the Pyg-mies out of the forest, for at least part of the time. Census-taking was not the only motivation behind the idea, of course, for the Belgians, like most modern men, felt compelled to "improve" the lot of these tiny Stone Age people living in the forest. With the Pygmies, there was no thought of exploitation, which has been the ultimate goal be-hind much "improvement" of uncivilized peoples. The Pygmies didn't have anything to exploit. But the social-worker impulse made the Bel-gians move some Pygmies to plantations on the edge of the forest, where they could grow their own crops and free themselves from their "bondage" to the village Negroes but at the same time be able to hunt in the forest. The idea was to make agriculturists out of hunting nomads, a transition that had taken tens of thousands of years of natu-ral evolution in most of the world. The genial Pygmies were willing to try. They worked the vegetable gardens set up for them, they sent their children to village schools — and they died like flies. Gardens are cleared areas, open to the sun, and the Pygmies could not stand so much direct sunlight. They suffered from dehydration, were suscep-tible to pneumonia and other respiratory diseases, and had no immu-nity against the malaria-bearing mosquito, which does not live in the forest. Bill Deans and other missionaries who understood what was going on protested to the Belgian authorities again and again, so the experiment was finally abandoned. The Pygmies went back to their forest, back to their symbiotic relationship with the village Negroes.

But that did not last long, for in these days there is really no going back to the old ways. Uhuru was followed by civil war and the resurgence of tribal loyalties that made a score of "countries" out of the artificially carved plot of earth that had once been King Leopold's private domain and later the Belgian Congo. Transportation systems broke down, and the village Bantus could not get the beer, salt and tobacco which they wanted and which drew the Pygmies to the vil-lages. They came out of the forest less and less. They missed the few amenities of civilization they had become accustomed to, but they could get along without them. Only a few decades before, they had taken one or two tentative steps out of the Paleolithic Age. It was easy to retreat those few steps, into the forest that had always sheltered and sustained them.

All around this protected area of the Ituri, old tribal jealousies and religions among the Negroes received new life through uhuru. When independence did not bring the utopia that had been promised, they reverted to their old ways. Witchcraft, which had languished, reawoke with new vigor. An old tribal religion, Kimbanguism, arose and spread among many tribes. Another religious sect, called Kitawala, spread so rapidly and aroused such devotion as to become a menace. Strangely enough, Kitawala was an offshoot of Jehovah's Witnesses, which missionaries had brought to Africa but which degenerated into a mish-mash of ancient superstitions, witchcraft, and old tribal loyalties. It was strongly antigovernment, whether the government was Belgian or Congolese, right wing or left wing, and the government took repressive steps to stamp it out, to little avail.

Islam exerted a strong appeal to many Africans, because many of its tenets, such as polygamy, fitted in with their ancient customs. There had long been centers of Mohammedanism in Africa. From the old days of the Arab slave trade in the nineteenth century, many Moslems had remained in Central Africa, marrying Negroes but retaining their religion. (They also brought Swahili, the language that, in one form or another, became the lingua franca of the Congo and other areas.) Stanleyville was the largest town with many *Aribisés*, as the Belgians called the followers of Islam, but there were others. I found that the Masai in Tanganyika were also attracted to the Moslem code.

The widespread turning to new religions or back to half-forgotten pagan belief resulted, in large measure, from the general disillusionment with uhuru. Many people were worse off than they had been under the Belgians. Some officials, however, were putting away private fortunes — in banks abroad or in the purchase of office buildings, bars, cafés that would still be profitable when they lost their political jobs, as they all expected to do. Bill Deans said that there had been a general moral breakdown throughout the country. Drinking, especially beer because it was the cheapest alcoholic beverage, had increased manyfold. That and other factors had led to an increase in prostitution. Bill knew of twelve converts from his school who had turned to prostitution in order to get money for more beer. And he is not the kind of missionary who objects to a little fun, even a little paganism, among people so recently converted; he doesn't look for evil where it does not exist.

Deans's mission at Nyankunde was larger than when I had seen it last, in 1954, with a small hospital now, a school, and a good-size printing plant for turning out tracts and Bibles in native tongues. There was a staff of converted Bantus, who worked hard, seemed happy, and obviously adored Bill and Dora Deans. After a few days there, Bill drove me to Lolwa, about two hours away, where Bill and Ella Spees carried on their missionary work. It was Spees who accompanied me deep into the forest for a visit with Pygmies. On the way back we stopped for breakfast at another mission, run by Mr. and Mrs. Gordon Searles, then had dinner at an orphanage run by Miss Margaret Dawes of Vancouver. She had both Bantu and Pygmy children in her institution, and had come to the conclusion that the intelligence of the Pygmy children was definitely superior to that of the Bantus.

Bill Deans picked me up at Lolwa and drove me to the medical missionary camp at Oicha, where I met one of the great men of Africa — Dr. Carl K. Becker, an American doctor from Doylestown, Pennsylvania. He had first come to the Congo in 1929 and, except for too few and too brief furloughs, had carried on his work there ever since. At Oicha there was a leprosarium that at one time cared for as many as four thousand lepers. While I was there, his dispensary handled the ills of two thousand patients a day. The doctor had several white assistants, and had trained a fine staff of native Bantus to help him. It seemed to me they all worked about eighteen hours a day.

Dr. Becker was about seventy years old, a genial, happy man — the kind of person everyone would automatically trust on sight. His wife, two or three years younger than her husband, had injured her leg some time before my arrival, but she could not let that interfere with her work — "There's just too much that has to be done." They did not have the proper splints or braces, so Mrs. Becker found two pieces of metal and made her own brace so she could hobble around.

Dr. and Mrs. Becker were so busy they scarcely noticed the coming of independence to the Congo. But six months later the American government, fearful of serious repercussions following the murder of Patrice Lumumba, ordered all United States citizens to evacuate. When the Beckers reached the border of Uganda, Congolese soldiers and officials pled with them not to leave. They promised that no trouble would come to him, insisted that they needed him desperately. So he went back to Oicha and carried on, even though he had great difficulty in getting needed medications. I asked Dr. Becker, before leaving, what diseases he treated other than leprosy. He smiled and replied, "You name it — we've got it."

Later Bill Deans drove me to the Epulu River to see *La Station des Okapis de l'Epulu*, a kind of sanctuary established originally by the Belgians for catching and studying the Congo's most unusual animal. I went into a compound with food for the twenty-four okapi there, but only a few were bold enough to come to me and get it. I remembered my first trip, in 1937, when I had been excited at seeing just one okapi at Pat Putnam's famous camp on the edge of the Ituri Forest. They are shy animals and don't look quite real, for the stripes on the hind legs suggest the zebra and the longish neck suggests a beast trying to become a giraffe. But the okapi's tongue is more like an anteater's, so long and sinuous and sticky that it can pull down succulent leaves almost a foot above its head.

I met the founder and for many years director of this station, Jean De Medina, a remarkable man whom I had heard praised by some of the best animal men in Africa. I had looked forward to this meeting, but it was a sad occasion. The day before our arrival, De Medina had received a letter from the Congolese government removing him from the management of the Okapi Station, replacing him with Pascal, a native De Medina had trained, and putting De Medina in the assistant's position. I don't think this would have bothered the man much if the work to which he had devoted his life could have gone forward properly. But the past few years had shown him this could not be. After independence he had been called to Stanleyville for some special work. When he returned to the Epulu, only two elephants remained of twenty-two that had been kept there. Native workers said that the twenty had died of some sickness. When De Medina asked where they were buried, his men said that God did not mean meat to be buried, but eaten. He knew that the elephants had died of "spear-sickness."

Meanwhile his okapi-catching staff had been reduced from ten to two men. So the many pits they had dug for catching okapi could not be serviced—the animals died if not taken from the pit in two or three days. In the middle of this discouraging recital, Bill Deans managed to whisper to me that De Medina's only son had been killed in the riots in Leopoldville, shortly after independence.

In spite of all this, De Medina gave us a light lunch on a porch overlooking the Epulu River. He talked about animals, and methods of catching animals for zoos throughout the world. He wanted everyone to be able to see all animals, although he disapproved of the way they were handled in most zoos in the world. He had been horrified, when he was a young man, at the methods for catching gorillas. Zookeepers wanted babies or young gorillas, and the only way to get them was to kill the mother, probably the father, and perhaps some other relatives. De Medina knew that this method would soon wipe out the small gorilla population. So he had developed the use of the Pygmy Bisenji dogs for hunting gorillas. These barkless mongrels had immeasurable courage and pertinacity. De Medina took eighteen or twenty of them on a gorilla hunt. When they found a gorilla family, the dogs started snarling and snapping and jumping at the huge beasts from all sides. The adult gorillas sent their young ones up a tree and tried to defend the trunk. But the persistent nagging of the dogs finally drove them off. De Medina then sent some young Africans up the tree with clubs which they never used. They wielded them threateningly, and the baby gorillas whimpered in fright, let go, and toppled into the nets De Medina had spread below.

De Medina did not think his method was by any means perfect. He told me about the new technique of a Swiss-American, Charles Cordier, who had devised guns shooting darts pointed with an anesthetic. With his sleep-inducing darts, Cordier could put the adult gorillas out of action without terrorizing them, and then catch young gorillas who were sleeping peacefully. But I heard later that the method was not as scientific as might be wished, for the amount of drug in the dart had to be gauged according to the weight of the animals.

When we were leaving the okapi station, the new director and former assistant, Pascal, came to me and said the station needed money, and he had been authorized to sell some of the okapi there. Perhaps I would know of some zoos in America that would like to have okapis. He would sell a female for five thousand dollars, a male for thirty-five hundred dollars. I said I would let him know if I found anyone who was interested.

After such a conversation, it was a relief to go into the Ituri and talk to the Pygmies. Bill Spees and I sat around a fire with three elephant hunters. While they ate, I listened to the sounds of the forest — the shrill, steady buzz of the katydids, the sharp chirps of crickets, the songlike talk of some colobus monkeys. I started at the eerily human cry of a tree lemur, and later at the call of a leopard, but the Pygmies scarcely seemed to notice these sounds. When an owl hooted, however, they cowered together and looked around in fear. Luckily, the owl went on its way without hooting again, or the Pygmies might have left us. They fear the owl more than anything else in the world, for they say it walks with evil spirits.

Bill Spees soon got the hunters talking — Akilimani, tall for a Pygmy, almost four feet five inches; Sasita; and Asani. Sasita told us about a close call he had had about a month before, when he, Asani, and another Pygmy had gone elephant hunting. After a time they found a group and chose one animal at the side. Sasita rushed in first to drive his spear into the elephant's belly. He turned to retreat, but the elephant's tail, in a freakish motion, caught around Sasita's neck and knocked him to the ground. The elephant whirled to finish him off, but moved a little too far (elephants have poor eyesight). Sasita rolled himself right under the big beast, between his legs, and lay there while the elephant looked around. As the creature started to move, Sasita was afraid of getting tromped on, so he slipped out. The elephant saw or smelled him, picked up a big log, and smashed it down. Sasita leapt out of the way, scurrying under the elephant again — sometimes the safest place in such a situation. All this time, Sasita's spear was in the elephant's belly, and at last the creature gave up and started to follow the rest of the herd. Sasita slipped away unnoticed and, except for some bad bruises, was none the worse for the encounter. The next day he and his companions followed the tracks and found the elephant dead about two miles away.

The greatest joy to a Pygmy is hunting elephants, the next greatest talking about it. But other animals provide some exciting tales on occasion. One day Akilimani was alone in the forest, looking for small game. He came upon a big buffalo that charged him so fast Ailimani was caught on its wide horns. The animal tossed Akilimani about ten feet, but luckily the horns did not puncture him. The hunter staggered to his feet, and the buffalo tossed him again. The third time the animal caught Akilimani on his horns, it did not toss him, but started to run off. As it passed under the breach of a tree, the Pygmy reached up and grabbed it, pulling himself to safety. The buffalo charged the tree for an hour trying to knock Akilimani down, but in spite of his wounds the hunter held on until the buffalo gave up and ran away. Akilimani was just barely able to make his way back to his camp.

I don't like to think about what happened in that part of the world shortly after I left. Everyone was fearful of what the next few months would bring. They brought control of the northeastern Congo by the rebel forces, tortures, atrocities, and mass killings. Bill Deans knew of more than five hundred men and women who were executed at the foot of Lumumba's statue in Bunia. He got out of the country just one day ahead of the rebel forces that took over Bunia. Dr. Becker's great medical mission at Oicha was destroyed, although Dr. and Mrs. Becker managed to reach safety in Uganda. So did other missionaries I had met — the Searleses, the Speeses, and Miss Dawes of the orphanage.

In time the regular Congolese forces retook the area from the rebels, and months later some missionaries were permitted to return. Bill Deans reported that he was happy to find that his staff of converted Bantus had more or less kept things going at his Nyankunde station. Dr. Becker and some of his staff, too, were back in the Congo, but they were now at Nyankunde, which was to become the mission medical center and training school for the northeast Congo. A smallpox epidemic had recently scourged the area. Bill wrote: "Army ants have invaded our house — we are turning them back with embers and kerosene. They travel, claws upward, like regimented soldiers in formation with a row of guards. They rapidly run up one's legs, pinching viciously as they ascend. In a home they eat everything that is meat or fat, dead or alive, particularly animal or bird pets, sometimes even native babies. Historic, classic Congolese punishment for a lying, thieving child: ten minutes on an army ant hill. It is reportedly a sure cure."

My most recent letter from Bill Deans was dated April 13, 1966. He had been kicked out of the Congo again and returned again since the last time I had heard from him — making this the third time. He wrote, in part, "You got your last trip into the Congo just in time. Poor De Medina, whom we met at the okapi station on the Epulu, was killed by the rebels, who then ate all the okapi and elephants. An expensive meal!" Bill went on to report more discouraging events.

But when I am overcome by thoughts of what has happened and what might again happen to what could almost be called my "second" country, I am solaced by the Pygmies. They have retreated more deeply into the Ituri, and come to the Bantu villages only rarely. No soldiers will penetrate their homeland, whether rebel or regular Congolese. The forest they love will give them sustenance and joy. There is peace in their world, if in no other place on earth.

5

Masai, Mangbetu, Mau Mau

THERE was no place like Africa for a study of the human race in all its diversity of shape, color, size and features, and in the infinite variety of dress, decoration, architecture, art, religion, morals, and manners. Africa was the home of perhaps the greatest of ancient civilizations; it is now thought to be the birthplace of mankind; and it was still the home of men of the Stone Age when I first visited it. It contains more different racial groups and languages than any other continent — perhaps more than all other continents combined. If you had spent just one week with each distinct tribe in Africa a quarter of a century ago, you would have visited for more than eight years. Obviously it is impossible to make reasonable generalizations about "Africans."

We Americans like to think of our country as containing many different racial stocks, but it hasn't a tenth of Africa's human variety. Some of that continent's racial strains have apparently remained fairly pure, but most have intermingled in an uncountable number of blends. Except for the desert areas and the Ituri Forest, the continent presents few barriers to movement; the races of Africa have been moving back and forth and around for centuries, conquering, being conquered, intermarrying, and running away. There were Bushmen, Pygmies, West African Negroes, Bantus, Sudanese and Nilotic Negroes, Hamites, Semites and the perhaps-white Berbers of the north. There are countless mixtures of these, such as the Hottentots, who are probably a blend of Bushman, Negro, and Hamite; the Masai, who are Hamite and Negro; the Batwa, who are Pygmy and Bantu; Ethiopians, who are Hamite and Semite, with some Negro; the Tibbu, who are Berber and Negro; the Luo, who are Nilotic and Bantu. The Azande and the Mangbetu are usually called Sudanese, but they probably intermingled with the Fula, who were in all likelihood a mixture of Berber and Negro. The aristocratic Watusi are pure Hamite, surrounded by Bantu and Pygmy and blends of those two.

As if a continent with four or five hundred tribes was not varied enough, Africa has welcomed Arabs, Persians, Turks, Indonesians, Indians, Chinese, plus French, English, Dutch, Spanish, Italian, German, Belgian, and Danish traders, missionaries, conquerors, and settlers, some of whom added their bloodstreams to the racial rivers of Africa.

Languages? There are over three hundred — not counting dialects. One can find small areas of perhaps fifty square miles, containing half a dozen villages, where four or five different basic languages are spoken. A few trade languages have spread over large areas, but there are variations in dialects even of these tongues.

Most of Africa has no recorded history. But one part of it — Egypt — has just about the longest history possessed by the human race. There was ancient Carthage, too, and the later Roman encirclement of the Mediterranean, followed in the Middle Ages by a thriving Arab civilization that even invaded Europe. But all of these were along the northernmost edge of the continent and are not characteristically "African." We now know that the interior of Africa once contained large and powerful kingdoms, but all disappeared except Ethiopia, and we know little about them. The British found a strong and well-organized kingdom in Uganda when they first went there, but it was not an advanced civilization by our standards. Other tribes, such as the Zulu and the Basuto, organized themselves into strong confederations, chiefly to oppose white men's encroachments. Almost every tribe has its legends which may well be founded in history; but it is difficult to tell how far back they go. The Pygmies of the Ituri Forest, for instance, say that their people originally came "from the north," but when and how far north no one has the faintest idea.

In some ways, the lack of known history makes visiting African tribes more interesting. You have few of the preconceptions you might get from reading a history of a people before seeing them, as I had tried to do in all my travels. Most of us, however, have other preconceptions so firmly rooted that we cannot eradicate them easily. We have a mental picture of a "typical African native," with dark skin, kinky hair, flat broad nose, big mouth, prognathous jaw, few clothes, many superstitions, a dislike of work or responsibility, a wonderful sense of rhythm, a childlike gaiety. A few Africans are like that, some are totally unlike that, others have one or more of those traits.

Even though I confined my visiting to a relatively small area of the continent, I found amazing variety. In the Congo alone there were Bantu, Nilotic and Sudanese Negroes, plus Hamites, Semites, and Pygmies — with blends. There were Baluba, Bakuba, Balunda, Babali, Bambole, Babira, Bahavu, Bambuba, Bakele, Bakusu, Basonge, and a dozen more beginning with *Ba*, meaning "people." There were the hot-tempered Walendu, who were tall and long-legged like most Nilotics but not as tall as the Hamitic Watusi. Other Nilotics were the Alur, the Logo, the Lugware, and the Kakwa. Then there were the Sudanese, among whom the Azande and the Mangbetu were the best-known tribes — and these were quite different from each other in language, costume, and culture.

There were Walese, Wanande, Warega, Wazimba, Wasongola, Walengola, Wanianda, Wagenia, and others whose tribal names began with *Wa*, also meaning "people."

I visited the Babira tribe, near Bunia in the eastern Congo, in 1937 and again in 1946 on the *Savage Splendor* trip. Most of us think of the Ubangi when we see plate-lipped women, but the insertion of large disks in holes in the lips is a custom of numerous tribes. The Babira *femmes à plateau* were friendly and accustomed to having their pictures taken. Little girls used to have their upper lips pierced and a small bone or stick inserted in the hole. As the girls grew, larger and larger plugs were inserted, stretching the lip more and more until by their teens the young ladies wore three- and four-inch wooden disks. To hold the disk in place, the women knocked out their four top center teeth so it would fit into a snug holder. With the disk removed, the lip hung down to the chin and revealed the wide dental gap, presenting at least to me just about as ugly a sight as the human face can offer.

Looking at these Babira beauties, I almost believed the tale that this practice originated when the Arab slave traders first came to Central

Africa. The idea was to make the women so unattractive that they would not be taken as slaves. In time, supposedly, the men of their own tribe began to find the decoration, especially with the disk in place, attractive. A plausible story but probably not true, because the lip-stretching seems to date back long before the Arab raids. And it is really not so different from other forms of mutilation practiced by primitive tribes; it just looks more repulsive to us. I saw a comparable practice among the Kuria tribe in western Tanganyika, whose men stretched earlobes in similar fashion. We filmed a Kuria medicine man whose earlobe was so stretched that the women of the tribe passed their newborn babies through the loop for good luck.

By 1946 I found fewer plate lips among the Babira than I had seen in 1937 — and none at all among young girls. By 1964 the last of the older women with plate lips had died, and the strange practice existed no more. And without the big lips, the women of the Babira were uninteresting.

On the other hand, a somewhat larger tribe, north of the Ituri Forest and not far from the border of the Sudan, was fascinating. The Mangbetu were Sudanese in origin, and had achieved a fine artistic expression. Moreover, their women were among the most attractive and appealing I have met in Africa. Just why they were so attractive is difficult to determine, but they undoubtedly had more sex appeal, without being obviously erotic, than women of most primitive tribes. Perhaps they kept their figures longer. At any rate, the proportion of young women with slim hips, firm breasts, and lithe bodies was greater among the Mangbetu than among other tribes, where only women between about fourteen and twenty-three were attractive by our standards. Perhaps part of the appeal came from the *nekbwe*, an oversize fan or undersize chair seat worn like a bustle on the buttocks. When Mangbetu women danced — actually a rather sedate and quiet dance except for soloists — the nekbwe twitched and shifted slightly at every movement, with a most alluring effect. This was enhanced by the fact that the nekbwe itself was pretty, being made of woven colored fibers in geometric or other designs.

Mangbetu women had great dignity, as did the women of the Watusi aristocracy, but there was warmth beneath it. The Watusi women were gracious, dignified, friendly, and far, far away. The Mangbetu women were gracious, dignified, friendly, and — one felt — might be very close. The Watusi aroused admiration; the Mangbetu aroused more fundamental emotions. They did not invite; they stimulated. Even their elongated heads were rather attractive, and when they were crowned with the elaborate and unusual hairdos of the Mangbetu they were quite stunning. When I first saw these women, their heads reminded me of the famous bust of the Egyptian Queen Nefertiti, but I thought this was because of the long headdress in that statue. Later, however, I saw in the Metropolitan Museum of Art the unadorned head of a daughter of the ancient Egyptian king Ikhnaton. The skull was so elongated that it had obviously been bound in childhood in the fashion of the Mangbetu.

Perhaps Mangbetu men found the women of their tribe as attractive as I did, for polygamy was practiced by those who could afford it. Tribal chiefs had anywhere from thirty to four hundred wives, and other important men enjoyed sizable harems. But the plebeians usually had only one wife each.

Although the Mangbetu seemed artistic and cultured, they once enjoyed an unsavory reputation for cannibalism. There has been much loose talk by casual travelers about cannibalism in Africa, but there was undoubtedly a good deal of it among many tribes. Such customs are hard to kill. In the case of the Mangbetu, there was more than just talk. There was good evidence. The distinguished German ethnologist G. A. Schweinfurth lived with and studied the Mangbetu during the 1870's and 1880's, when that tribe was living as it had for centuries, untouched by civilization. The scientist, wishing to take back to Europe bones and skulls for his studies, offered the tribesmen copper, which they valued highly, for human bones left over from their feasts. In a short time he had accumulated a great pile, although he was disappointed to find that most of the skulls had been shattered so the Mangbetu gourmands could get at the brains — a great delicacy. Still, he brought home forty excellent skulls out of the hundreds he collected.

No doubt eating human flesh among the Mangbetu has long since ceased, but on my first trip I received some vague and confusing answers to my questions about it. One missionary, who knew the country and people well, told me, with a not-to-be-taken-too-seriously look in his eyes, of the Mangbetu wife whose husband died. Instead of burying him, she made a stew of him and invited all her friends to the feast. "You know," she said to a guest, "this is the first time I really appreciated my husband."

Of course, the chance to eat human beings rarely if ever presents itself any more. For decades, there have been no old-fashioned tribal wars, no raids, no captives. But when Schweinfurth first discovered the Mangbetu, their king, Munza, treated himself almost daily to a meal of a tender child. Along with this habit has disappeared also the Mangbetu greeting that Schweinfurth reported. They held out their right hands, said *"Gasiggy,"* and cracked the joints of their middle fingers. I saw nothing like it, but I was allowed to film a Mangbetu mother binding her baby's head with long strands of raffia to elongate it.

During the first years of life, when a child's skull is still pliable, the raffia bindings are worn almost all the time, forcing the skull to grow up and back in a not unattractive oval. Doctors say that this alteration of nature's intentions has no bad effect on the brain or intelligence, but it does give the eyes an oriental slant and make them pop slightly. Despite the fact that medical men said head-binding was harmless, Belgian authorities discouraged the practice, so more and more children grew up with normal heads. By 1946 I saw fewer children wearing the raffia bindings, and by now the practice has stopped.

The Mangbetu were fine artists, musicians, and dancers. The house of Chief Ekibondo, in a village not far from Paulis, had walls of plaster, and even the poles supporting the roof had been covered with plaster to make them into square pillars, upon which were painted in black and red various designs suggested by animals — crocodiles, snakes, and fish. Geometric patterns, complicated but uncluttered, covered the plaster walls. Even the smaller houses were attractive cylinders with conical thatched roofs, their plaster walls decorated almost as beautifully as the chief's.

I first met Ekibondo in 1937 and found him pleasant, cooperative, and almost too eager to see that his musicians and dancers performed just right for my cameras. The town of Paulis had undergone great changes by 1946, for in World War II it became a truck terminal for the shipment of huge quantities of ammunition and supplies overland to the Allied armies in North Africa. Much of the evidence of this modern bustle had disappeared but its influences remained. Ekibondo was dressed in European trousers; he wore a wristwatch. He was happy to change into his native regal attire, with woven fiber cap decorated with brilliant feathers, and the voluminous bloomer-like loincloth made of pounded bark. He gathered his court around him, including several of his seventy wives, brought in the orchestra and the dancers. Altogether he put on a good show, and I obtained some excellent footage.

The Bakuba are a Bantu tribe living in the south central part of the Congo, in the Kasai province. They are well known because more of their artwork has been collected by museums and connoisseurs of Europe and America than that of any other tribe. Their sculpture and wood carving are astonishingly beautiful; the designs in their cloth, their mats, and even the raffia walls of their houses are colorful, imaginative, and quite "modern" in feeling; their embroidery, a rare art among African tribes, is intricate and lovely. One of the finest pieces of art I have seen is a Bakuba mask carved in wood and decorated with colored beadwork.

The importance of art to the Bakuba themselves is illustrated by the fact that among the king's council there were representatives of various arts and crafts, including sculptors and legend-keepers, or historians. Bakuba legends, which are memorized and passed on from generation to generation, go back much further than those of most tribes and can sometimes be tied to known historical events, so we have an inkling of their history. Among the legends is one of the creation telling how their original king, or *Nyimi*, came down to earth from the creator of earth and heaven and all things. It bears striking resemblances to the creation stories of many other religions. Among the Bakuba, too, there is a flood legend similar to our own.

The Bakuba love beautiful ornaments — beads, feathers, metal pins, rings, and bracelets. When I was there in 1954, the king, a monstrously fat man, wore more than anyone else on his capacious body. He also wore an expression of great weariness and boredom. He was so restricted by tribal customs and traditions and ceremonies that he could scarcely move. I filmed him sitting down on the back of a slave, which he must always do. His feet were not supposed to touch the earth, so other slaves strewed mats before him as he walked, or carried him in a litter. One important sign of his royalty and divinity was a pair of big rings worn on his right big toe.

It was this king who built the first native African museum, to house his own priceless collection. It was a praiseworthy venture, for as time went on the Bakuba were gradually losing their great artistic skills. I don't know what has happened to the Bakuba king's museum, for there has been much fighting and looting in his area. I hope the new government has managed to keep it intact.

The Masai, who live in Tanganyika and southern Kenya, have been much photographed and written about because they are handsome, proud, and romantic. Even after they had been forced to abandon their warlike habits, they were appealing. The British officials of Kenya and Tanganyika before independence considered the Masai extremely difficult, but they spoke with admiration of their pride and even insolence. I knew one official in charge of a Masai preserve who always talked of "my Masai," as one would of a talented child who was a holy terror. The British recognized in the Masai another people who, like themselves, were born with the unshakable conviction that they were a superior race. Even the lowliest Masai felt certain that he occupied a plane far above other human beings.

The self-confidence of the Masai is the kind that has been part of a people's heritage for centuries, but we don't know their history that far back. They are probably Hamitic in origin, with possibly some strains of Nilotic and Bantu. Not too long ago — a couple of centuries perhaps — they moved down from the north as conquerors. During the nineteenth century they were the top dogs in East Africa. They had overcome all the Bantu tribes in their way; they kept making raids and extending their territory; and they scared the slave-trading Arabs so thoroughly that they detoured around the Masai and no Masai was ever enslaved.

This period of dominance is still reflected in the walk and bearing and glance of the Masai *moran*, or warrior. He is tall — six feet or more — thin, well-proportioned, and walks with a graceful loping stride. He wears a dark cloth loosely thrown over one shoulder, except for lion-hunting, when he strips for action. He glows with a kind of reddish-orange hue from the ocher mud that he smears on his body and on his hair, which is gathered into three or four small pigtails. He doesn't tattoo his body and wears relatively little decoration. Pierced earlobes sometimes are stretched until they are long loops, from which dangle heavy ornaments of copper or iron.

This was the professional warrior, part of the Masai standing army, which consisted of every able-bodied male between the ages of eighteen and thirty. This was all very well when the Masai were rulers and conquerors, but in more recent times it became rather troublesome to have such a large body of professional warriors with no one to fight.

The Masai moran was trained from boyhood for his fighting period. At about fourteen he went through a painful and rigorous circumcision ceremony, remarkably like that of primitive tribes elsewhere in Africa and as far away as South America and New Guinea. As he approached his eighteenth year, he allowed his hair to grow — up to that time it had been shaved off, as with all Masai except the warriors. Finally he went out on a lion hunt with some of the veteran warriors and that traditionally made him into *el moran*. Eventually the British put a stop to the old lion-spearing ventures; I don't know what substitute feat the Masai decided on to qualify a young man for the warrior band. At any rate, a warrior devoted his life and thoughts to being a warrior and nothing else. He could not marry. He could not live with his family, but instead lived at a special *manyatta*, or village for fighting men. But this did not mean Spartan-like abstinence on his part, for he may have had one or more girls living at the manyatta, too.

Girls living with the warriors were usually so young that they had not reached puberty and so could not conceive. When they approached that age, they withdrew from the moran manyatta, went through a rigorous circumcision rite of their own, and were considered marriageable. After the rite, they were supposed to remain chaste until married, and faithful afterward except when, as often happened, the husband gave permission for his wife to entertain a guest or friend.

For ten or twelve years the young Masai man was a warrior without wars. In his late twenties he retired, cut off his pigtails, and married. If he was smart and respected, he might become one of the clan elders or eventually be elected headman. Women didn't have much to say among the Masai, but were on the whole rather well treated. They gave themselves their own punishment, so far as I could see, by wearing pounds and pounds of decoration, usually thick copper wire formed into rings around legs, arms, and neck. Each limb might carry up to fifteen pounds of copper, and once put on it was never taken off. Some women carried such loads around their necks that they had to support them in wooden frames when they lay down to sleep.

The Masai are cattle herders and blood drinkers. A few groups of this once large tribe, isolated from the others in the course of migrations and wars, have turned to agriculture and a settled life, but the majority are pastoral folk who consider it degrading to hoe the earth. Wealth and prestige depend largely upon a person's cattle, but unlike the Watusi, the Masai count the number of cattle only and pay little attention to the quality. Masai cows are generally a sorry-looking lot, and their milk production is not large. But most of the sustenance of these natives comes from the cattle. Milk in its many forms — cheese, smoked milk, butter, clarified butter called *ghee* — form the basis of most foods, but the most prized dish is blood drawn from the jugular vein of the cattle. It may be taken straight or mixed with milk into a kind of thin porridge. This high-protein diet may account in part for the lean muscular appearance of the Masai.

Cattle are the focus of life for all Masai. Even the lion-hunting, for which they were famous and through which a young fellow proved his manhood, stemmed from cattle-keeping, for lions went after the cattle. Whatever steals a Masai's cattle is the enemy, and the lion is the arch enemy. These magnificent hunters never hunt anything else, and they do not eat the meat of any game.

The British government's troubles revolved much of the time around cattle. The Masai were not very cooperative about protecting their cattle from the rinderpest or the trypanosomiasis carried by the tsetse fly. They moved their herds onto game preserves or other restricted areas when they thought they could get away with it. And they resisted the government requirement that they sell a certain number of their cattle each year. Since the cattle used so much of the land and constituted a primary nutritional resource of the area, they had to be used to support the population.

When the requirement that the Masai sell some cattle first went into effect, the wily natives invariably picked out the worst of their animals for sale. So the government stepped in and said that its officials would select the cattle to be purchased, but they would choose a representative group, good, fair, and poor. This system worked well most of the time, but the British had not taken into account the fact that sometimes a Masai herder became deeply attached to one or two particular cows, much as one might feel toward a devoted dog or other domestic pet. When an official would inadvertently pick one of these pets for purchase, the Masai owner would be disconsolate and would plead that his pet be spared. Take any other, even a fatter one, but not this cherished creature.

The officials, at the outset, agreed to a substitution when this situation arose, but the Masai decided they could use this trick by claiming that every fat, sleek, and hearty cow was a special pet. Being excellent actors, like most primitives, the Masai would weep and plead with great urgency, but in the end they went too far. One official, Major Hugh Grant, had been tricked many times, so he finally laid down the law — no more substitutions.

Then he picked a favorite cow of one Masai herdsman, who begged for a substitution. But the major was adamant, so the Masai raised his spear, hurled it at Grant, and impaled him against a wall.

I saw my first Masai in 1937, and felt the same admiration for them that almost everyone does. There's something fine in the sight of two or three Masai moran striding across the plain with their long, thin spears and tough colorful shields. By 1954, most of the Masai in Kenya and some in Tanganyika had been deprived of both shield and spears, so they could not go on raids or hunting lions. Some of the men carried staffs instead of spears, but they were not as satisfying, by any means.

My first visit to a Masai village brought considerable dissillusion-ment about them. The first view of a manyatta is striking, for all you can see is a big circle of tangled thornbushes, ten or twelve feet high, designed to keep cattle in and lions out. Inside the circle, I saw a clus-ter of flat roofed huts made of earth and dung — with plenty of odor to confirm the latter. There was more smell than just cow manure, however; this was accounted for when I learned that the Masai use cattle urine for washing. They do not waste any of the products of their herds.

I wanted to look into one of the huts, unprepossessing though it was, so made my way through a cloud of flies that had found a para-dise on earth. The Masai do not seem to have a well-organized or sys-tematized religion, but they believe that the spirits of their ancestors abide in all living things — except the lion. Even flies are creatures that may bear an ancestor's spirit, so they must not be molested. The Masai will not even shoo them away.

The doors of Masai huts are low, so I got down on my hands and knees to crawl in and have a look. I could not see much, for there were no windows, but a fire was burning dully, filling the place with smoke. A calf mooed at me from a far corner, but I did not investigate further. The smoke made my eyes smart, and the smell was considerably stronger inside than outside. The floor of the hut was made of manure, damp and sticky!

My curiosity about the Masai temporarily evaporated. But as I went on my way to Ngorongoro with three fine Masai guides my perspective returned. And I was busy enjoying the incomparable sights. Ngorongoro is one of the world's largest craters, twelve miles by thirty-five miles in size. Its flat bottom contains a good-sized river, two lakes, and at that time an estimated one hundred thousand head of game of great variety. The first white man discovered it in 1892, but it was not until after World War I that T. Alexander Barns wrote the first thorough description of it. Since then someone had built what was euphemistically called a road up the outer slope to the crater's rim, but after that all the going was on foot. Not many people had descended to the crater floor. I wanted to see what was there and film the game.

So Cézaire and I drove from the town of Arusha, in Tanganyika, past Lake Manyara with its thousands of flamingos and pelicans, and into the thick forest on the slope of Ngorongoro. We went slowly over nine miles of twists and turns to the lip of the crater, eight thousand feet above sea level. There the government had built several thatched rest houses for its game wardens and travelers. It was almost dark when we arrived, so we could see little, but the view brought by the dawn was breathtaking. I had not visualized that the floor would be so far below us, but there it was — all hundred square miles of it — two thousand feet down. Ngorongoro must have been the tallest mountain in Africa to leave such a crater when it blew its top on some dateless yesterday.

The three Masai guides I had arranged for arrived — they had climbed the nine-mile slope to the rim — and led us down a trail that they said had been made by rhinoceroses. If they shouted *"faru!"* we were to climb the nearest tree. This is one beast that even the brave Masai does not want to encounter. But we saw no animals on our descent, perhaps because we made so much noise and the growth was too thick for us to see any distance. Suddenly we emerged from the bush, found ourselves on level ground, and saw the vast floor stretching before us.

We stepped out on a thick green lawn of clover that bounced resiliently as we walked across it. It was close-cropped, almost as even as a golf fairway — and soon I saw why. Off to the right was a herd of several hundred zebra, quietly eating clover. Near them was a herd of wildebeest, often found grazing near zebra. The animals looked up at us but, since we did not come closer, they were not disturbed. I stopped to take some pictures and they went back to their grazing. When we started on again, one of the wildebeests took offense and trotted away, though not in a hurry, and the others followed him. The zebra decided to go along, and for several minutes the crater resounded with the muted drumming of hoofbeats on the grass.

We walked through an acacia forest and then into fields of white and red clover that came up above our ankles. Its growth was so lush that even all the animals in the crater could not keep it cropped. And there were plenty — zebra, hyena, leopard, elephant, rhino, hippo, buffalo, cheetah, baboon, and scores of varieties of antelope.

In 1946, when we were filming *Savage Splendor*, I wanted to shoot a Masai lion hunt. I knew that they had increased because of lax supervision during the war, and I had heard descriptions of them from old-time white hunters. These brave men all swore that they could never summon the courage that seems commonplace among the Masai on such a hunt.

When a lion killed a cow, ten Masai moran tracked the killer. They might locate it in a thick undergrowth, into which they threw rocks until the beast leapt out to get away. In a flash, the Masai hunters were after it, and the lion soon turned to attack its pursuers. The hunters encircled the animal, closing in on it step by step, shields held before them, spears poised to strike. When the men were ten or fifteen feet away, the lion usually chose one to attack, one that he would try to kill in order to escape. With three twitches of the tail the big cat leapt, and the hunter facing it dropped to one knee and lifted his shield to bear the force of the pounce, while hurling his spear at the lion in midair. Even if the spear hit its mark, it did not stop the beast. The big body landed on the shield, the claws raking and scratching. The others hurled their spears until the lion looked like a pincushion, but the man who took the lion's attack was usually mauled, sometimes killed. The other hunters, after flinging their spears, rushed in with their *simis*, double-edged knives about two feet long, and hacked away at the lion until it was nothing but hunks of bone and flesh and a mass of bloody fur. They didn't care about skins or trophies — only about dead lions.

The hunters came back home happy and triumphant, proud of their wounds and their bent spears. The man who took the charge was a special hero, but on occasion there was one who took precedence even over him. This was the man who grabbed the lion by the tail. If the encircling ring of hunters got close enough before the lion sprang, one man might rush forward, snatch the animal's twitching tail, and haul back on it with all his strength. At this instant, of course, the other hunters closed in swiftly with spears and knives, trying to kill the lion before it could whirl and claw the tail-holder. While this procedure sounds silly, it can hamper the footing of a lion enough to spoil its pounce. It is a method not infrequently used in hunting other animals.

No one had ever taken films of a genuine Masai lion hunt in color, but, much as I pleaded for permission in 1946, the authorities denied me. In 1954, I was more hopeful because I was better known; it was clear that I wanted an accurate film record of the event. I marshaled all the recommendations possible from some important and influential people, resulting in a great deal of help in other projects for my film *Zanzabuku*, but not in filming a Masai lion hunt.

Finally at Monduli, about fifty miles from Arusha, I filmed a sequence that proved more dangerous, if not more exciting, than a lion hunt. The headmen from three Masai manyattas brought some of their moran together, with shields and spears, for a war dance. (In this remote area, the Masai were still allowed to carry weapons.) Dave Mason, one of my British cameramen, was with me, so I expected to get some good and varied shots.

The Masai had no musical instruments except drums, but they gave out a persistent beat that was hypnotic in its effect. The dancers became more and more ecstatic as the dance progressed, flinging their arms out with great abandon and throwing their heads back violently. When I saw the wild look in some eyes I recalled stories I had heard about the occasional effect of the war dance on some Masai moran. The resurgence of the old war spirit sometimes sent a few warriors into uncontrollable fits like epileptic seizures.

Nothing like this happened in my shots, but I had an idea — to select just a few men and give them some action that would arouse their spirits as the dance did. If these out-of-work warriors were excited by recollections of war, maybe a charge as if against an enemy in battle would do the same thing. Through the interpreter I spoke to the three headmen, to learn if such a charge would be authentic, if the Masai method of battle included a running attack with spears held high. It did indeed, the headman assured me with a smile, and the moran surrounding us agreed.

So we set up the scene, selecting a low hill for the warriors to come charging over the crest of, with two cameras set up on flat ground about fifty yards below the crest. Then I chose ten particularly fine specimens from among the warriors, explained the plan to them, and they retired over the hill. The other Masai lined up at one side, out of camera range but close to the projected line of march.

The signal was given and, before we saw the warriors, we heard their wild whoops, so the cameras were started. The Masai burst over the top of the hill running at breathtaking speed, holding their shields in front of them and brandishing their spears on high. It made a thrilling spectacle, and I was delighted. Straight toward us the men raced, two or three in front, the others strung out behind. They were forty yards away, thirty, twenty — and I could see plainly the expressions of frenzy on the faces of the leaders, the gleam of joyous ferocity in their eyes. Suddenly I knew that the first man was no longer acting. He was really charging me. He was going to pierce me with his spear. Perhaps it was the fleck of foam on his lips that told me, but the wild look in his eyes was that of a man who has taken flight from reality.

I was too terrified to move, and there was scarcely time, anyway. But the other Masai standing alongside acted with speed and decision, for they saw what was about to happen. When the charging warriors were only about ten yards away, several of the bystanders hurled themselves at the first two runners and knocked them to the ground.

"Dave, get it!" I called to Mason, who was already turning his camera on the scene where the Masai who had saved us were with difficulty holding down the two writhing, kicking warriors, both of whom were frothing at the mouth. One still jerked his arm violently as if throwing a spear. His eyes were turned up so that I could see only the whites. He was a pitiful if frightening sight. The other warrior recovered from his seizure more quickly, and was soon nursing a deep gash in the calf of his right leg. He had stabbed himself with his own spear as he fell.

Within a few minutes both men were calm. Their frothing and panting stopped, as well as their struggles to free themselves. But when they got to their feet, their eyes were vacant and glazed, and both acted bewildered.

Some months later, when I was telling someone about this incident, I learned of a similar occurrence during the filming of *King Solomon's Mines* in Africa. At one point, the cameramen on that film had abandoned cameras and everything to run from a surging mock attack of Masai warriors.

The Masai have gone from hunting to the domestication of animals as a main way of life, but they have never developed an agricultural society. They plant no crops. For the most part, they have for more than half a century rejected the available products and ways of the modern world — its clothes, foods, dwellings, morals, and values. Even money still means little to them, for they buy almost nothing.

One contribution from the outside world has, without intention on the part of the Masai, had a significant influence on them — venereal disease, introduced by the first railroad builders in East Africa. Because of the Masai custom of offering a wife to any guest in a manyatta, regardless of tribe or race, venereal disease spread rapidly, infecting in time an estimated ninety to ninety-five per cent of the Masai population and causing much sterility. This resulted in a decrease in the birth rate and then in the taking of Kikuyu wives by many Masai men, at least in Kenya where their lands adjoined. So two ancient and bitter enemies found themselves related — an unimaginable state before the advent of venereal disease. The British authorities finally set up clinics, gradually reducing the incidence of venereal disease to about ten per cent among the Masai.

The Masai have shown little interest in uhuru in both Kenya and Tanganyika, and independence has not changed their lives significantly. Only a handful in Tanganyika have wanted an education and entered into public affairs. The vast majority still lead semi-nomadic lives, taking their herds to good grazing land or to water. Some of them occasionally steal cattle, mainly to prove they can do it for old times' sake, and to show off to each other and their women. A Masai legend says that in the beginning all cattle in the world belonged to the Masai, and underneath they still believe this is true, or should be. A Masai moran may still commit murder over a pet cow. But the tribe was never, after its initial subjection, a threat to colonial authorities, even during the uprisings leading to independence, and they are no real problem to the present native governments.

Carr Hartley told me about one surprising development among the Masai in Kenya in connection with independence. "During the agitation leading up to uhuru," Carr said, "the British realized that they should prove to the Africans the value of the gold mine we have here in our game population. So they gave over to the Masai two big game parks, at Amboselli and in the Mara Valley. You know them both — wonderful reserves for wild animals. Well, in spite of the fact that the Masai cattle had always driven game out of good grazing lands, the Masai realized the value of the game parks, and they are now doing everything they can to preserve the game as well as feed their cattle. I think the Masai will turn out to be a great asset to this country in the future."

About six hundred miles north of the Masai country lives another tribe of herdsmen — the Turkana, tall, thin Hamites with some infusion of Nilotic and Bantu blood like the Masai. And they had a heritage of raiding and war more recently active than that of the Masai. I became interested in the Turkana in 1946 and again in 1954, when I met some of them working for Carr Hartley on his animal-catching farm north of Nairobi. When filming *Zanzabuku*, I decided to visit Turkanaland, although it was a long and difficult haul up through Kenya into its Northern Frontier Province. We drove down a twisting road that wound two thousand feet from the top of the escarpment to the bottom of the Rift, quite wide at this point. We had to cross a broad desert — the chief reason for Turkanaland's being so completely isolated from the rest of Kenya — and go through part of the Suk Closed Area, from which visitors were excluded except by special permit. The entire trip, in fact, required government sanction.

Turkana country is not much better than desert land itself, arid, rocky, barren of almost all but scrub growth. At the northwest corner, where the mountains begin, and along the banks of two sizable rivers, there is more varied vegetation. But both rivers are likely to be dried up for seven or eight months of the year. The natives dig wells and waterholes along the dried-up beds, for there is usually some water not far below the surface.

Once the Turkana were great warriors, and there was much fighting as recently as the twenties, when the British finally stepped in forcefully to end it. Once, too, the population lived principally on meat from wild game, but they killed out their rather sparse larder and had to become herdsmen. Their cows can get enough pasturage only in choice areas near the foothills, but sheep, goats, and camels seem to find enough to eat. The Turkana milk all these animals, and tap their arteries to obtain blood, which they usually mix with milk before eating. And they slaughter some animals for meat — sometimes more than they breed.

Turkana women try to cultivate small garden plots if they live near the rivers, where they may raise a little kafir corn. Fortunately, there are dom palms in the region, whose nuts give food, and also twenty or more varieties of bushes with edible berries, some of which grow all the year round. The women make a pounded and dried berry meal which they can store, mixing it later with blood or milk or both to cook into cakes.

When we finally reached Lodwar, the administrative center for Turkanaland, we were warmly greeted by District Commissioner Whitehouse. Lodwar consisted of only a few buildings in the midst of dreary country. From my window in the commissioner's house I looked down on a small building in a compound guarded by native soldiers. It was the prison of Jomo Kenyatta, who had recently been convicted as the leader of the Mau Mau terror and who was to become, in a few years, the Prime Minister of the independent republic of Kenya.

The Turkana village near Lodwar was colorful, and the men and women so strikingly photogenic that I knew the long trip would be worthwhile. The men were tall — most of them over six feet — strong, and graceful. Some were completely naked, while others wore a kind of toga knotted at the shoulder. Most men wore smooth ivory plugs in their perforated lower lips, objects that looked from a distance like golf balls fixed just below the mouth. Somehow they were attractive, standing out vividly against the reddish-brown skin. Many men also wore earrings, leg bands, arm bands, and necklaces of wire and beads. They all carried thin, graceful spears — many had two — and rectangular shields made of heavy leather, some decorated with big, black ostrich-feather balls at the top. Each young man when fully dressed had a little wooden stool slung from his left wrist, which he used to sit on or as a headrest to protect his precious coiffure when lying down. I saw other weapons — knives, clubs, and a strange semicircular knife attached to the right wrist — a devastating weapon for in-fighting. There were also some wickerwork shields, which I learned were used in stick fights between one Turkana and another, a favorite sport.

White and orange headdresses were the most striking ornaments of the Turkana, usually made of waving ostrich plumes. They were the crowning glories of elaborate hairdos which, I learned, were only modest and skimpy versions of the startling coiffures worn seventy years before, when Europeans first saw them. Then the hair had grown long and had been plastered with mud to form a huge chignon, which hung down as far as the waist and was decorated with a kind of snood made of feathers. From the top of this device came other plumes and even wire halos with feather balls suspended over the top of the head.

While the hairdo has shrunk to a good-sized mud-plastered bun on the back of the head, the feathers and waving plumes remain — and on top of a tall man they are striking, the most spectacular I had ever seen until I went to New Guinea and saw the amazing bird of paradise headdresses there. Turkana women don't go in for much frippery; they shave their heads on the sides and twist what hair is left into greased curls that hang down like an old floor mop.

After getting acquainted, we started our camera work. We shot some hunting scenes involving leopards and hyenas, which go after Turkana livestock and thus are the prime enemies. Soon men, women, and children started streaming in from other villages, and the dancing began. I have seldom seen any group that loved dancing more than the Turkana. They were always eager to dance for the cameras, and once after we had filmed during the good light for several hours we knocked off and told them their work was done. But there was no stopping them. They kept going all evening and most of the night, and the next day put in another four hours' dancing.

After some time around Lodwar, we drove to Lake Rudolf, about forty-five miles to the east. It is a large lake with no known outlet, containing an alkaline water that abounds in fish, crocodiles, and hippos, and is loved by thousands of birds. The Turkana settlements on the shores of the lake were comparatively recent, and so was fishing as an occupation. Although this tribe had a difficult time finding enough food in its arid land, it had never taken to fishing, had not even considered fish edible. British authorities had finally persuaded some of them to migrate to the lake and eat fish. They brought in nets and other equipment, and gave instructions. The teaching had borne fruit, for there were several Turkana villages on Lake Rudolf, and more and more fish were being caught — and eaten.

One day when we had stopped filming because of the diminishing light, we were watching the Turkana fisherman haul in a netful of fish. As the net neared the sandy shore we saw a violent thrashing in the water and wondered at the size of the fish that could raise such a commotion. But it was no fish. It was a crocodile that had been netted. It had played possum in its customary fashion so long as it was some distance from shore, but as the net forced it onto the sand in shallow water it struggled to escape. For three days we tried to get this scene on film, but never made it. When there was enough light, there was no croc, or it escaped around the end of the net, or the Turkana speared it before we could get our cameras close enough and in action.

It was pleasant at Lake Rudolf, where we stayed in thatched huts on a sandy spit jutting out into the lake. After work we sat beneath the palm trees or went swimming — always keeping a wary eye out for crocs — and watched the magnificent sunsets. I felt as remote and removed from the modern world as I had in the Ituri Forest. But for three weeks of work we got just one three-minute sequence in *Zanzabuku*.

The Kikuyu, the largest tribe in Kenya, could not be considered primitive even at the time of my first trip to Africa in 1937. They had been in close contact with civilization for several decades and had accepted its influence instead of rejecting it like the Masai. But the vast majority was illiterate, lived at the lowest subsistence level, and retained many old customs and beliefs even if these were sometimes mingled with a few concepts from Christianity. Their veneer of civilization was tissue-thin, and was easily broken through at the time of the Mau Mau rebellion in the early 1950's.

Mau Mau was a movement of terror, secrecy, and mumbo-jumbo rituals, which has had its counterparts in almost every primitive society. (And in many civilized societies, as well, I must conclude, when I think of the Mafia, the tongs, the Ku Klux Klan, and others.) You can find countless evidences of the great power of medicine men, witches, or whatever they are called. And not just in the old days. Shortly after my 1954 trip to Africa, for instance, there was a wave of witch

killings in Uganda. Seventeen years before, on my first trip, I saw in a
jail in Irumu, in the Congo, seven members of Anyoto, the secret society of "leopardmen" that had been in existence longer than anyone
could remember.

In 1934, the town of Beni endured a reign of terror from the leopardmen, who killed forty-two Africans in three months. Since leopards infested the nearby forests, it was some time before the deaths
were ascribed to the secret society. But leopards do not go on concentrated killing campaigns. Only humans do that. It was learned that one
witch doctor had instigated twenty-three of the murders, and the
chief of a neighboring tribe was the head of the local Anyoto chapter.

What did the leopardmen do? They killed other human beings in a
way to make it appear that leopards had done the job. The killer wore
a leopard skin, a caricature of a leopard mask, and an iron or bone
bracelet with four sharp, curved knife-claws. Some killers even carried pieces of carved wood "paws" to make leopard prints in the earth
around a victim. Members of the secret society usually killed the han-
diest person, leaving the marks of the leopard; a majority of the victims were women, who often had one breast clawed off and taken
away — a sure clue that the killer was human rather than animal.
Sometimes the breast was taken to the Anyoto leader as proof of killing; sometimes it was eaten. In some areas the eyes of victims were
taken and boiled with the claw-knives to give the killers night vision.

During the day, the leopardmen appeared to be normal, respected
members of their communities, and no member of Anyoto would bear
witness against another. There was usually no significant pattern to
the killings that might offer clues. But when I was in Africa in 1954,
the Belgian authorities had finally managed to stamp out Anyoto in
the Congo except for occasional small flare-ups. It may well rise again
in the Congo's time of turmoil and terror.

When one considers Anyoto and other similar movements, Mau
Mau in Kenya in the early fifties is not too surprising. There was one
striking difference — Mau Mau killings had a pattern, a definite objective. They were intended to terrorize and drive white men out of
Kenya. That a hundred times as many Kikuyu were killed as white
does not alter this fact, for uncooperative Africans had to be terror-
ized into submission and silence. Many took the Mau Mau oath in
gruesome rituals, even though they did not want to, because they

were filled with fear of human and — more effective — spirit reprisals.

So much has been written about the Mau Mau that I will confine myself chiefly to my own and my friends' experience. The terrorist movement was started by the Kikuyu aided by two smaller allied tribes, the Embu and the Meru, with the help of some Masai who had intermarried with the Kikuyu. Many white men, women, and children were slaughtered, cattle killed, farmhouses burned. There were gruesome tales of revolting and sometimes erotic initiation ceremonies of Mau Mau members, some of which were no doubt close to the truth, since the movement was calculated to cause a resurgence of latent superstition and sorcery. In 1952, British authorities decreed a state of emergency throughout Kenya, called up men for a special police force, and tried to create some kind of radio communication system for isolated farms. Many Britishers sent their families back to England for the duration of the emergency.

When I arrived in 1954, I was warned against going with my crew to Carr Hartley's animal farm at Rumuruti, in the heart of the Mau Mau country. Authorities required that we carry guns at all times. I stated that I had never found it necessary to carry a gun on my expeditions to Africa, but now I had to do so as a safety precaution against men, not animals. Moreover, strict rules demanded that one must carry his gun at all times — to meals, to the bathroom, to bed — so that it might not be stolen. The Mau Mau were desperate for firearms.

I could not quite believe that I might be attacked by a band of terrorists, nor could my staff. So we went on our way out of Nairobi. At Hartley's I stayed in a *rondavel*, or small thatched cottage, near his house. My crew stayed at a local farmer's club about ten miles away, a building surrounded by barbed wire entanglements to discourage possible attackers. A nearby building was temporary headquarters for special police installed in what they knew to be one of the worst Mau Mau areas.

I learned that Carr Hartley himself, who was the kind of man to pooh-pooh most threats, had twice been ambushed by Mau Mau bands on his way to or from his farm, and had escaped both times only because the attackers had so few guns and were such bad shots.

Shortly after our arrival at Hartley's, the district head of police called on me and strongly urged us to leave. "I don't like to feel responsible for your lives," he said. "You are living within five hundred yards of an almost impenetrable swamp where scores of Mau Mau are hiding. There are wild animals all over East Africa that you can film safely. Go there."

He was right, but I had already decided upon centering the animal sequences for *Zanzabuku* around Hartley's son, thirteen-year-old Mike. My "scenario" called for Mike, and I could come up with no substitute idea. So after consulting my crew and hearing their agreement, I decided to stay and do our work, taking all possible precautions.

So we went ahead. After a few days of filming, however, another incident occurred that shocked and discouraged us. The police arrested more than twenty of Hartley's workers, among them the head man, Wilson. We were all shaken to know we had been working side by side with Mau Mau terrorists who had taken a sacred oath to kill white men. They were no doubt waiting for instructions from the swamp so a concerted attack could wipe out all the whites on the place. Hartley was not too surprised, for he knew that many farmers had found their most trusted workers to be among the Mau Mau.

Next Carr's half brother, Gordon Pollman, a superb handler of wild animals and a great help in our work, was called up for duty with the special forces combating the Mau Mau threat. After some petitioning, the authorities postponed his service for one month because he was in the middle of our project.

Then one day a faithful African warned Hartley that his place was going to be attacked that evening by a band of Mau Maus from the swamp. Our work had ended for the day and my crew had driven home to their fortress. Hartley called everyone into his home. There we armed ourselves and waited for the attack. We did not listen to the wireless, a common evening entertainment, because its noise might have obscured sounds of approaching attackers. Some of us tried to play cards but had little heart for it. We talked in desultory fashion, listened intently during the long silences, and wondered what might happen. I was amazed to see the quiet calm of the women, Mrs. Hartley and her sisters, Dulcy Wedd and Thelma Randall, and Hartley's secretary, Nancy Drew. The attack never came, probably because we were prepared and well armed. The next morning Carr found that some of his cattle had been slaughtered to supply food for the nearby Mau Maus.

The incident apparently gave Carr Hartley an idea. He must have been the kind of child who sets off firecrackers under old ladies' chairs, and he still had a fondness for practical jokes. The evening after the false alarm, I was sitting in my rondavel writing letters. Darkness had not completely fallen, but one could not see far. The animals had gone to sleep and the whole place was quiet, as only a remote farm can be. Suddenly the air was split by a piercing scream, a scream from Carr Hartley himself, somewhere outside my rondavel.

"Mau Mau!" he yelled. "Mau Mau!"

I snatched my gun from its holster and tore out of the rondavel at top speed, only to collide with the chunky, barrel-chested Hartley. The big man burst out laughing, and his laugh boomed over the plains. Others came rushing from the main house, and Hartley, still laughing, explained how funny I had looked racing out of the hut, gun in hand. Nobody else thought it was very funny. I put the incident down to an unusual — to say the least — sense of humor, but later I decided that it was his way of trying to relieve the tension. If so, it didn't work.

The next evening at dinner, Hartley left the table a few minutes ahead of the rest of us. His secretary said she thought he was planning another stupid Mau Mau joke for me, so we all followed him outside before he had a chance. There he stood, grimly serious for a change, staring down at the blacker-than-black patch of swamp where the Mau Mau were in hiding. We saw a flash of light, then another and another, in a rhythm that must have been a code of some kind. The men in the swamp were definitely signaling to others on the farm or beyond. Hartley pulled out his flashlight, pointed it toward the swamp, and flashed it on and off, as if he too were sending a signal. There was no code in his flashes, but he let the Mau Mau know that Carr Hartley had seen *their* signals and was ready.

End of practical jokes. And also end of Mau Mau difficulties during our stay at Hartley's place. But we never slept very soundly all that time.

After leaving Hartley's, I was in Nairobi for a couple of days before going into Tanganyika, and had lunch with Diane Hartley, widow of Carr's younger brother, Lionel, who had been one of my white hunters and guides during my 1946 *Savage Splendor* expedition. Lionel was later warden of Tsavo Game Park, and was killed in the crash of a light plane while on the way to try to save a sick elephant. Diane had continued to live in Kenya and had even gone into the animal-catching business. At lunch she told me the following story.

In October, 1954, just a week before I talked to her, Diane had gone to visit her mother and stepfather, who owned a farm at Kiber-eri, near the town of Nyeri in strong Mau Mau country. Her step-father, seventy-year-old G. A. Leakey, was not worried, however. He had always trusted the Kikuyu and had even been made a blood brother of the tribe. He could not believe that harm would come to him who had always befriended them, so did not barricade his farm or keep a gun always at hand. On government instructions, he *did* have in one bedroom a battery-operated rocket signaling system, but he never expected to use it.

The day after Diane's arrival, she and Mr. Leakey and her mother were having dinner when about thirty Kikuyu, armed with long knives called *pangas*, burst out of the scrub growth behind the house. They slashed to death a Kikuyu cook at the door and rushed inside. Diane and her mother ran to the bathroom, which had a removable section in the ceiling for gaining entrance to an attic. Diane's mother pushed her up, but before she herself could climb to safety the Mau Mau found her. They snatched Mrs. Leakey, without seeing Diane in the attic. Since she had arrived just the day before, it is likely that the raiders did not suspect that she might be there. In any event, they strangled Mrs. Leakey on the spot, dragged the body outside and hacked it with their pangas until it lay in a pool of blood. They did not kill Mr. Leakey, but carried him off with them.

It was all over in a few minutes, and Diane rushed to the bedroom to send up the signal flares. They were seen from a government sta-tion a few miles away, but meanwhile Diane raced to the next farm to make sure help came. It was there in short order, but it was too late for Diane's mother or the cook who had been killed. There was no trace of Mr. Leakey. Of five servants, three had vanished.

An intensive hunt for Mr. Leakey took place, with as many as two thousand security men combing the woods and hills for miles around the farm. They finally found some of his clothing in a cave, where they also captured a Mau Mau who was believed to be the leader of the raiders. They learned that the old gentleman had probably died in a sacrificial rite. A native woman in the area, who said she was a prophetess, had gained great influence over the local Mau Mau. She had said that if a prominent Englishman could be captured and buried alive in a sacrifice, Mau Mau fortunes would prosper. Mr. Leakey, along with several goats, had apparently been buried alive in this primitive ritual. The authorities were sure enough of this story to give up the search for him.

In spite of her horrible ordeal, Diane found one thing to be thankful for. Her two children had been expected to visit the farm the next day. If the Mau Mau raid had come just one day later, she felt sure they all would have been killed.

Diane continued in the animal-catching business, becoming known as an absolutely fearless woman who had an uncanny understanding of animals. For a time she was laid up after suffering a broken neck in a truck crash, but she managed to go back to work. Late in 1960 she got an order for two cheetahs to be used in a movie, caught them, and delivered them to a game farm near Arusha, in Tanganyika. While there she called on a lion that was an old friend — one that had been born and brought up in captivity and used in a number of movie sequences. Diane had handled the animal many times and considered it such a pal that she always dropped in to say hello when she was near. So on this occasion she entered its compound, calling and talking to the lion. It lifted its head and sniffed, and Diane thought it was recognizing her familiar scent. But it was actually sniffing something else — blood. Diane had forgotten that she was menstruating at the time. She approached the lion, and the lion approached her. Suddenly it leapt upon her, bearing her to the ground in an obvious attempt to mate with her. She wrestled it half off her, as a friend rushed in to help. Diane got to her feet and the lion pounced again. As she went down this time, her head struck a rock and her neck broke where it had been broken before. So she was unaware of what happened after that. The lion clawed and mounted her, and finally sank its teeth in her throat, as male lions do when mating with a female.

An attendant shot the supposedly tame lion, but that was the end of Diane Hartley, who had more than her share of tragedy in a short life. White hunters of Kenya and Tanganyika called her one of their own; she was probably the only woman they would dignify with the title of "white hunter." Carr Hartley, in telling me about this incident, spoke of her as "a noble and fearless woman."

Back to the Mau Mau terror. The white settlers of Kenya did not panic and leave, as the leaders had hoped. Some sent their families away, but they stayed on and fought, even though many had doubts as to how much longer they might remain in Kenya as permanent residents. Jomo Kenyatta and several others were tried as leaders of the rebellion and convicted, imprisoned, and exiled. Even at the time there were serious doubts about this verdict, although the trial was certainly legal. In any event, the killings died down, and the emergency was ended. Men called up for the armed forces went back home. But life was not the same as it had been in the old days. The more intelligent Britishers knew that the end was coming, that sometime the country of Kenya would be turned over to the Africans to rule. They hoped that the government would intensify its efforts to educate and prepare Africans for the responsibility of government, that in the interim cooperating councils or groups in various fields might enable Africans and whites to come to some agreement about the future. But most African nationalists were understandably impatient, and too many whites were diehard colonialists.

It was not an easy problem to solve. It was not even easy to assess blame. When the British first came to Kenya they found thousands of square miles of beautiful farm and grazing land unused. They "bought" the land from the Kikuyu, but they did not realize that the Africans could not possibly understand what "buying" meant, as all lands were tribally, not individually, owned. The white settlers worked hard. They developed magnificent farms, producing far more goods than the land had ever given before. Most of the natives benefited from this increased production, from the health care and other services introduced by the British. But they were still, in the main, servants, menials, underdogs. No matter how well treated they might be, they were outcasts in their own land. Those who became educated and learned new techniques — through help of the British — were the ones who rebelled most, for they saw what could be done with their land.

The British increased African representation on governmental councils, but they retained control. Many British officials — and nongovernmental men — tried hard to advance capable Africans. They hoped that the transition, the turning over of power, could come gradually, with cooperation. But the exploited and deprived never really believe it when their "masters" tell them to be patient and wait a little while. There was a movement for freedom and independence sweeping the world, and Kenya was not isolated from it.

Jomo Kenyatta was released and was elected to the parliament at the next election. He — the presumed Mau Mau leader — astonished most Britishers by being moderate, cooperative, and nonviolent, while pressing for independence as quickly as possible. He has surprised them further since becoming Prime Minister by continuing to be moderate and cooperative, though firm and strong for his beliefs. His government has encountered many difficulties, chiefly economic. Shortly after uhuru there was a small armed rebellion, quickly suppressed with the aid of British soldiers that he called for. The same sort of thing happened in Uganda and Tanganyika. In Zanzibar a revolt was successful, but in a short while that country joined with Tanganyika to become one nation, Tanzania, under the presidency of Julius Nyerere of Tanganyika.

Kenya faced more difficulties after independence than her sister states. Uganda had had a well-organized government before the British took it over, so its people had some heritage of national unity. Tanganyika, once a German territory, had been mandated to Britain by the League of Nations and then the United Nations, so it was subject to regular international inspection. Its European settlers had always assumed that the country would in time be turned over to native African rule. Its white farmers were scattered about the country, rather than concentrated in one area like the "White Highlands" of Kenya.

At the time of independence, Kenya contained about 60,000 white Europeans, 300,000 Indians, 30,000 Arabs, and 6,000,000 Africans, of whom the Kikuyu were the majority, with the Luo second in importance. These tribes were ancient enemies, but despite their many differences, the two joined forces to achieve independence. Kenyatta, a Kikuyu, has held them together effectively, but many people expect trouble when he dies — and he is an old man. The two most prominent men in his government are Udinga and Tom Mboya, both Luo, both intelligent, both ambitious. The question is, will the dominant Kikuyu accept either Udinga or Mboya as Kenyatta's successor? If not, would the Luo accept anyone else?

During my 1964 visit to East Africa, I talked to many people, white and black, about the present and the future, among them Carr Hartley, who was active in both Kenya and Tanganyika; Sir Charles Markham, stepson of the great Lord Delamere, the "founder" of Kenya, and himself active in politics before independence; to Tom Mboya and other Africans; to Colonel Mervyn Cowie, head of Kenya's game parks and one of the few prominent whites to become a Kenya citizen, to the dismay of many diehard colonialists; to representatives of other countries, trained as perceptive and objective observers; to farmers, ranchers, and businessmen.

Sir Charles Markham told me that ninety-five per cent of the white farmers would sell out and return to England if they could, but the government purchasing regulations made selling at a reasonable price difficult. I know that Lady Betty Markham, whom I also visited, wanted to sell her beautiful four-hundred-acre ranch, eighteen miles from Nairobi. Dulcy Wedd, Carr Hartley's sister-in-law, whom I had known in 1954, would have liked to sell the unusual business she maintained in western Kenya — she caught monkeys to sell throughout the world for research. But I got the impression that many Europeans thought all *other* Europeans wanted to leave, whereas they planned to stay, apprehensive though they might be. They all expected discord and even some violence, with the Indians being the primary objects of hate rather than the English.

In African eyes, the Indian merchants, bankers, and middlemen were not productive in any way; they just got rich. Most Englishmen, on the other hand, *did* produce goods on their farms or in their mines and factories, and many taught their skills to Africans. Unrest seemed most likely to express itself violently among young Africans who had had a little but not much schooling, who had expected uhuru to bring Utopia, and who were bitterly disappointed, often not as well off as they had been under colonialism.

The new Kenya government had great plans for resettling African farmers on lands bought from Europeans, but progress was slow. The Kikuyu made excellent farmers if trained, but too few were trained. Still, many small African farmers were working together in a kind of cooperative, and some big farms were doing well under African management.

Most white settlers in Kenya agreed that African officials were learning how difficult it is to govern and to improve the standard of living of their people fast enough. They were becoming increasingly aware of the contributions of Europeans in economic aid, taxes, and know-how. Carr Hartley thought they were fast learning the value of Kenya's "little gold mine, its wild life," which brought in tourists who spent five to ten million pounds a year. Colonel Cowie thought progress was far too slow in this field, and he agreed that tourism could be the greatest revenue-producer for the country. When I arrived, the New Stanley Hotel in Nairobi was jammed, with piles of luggage in the lobby, and there was an air of bustle and prosperity in that city.

No one, African or white, seemed overly worried about Communism, though the Russians and Chinese have both been active in East Africa. I heard that Russian, Czech, and Polish technicians had acted more condescending to the blacks than the British ever had. And that the Chinese, who appealed to Africans as "colored" brothers opposing white domination, were considered "white" themselves. But the new nations were willing to accept financial and technical aid from anyone who would give it, while fiercely maintaining their independence. Their chief international interest seemed confined to Pan-Africanism.

Tom Mboya, Minister for Justice and Constitutional Affairs in Kenya, gave me a taped interview in which he emphasized that the United States should base its relations with African nations on direct dealings. He felt that too often we had considered primarily the wishes of the former colonial powers, England, France, and Belgium. He asked the United States to accept and even support Africa's policy of neutralism. He agreed that the new nations needed help, but insisted that it come without political strings attached, without condescension or a "big brother" attitude.

Many Europeans felt that if the Kenya government could move ahead without serious internal strife for two or three years and with substantial economic aid, they'd make a go of it, and the future would be good for whites and Africans alike. Sir Charles Markham, who had numerous business interests in Kenya, where he had lived for thirty-six years, said to me, "I love this country. I think of myself as an African who happens to have a white skin. I'm going to stay."

The situation was more encouraging in Tanganyika. August Kuenzler, the farmer and game-catcher who was so helpful when I filmed *Zanzabuku,* told me, "I've lived here thirty-five years. I think there is a big future for the white man in Africa. Newcomers don't believe it, because they've heard so much violent talk against the white man. But the blame for the past had to be put somewhere. The government is learning how much it needs the Europeans, who will be more welcome in the next few years."

Carr Hartley told me that the Tanganyika government was most cooperative and farseeing, at least concerning his main activity — game preservation. Its chief game warden was an African, intelligent and capable.

Russell Douglass, former white hunter, game warden, and now owner of the hotel at Lake Manyara, agreed. "Most European settlers in Tanganyika feel safe," he said. "I think Tanganyika has a great future. No, I don't think there's much danger from Communism — its concepts just don't fit in. But here's an interesting development. Many concepts of the Mohammedan religion *do* fit in — polygamy, the method of slaughtering cattle, and other customs. More and more Africans here who had been converted to Christianity as children are turning to Islam as they grow up."

6

Wild Life

NEAR the end of my first trip to Africa, I realized that I had not seen a lion. I had photographed a gorilla, had fed an okapi, and had seen and filmed scores of other wild animals. But to spend months in Africa without seeing a lion was like visiting Maine without eating a lobster, or going to Bali without seeing a dancer. So Cézaire and I quickly revised our itinerary and headed east for the Serengeti Plains in Tanganyika, passing through Kenya on the way. We couldn't *miss* seeing lions.

We saw them, but we did not anticipate that we would see Simba first on a black night on a narrow road that seemed to be miles from nowhere. We had stopped at a rhino-hunting camp on the Namanga River, in southern Kenya, where we had some beer and delicious avocadoes. Our British hosts assured us that the area was teeming with lions. We drove on as the sun set, but a full moon lit the road clearly when it came out from behind the clouds. We saw a herd of zebra, antelopes of great variety, a family of baboons that barked at us angrily, and a herd of giraffes that stared at us curiously.

Suddenly a huge animal leapt across the hood of the car. Cézaire jammed on the brakes, shook his head, and backed up to see if he could learn what had happened. His headlights picked up a lion, sitting seven or eight yards off the road, blinking his eyes in the bright light. I think he was as startled as we were, but he didn't look angry. After a few minutes of mutual staring, the lion walked closer, sniffed the bumper of the car, and ambled off into the bush.

Cézaire and I shook hands happily. We had seen a lion!

We drove on slowly, and the lights showed us two lionesses standing at the side of the road. We stopped about fifteen feet from them, and they did not seem to mind the bright lights. One turned to the other as if to make a comment, but the second was bored. She opened her mouth in a prodigious yawn.

Out of the corner of my eye I caught a movement just outside the open window of the car. A lion sauntered by close enough for me to touch him. He joined the two lionesses and turned to look at us. For five minutes — and that can seem like an eternity in such a situation — the lion family stared at us and we stared at them. I could see them breathe, shift position slightly, lift their noses to sniff the night air, turn to one another as if in whispered conversation. Finally the bored lioness walked up to the front of the car to smell it and make sure there was nothing she had missed. Her friend followed her and then both walked off into the bush. The lion gave us a last look, then leaped lightly over a thornbush and disappeared.

This was a fascinating introduction to lions, but there was one trouble — I could not film them. The next day, however, we came upon a pride of lions in the Serengeti Plains — two males, four females, and a toto about six months old. Cézaire stopped the car and the group ambled toward us to examine us more closely. When they were about twenty-five feet away, Cézaire picked up the Leica to get a shot. At his movement, six of the pack bounded away up a hill yipping and the seventh took off across the plains in the opposite direction, his tail between his legs, yelping like a scared dog. What kind of lions were these?

Later I asked District Commissioner Russell Douglass about the cowardly lions. "That's rather unusual," he said, "but I think I can explain it. A few nights ago a large pack of lions attacked a Masai manyatta and killed many head of cattle. I sent out some soldiers who shot a number of the gang. Your seven had probably been a part of it. When they saw someone raise an arm with a camera, they associated the movement with guns, by which their friends had recently been killed. So they took off in a hurry, forgetting all dignity."

Nonetheless, I did get some good footage on my first trip and on later expeditions I saw the king of beasts in a more favorable light. I became convinced that the lion is genuinely a king, and that he shares many characteristics with that other king of the earth, man. Both are insatiably curious, both are convinced that the world and everything in it was arranged for their comfort and pleasure, and both are quite concerned about their social standing and what the neighbors will think.

I recall one late afternoon during my 1946 trip, after a satisfying day of filming lions. David Sheldrick and Mark Williams were my guides and white hunters and we had as a native gun-bearer Mafuta, whose uncanny understanding of wild animals had made him one of the most famous of African guides. We sat in front of our tents on the edge of an acacia grove, looking out over broad grass-covered veldt, with a thick forest to our right and some scrub growth along a *donga*, or occasional brook, on our left. It had dried up, but there were still a few waterholes where animals came for a drink before dusk. We were relaxed and silent as we had our tea. Then Mafuta touched my shoulder and said, "bwana!"

I looked along his pointing finger and saw a strange procession that crested a rise of ground about two hundred feet away and headed for the donga. The central figure was a lion, one of the most majestic I have ever seen, huge and black-maned. He walked slowly and deliberately, with the subtle grace and latent power of all cats — but above all with great dignity.

The lion did not see us, or if he did, he did not deign to acknowledge our existence with a glance. He did not, indeed, seem to recognize the existence of any other living creature, although he was surrounded by a throng of jeering animals that usually served as his tastiest meals.

I say they jeered, although they made no sound. Just in front of the lion cavorted three wildebeests, the awkwardest of all antelopes, with their wrinkled skins and grotesque beards and the impression they give of being assembled from spare parts of other animals. On this occasion they were acting as comical as they look, kicking up their heels clumsily, almost in the lion's face, and leaping as if they thought they were graceful impala. They were so close to the lion that I wondered how they could have forgotten that a wildebeest is a lion's favorite food. But this lion did not notice them, even when they kicked up clouds of dust before him.

Behind the lion came four or five slope-haunched topi, their reddish-brown skins glistening in the sun. They made mock charges toward the king of beasts, darting swiftly within ten feet of him, taunting him with their lack of fear. Flanking the lion on either side were six or eight Thomson's gazelles, graceful little "Tommies" with long slightly curved horns and eternally twitching tails. On this occasion their tails were wagging twice as fast as usual and each flick was an insult flung at the haughty lion.

There was only one possible interpretation of this scene, and we all agreed on it. The lion had recently awakened from his afternoon siesta beneath a bush on the edge of the forest and found that he wanted a drink. He headed across the plain for the waterhole. Several herds of animals had seen him. They knew either that he had eaten recently or could not, in any event, catch them in broad daylight on the open plain. They seized the opportunity to taunt and humiliate him, with every mocking gesture, with every kick of their heels and flick of their tails.

The lion could do only one thing — ignore completely the actions of these small fry, these impudent creatures he could kill with one blow of his paw. They did not exist. Just once, in that long and embarrassing march to the waterhole, did he stop. Then he looked contemptuously at the topi behind him. All the other animals stopped, too, and stood stock still. Then the lion decided that the topi was too far away for one spring, and he might make himself look silly. He turned forward again and resumed his dignified walk. The lion finally disappeared in the bush near the waterhole, and the other animals went on with their grazing.

A lion *must* keep his dignity at all times — except for the cowardly seven I saw on my first trip — and it is dangerous to make him lose face. The lion on his way for a drink of water was certainly annoyed by the small creatures around him, but he would never lower himself to show it. Ace DuPreez, who knew animals about as well as anyone I have met and who helped me so much on my filming of *Zanzabuku*, told me of an incident that showed how important his dignity was to a lion. Ace was a husky, baldish, blond man, just under forty. He had been born in Kenya of a French Huguenot family. He was a gold miner and honorary game warden in the Mara Valley in Tanganyika.

"Once I came upon a lion in the grass," Ace said, "much to the surprise of both of us. The wind was just right, so he had no warning that I was near. We stood about ten feet apart, staring at each other. Then he haughtily turned to one side, going behind a tall anthill as if he were going that way in any event and my sudden appearance made no difference to him. But I was able to peek over the top of the hill, which he didn't realize. Once he thought he was out of sight, he dropped his dignity in a hurry and ran like a scared rabbit. So if you come upon a lion unexpectedly, remember that the lion wants to avoid trouble as much as you do — unless he's starving or it's a lioness with cubs. But don't back him into a corner or what he might think is a corner, and don't do anything to make him look silly. He's the king and he knows it, and he must act like a king. But, on the other hand, don't depend on a lion's always acting the way I saw."

That's the universal refrain of all who know lions — they are often unpredictable. Allan Tarlton, noted white hunter and expert on snakes, even came upon a lioness with cubs without getting hurt. He was hunting guinea fowl with a twenty-two rifle, when he almost stepped on a lioness suckling two newborn cubs. The lioness sat up on her haunches, with one cub still clinging hungrily to her breast. Tarlton saw the blazing ferocity in her eyes, the twitch of her tail, but he just stood still. His twenty-two was ineffectual against a lion — particularly a lion only seven or eight feet away. Running away would have certainly been a fatal move. So he just waited for the lioness to spring. She didn't. She just stared. When there was no threatening move toward her or her cubs, the fire died slowly out of her eyes and she relaxed slightly. Tarlton moved very slowly to one side, into some tall grass, and quietly walked away. The lioness looked after him a moment, then settled herself again, as her cubs went on with their interrupted meal.

Despite this experience, Tarlton advised me that no one should take for granted either the tameness or apparent amiability of a lion. (Diane Hartley, unfortunately, did.) He recalls that three of the hundred lions he has shot were man-eaters that the government requested him to go after, as professional hunters are asked to do whenever these psychopaths among lions are discovered. They are discovered, of course, only because they have eaten someone, making it too late for the digested man but safe for everyone else in the neighborhood. It was once thought that man-eaters were lions too old or sick to catch their normal fleet-footed prey, but it is more widely believed now that once a lion has tasted human flesh, he is not satisfied with anything else. So when a lion kills one person, strenuous efforts are made to hunt him down before he can indulge his new appetite further.

The most famous man-eaters were definitely connected with the advent of civilization. The man-eaters of Tsavo held up construction of the railroad from the coast into the interior of East Africa in 1899 because they ate so many workers. Colonel J. H. Paterson, who eventually wiped them out, thought that the laborers might have started the whole thing because they did not bother to bury properly a few men who had died on the job of tropical diseases; they just left them in the tall grass or among the thornbushes. Along came some lions, ate the flesh they found, and liked it. They wanted more of the same and went looking for it, even to the extent of occasionally dragging a screaming African from tent or hut.

Fortunately, man-eating lions are rather rare, and I never, to my knowledge, encountered one. On my 1954-1955 trip, when we were going to Ifakara, a Wasdamba village on the Kilombero River, to film the native harpooning of hippos, we learned that five Africans had been killed by man-eating lions shortly before, one of them within a hundred yards of a church mission. I was glad that we were not searching for lion pictures there. It is one thing to approach on foot within twenty feet of a normal lion who might look on me as little more than a prying nuisance, and quite another to move up close to a lion that might consider me a great delicacy.

While the danger of encountering a man-eater never entered my head when I was out in the field looking for lions to film, there was always the chance that a lion might be in pain or a foul temper from any of numerous causes — ulcerating tooth, porcupine quills in his footpads, a lost girl friend, or a plain stomachache. Lions are subject to moods like people, though cause and effect may be simpler and more direct. You do run into a nasty-tempered lion on occasion, ready to slash at mate, friend, or annoying man with a camera. Such beasts are called *kali*. They are not psychopaths like the man-eaters, or rogues that seem to have gone completely crazy. They are just bad-tempered animals — at least, for the moment. And they are not to be trifled with.

Sometimes I could sense when an animal was kali, but I did not rely on my own judgment. A look in the eye, a twitch of the tail, a kind of nervous tension would give me warning. Then I'd look at my gun-bearer, Mafuta, if he had not already cautioned me. Mafuta could always tell. He even scowled and looked bad-tempered himself, as if sharing the animal's emotions.

I never knew anyone who understood animals instinctively as well as Mafuta. He could put himself in the place of animals so that he felt what they felt. On my 1946 trip, a lion was wounded and disappeared into the bush. It is absolutely essential, and also quite dangerous, for a professional hunter to follow and kill the wounded creature. Mafuta knew just where the suffering and bloodthirsty lion would be hiding, waiting to spring on his pursuers. I asked him how he knew. He shrugged and said, "Well, that's where I would hide if I were a wounded lion."

Allowing for a few exceptions and for their unpredictability, lions are generally quite tolerant and even amiable creatures. They are intelligent and adaptable. They have learned to recognize the horn toot of a particular truck bringing them meat, and they will even jump up in back of the truck before it stops, to get at the food. In some parks, like Kruger in South Africa and Nairobi in Kenya, they sometimes act like the bears in our Yellowstone Park. It doesn't take lions — or any other animals — very long to realize they are in a safe place. Occasionally, of course, some foolish person is beguiled by the lions' placidity into thinking they are completely tame. He gets out of his car, contrary to regulations, and goes too close. Even then, the lion is most likely to move away, but he may become annoyed and maul the human pest. A man outside a car is not at all the same thing to a lion as a man inside one. It appears that the lion of the parks looks upon the automobile as just another creature that has never hurt him and with which he has become familiar.

The lion's prey knows that a lion is thoroughly inoffensive when he is not hungry. I've seen herds of topi, wildebeest, hartebeest, zebra, and "Tommies" grazing within seventy-five feet of a pride of lions without even keeping a wary eye on the big cats. The lions were full of food. I think that antelopes and other lion prey know through a sense of smell when a lion is satisfied and when he is hungry. The glandular activity of a lion digesting a meal is certainly different from that of a hungry lion getting ready for a quiet stalk and a flying charge.

The animals that are not considered edible by the lion show no fear of him. A hyena will keep out of a lion's way because lions obviously don't like hyenas. But they don't kill hyenas and never eat their flesh. When these scavengers come too close before a lion has finished eating, the annoyed king will take a swipe at the hyena or make a short charge to drive him away. But lions seem to like jackals and have been reported to toss them bits of meat while they are still eating. Lions have fun chasing vultures away from the remains, but they never try to kill the birds.

I've taken many good pictures of lions from trucks, some quite close. But while the creatures are beautiful, they are not good subjects for a film when they don't move except perhaps for a slow amble or a big yawn. So in 1946, when I was shooting sequences for *Savage Splendor*, I went to wild country west of Narok, in Kenya not far from the Tanganyika border. David Sheldrick, Mark Williams, and Mafuta were with me. We traveled in a truck and a safari wagon which had open sides and a hatch in the top to facilitate filming. The first night we camped out, two lions wandered up and padded around our tents, but caused no trouble. I was somewhat uneasy, I must confess, but my three experienced guides said the lions were just curious. "They have an insatiable curiosity," Sheldrick said. "Almost as bad as human beings."

In the old days, when most hunters thought lions were naturally ferocious, they tried to surround their camp with a tangle of thornbushes, which served only to titillate the lions' curiosity, so they tried to break in. The men were scared, shot at the lions, and came back to tell how the beasts had attacked them during the night.

It took a long time for people to learn enough about lions to give up building walls around their camps. With the Masai it's different, of course, for they have cattle the lions would like to eat.

The next morning we were out early looking for lions and found three within twenty minutes, a male and two females lying under an acacia tree. Sheldrick suggested that we get some bait to entice them into the open, where we could film them. This was easy, for in that country there were herds of zebra, topi, wildebeest, hartebeest, giraffe, Thomson's gazelles, eland, and other animals almost everywhere we looked. Mark Williams shot a topi — the first animal I had seen shot in all my travels, and I didn't like it.

By the time we started to drag the topi behind the truck, vultures were circling above and following us. We drove as close to the tree sheltering the lions as we could without chasing them away, then hitched the chain to a small tree in the open, where the lions could see and smell the meat. The chain would keep them from dragging it back into the shade before eating. We retired a short distance, waiting for them to come out. But they did not move.

"They must have eaten recently," Sheldrick said. "They aren't hungry."

The vultures circled lower and finally skidded to an awkward landing about ten feet from the carcass. They knew the lions were watching, so kept their eyes on the beasts. We hoped that the sight of the vultures at the meat would bring the lions out, but they just lay under their tree as if enjoying the sight. In disgust, we headed back for camp, and by the time we returned the vultures had finished the topi. The lions were asleep and merely lifted their heads when they heard us approach. I was not interested in filming lions resting in the shade of a tree.

After many days filled with such futile efforts, we found a pride of five lions, including two males with beautiful manes, under a small cluster of trees. Sheldrick shot a wildebeest, and we brought it back near the lions. There was no tree to tie it to, but we left it in the open not far from the lions and retired in the truck. A few lions came out almost at once, chased away the approaching vultures, and started to feed. We edged up in the truck with both cameras going, getting a good shot of a lioness, annoyed at the vultures, chasing them away.

As we drove closer, the lions kept looking up nervously, so we decided that if we went further they would bolt. I decided to go closer on foot. Sheldrick and Mafuta agreed it would probably be all right, and stood ready with their guns to cover me.

The lions did not pay much attention to me when I stepped from the truck, but they glanced up now and then as I moved slowly toward them, stopping to film them every few steps. The whirr of the camera in the truck behind me told me that my cameraman was getting both me and the lions on film. When I was about twenty feet away, all the lions looked up from the carcass, blood dripping from their jowls. They obviously did not like my being so close. At such times you have no way of knowing if the lions are going to return to their eating, retreat, or charge. If their decision is the last, it happens in about one second. There was nothing I could do but freeze.

I knew that David and Mafuta both had their big guns trained on the lions, ready to shoot the instant one of them made a move toward me. But could they handle five lions? Luckily, five lions rarely charge at once. One of them, probably a female, would have been first, or perhaps two might have come for me while the others waited to see what would happen. So the hunters, with their double-barreled rifles, might have been able to take care of four lions before the cats could reach me, provided each one shot at a different lion each time.

Happily, there was no need to test their ability to get four lions in one second. One lioness lowered her head and sank her fangs in the wildebeest's haunch. The other lions looked at her and decided not to let her have it all. They went back to their meal, apparently forgetting all about me. But I had no stomach for trying to get any closer. I backed up slowly until I could turn and get in the truck.

After that, our luck turned and we got more lion sequences. One day vultures in the sky led us to a spot where eight lions were feasting on a zebra they had killed. Another time we came upon a fine lioness with a cub about six months old. They retreated into the edge of the bush at our approach, and we saw other lions there without being able to count them. I came up quite close to the lioness and her cub, filming them from about eighteen feet.

Hoping to get the rest of the cats in to the open, we went for bait and put it nearby. This time we brought two carcasses and placed them about twenty feet apart. We hoped that the lions would go to one, vultures to the other, and that some of the lions might run back and forth chasing the vultures away. This would make good footage for the lion sequence.

Only the lioness came out to the bait, however. When the vultures went after the other carcass, the lioness didn't chase them. If she was so tolerant of vultures, I decided she would tolerate a cameraman, so I went on foot to within about fifteen feet without seeming to disturb her. But apparently I was downwind, and she was so busy eating that she was not even aware of me, for when she suddenly looked up and saw me, she was obviously astonished.

Astonishment was quickly replaced by anger, and I saw what Tarlton had meant when he had spoken of fire in an angry lion's eyes. They were burning flames. She raised her tail slightly and flicked it twice. This really made me freeze, for I had always been told that three twitches of the tail was the prelude to a charge. I never found out, for she gave only those two twitches. We stared at each other for fifteen seconds that seemed like minutes. Then the angry young lady decided to go back in the bush with her cub. As soon as she was there I retreated hastily to the truck.

Gazelles, antelopes and other prey of lions are much easier to film than lions themselves, but no matter how beautiful they are, they are not dramatic enough for more than some establishing shots in feature films. They are, however, among the most satisfying and thrilling sights in Africa, for they usually live and travel in large herds. Today they have been thinned out considerably, and you have to travel farther to see really big herds. I would have to travel a long way to see once more a herd like the three hundred zebras that stampeded before my eyes in 1946.

The variety of African animals seems unlimited. Just think of the kinds of antelopes one can see there, without even specially searching for them. The reddish-coated hartebeest, with curved and pointed horns; the big and ungainly wildebeest (the gnu of crossword puzzles) with horns that curve down and out, and with long hair on the throat that makes him look bearded; the shiny-coated, slope-haunched topi; the little duiker, which means diver, so called from its sudden graceful dives into thick brush; the agile rock-climbing klipspringer, only about two or two and a half feet tall; the tawny oribi, with straight horns; the rabbit-sized dik-dik, so swift that you can scarcely see him when he puts on steam; the large waterbuck that lives along the banks of streams and is a good swimmer; its relative, the bushbuck, smaller and swifter; another relative found chiefly in Uganda and called the kob; the good-sized oryx, with long straight horns sloping back over the forehead; the long-necked gerenuk, with thick horns; the medium-sized impala, a prodigious jumper, with particularly graceful curved horns; the big eland, sometimes weighing as much as fifteen hundred pounds; the situtunga, which spends most of its time in the water with only head and horns above the surface and whose hooves are specially elongated to enable it to walk in soft mud; the steinbok or stembok; the kudu, of which I have seen only that called the lesser and not the greater; the bongo, probably the biggest of all

East African antelopes; and finally the loveliest of them all, Grant's and Thomson's gazelles.

All these are meat for lions, although they have preferences. The waterbuck is not very palatable, the dik-dik is not a mouthful, and even the "Tommies" offer so little meat as to be scarcely worth a chase unless there is nothing else around. Aside from the larger antelopes, lions love ostriches and zebras.

Lions are not the only enemies the antelopes have. The smaller gazelles are favorite dishes for cheetahs, hyenas, and wild dogs. And leopards will eat almost anything — even the meat of the hyena.

Leopards like dogs, too, as well as other domesticated animals. So they often hang around close to villagers or farms, which they raid. Leopards do not seem particularly impressed by men, or afraid of them, although they usually avoid contact if they can. A favorite food is baboon meat, which brings up a problem in the economy of many areas. Baboons are a nuisance and a destructive menace. So are leopards. If you kill off the leopards, baboons multiply by the hundreds and drive everyone crazy, ruining crops of all kinds but killing no living thing. So you must let the leopards live to keep down the baboons, even though they may steal your dogs, your cattle, and even an unwary worker or his children. Game conservationists in parks and restricted areas try to keep the two in proper balance.

Leopards are among the most beautiful of all four-footed animals, but they are a difficult challenge to hunters with either guns or cameras. They prefer hunting at night, and they are so fast one often gets no more than a glimpse of them. I saw quite a few leopards, for example, during my weeks in the Mara Valley in 1954, but I did not get a camera shot of one of them. Ace DuPreez and I were walking along a faint animal path through tall grass and thick bush when we heard a bleating noise, a sound of great distress. There was a rustle of leaves, and a leopard flashed across our path with a small animal in its mouth. My hand did not even have time to move for my camera.

A little behind the leopard came two roan antelopes, male and female, and we knew that the leopard had snatched a baby antelope whose mother and father were in pursuit. At this moment, of course, all the animals were oblivious of our presence, so we crashed our way through the bush trying to follow them and see what happened. In a short while we found the father and mother antelopes. They had given up the chase and were wandering about forlornly.

The only chance I had to make films of a leopard came when I was working on *Zanzabuku* at Carr Hartley's game farm in Kenya. He had trapped a magnificent specimen shortly before my arrival and kept him in a strong cage in the compound. Hartley and his young son, Mike, who played a prominent part in my film, had named the leopard Chui, the Swahili word for leopard. He was not tame, by any means, but his wildness seemed to have been tempered somewhat by kind treatment and good food since his capture. My one worry, in fact, was that he was too mild a beast to make a good movie sequence. I was not interested in pictures of a leopard purring and licking one's hand. He did not purr for me when I first visited his cage, but he let me put my hand through the bars and scratch his ears.

But the next time I saw him he was quite different. I was walking around the compound with Mrs. Hartley's sister, Dulcy Wedd, and as we approached Chui's cage he snarled, laid back his ears, lashed his tail, and sprang against the bars. I talked soothingly to no avail. The beast obviously had just one thing in mind — to get out of that cage and kill both of us.

Maybe Chui would make a good movie star after all, I decided. I tried visiting him the next day alone, thinking that perhaps he didn't like women. He snarled at me just as viciously, so I decided to go ahead with an attempt at pictures in Carr's big enclosed arena about three miles from his house and animal compound. To tempt the leopard into action, we decided to use his great fondness for baboon meat. Carr had in his private menagerie a mother baboon, with her baby on her back and a slightly larger adopted baboon child at her breast. We did not use the animals themselves for bait, but their smell.

We trucked the unfriendly leopard in a strong cage to the arena, then took the baboon and her children to another spot about a hundred feet away, in sight and smell of the leopard, which paced eagerly back and forth in its cage. In a while, we removed the baboons from the arena, through a gate on the far side, away from the leopard. The cameramen were stationed at strategic spots within the arena, and several of Hartley's helpers were ready, further along, to try to keep the leopard on a course that would be within camera range. I stood with Hartley close to the path Chui was supposed to take on his way to the spot where the baboons had been.

Since we had already taken some shots of the baboon and its children, we hoped to establish the idea that the leopard was after them.

The soundest way to bring the idea home was actually to make the leopard *go* after them. He would, we hoped, spring immediately to the spot where he had seen them and could still smell them. Then he would follow their trail to the far gate, where he would get some meat, even though not his favorite baboon. It was a good plan if it worked, but few animals act with men around as they would in their normal environment. At the last moment, instead of thinking about the leopard, I thought about myelf. I asked Hartley, "What if the leopard comes for us?" He answered, "Stand absolutely still. Don't move an inch. He'll probably go on past, since you don't smell like a baboon. And anyway, I'll take care of things."

The leopard was released from his cage and came stalking swiftly down through the trees and underbrush along the route we had intended. Chui was an impressive creature. Beautiful as he had seemed in his cage, he was far more spectacular out in the open, moving ahead almost like liquid, and I was delighted to see two cameras trained on him from different angles. Once he slowed down and darted quick and uncomfortable glances at the humans around, but the smell of baboon overcame his worries, and he went straight for the spot where the baboons had been. This brought Chui within about fifteen feet of Hartley and me, and I held my breath as he passed. But he went on his way.

He sniffed at the spot, looked up, and started off in the right direction, more swiftly than before. He didn't want that baboon to get away. Then quite suddenly he veered to the right, away from the baboon's trail and almost out of range of our cameras. Perhaps the wind shifted and fooled him, or our presence threw him off. Hartley signaled to one of his African helpers up on a hill to move toward the leopard in an effort to turn Chui back to his route. His experienced men would have known that wild animals usually turn aside when men approach, but this was the time when his best people had been arrested on suspicion of being Mau Maus.

The inexperienced fellow tried to do what Hartley signaled. He took half a dozen steps toward the leopard's path, at right angles to it. Chui *should* have angled off to the left, back toward the gate and into camera range. But he didn't. He stopped, faced the man, and lashed his tail in annoyance. This was too much for the African, who was seized with sudden fear. Hartley and I could sense it a hundred feet away, and I'm sure the leopard sensed it, too. Fear made the man do the worst possible thing — run away. If he'd had the courage or experience to hold his ground, Chui would almost certainly have continued on his way. But when the fellow panicked and took to his heels, the leopard was after him. In two terrific bounds Chui was on the man's back, knocking him to the ground. Hartley was already racing for the spot, with me not far behind. As we rushed up, the leopard turned the man over and tried to sink his fangs in the throat.

It was a tough shot for Hartley to make, with man and beast so close together, but he did not hesitate. His first bullet struck the leopard, who leapt off the native and bounded away. Three more quick shots dropped the animal about ten feet from us.

The man was horribly mauled and bleeding profusely, but still alive. Hartley ordered men to carry him at once to a truck and rush him to a hospital — a long trip, but his only hope. The man hovered between life and death for weeks but finally recovered. This was the first serious accident on any of my expeditions.

A couple of years after my 1954 trip, young Mike Hartley found and captured a two-week-old leopard cub. He bottle-fed it for months, mothered it to the extent of taking it to bed with him at night to keep it warm. The nights often get quite cold there, even though Hartley's farm is exactly on the equator. As the cub grew into a full-sized leopard, Mike and he remained great friends. Chui (he bore the same name as the leopard that had been killed during my filming) and Mike romped and played and wrestled together almost every day.

This went on for about five years, and everyone agreed that if ever a wild animal had become tame, Chui was the one — at least so far as Mike was concerned. Even when the young man went off to school, he wrestled with Chui on his holidays, when the leopard was obviously overjoyed to see him. On one school holiday, Mike brought some boys and girls home with him. They had all heard about the pet leopard and wanted to see Mike wrestle and play with it. Mike was not averse to showing off in front of his girl, but would have romped with Chui in any event. But Mike did not know that just before he went to Chui's cage some tourists had been annoying the animal. Hartley's farm was well known, and tourists often stopped off to see and photograph the animals. Uusally there was an attendant around to see that the visitors did not annoy the wild creatures, but on this occasion there was no one to stop them from poking sticks and throwing stones at Chui in an effort to get him to snarl for their cameras.

Just after this business, Mike walked in to say hello to Chui. The angry leopard pounced on Mike viciously and began to maul him. Mike screamed, and his brother Pat and an African cookboy raced for the compound, both rushing in at the same time. Pat grabbed Chui by the neck, the African pulled his tail. Once they got him off Mike, Pat staggered the beast with a kick in the head, enabling the boy to get Mike out of the cage. By that time Hartley was there. On examining his youngest son, Hartley found eight bites through Mike's right arm. "I could put a pencil clear through five of them," he told me.

There were three bites in Mike's left arm, two in one leg, one in the other, and his back was lacerated from neck to waist by the leopard's sharp claws. For half an hour Hartley dressed Mike's wounds to stop the profuse bleeding, then drove him to the hospital in Nairobi — a hundred fifty-two miles in two hours. Mike required several blood transfusions, but was out of the hospital in a few weeks. A year later, when he came to the United States on business, he visited me in my New York apartment and stripped to show me his wounds when I asked about his experience. Even though healed, his back made me shudder.

Another member of the cat family that is an excellent hunter is the cheetah. I saw few of them during my trips, and today they are in danger of becoming extinct. The spotted creatures with astonishingly long legs are considered to be the fastest of all land animals, having been clocked at upwards of seventy miles an hour. Once when we were out in the truck we came upon one that ran from us, and we tried to race it. It left us far behind in less than a mile.

The cheetah is not as dangerous to man as the lion or leopard, partly because its claws are rather blunt, like a dog's instead of sharp sabers. Although it can climb trees, it is not good at it. During my 1954-1955 trip, a small cheetah tried to get away from us by climbing a tree, but it kept slipping down. Young Mike Hartley reached up and grabbed it by the tail and pulled it down so that some helpers could grab it and take it back to the Hartley farm.

For many years it was thought that lions could not climb trees, or at least that heavy male lions could not. But Colonel Mervyn Cowie proved that they could, some years ago, by tying meat higher and higher in the branches of a tree and observing from a nearby tree platform. On my 1964 trip, when I visited Russell Douglass at his hotel near Lake Manyara Park, he showed me an acacia forest where ten or twelve big lions were draped over the branches about thirty-five feet above the ground. They were resting, and looked perfectly relaxed. Douglass told me that the lions climb up there to get away from the tsetse flies, which never go more than twelve feet above the ground.

I've mentioned that hyenas go after small antelopes for food. They also like ostrich eggs; and they have been known to follow a zebra about to give birth so they can snatch the baby when it is born. But the bulk of a hyena's diet is carrion — dead flesh of almost any kind, animal or human. They follow hunting lions so they can eat whatever is left over. Revolting though their habits may seem to us, hyenas do serve a very useful purpose in the wild by cleaning it up and keeping it clean. Nothing can lie around and rot for long within miles of any hyenas.

I saw many hyenas, of course, during my lion-filming forays, and I didn't like them. In the first place, a hyena is thoroughly unattractive, with its moth-eaten coat, its huge head and strong jaws so out of place in front of a skimpy rear end that looks as it were made for a much smaller animal. They always appear to be cringing. Their cry in the night is chilling, like a maniac's laugh. And they smell to high heaven.

At Hartley's farm in 1954, I changed my mind about hyenas — at least about one hyena I came to know. His name was Eric, and he had quickly become a pet after Hartley caught him. While I was there, he had the run of the place, and everybody loved him for his playfulness and pixie sense of humor. At first I found him just as ugly as other hyenas, even though he didn't smell. But his personality won me over. And he knew it, for he attached himself to me for the rest of my stay there. One of his favorite tricks was to sneak into my rondavel while I was writing, snatch up my hat, and dash out with it. He was quiet about it, but he always made a noise on the way out, to make sure I would chase him.

I could never have caught him if he had not wanted me to, but he let me grab him and tussle and finally take the hat from his big, snapping jaws. Once he took a shoe which I desperately needed, and dashed into a clump of cactus where I could not follow. When he felt he had teased me long enough he emerged with the shoe. He let me give him some hard slaps on his rump. This showed him I was angry, so he didn't steal anything from me for a couple of days.

Eric used to play for hours at a time with a big shepherd dog of Hartley's. The dog sometimes mauled the hyena rather badly, but Eric never used his sharp teeth and strong jaws to retaliate. He knew that if he did he would lose the dog as a playmate.

On my 1964 trip I asked Hartley about Eric. "Yes, he had quite a personality, that one," Hartley said. "I never saw another hyena like him. I sold him some years ago to an outdoor zoo in Europe. Those people got a prize."

From a distance, the wild dog looks something like a hyena, but his character is quite different. The wild dog is a killer, not a scavenger. He is brave, willing to tackle something three times his size even when alone. Usually, however, wild dogs travel in packs of five to twenty, occasionally up to a hundred. Short-haired, big-eared, and spotted irregularly with black, white, and tan, the wild dog, or lycaon, is not handsome. Built for speed and endurance, he can outrun almost any animal on the plains.

When they are chasing a fast antelope, baying like hunting hounds, the dogs work together perfectly. One leader sets a stiff pace right behind the fleeing prey, while the others lag behind a bit. When the leader tires, he drops back and another takes over. When the antelope begins to falter, all the dogs come alongside and slash with their teeth at the flanks of the doomed animal, ripping the skin until the intestines fall out. I've never heard of wild dogs attacking a human being, but natives always give them a wide berth.

Once we saved a zebra from this kind of death. We were driving across the plain and saw a half-grown zebra standing alone — unusual because they are always in herds. We drove closer, slowly so as not to panic the animal, which had been abandoned by the herd when it could not keep up with it. It was frightened when we got out of the truck some distance away, but it was also desolated at being left alone. Hesitantly, in desperation, it walked toward us and finally got near enough for us to pet it. It was unsteady on its legs, though we could not see what injury or sickness it suffered from.

There was nothing we could do for it, so we drove on. About a mile away we saw a pack of wild dogs loping along in the direction from which we had come. In a few minutes they would catch the scent of the lone zebra and would be on it, ripping the flesh from its bones, tearing open its belly to get at the entrails. We turned and drove back. Ace DuPreez put a bullet through the zebra's head, to give it a quick death.

On my first trip to Africa I was able to see Lutembe. The grand old girl was dead when I returned in 1946, or was presumed dead since she no longer came when called. For at least three generations this famous crocodile had never failed to answer to her name.

You think of wild animals in African parks and reserves as being somewhat tame, but I doubt that anyone will find there a friendly crocodile. All animals and humans seem to dislike the creatures, and white men have carried on a war of extermination for several decades — a war that has apparently changed the crocodile population very little.

I found Lutembe in the fishing village of Dewe, on the shores of Lake Victoria. I couldn't quite believe the stories I'd heard about her, and half expected to find a stuffed skin or at best a toothless old beast in an enclosure. But there was no phony crocodile on hand when I found its African master. He said he'd have to call up Lutembe, which he would be happy to do for a modest fee.

Gathering up an armful of dried fish, the man led the way to the shore, where he looked out over the broad waters of the lake, cupped his hands to his mouth, and shouted long and loud, "Lutembe!"

The name echoed over the choppy waves. The young man called again and again. Still nothing could be seen. I shifted uneasily, and received an admonition to be patient. For ten minutes the call to Lutembe rang out over the lake. Finally the African pointed triumphantly and turned to me with a smile. I saw a commotion far out in the water, as if someone were swimming vigorously. In a few minutes I could make out the snout that ploughed through the waves directly toward us. As it approached the shore, I saw the moving tail, the big jaws, and the serrated hide of a crocodile. The beast heaved itself out of the water and lumbered toward the man. I stood a few feet away, behind the pile of fish, filming the incredible performance.

The crocodile was about fourteen feet long, huge and hideous, especially when it opened its cavernous mouth and revealed its sharp teeth. I thought it was glancing hungrily in my direction, but I soon realized its interest lay in the fish behind which I stood. The man reached for a fish, thrust it in the croc's jaws, his hand coming within inches of the teeth that chomped down on the morsel. Fish after fish went into the bottomless pit. Finally the creature's master took hold of the crocodile's tail affectionately and sat down on it. One swish, I thought, and he would have been tossed into the lake.

"How old is he?" I asked.

"She, bwana," the man replied.

"Well, I don't know how you can tell, but *she*, then. How old is she?"

"Five kings — Kamanya, Suna, Mutesa, Mwango, and Daudi Chwa."

I had no idea how long Buganda kings normally lived, but I found out later that this span would mean about a century and a quarter. While probably an exaggeration, I had heard that the young man's grandfather was the first to make a pet of Lutembe by tossing fish to the ordinarily irascible croc. The creature quickly became accustomed to her daily handout and visited that spot on the shore regularly. In time she learned the name "Lutembe," and came when called. After the original crocodile-tamer died, his son inherited Lutembe, or Lutembe inherited him. That man's son was the present owner.

"What would happen if I fed Lutembe?" I asked.

"She would eat, bwana," the man said, getting off his pet.

I asked him if he had ever handled a camera. He said no. So I showed him how to point it, how to push the right button down. He aimed the camera at Lutembe and me, and I gingerly picked up a fish and held it out to the crocodile. Lutembe moved toward me with a speed that made me recoil. I had not realized that crocs were so fast.

I flipped the fish into the open mouth before Lutembe reached me, and backed away a few steps. The croc was either disappointed in the small morsel or disturbed at my distrust. In any event, she slithered off into the water and began circling around. Wondering if she would snatch at something thrown in the water or perhaps even retrieve it like a pet dog, I picked up a stick and tossed it playfully in her direction. But instead of landing in the water in front of her, it hit her back and bounced off. Instantly, as if in a huff, she turned and headed full speed toward the middle of the lake.

"Bwana, you should not have done that," the man said, handing me my camera. "You hurt her feelings." He called pleadingly to the fleeing crocodile, "Lutembe! Lutembe!"

Although my stick made little impression on the croc's tough hide, I felt like a bad boy when Lutembe refused to return. But her master persisted, calling lovingly to Lutembe, who finally decided that her temperamental conduct might be depriving her of dessert. She buried her pride and circled back to shore, where her master stuffed her until she could have no complaints. Then she lay contentedly in the sun, opening wide her enormous jaws so the rays of the setting sun shone directly down her throat — a most unusual kind of sunbathing.

And that's the way I left her. Just what caused this particular crocodile to become friendly with men, although all others obviously fear or hate humans, is not clear. She was probably the only crocodile that ever met human beings who acted friendly, instead of trying to kill her. Why it occurred to that first man to be nice to a croc is incomprehensible, for they are generally as ugly-acting as they are ugly-looking. More Africans are killed by crocodiles than any other wild animal, because they go into so many streams and lakes, fishing, bathing, or fording. Snakes are probably the second most common killers, since bare legs and feet offer ready targets.

I've seen and filmed hundreds of crocodiles since my experience with Lutembe, but I never let her apparent tameness lessen my caution in dealing with them. Another incident from my 1937 trip showed the foolishness of taking chances with them. Cézaire and I had arrived at Pat Putnam's camp on the Epulu River, on the edge of the Ituri Forest. Although this unusual American who had lived so many years in the tropical forest was away in the States, two servants were in charge and made us at home.

It was swelteringly hot, so Cézaire suggested a swim in the river, but I wanted to take some pictures of Putnam's two rare okapi, kept in a stockade, while the light was still good. Although some of these rare animals have since reached the zoos of the world, they had at that time been seen by few people. As I was leaving the stockade, I heard Cézaire shouting. There was such fright in his voice that I abandoned my camera and tripod and raced for the riverbank. Cézaire was about thirty-five feet from shore, treading the coffee-colored water and splashing furiously with his hands. Two Pygmies were jumping up and down on the bank, adding their shrill cries to his. Suddenly I saw the cause of the commotion — a huge crocodile scarcely ten yards downstream from Cézaire and swimming steadily toward him against the current. If Cézaire made a dash for shore, the crocodile could put on a little speed and snatch him. Our only hope was to frighten the big monster off.

I picked up a rock and let fly, but my aim was bad. Still, the croc slowed down a little at the big splash in the water. The Pygmies, following my example, started flinging stones, and we all kept up a terrific din. The beast did not slow down, but at that moment a stone caught him squarely on the snout. That was enough for him. He turned and retreated.

"Come on, Cézaire, come on!" I shouted. "Now's your chance."

While we kept up the rock barrage, Cézaire started flailing the water arm over arm, his feet beating like a paddle wheel. I pulled him from the water, and he stood there trembling, unable to speak for several minutes. It may seem foolhardy to go swimming in waters known to harbor crocodiles. But since almost all rivers and lakes contain them — except for lovely Lake Kivu and a few other favored spots — people swim and fish in spite of danger.

I always found it amusing to watch a big group of hippos together, in clusters of fifty to a hundred, provided I sat in some safe spot, away from their regular tracks from the waters back to their feeding places. The first time I enjoyed such a scene was in 1937, when we drove to the Rutshuru River in Congo's great Albert National Park. As we drove toward the river, we saw here and there great mudholes from each of which a set of parallel tracks led toward the water. They were hippo tracks, and since an adult hippo may weigh as much as four tons, they were quite deep.

A hippo isn't afraid of anything, even another hippo. He can break a lion's or a crocodile's back with one crunching bite of his gigantic jaws. He'll try his best to do the same to another hippo if he thinks his mate or his favorite sunning place is being appropriated.

Cézaire stopped the car on a high bank above the river, and I gasped at the sight below me. There were hundreds of hippos in the river, along the muddy banks, on little islands and sandbars. The water was full of them, diving, squirming, snorting, and cavorting, obviously having a good time. One would sink below the surface with contented gurgles, emitting huge bubbles, only to come up a few yards away puffing and blowing. Another would dive and be gone, apparently forever. A hippo can remain submerged perhaps ten minutes — some authorities say much longer — can swim under water with grace and agility, or walk along the bottom.

I found a spot where the reeds and bushes along the shore grew thick and high, so I could get near the hippos without being seen. Not far away a tremendous bull hippo slept with his head resting on another's back. A huge scar, looking red and fresh, ran down his side, the memento of a recent battle. My camera was going, and I suddenly saw in my viewfinder something riding on top of the water. When I looked directly, I saw it was a baby hippo, small and almost pink, riding on the back of its mother, who was sedately swimming downstream with only her snout and eyes showing. She deposited the young one on a sandbar and nudged away a few friends to make room for it. Then she lay down herself and almost squashed her baby to death. It squealed, the big hippos nearby shifted slightly and reluctantly, and the baby went to sleep.

On another sandbar a mother was playing with her baby, letting it slide down her back into the water, then helping it up for another go. I was diverted from this scene by some thrashing on my left. I saw a pair of hippos not more than fifty feet away. Only the back and ears of the female showed above the water, and the male was in an undignified but for him quite natural position on top of her. So I caught them *in flagrante delicto* in my telephoto lens. The amorous gentleman must have become aware of it, for he turned his head in my direction and threw a nasty look at me. But I had a rare sequence, even if it could not be used in a film for general public distribution.

On my 1946 trip, Commandant Ernest Hubert of Albert National Park took me down to the Rutshuru again to see the hippos. We drove in my truck, with one of Hubert's African helpers walking ahead. The truck proceeded slowly because of the many rooks and anthills hidden in the grass, so the native was a couple of hundred feet ahead. Not far from the river, a big bull hippo materialized from a mudhole, looking like a giant self-propelled piece of the wet earth he had been lying in.

The hippo was to the left of the truck and some distance ahead.

The helper was directly between the hippo and the river, and the hippo didn't like the idea. He headed for the man on the run. Although his gait was awkward and lumbering, the beast covered the ground at a remarkable speed. The man started running back toward the truck, but it looked to me as if the hippo might cut him off before he reached us. Hubert apparently thought so, too, for he leapt from the truck and ran toward the hippo. He had no gun or weapon of any kind, but he went at the four-ton monster as if he intended to put it across his knee and spank it.

When he was about seventy-five feet from the hippo, Hubert stopped, waved his arms wildly, and shouted at the top of his lungs, "Hey! Hey! Hey!" The big brute slowed down, came to a stop, looked at Hubert and then at the helper, who had just about made the truck, and turned to one side in a huff. It was difficult to credit my own eyes, but I could believe now the story I had heard about the angry lion that had once charged Hubert — how the commandant had just held up his hand imperiously and shouted, "Stop!" Other times, he diverted charging beasts by throwing chunks of mud at them.

Ace DuPreez was, in his way, as amazing as Hubert in dealing with animals. During the filming of *Zanzabuku* we came upon a herd of a hundred or more hippos in the Kazinga Channel between Lakes George and Edward in the Queen Elizabeth National Park in Uganda. Ace wanted to help me get some good footage, so he said he would get into a little rowboat and float down into the middle of the herd. I protested, since he would very likely get tipped over by one of the huge beasts.

"That's a good idea," Ace said. "If they don't tip me, I'll tip myself."

There was no stopping him once he got an idea in his head. He stepped into the little boat and pushed himself off from shore. We scrambled into a larger boat behind him, and were busy filming him as the current took him toward the herd of hippos. He was only a few yards away when the first hippos saw him and submerged. Some swam away, but I was afraid that one that had submerged might come up under his boat and tip him over.

Suddenly Ace signaled with a hand, the boat tipped, Ace lurched as if trying to keep his balance, and then tumbled over in the water. He started swimming for shore about two hundred yards away. I expected at any moment to see a thrashing in the water, a huge gaping mouth, and then no more Ace. But the hippos around him submerged and swam away from this unnatural disturbance in their water. By the time they came up again, Ace was near shore, and they just looked at him inquiringly. A few snorted loudly.

Ace pulled himself up on the shore, dripping and muddy. We circled around in our boat to pick him up. He had not had to tip himself over, as a hippo obligingly had done it, but he was sure they would not hurt him since they were protected in the park and had not been hunted for years.

A few days later, Ace and I, with one of my cameramen, were out on the plains looking for a herd of buffalo when we came upon a muddy pool overflowing with hippos. There must have been about fifty of them, but they were so covered with mud and so overlapped on each other that we could not make out the details. I started to film the scene, but Ace said it would look like nothing but a seething hill of mud. We should try to detach at least one hippo from the mass.

He took a few steps toward them, and one big bull stirred, lifted its head, and bellowed. Ace stopped for a moment, then went on. The muddy mass heaved again, and the big bull moved away from it, faster than we had anticipated. It was suddenly racing toward us, its head lowered, its tiny eyes blazing. We turned and ran for the truck. The driver angled toward us so we could leap aboard — just a few feet ahead of the angry hippo. Luckily the cameraman in the truck had recorded the whole scene, with more action than we had bargained for.

While hippos were often interesting and sometimes dangerous, they could not hold a candle to rhinos in either department. A rhino will eagerly attack a two-ton truck — and sometimes win the battle. He has been known to charge a railroad train, but has never derailed one. The theory that all wild animals will let man alone if not annoyed or hunted is put to a severe test by the rhino, who seems to go around permanently angry. On the other hand, Carr Hartley had two large tame white rhinos that allowed people to ride them.

There's no way of knowing what a rhino will do, and that's what makes him so dangerous. Half the time he will charge a man anywhere near him, whether there has been provocation or not. And when a rhino charges, he means business. He's fast, agile, and determined. Why is he so belligerent? He is not very bright, and his eyesight is poor. He cannot see anything clearly until it is about ten yards in front of him. But the rhino makes up in courage what it lacks in brains, and a keen sense of smell compensates for its poor eyesight. If you approach a rhino downwind, as any sensible person does, the animal is not aware of you until you are quite close. He dimly makes out the menace in front of him; and he seems to figure that if there is danger there, there is also danger behind him and to the right and left. So he charges to break out of the supposed encirclement. Don't think that because he looks so bulky and clumsy you can dodge out of his way and his speed will carry him past you. He can wheel and turn in his own length, no matter how fast he is going.

All other animals make way for the rhinos. If *faru* and *tembo* meet on a narrow forest path, the elephant will detour. I doubt that a rhino could do much damage to an elephant, but the elephant will still decline an engagement. All Africans feel the same way about the rhino. The Masai, bravest of the brave, who kill charging lions with spears, fear only one animal — the rhino.

Perhaps it was foolhardy of me to set out to provoke a rhino to charge me, but a rhino sequence is nothing unless he is charging. He's an ugly brute, and nobody enjoys looking at him in repose. With his thick hide that fits so badly that it seems to be made for some other creature, and his long, forward-sloping horn placed in the most un-likely position near the end of his nose, a rhino would look like an amusing caricature if he weren't so obviously cantankerous.

On my 1946 *Savage Splendor* trip, Lionel Hartley, my white hunter and guide, tried to help me get some footage of a rhino charg-ing, but it was not easy. There were so many essential elements in my planned scene that we never managed to get them all together at once. There had to be, first of all, the rhino. Then there had to be a good tree for me to climb when faru charged me, plus a safe spot for my cameraman, preferably another tree, from which he could film me, rhino, and the tree I escaped to. And the light had to be right. Hart-ley, of course, planned to cover the whole thing with his big .475 gun — it took a mighty jolt to stop a charging rhino, and there was rarely time for a second shot.

We went out in a truck and saw our first rhino right away, but he heard the motor and didn't like it, so ambled out of sight. A few hours later, after watching a fine pride of lions, we sighted a big bull rhino about two hundred yards away. When we stopped the truck, he retreated.

As we jolted about the countryside for several more hours, I began to express doubts about the ferocity and even the presence of rhinos. Suddenly a big rhino lunged at the truck from behind a bush. But the truck was going fairly fast, and Hartley stepped on the accelerator, so the rhino missed. He took up the chase, however, and came so close to the rear of the truck that one of the Africans sitting there rolled over to get as near to the truck cab as possible. Hartley speeded up more and we finally pulled away from the angry beast, who might have toppled us with a charge against the side. While this was exciting, we didn't get a camera shot. The rhino had not given us time to get set.

During the next few days, this sort of thing happened a number of times — a rhino suddenly charging from the bush — but these meetings were unproductive photographically. Hartley explained that we had to find a rhino quietly feeding, approach him downwind, find the necessary trees, then let the rhino know we were there, whereupon he would charge. After several days we came upon a feeding rhino who did not hear or see us. We watched the little tick birds walk up and down his back picking lice from the folds of his hide, and hoped they would not take flight. They are alert, and often serve as the rhino's eyes. If they became alarmed, they would fly up with little cries and head in our direction, and the rhino would know where to look for trouble.

We inched the truck to within a hundred yards of the animal. From here the cameraman could film the scene with relative safety, since the rhino would presumably be charging me rather than the truck. We found a tree off to the left that I might climb, but Lionel decided it was too fragile; the rhino might knock it over. Farther away we found a tree that was good, but it was out of position for the cameraman. So we switched around, put the cameraman in the good tree, and decided that I would run for the truck. All set at last, I walked slowly toward the feeding rhino, shooting film with my own camera. I wanted to catch that moment when he looked up, saw me, and started his charge. Then I'd fly and hope to make the truck in time.

He finally looked up, all right, but instead of charging he just turned and trotted away into the bush. We had lost a couple of hours!

Later we came upon another big bull feeding. He looked peaceful to me, but Hartley said the animal was kali and ought to be "full of fun," perhaps because it was the rutting season, when rhino bulls are nervous and irritable. Among rhinos, the female is the aggressor in lovemaking and will chase an attractive bull for miles, then butt him furiously until he gives her what she wants.

We found a tree for the cameraman and a sound tree for me about forty-five feet from the rhino. The light was right, and Hartley stationed himself to cover me. I approached the rhino, but the wind was wrong and he had no idea I was there. I picked up a stick and threw it at him. It fell short, but faru heard the noise and looked up, eyeing me suspiciously; but he did not charge. I threw a rock, which came a little closer and angered him. As he lowered his head, I was sure he was going to charge, and took off for my tree at full speed. I grabbed the lowest branch, swung my right leg up over it, straining a muscle badly at the same time. Breathless but safe on the branch, I turned and looked back. The rhino was in the same spot, staring at me wonderingly!

Hartley said he too was sure the rhino was about to charge, but I ran one second too soon. If the charge had started, the rhino would not have stopped, but I ran just before he moved, and this confused him.

We didn't give up. I approached the rhino again, though he did not seem very interested. Hartley sent a helper to circle around in back of the rhino, hoping the animal would get his scent, feel surrounded, and charge me. The helper climbed a tree to reconnoiter, then saw a sleeping cow rhino, the mate of my friend, near the foot of it. Hartley and I did not know this, of course, and Lionel could not figure out the helper's signals from the tree. The man was afraid to go down for fear he would waken the sleeping rhino, which might charge him; or she might have charged me suddenly from the side, cutting off my retreat to the tree.

But I could not get a rise out of the feeding rhino. *He* knew that he was not surrounded, for he had left his mate asleep back in the bush a little way. The light was growing dim and finally the big rhino, his belly full, turned and went back to awaken his mate. They went off together.

On my 1954-1955 trip I was more successful in filming rhinos. In Arusha, Tanganyika, I met August Kuenzler, a Swiss who had come to East Africa in 1929 and had eventually developed his business of capturing, and training for zoo life, many kinds of wild animals. He was one of the first to capture baby rhinos, elephants, and other animals without killing the mothers — once considered impossible but now required by law in Tanganyika. Kuenzler had trained a remarkable assistant, Pellegrini, who had become perhaps the finest game capturer in that part of the world. We were permitted to accompany Pellegrini on a number of game-catching ventures, and on one of them we filmed a touching scene with two rhinos.

Pellegrini, using a technique similar to that of Carr Hartley in Kenya, lassoed a big cow rhino, using a noose on the end of a long pole, which he handled from the back of the truck as it sped along beside the animal. During the ensuing struggle, the truck bogged down in a deep hole and could not move. Pellegrini descended and at great risk slipped another rope around one of the beast's hind legs. He and his men had almost immobilized her when they were interrupted by a huge and angry bull rhino who had come to rescue his mate.

The cow rhino, fastened to the truck with a stout rope, tried desperately to get away, tugging until it seemed she might tear off her leg. The bull rhino watched her from about thirty yards away, then decided the situation called for action. The men all clambered into the doubtful safety of the truck as the big rhino prepared to charge. With lowered head, he quickly picked up speed until he was thundering down on the truck like an express train. If he had struck the side of the truck he might have tipped it over, but fortunately he aimed for the front and smacked the heavy grillwork with such force that the vehicle was almost shaken out of its pothole. Bewildered and perhaps a little dazed, the rhino backed off and surveyed the situation, nervously eyeing his mate and the truck which seemed impervious to his blows. Then once more he charged and crashed against the front of the truck.

When he backed up again, he looked genuinely bewildered as well as frustrated and angry. He shifted uneasily on his stubby legs and looked about, as if puzzled. Then for the third time he hurled himself against the front of the truck. I was touched by the terrible beating the male was taking. If I had been in charge, I would have been inclined to free the cow rhino. But we were guests of Pellegrini, and he was determined to keep his valuable captive.

But he decided that he should try to get rid of this persistent and dangerous male. He took a slender pole about fifteen feet long and, standing in the truck, waved it menacingly toward the rhino. I can't understand why a waving pole should intimidate a rhino, but it seemed to. The beast backed away a few yards, then held his ground. Pellegrini got down from the truck and advanced toward the rhino on foot, slowly and cautiously, all the time waving the pole.

The rhino backed away, confused by the approaching man and the strange thing reaching out in the air toward him. He might have become even more angry and charged, of course, but Pellegrini knew what he was doing and showed great courage. The animal kept moving away and, just before disappearing in the thick bush, turned for one last look at the mate he had tried so hard to rescue.

The most exciting rhino sequences were filmed during my stay in the Mara Valley, in northwestern Tanganyika, where Ace DuPreez operated a small gold mine and where he was honorary game warden. He was a kind of unofficial "king" of the Mara Valley, which contained twenty-nine species of animals in an area of thirty square miles, most of them in abundance. There was every kind of terrain, with the river, thick forest, rocky plain, swamps, hills, and valleys. There was no road, but Ace got around with a Jeep and a battered old five-ton truck with four-wheel drive. And I had one of our Power Wagons.

Ace knew animals. Not as Mafuta, the gun-bearer, knew them, for his knowledge was specially useful to the hunter. Not as Kuenzler and Pellegrini and Carr Hartley knew them, for these men were spectacularly gifted in capturing them alive and unharmed. Ace did not hunt or capture them, except when his job as game warden made it necessary. He just lived with them every day, and he knew how they lived their day-to-day lives.

At the time the Mara Valley was a "controlled" area, rather than "restricted." There were no rigid prohibitions as to the hunting or filming of animals, so we could do what we pleased to get the films we wanted — especially since the man in charge would be helping us.

One day Ace was driving the Jeep, with Canadian cameraman Johnny Coquillon beside him and the rest of us following in the Power Wagon, when two big rhinos charged out of the bush at the

Jeep. Johnny got the charge in his camera, and from the truck we got the whole scene. One rhino finally gave up after a good deal of racing back and forth, but the other was more determined. He charged the Jeep again and again, missing it only by inches. Johnny had absolutely no protection from the big horn that came tearing at him. The Jeep was low, putting Johnny at just the right height for a horn thrust. But Johnny kept filming throughout, getting some magnificent shots. And Ace's maneuvering of the car was uncanny.

Finally the rhino succeeded. His horn caught the rear of the Jeep about a foot behind Johnny. Ace and Johnny tumbled out on the other side, Johnny clutching his precious camera, and we speeded up the truck to close in on the furious rhino, who was busy poking holes in the Jeep and one rear tire. He charged us, and we pulled away. He followed us a short distance and then turned back toward the Jeep. Johnny and Ace had run away meanwhile, so we breathed easier and stopped the truck. The rhino pounded away at his first enemy, the Jeep, so I got out of the truck and approached him on foot, filming as I went.

I was about forty feet away when the rhino saw me. He didn't hesitate, but lowered his head and raced for me, puffing with that sound that everyone had described, accurately, as like a steam locomotive. I ran for all I was worth, slipped once, scrambled to my feet, and leapt into the truck about five feet ahead of the rhino, who struck the vehicle a glancing blow that did little harm. The truck took off fast enough to make the exhausted rhino give up the chase. We picked up Johnny and Ace, caught our breaths, and congratulated each other on the action shots we had taken without harm to anyone. There was no gun coverage during this filming. Ace's and Johnny's cool courage inspired all of us.

An aroused buffalo may be just as vindictive as a rhinoceros, but he is more predictable. With the rhino, you are dealing with stupidity and deficient senses, so many of his actions appear silly, incomprehensible. The buffalo knows what he is about and you can tell that he does.

When you come upon a herd of buffalo grazing they look from a distance not unlike a herd of domestic cows, peaceful and contented. You can often spot a herd from a distance, even in tall grass, from the white egrets flying overhead, then settling on the animals' backs to pick the lice from their hair. When you first see a buffalo close up you can't help admiring him, for he is a magnificent creature, weighing up to two thousand pounds and all muscle. His sweeping ebony horns are as thick as an arm at the base, and taper to fine points.

Some people have said that the biggest danger from a buffalo herd is a stampede, but they don't commonly attack en masse. A lone buffalo usually makes the charge, although others may stay close to take up the battle if necessary. My experiences in filming them, in Albert National Park, the Mara Valley, and elsewhere, tends to verify this. The others looked, but made no menacing gesture when they saw that one of their number had the matter in hand.

All Africans have a healthy respect for the buffalo, and hunters generally place him number two, if not number one, on the list of most dangerous beasts. And most animals refrain from tangling with a buffalo, though a lion that is hungry enough and can find no smaller prey will sometimes attack. This is a battle I'd like to see, for it is just about as even as one can imagine. The bones of a lion and a buffalo have been found side by side after a battle in which both of them died.

Everywhere I've gone in Africa I've seen elephants. They are great travelers, and are at home in all kinds of country. They like the great plains covered with low bush and elephant grass; they seem equally comfortable in thick jungle like the Ituri Forest. I've seen a huge elephant push through almost impenetrable forest growth silently and without disturbing many leaves. And I've seen one clamber up a steep mountainside with speed and agility, if not with grace. Elephant trails are as well engineered as any route could be, as surveyors learned long ago.

Unless wounded, attacked, or protecting the young, elephants are not very belligerent. They are so big they have few enemies, if any, and they are undoubtedly the most intelligent of wild animals. They possess great dignity, despite their wrinkled and ill-fitting skins, their baggy Charlie Chaplin pants, and their ridiculous little tails. They are somewhat sentimental, too. A male will travel miles to visit the spot where its mate died or was killed.

Elephants are among the few wild animals that consciously help others of their species besides their mates. If one elephant is hurt, others will gather around solicitously and try to help. I once saw a young elephant try to uproot a tree to get at the succulent roots, and when it proved too tough for him, go away to find a friend to help. Together they uprooted the tree and feasted. I have seen elephants help a wounded comrade from the field of battle, and so has Allan Tarlton and others whose word cannot be doubted. If an elephant is wounded and falls to his knees—so long as he does not actually collapse—two other elephants will come along, one on either side of him. Pushing against his body, they not only lift him to his feet but support him as they walk away seeking safety.

Elephants can cause much damage to farms and plantations. They need a tremendous amount of food to keep their hulks going, and the quantity must be extra large since they are vegetarians. They spend about fourteen to sixteen hours a day eating — lazily and slowly, but still eating — with stomachs rumbling. I've passed through spots in the forest where a herd of elephants has been eating; it looks like complete devastation. The forest grows again quickly, but not a farmer's plantings. When herds are repeatedly destructive in a neighborhood, officials sent out professional hunters to drive off the beasts, shooting several if necessary.

Elephants love water. They like to wallow in it and squirt it over themselves. In most places the water is muddy, so elephants regularly coat their hides with mud the color of the earth nearby—making even a creature that large hard to spot sometimes. At Mudanda Rock in Tsavo National Park, for instance, all elephants look pink or red, because that is the color of the earth in that area.

In 1946 I visited Gangala na Bodio, in the northeast Congo, where Belgian authorities had started an elephant training school despite the fact that most people thought African elephants could not be trained for work as Asian elephants can. They had a plentiful supply of the big animals in nearby Gambara National Park, where elephants were protected. And they *had* succeeded in training them.

To catch the elephants they used American cowboy techniques, cutting a few animals away from the herd and lassoing them. But lassoing an elephant, with its long trunk and big ears, is almost impossible, so they went for the leg. Elephants between twelve and twenty years were preferred, because they were old and strong enough to stand the shock of capture, but not too old to learn new tricks.

Lassoed elephants fought hard, and some died of fright or heart attack. So every effort was made to keep the procedure as gentle as possible. The biggest help came from monitor elephants, already trained and reliable. Each monitor had his *mahout*, or *cornac*, as he was called in the Congo. A monitor elephant stood on each side of the captured animal, and a rope was tied around the young elephant's middle and around each monitor's neck. When the captured animal bucked or held back, it hurt the monitors, so they punished him, argued with him, and in some way told him to stop being so stubborn. Meanwhile the cornacs talked soothingly in the way they had learned to talk to elephants. By the time the new elephant got to the school he was usually less rebellious.

Food and plenty of water did a good job for the next few weeks. The captured elephants came to know their cornacs, who brought them their meals each day, hosed them off, filled their pools. Then the training period began. One cornac did the whole job for one elephant, with the help of the monitors. Elephants obviously became fond of their cornacs, even when they were still suspicious of other humans.

Even in 1946 there were beginning to be doubts about how economical elephants would be for working purposes. They required so much food, and took such a long time to eat it, that production was small in proportion to consumption. It was suspected that tractors and bulldozers might be better, even with the high price of gasoline in Africa. Then came uhuru, and the Congolese government abandoned the elephant training program.

On my 1954-1955 expedition we went with Pellegrini on several elephant hunts. First we established a base camp in good elephant country where the animals were not protected—trackless country through which trucks could travel. I would not have dreamed that trucks could ride through places Pellegrini took us, but he could take a truck almost anywhere, usually at a fairly high speed. He skirted swamps, and stopped angrily at ten-foot-deep ravines, but rocks, stumps, underbrush, potholes, streams, and washboard-packed earth did not even slow him down. Twice in one week he broke springs on his truck, but he had spares and replaced them himself, after a full day's chase in the broiling sun.

We usually had Dave Mason in the catching truck, driven by Pellegrini or one of his men, and another cameraman, Freddie Ford, Jr., in a second truck that followed. Men with precious cameras clutch them in their hands, and cannot hold onto anything. At the end of a day's hunting we were all battered and sore.

When Pellegrini spotted a herd in the distance, he examined it carefully. Sometimes he said, "No, we won't go after that one. I don't like it." I never figured out how he reached his conclusions, but once he had chosen a herd as satisfactory, he headed toward it in the trucks, keeping the wind right so the animals would not run away too soon. As he approached, with the truck crashing through the low brush, skipping from furrow to furrow in the hard-baked earth, he picked out the elephant he wanted. While one truck scattered the herd, Pellegrini maneuvered his to cut his choice away from the rest. Finally he came alongside the racing elephant and threw his rope to catch it. If he made it, only a small part of the job had been done. He had to get the elephant in a crate, get the crate loaded on a third truck, drive it fifty miles to a mission where he had built a stockade. Later he would have to move his whole catch — five or six young elephants — to Arusha.

Twice my cameramen were almost killed. Once, after an elephant had been caught, the rope holding it was temporarily tied to the rear of the second truck. Dave Mason was standing with his head, arms, and camera above a hatch in the top of the truck when the captured animal darted for the front of the truck, scraping the rope across the top. With an elephant tugging on it, the rope might well have decapitated Mason if he had not moved like lightning. The rope caught the back of his head, smacked it against the front of the hatch, and scraped over the top of his skull. He fell down in the truck with blood streaming from his nose, half-conscious, but the first thing he looked for was his camera, with the film he had just taken.

Another time, Freddie Ford, Jr., had lashed himself to the struts at the back of the catching truck so he could get some pictures with the truck in motion. In the midst of the cutting-out operation, one of the big elephants became angry and started to chase the catching truck. The driver, intent on the prey ahead, did not realize that he was being pursued, but Freddie, tied securely, saw the angry elephant bearing down on him, getting closer and closer. In spite of the danger, he kept filming the pursuing elephant. The beast came so near that he began stretching out his trunk for Freddie, and the tip of the trunk was only about four feet away. Pellegrini, driving, suddenly realized what was happening and stepped on the gas.

In Africa there was no end to the wild animals. I saw so many that I have to go back to my films to recall all of them. There was the pet eland at Carr Hartley's who took a cigarette gently from my mouth and ate it, the two wise owls there who commented on everything they saw, disapprovingly. There was the lion cub Mike Hartley discovered. We had been out in the truck, and he saw the cub stagger from under a bush. We stopped and looked around cautiously, for a lioness rarely leaves such a young cub alone. She can get papa to baby-sit sometimes, and she can usually find another lioness to take over for her. This time there was no adult lion around, so Mike scooped the cub up in his arms and we went back to the farm. There Mike tried to feed it from a bottle, but the little cat could not figure out what it was supposed to do. Then I recalled a time when I saw a Jivaro headhunter's wife in South America nursing a baby and a puppy at the same time. We went to a camp of the Turkana, where we found a nursing mother. She readily, smilingly, put the lion cub to her breast.

Then there were giraffes, ungainly and ridiculous creatures really, but remarkably graceful as they lope across the plains against the sunset with a rocking-chair gait in slow motion. We went on a giraffe-hunting trip while at Hartley's farm, and filmed the whole bit — lassoing from the end of a pole, slowing to a gradual stop, native helpers dashing out and grabbing the animal by the tail. It was a hard job getting the giraffe into a crate and up into the truck, but he was fairly amenable. And we got a wonderful shot of the animal leaning over to pluck Gordon Pollman's hat from his head just for the fun of it.

There was the baby ostrich that I saw fight its difficult way out of its big eggshell after three days. And on the subject of birds, it took me three trips to get the films I wanted of the beautiful flamingos that feed on three saline lakes in East Africa — Nakura, Elmenteita, and Hannington. I approached a lake, and thought I saw a blanket of pink water lilies strewn over thousands of square yards, moving slightly. Then when I came closer, a few birds on the periphery became disturbed and took off. A flamingo, like most big birds, requires a long runway to be airborne, so the creatures in the middle of the flock could not move at once. The outer edges of pink moved first, with a great whirring of wings and splashing of the water. Then the others gradually followed in a great slow wave that became a pink cloud between me and the setting sun.

We filmed pelicans, egrets, different kinds of ducks, hornbills, cormorants, darters, terns, gulls, eagles, bustards, francolins, grouse and partridge and quail, hummingbirds, sunbirds, widow birds, blackbirds, cuckoos, doves, warblers, Egyptian geese, plovers, herons, crested and other cranes, snake-hunting secretary birds, and parrots of endless variety. But we did not film a single insect, of which there are hundreds of thousands of varieties.

Snakes? Yes. I had seen many, but had decided that filming one was almost impossible, unless it was a python, the only kind big enough to show up on film. On my 1954-1955 trip I found the only man who could help me — Allan Tarlton.

He had been a famous white hunter, but he had one peculiarity — he liked snakes. Most people hate them; Carr Hartley, for example, who fears no animals and makes pets of rhinos and hyenas, has such a sickening aversion to snakes that he must turn over to another man any business involving them.

For thirty years, however, Allan Tarlton had been fascinated by snakes and had kept every African variety in captivity at one time or another. He made a business out of his love of snakes, supplying venom for firms all around the world. At one time he "milked" up to four hundred snakes a day of their venom. He had been bitten many times, and had developed a remarkable immunity, but it had the undesirable effect of altering his blood so that one bee sting might kill him.

When I met Tarlton in Arusha, I asked him if it would be possible to film a python in a scene involving men. He said yes, because a python has sharp teeth and powerful jaws but injects no poison. He kills by clamping his jaws on a victim to hold it, then wraps his tail around a tree or rock to give him leverage, coils his body around his prey and crushes it to death. "Never let a python hook his tail on anything," Tarlton said, "for without that leverage it can't squeeze a lemon. Of course, you try to avoid the bite, too, because it hurts even if it doesn't poison."

But pythons live in thick growths where there is almost no light. Tarlton said he would bring a python out where there *was* light and space. We found a good spot, set up cameras, and Tarlton and his helpers caught a python in the bush, brought it out and placed it on a low branch of a tree. Tarlton and I moved off a way. The cameras started turning as we walked toward the tree and saw the python.

Close-up of python. Decision to capture same. As Tarlton came close, the python suddenly shot its massive head forward, and the man ducked it like an expert boxer, without retreating. The snake coiled its body back for another thrust and again missed Tarlton by inches.

Apparently feeling that it could battle better on the ground, it slithered down the tree trunk and made for us with speed and determination. But now Tarlton had the python where he wanted it. It unleased a vicious blow at the man's legs. He sidestepped it and, with a speed equal to the snake's, grabbed its neck with both hands. A moment later I leapt on the python's body, holding onto its writhing tail for all I was worth. It was sickeningly cold, twice as thick as my arm, and had amazing strength. But I held on. The natives ran up with a gunnysack and with their help we shoved the writhing python inside.

In the years after my *Zanzabuku* expedition, I read more and more articles about the depletion of wild game in Africa. According to the articles, the game population declined dramatically after the achievement of independence by many African nations. Some governments could not or would not carry out conservation measures.

It was hard to believe that things were as bad as newspapers and magazines said. But when I returned in 1964, I drove a thousand miles through the northeastern Congo, including a trip across the Albert National Park, once teeming with game. I saw almost no wild animals on that entire trip. There were many reasons. For one thing, tribes that had been relocated at the time the park was created thought that *uhuru* meant they could return to their ancient hunting grounds. Many of them did, and the central government, facing a multitude of problems and civil war, made only feeble attempts to keep the Congo's parks intact. Poachers streamed in by the hundreds, killing mainly for meat. European game authorities were ousted or replaced by inexperienced Africans. I hate to say it, but I would not be surprised to see the Congo lose its best game preserves and much of its game.

In Uganda things were much better, for the government was maintaining the Queen Elizabeth Park despite a great increase in poaching. It was learning, too, that the park attracted tourists, and tourists brought money.

Colonel Mervyn Cowie, director of parks in Kenya, was worried, though the government was becoming convinced of the necessity of preserving wild game.

"Of course the game has decreased tremendously," he told me. "There were areas I knew as a young man that literally teemed with game, where there are no animals now. Much land has been taken over for farms and ranches. That's necessary, of course, because Kenya needs food. Some people say that the animals that used to roam on farm lands have gone into the parks, but we know the park population has not increased. We must zone all land in Kenya, with certain areas for farming and ranching, others for the total protection of wild life."

The New York Zoological Society has recently donated a small airplane for the use of the game wardens, and both Cowie and David Sheldrick had learned to fly it. Sheldrick told me it was useful in Tsavo National Park for tracing animal movements, estimating populations, checking on water supplies, and spotting poachers.

Poaching is a most serious problem, with elephants and rhinos being the chief prey in East Africa. Rhino horn has become more valuable than ivory, for hundreds of thousands of people in Asia believe that ground rhino horn is a powerful aphrodisiac. And it is really not even horn, but hard, compacted hair. A poacher may get ten to twenty pounds for a rhino horn, the trader who ships it out forty or fifty, and the eventual seller of the powdered product hundreds. So it is a profitable though illegal business, as is the selling and export of elephant tusks.

Carr Hartley thought the punishment for poaching had to be more severe in Kenya, as the customary ten-pound fine, plus perhaps two months in jail, was an insufficient deterrent. In Tanganyika fines had been increased to a hundred to two hundred pounds, plus two or three years in jail. Both Hartley and Cowie agreed that the real villain was not the poacher so much as the trader, or middleman, who rarely got caught.

Everyone agreed that the game situation in Tanganyika was the best in East Africa. But there were serious problems in addition to poaching.

"The human and animal populations are increasing," August Kuenzler told me. "Both need more water and in many areas it is scarce. We must have more farm land and more park land, both. The government is trying hard and generally doing a good job."

Carr Hartley agreed. He and his four sons were working on a great conservation project for the Tanganyika government — catching rhinos and moving them to a large island in Lake Victoria. The inhabitants of a few fishing villages there were relocated on the lake shore. Rubanda is an island of fifty-eight thousand acres, with plenty of vegetation and water. The government was planning an airstrip and lodges for tourists, and in time the five-day lake boat-trip would include Rubanda in its itinerary.

"As the rhinos increase," Hartley said, "we can take off breeding pairs to restock other parks. And we'll have other animals on the island, too — elephants, and almost everything but carnivores."

On another island Hartley and the government plan to put cheetahs, fast becoming extinct. But since they are meat eaters, the island must also have "Tommies" and other antelopes, and wild pigs. With experiment and study, a natural balance can be achieved.

So there is hope for the wild life of East Africa. In 1964 it was a joy to be driven through the Nairobi Park by Colonel Cowie. Then I drove down to Arusha, and a group of giraffes loped across the road in front of my car. At Lake Manyara Park I saw a pristine forest with much game — elephants, hippos, giraffes. I saw a leopard at close range stalking some impala, who spotted him just in time.

I drove to Kuenzler's farm for a visit, during which I learned that Pellegrini had left him to buy a coffee plantation with some Italian friends. But he was not too happy out of the animal-catching business.

I stopped at the Namanga Rest House where Cézaire and I had tarried in 1937, and ate the same food — beer and avocadoes. I wanted to see Cézaire again on my 1964 trip, but learned that he had recently died after an operation. I heard that Ace DuPreez had moved to South Africa when the Mara Valley became a national park. And I saw Mike Hartley, a husky, handsome young man, with his bride, a singularly beautiful girl.

Jan Smuts was right when, in 1936, he urged people to come to Africa before it was too late. In less than three decades, the primitive world has almost disappeared. Millions of Africans were skipping ten thousand years in their leap from the Stone Age to the Atomic Age.

But there were still trouble spots — the Portuguese territories, South Africa and Rhodesia are festering sores; their futures are at best uncertain. Not all African countries have rich resources. Many are small, arid and barely capable at present of producing scant crops and lean livestock. Faced with a steady increase in population, even the well-endowed nations are finding that economic development is proving to be far more difficult than the winning of political independence. In addition, many governments have proved unstable, as has been evidenced by the military takeover in the Republic of the Congo, Nigeria and in several other countries. There are quite a number of able leaders who are gaining rapidly in maturity and competence, but among other problems they are faced with inveterate conflicting tribal loyalties. But the people of Africa have energy, adaptability and determination, and though there will doubtless be more strife, bloodletting and crises, eventually progress and some degree of stability should result. Unfortunately, I cannot say this about some other areas of the world where I have witnessed the gradual end of the Stone Age. In these places the hand of civilization has brought sickness, death, lethargy, despair.

The wild animal life of Africa will never again be what it was when Carr Hartley was a young man. He told me that within a few miles of his farm, he could have been blindfolded, whirled around, and told to shoot — and he would have hit some wild creature. But there will still be much wild game protected in vast parks or preserves in Uganda, Kenya, Tanganyika, and perhaps elsewhere. These sanctuaries will be an increasingly alluring tourist attraction, unlike anything to be found elsewhere in the world.

But there are no parks for the preservation of Stone Age man except the Ituri Forest. This will be the last retreat of true primitives — my friends, the Bambuti Pygmies. It will be a long, long time before they join the rest of the world.

II
SOUTH AMERICA

ATLANTIC OCEAN

VENEZUELA

COLOMBIA

Negro River

Quito

ECUADOR

Pifuayal
Iquitos

Barranca
Borja

Marañón River

Amazon River

Manáos

Madeira River

Tapajós River

Xingu River

BRAZIL

Belém

PERU

Lima

Cuzco

MATO
GROSSO

Rio das Mortes

Tocantins River

Bahia

Lake
Titicaca

La Paz

BOLIVIA

Cuiabá

São Lourenço

Brasília

PARAGUAY

Paraná River

Paraná River

São Paulo

Rio de Janeiro

CHILE

ARGENTINA

PACIFIC OCEAN

SCALE IN MILES
0   200   500

COLORADO
INDIANS

JIVARO
INDIANS

YAGUA
INDIANS

UPPER
XINGU
TRIBES

BORORO
INDIANS

1

Curaka Chumbika

THE YEAR was 1940, and Europe was at war. Hitler's troops had swarmed over France, and it looked as if the whole world would be engulfed soon. Walls would be built over which no traveler could leap, and if I went anywhere it would probably be at Uncle Sam's direction and in his uniform. If I were going to get in one more expedition, I'd better hurry.

In 1939 I had spent a month in Mexico, visiting and filming ancient Aztec and Mayan ruins, about which I had been reading. This led me to more reading about ancient civilizations in Latin America, and inevitably I went from ancient cultures to primitive peoples. There were many in South America that fascinated me, most of all the headhunting Jivaros living in a vast wilderness on the eastern slopes of the Andes, where the headwaters of the Amazon rose.

In two weeks I arranged business matters with my secretary, Louise Smith, booked airplane passage to Quito and Lima, bought four thousand feet of 16-millimeter Kodachrome, and engaged in enlightening but all too brief talks with Dr. Herbert Dickey, who had lived a quarter of a century in South America, and Dr. Harvey Bassler of the American Museum of Natural History. Both suggested interesting tribes to visit, and both doubted that I could reach the Jivaro country. The area has been in dispute between Peru and Ecuador for more than a hundred years, and at that moment the dispute was growing hot. It would be difficult to get official permission from either government, but I decided to try it.

At Quito I learned that I might be allowed to climb over the Andes and down into the land of the Jivaros, so far as the government was concerned, but it might not be worth it. Two emphatic and opposed warnings were given me — if I went one way I'd find headhunters so "tamed" by contact with civilization that I'd see no true primitives; if I took another route I might never come back, as the Jivaros in that section bore an active resentment toward white men.

"Go in the front door," I was advised, "from the Amazon side, through the Pongo de Manseriche. There have been few killings over there since the Borja settlement was wiped out in 1865 — except for isolated incidents with rubber workers around the turn of the century."

So I flew down to Lima, where I was fortunate enough to meet President Prado of Peru. I not only received government permission to visit the Jivaro country but was told that a navy plane would be at my disposal in Iquitos, a Peruvian town on the upper Amazon. An American pilot in Lima warned me against crossing the Andes in the antiquated Peruvian planes—and it was no fun to be flying in a cloud and suddenly see a mountain peak materialize straight ahead. But the rather casual and relaxed pilot felt his way through safely — only, I feel sure, because I sucked in my breath at the right moments.

In Iquitos I suffered for one full week from that greatest affliction of the explorer, official red tape and delay. The authorities in the isolated frontier town were unconcerned about certain requests from the capital. They were courteous, kindly, friendly, but they saw no reason for hurrying. The government man sent me to the army, the army to the navy, the navy back to the government man. During this time I enjoyed the company of young Lieutenant Benavides, the handsome navy pilot who was to fly me up close to Jivaro country. The town was interesting for a day or two, but then I had seen it all. It was a relic of the great rubber boom of decades before, when the forest around the upper Amazon and its tributaries supplied most of the rubber for the world. Peruvians, Moroccans, Chinese, Spaniards, Italians, Germans, British, and Americans had joined the Amazon rubber rush, as they had followed gold rushes all over the world. When the Malay and Dutch East Indies plantations began producing rubber, the bubble burst and Iquitos shrank to a frontier town doing a small trade in mahogany, tagua nuts, copper, and Sea Island cotton.

I played cards, made friends, bothered officials, ran into my old friend Ruth Harkness, who had brought the first giant panda back from Asia — and lost my movie camera!

I was in a small launch filming the river life. The Bell and Howell was set up on a tripod, its heavy telephoto lens in place, and I scanned the shoreline for good background shots. Suddenly the bow of the launch was caught in a small whirlpool and whipped sideways. I grabbed the gunwale, the Indian at the wheel shouted, and I turned to see the tripod tipping over. I lunged, and just touched the tip of one leg as camera and tripod hit the rail and dove into the water.

The water was too deep and the current too swift to think of trying to recover it. I was crestfallen. Moviemaking was not then my primary objective, but I had never traveled without taking pictures.

There wouldn't be a 16-millimeter motion picture camera in Iquitos, I felt sure; and it would take weeks, at least, to have one sent in. But I told people about my loss and someone finally mentioned an old English trader who had once owned a movie camera. I found the company for which he worked and there learned that he was upriver for several weeks. Yes, he had a movie camera, sometimes took it with him on his trips. I went to the trader's house and talked with his Indian wife. After much pleading, she searched through an old trunk and came up with an old-fashioned Ciné-Kodak.

She wouldn't sell it, but she would lend it. I gave her a hundred-dollar deposit to insure return of the camera, and went back to bothering the officials. I had no way of knowing if the camera would work.

An official for whom everyone had been waiting returned to Iquitos from wherever he had been. I got my permission at last, and Lieutenant Benavides, mechanic Serafio, and I took off in the single-engined, pontoon-equipped plane, pointed toward the headwaters of the Amazon and Jivaro country.

After five hours of flying we reached Borja late in the afternoon. Borja was only an army post, but there had once been a town there. In 1865 Peru had encouraged its establishment, transporting a hundred settlers and their families with supplies and equipment by steamer; the steamer was to return every six months. At the end of the first six months the steamer found a bustling little town. Houses had been built, crops planted. Six months later it found charred ruins already being covered by jungle growth. There were a good many bones, too, mostly of men. The Jivaro Huambiasas had burned the town, killed the men and old women, taken the younger women and a few children along with them. Nobody had ever tried again to build a town so close to the Jivaros. The army post was there not to disturb the Indians but to keep an Ecuadorian post out.

The officers at Borja greeted me warmly, for they rarely saw a new face. They brought me a guide, a *mestizo* or half-breed, named José, who would take me into Jivaro country and, we trusted, out again. The army post's launch was to carry me through the Pongo de Manseriche and up the Santiago River about sixty miles, after which we'd have to walk.

The Pongo is a deep gorge through which plunge the gathered waters of many mighty rivers that have joined to start the Amazon on its trip to the Atlantic Ocean, three thousand miles away. In its short course through the Pongo, this torrent forms many small and two mighty whirlpools, the latter named by the Indians Atun Huacangui (Thou Shalt Weep Greatly) and Asua Huacangui (Thou Shalt Weep Bitterly).

The launch navigates these turbulent terrors, one at a time, by sticking its prow into the swirling circle at just the right point, getting itself jerked around to a near crash against the rocky wall of the gorge, then emerging from the tugging pull of the waters on the other side. And that is the trick! Getting *into* a whirlpool is easy. Getting out requires perfect timing and steering and a sudden burst of power from the engines. You might think you'd have another chance going around if you didn't make it the first time, as on a merry-go-round. You would, but your launch would then be further from the rim and closer to the vortex and going faster. We made it through both big whirlpools the first time.

Once through the Pongo, the trip was easy enough, although the launch had to work hard against the strong current of the Santiago. And in time I was walking along a jungle path chosen by José, followed by two bearers with some equipment and some gifts I hoped would please the men I was about to visit. But what would please a man who cuts off another man's head, shrinks it to the size of his fist, and then dances around it?

I trudged up a hill, keeping my eyes on the broad, leathery bare feet of the guide. In the Jivaro country, the earth, which has lain flat and even throughout most of the Amazon basin, begins hunching itself up into rolling hillocks, as if preparing for its mighty leap upward to the twenty-thousand-foot peaks of the Andes, just a few miles to the west. I was walking up and down almost as much as forward, and the sweat streamed down my face and neck, occasionally engulfing some of the smaller insects that swarmed in for a bite.

A sudden chattering and scolding from the branches above startled me, and I stopped a moment to watch a troupe of reddish-brown howler monkeys scatter, turning occasionally to glare venomously and squeak indignant protests at having been disturbed. As I looked up, a small splash of red caught my eye, a welcome sight after the monotony of green — light green, dark green, medium green, glossy green, dull green, but always green. It was an orchid exploring for sunlight near the tops of the mighty trees. I didn't expect to see many during the dry season, when the rainfall drops to a low of eight or nine inches a month. As we walked on I saw other darting spots of bright color, toucans, parakeets, and blue and yellow macaws that squawked at us.

We had been walking about an hour and a half when it happened. Maybe I was growing tired and careless about watching my step, but I don't think even a native would have seen it. My guide missed it because he was lopping off an elephant-ear that grew in his path. I stepped around the huge leaf and into nothingness. One moment my feet were on the good solid earth. The next instant they were treading air, kicking for a footing that didn't exist. As I crashed downward, I felt a sharp blow against my right leg, another against my side; I heard cloth tearing and the crunch of breaking wood.

Sprawled awkwardly at the bottom of a pit about four feet deep and three feet square, I looked up to see the three frightened faces of my guide and bearers peering down at me. I sat still for a moment while my heart found its way back to its accustomed place, but when I felt the stinging bites of the red ants crawling up my arm I scrambled to my feet. José pulled me from the pit and I took inventory of myself. No broken bones. Not even a sprained ankle. My right trouser leg was ripped about six inches, revealing scraped skin but no blood. My side felt as if it had been hit with a baseball bat, but the ribs were intact.

My hand still clutched the old movie camera. It must have banged the bottom pretty hard and now I would be even more doubtful of it. José was lying flat on the ground, fishing with a stick for my hat, which sat jauntily on top of a broken lance. When he retrieved it, I examined the pit. Three hardwood lances with very sharp points had been imbedded in the bottom, points upward. They had poked and scratched me, but had broken under my weight. José looked worried, however, and got one of the broken lances for examination, scrutinizing the sharp end closely. He smiled and handed it to me. It was so old that whatever poison might have been on the tip was ineffective.

I hadn't thought of that, although I had heard of these Jivaro man-traps, with lance-ends dipped in curare. The *mosertinyu whua*, or hole of death, was dug on a path along which a clan might expect attackers to come. Covered with twigs and leaves, it was almost impossible to detect, especially at night when most Jivaros stage their raids.

For a moment I wondered if we might walk into a *tambunchi* trap, too — eight short chonta palm spikes fixed to a strong sapling bent back like a bow and secured by a thin liana. Another connecting liana on the ground releases the spring when a trespasser's foot touches it, and the spikes tear into his face or chest. Then I concluded that any such trap would probably be as old as the pit, and the liana would long since have rotted.

We resumed our journey, but I noticed that even José walked a bit more cautiously and that his eyes constantly darted from path to trees and back to path again. He appeared puzzled, too, and hesitated once or twice as if uncertain of where to go next. When I asked him if something was wrong, he said the path had not been used for a long time but that we should be close to the house, *jivaria*, of a chief named Cajeke.

We went forward again, and soon saw the faintest hint of light ahead — and that meant a clearing. José started calling "*Whe-dee! Whe-dee!*" to tell our unexpectant hosts that friends were arriving.

I joined in with fervent *whe-dee*'s of my own, for as the moment drew near for the meeting I had traveled so far to attend, I felt the usual butterflies in my stomach. The time of greatest concern in dealing with a hostile group is the first moment of contact. Indeed, the hostility may come flying through the air in the form of a bullet or an arrow even before you think you have made contact, as the natives are sure to have heard the crashing, bumbling approach of the white stranger long before he sees or hears them. In the case of the Jivaros, shouting "I come! I come!" was a reasonably sure safety device. Many Jivaros dislike white men, but they are worried primarily about other Jivaro enemies, who never announce their approach but prefer to creep silently in the night.

You might think that clever and alert Indians, never loath to use deceit against an enemy, would take to shouting false *whe-dee*'s as they came to attack. Such tactics, however, would violate the Jivaro's nature and tradition too much. The only way to fight, he is convinced, is by stealth and ambush. The deceit would also destroy a valuable tool of communication. Some Indians do travel, for one reason or another, beyond their clan's territory; others get together for a truce talk occasionally, especially if they want to combine forces against a more threatening enemy. Two feuding tribes called off their own hostilities just one year and four months after I trudged up the hill shouting hopeful *whe-dee*'s. The purpose was to massacre seventy-seven placer miners who had stepped a bit too far into Jivaro territory. After wiping out the gold-seekers, as Jivaros had been doing for three hundred and fifty years, they probably resumed their own feud. Meanwhile the *whe-dee* had been useful to them.

José slowed down, but I was right on his heels, looking over his shoulder eagerly for my first sight of headhunters, expecting to see a cluster of men with ready weapons. But I saw no one! I stood at the edge of the clearing. Near the center of the three- or four-acre area stood the jivaria, or *hea*, communal house of an Indian family.

We walked toward the house. The jivaria was about sixty feet long and thirty-five or forty feet wide, with parallel sides and rounded ends. The walls, made of tough chonta poles imbedded in the ground and lashed together with lianas, were about ten feet high. The roof, sloping down from a center ridgepole, was thickly thatched with palm leaves and extended over the walls, making eaves about two feet deep. I could see a narrow door at the end nearest us, made of two thick slabs of wood. It was closed tight. I asked José where everyone was.

"They have gone," José said. "Cajeke is dead!"

Cajeke was the *curaka*, chief of his clan. But how did José know he was dead? The guide pointed to the overgrown clearing, reminded me of the little-used path and the neglected pitfall.

"They would not leave this house unless Cajeke had died," José said. "He is inside, and his people have built another house somewhere else."

I wanted to see. While José and the bearers stayed behind, I walked to the door, which was kept shut by two big rocks. Crude figures of animals and humans were scrawled on the door to ward off evil spirits. I moved the rocks, swung the heavy door, and stepped inside. It was so dark that I could see almost nothing until my eyes adjusted themselves, but my nose twitched against the musty smell of decay.

First I saw, near the walls on either side, the wide platforms that served as beds. Next the tall chonta trunks that supported the ridgepole of the house. And then I saw Cajeke. I could not see the curaka himself, of course, but I knew that he must be inside the canoe that hung on end from the roof. The top of the canoe had been covered with bark and palm leaves tied in place with vines, so the body was completely enclosed. Some Jivaros put the bodies in hollowed-out logs, others in a kind of bamboo coffin; but no matter what the receptacle, it was usually hung from the roof of the jivaria — a chief in an upright position, an ordinary man in horizontal position. Cajeke slept upright, like a good curaka.

I stepped closer to the covered canoe and saw the pottery jars, from which a squirrel whisked away in fright. Here Cajeke's family had left food and *nijimanche*, the fermented manioc beer that is the staff of life for all headhunters. Tied to the upright nearest Cajeke's coffin stood his blowgun, and suspended from hooks were a sheaf of darts, a gourd of cotton, and a small gourd of poison. Near at hand was the dead warrior's lance.

By this time I could see fairly well in the dim light. At the far end of the house there were other platform beds partially enclosed with bamboo walls. These were the beds in the women's section. There was little else to see — a bench or two, the cold gray ashes at the ends of three logs arranged like the spokes of a wheel. The rest of the house had been stripped. It was clean and neat, the hard-packed earth floor appearing to have been swept carefully.

I went outside, and José told me he had found the path to the new jivaria. I told him I had seen fresh bananas inside.

"Yes, they leave food every month for two years," José said. "They know he is grateful for the food and nijimanche because he has eaten it when they come."

I thought of the squirrel I had seen. There were doubtless other visitors, too, and the liquids would evaporate in a month. But I said nothing of this to José. "Why do they keep it up for two years?" I asked.

"It takes two years for him to be a jaguar," José answered simply.

"Oh, so Cajeke is a jaguar now," I said. I knew that the Jivaros believed in the transmigration of souls.

"Probably he is a jaguar," José said. "He was a brave curaka who had taken many heads, so he could be a jaguar if he wanted. And it takes two years for a jaguar to grow enough to take care of himself in the jungle. That is why they can stop taking food after two years. He can take care of himself then."

"But I thought the Indians feared and hated the jaguar," I said. "They try to kill it. Doesn't that mean Cajeke's family might kill him a couple of years from now?"

"Oh, no, for Cajeke will go to the land of the hated Aguarunas and trouble them," José explained. The Jivaro plans to go on attacking his enemies even after death.

We walked down the hill from the abandoned jivaria, across a short stretch of flat land, leaped over a tiny stream, climbed up and down another hill. After about three miles José suddenly started calling *whe-dee!* again.

José stopped suddenly at the edge of a clearing. I looked over his shoulder and saw a strong and sturdy Indian standing alone about ten feet in front of the door to a jivaria. He wore only his *itipi*, a kind of wraparound skirt reaching from waist to just below his knees. His dark hair was banged over the eyes and parted into three short braids on sides and back. Toucan feathers hung in the rear braid, their bright colors vivid even at a distance.

I saw three women and two children scurrying through a door at the other end of the jivaria, looking over their shoulders as they disappeared. Then from the other side of the clearing appeared three more men, who stopped when they saw us. Two carried blowguns and one a single-barreled shotgun. They watched and waited — for a clue, I thought, from the man in front of the jivaria. He had no weapon, but his angry scowl was as piercing as a chonta lance.

"Chumbika," José said to me quietly.

"What's that?" I asked, almost in a whisper, feeling as if I should not move or speak under the searching look of the first live head-hunter I had ever seen.

"Chumbika," José repeated. "Cajeke's son. He is curaka now."

The young Jivaro chief turned and strode into the jivaria, leaving the door open behind him. The men on the edge of the clearing seemed to relax a bit but did not move. Instead I saw them reach into little satchels of monkey fur which were slung over their shoulders. They began to comb their hair!

"Chumbika has left the door open," José said. "That means we are welcome to enter the house. But maybe we should wait a few minutes, to give him a chance to dress up."

The three warriors who had probably been returning from a hunt were now smearing red dye on their faces, the kind made from achiote seeds and used by many South American tribes. As we walked toward the door of the jivaria, I saw one putting bright feathers in his hair, another arranging a collar around his neck.

José stepped through the door first. I followed and then came our two bearers. We stood just inside the door, and I peered ahead in the dim light. Chumbika, I saw, had taken a moment to adorn himself with a beautiful crown of multicolored feathers. He sat on a stool near one of the center supporting poles of the house, facing us but not looking at us. He was busy sharpening a chonta lance with a shell.

Beside him sat another man, wearing a crown of monkey fur. His wrinkled face was covered with reddish-brown achiote dye and many broad black lines. He was busy weaving on a loom about three feet square, passing the shuttle rapidly back and forth.

Neither man spoke a word or indicated in any way that he was aware of our presence. José sat on a stool to the left of the narrow door, and I sat on a platform bed just a little to the right. The two bearers, at José's direction, moved to the other side of him, put their bundles on the ground, and squatted beside them, leaning against the walls.

I was uneasy, but not really apprehensive, for I was confident that a white man who came to the Jivaros unarmed, bearing gifts, seeking neither gold nor women, would be safe. There was always a chance, of course, that if there had recently been death, illness, or serious accident in the clan, the visitor might be blamed. To the Jivaro, bad things are caused by bad spirits sent by some enemy, known or unknown.

I looked around at the other Jivaros in the house, searching for a face in which I might find that flicker of warmth that sometimes flashes between two strangers. But no one was looking at me. The three men who had been hunting came in the door, put away their weapons carefully, then took seats against the wall at the left, saying nothing to anyone. At the other end of the house I could see women bustling about — there must have been more than a dozen of them, of all ages. An equal number of young children were there, too, and about four dogs, scrawny and abject, tied to the beds in the women's section.

After a ten-minute silence, one of the women walked from the other end of the jivaria, took up a gourd or bowl, and filled it with a liquid from a very large pottery jar that stood on the floor not far from Chumbika. She took the bowl to José, who drank deeply from it. As I watched, I realized how thirsty I was.

"This is nijimanche," I told myself, "beer made from the yuca, chewed by the women, spat into a bowl, fermented by their saliva. Can I drink it?"

The woman brought the bowl to me, and I took it in both hands. I wanted a drink badly, and I thought that I should drink anyway, for the sake of courtesy. I put the bowl to my lips and took a tentative sip. The taste of the nijimanche wasn't bad at all! It had quite a rich, malty flavor. I took a deeper drink, not even thinking about how it was made. People are silly about such things anyway, I told myself. What's wrong with saliva?

Still no one had spoken. The woman took bowls of nijimanche to the two bearers, and then retired to the women's section of the house, where I saw a fire burning and heard pots boiling. The women turned and looked at me curiously once in a while, and made comments to each other and laughed.

Suddenly I felt tired and impatient. Had I gone through all this just to sit and say nothing? A formal greeting according to the established Jivaro custom was well and good, but this was carrying things too far. What could possibly be the purpose behind a silly custom like this?

My eyes were heavy, almost closing. I had sat there, I suppose, no more than fifteen minutes, but it seemed like hours. I yawned heavily. Chumbika put down the lance — I thought that by this time he should have whittled it down to the end. The young curaka stood up, dignified, strong, defiant. He took his stool, stepped in front of José, put the stool on the ground, and sat down. He still did not look at José.

"*Winiti!*" he shouted loudly, as I almost jumped off my platform. Had I known then that the word meant something like "I see you have come," I would have been delighted. But I felt that the word was part of the traditional method of greeting a stranger. I learned later that Chumbika had waited more than the normal time before speaking just because he was disturbed at our arrival, for reasons I did not know until the next day.

José knew that Chumbika's one word had been the signal that he could talk, so he began to talk, in a voice as loud and unnatural as Chumbika's. I saw José stumble now and then, searching for a word, heard him lapse into Spanish. The Indians did not seem to notice, for they were paying no attention at all. From the bits of Spanish I heard I could tell that José was talking about my coming to Borja in the big bird, about going through the Pongo in the launch, about our trip through the jungle.

Chumbika's right fist was clenched, with the knuckles held against his lips. Occasionally he spat through his fingers vigorously. As José kept on talking, Spanish taking over more and more from the Jivaro tongue, Chumbika began to smack his lips and make clucking noises with his tongue, spitting more and more frequently. Then he started interjecting short grunts when José paused briefly to catch his breath. The grunts turned out to be words — "*Tsa!*" and "*Ho!*" and "*Tcah!*" It seemed as if he were making comments on the tale José told — "Is that so" and "No! You don't say." And that is exactly what he was doing, even though he did not comprehend all of José's words.

My guide's shrill recital came to an abrupt end, but Chumbika allowed only a few seconds of silence. He began to speak, loudly, insistently. The ceremonial nature of this whole business was evident in the way he spoke.

Chumbika orated somewhat longer than José had, and finally stopped with the same abruptness, turning and going to the big jar of nijimanche for a drink. José rose from his stool, sighed, and smiled at me.

"It is all right now," he said, and walked over to speak to one of the other men in the house. The ceremony was over, and I knew that I could move about the house freely — except for going to the women's section — and make myself at home.

I stood up to stretch, feeling rather left out of things even if I did have the freedom of the house. I knew that Jivaros are generally hospitable and warmhearted, filled with good spirits most of the time. Therefore it was apparent that Chumbika was more than just conventional. He was definitely not friendly, as his first scowl had indicated. He had returned to his stool after drinking, and was talking with the old fellow, who still worked at his loom. I looked at him, hoping that he would glance in my direction, perhaps smile, give me a chance to get acquainted. But he studiously kept his eyes away from me. Then I noticed something I had not seen before: several new scars — they might have been severe burns — on his right arm and on his chest. The right cheek looked burned, too. Perhaps José could learn later what had happened to the young warrior.

Then I remembered the gifts. I should have distributed them just as soon as the formalities had ended. The bearers opened the bundles as I directed, and most of the Jivaros crowded around, men, women, and children — except for Chumbika. Even the leathery-faced old one left his loom to get his share. They did not push or crowd, but they were eager. I handed mirrors to the men, who are much more concerned about their appearance than the women, to whom I gave safety pins and beads. The safety pin is one product of civilization they can understand and appreciate. For the kids I had colored marbles, which they loved, and rubber balls in which they were uninterested.

I turned to another bundle and took out some fishhooks and scissors, then a dozen pieces of red cloth which I handed around. I should have brought twice as much cloth, obviously. Each Indian took solemnly what I handed him, examined it carefully and said nothing. They expected presents from visitors as a matter of course. Their appreciation would be shown in practical ways later, if they were pleased. I got more reaction than I expected when I had handed around my last gift but one. These were cigarette papers and small sacks of tobacco. The Jivaros grow tobacco and make long rolled cigars or, more frequently, infusions of tobacco and water which they snuff up their noses or drink. But they knew about cigarettes and were rather adept at rolling their own. When some men started to light them at the fires in the hea, I took out my lighter. It created a sensation, and I knew they could not have seen one before. They chattered to each other about it, laughed and exclaimed each time I closed it and lit it again. Even Chumbika, who had joined in none of the gift-taking, looked up at it.

At that moment I took to Chumbika the knife I had brought along. He took it without glancing at me, looked carefully at the blade, tested it with his finger soberly, and then started sharpening his lance with it. That meant he liked it, but he showed no change in his attitude toward me.

Most of the men, women, and children were drinking nijimanche now, and there was a general buzz of conversation interspersed with a good deal of pleasant and easy laughter. The women brought forward jars of food and everyone ate — boiled yuca, the tuber that supplies so much food and drink for millions of people in the Amazon basin, and monkey stew. Meat stew is meat stew, and its tastiness depends upon the meat. Monkey meat is good. My chief objection to the stew was to a little arm and hand I saw floating around in it.

Despite the general feeling of friendliness that filled the jivaria, Chumbika remained quiet and aloof. At one time I saw a woman, probably one of his wives, approach him and speak to him as if urging him to throw off his hostility. She pointed at me once as she talked, at which he scowled angrily and spoke heatedly. He kept showing her the scars or burns on his arms and chest as he did so. I could not figure it out.

I decided it was time to try "Milonguita." There was one rather bulky item that remained in the bundles, a freakish kind of thing to haul into a tropical jungle on a visit to headhunters. I would never have owned the gadget but for my enforced stay of a week in Iquitos with almost nothing to do but fume at delay. I bought gifts for the Indians and a few supplies at different trading posts in the little town. When I had everything I needed, I still went back to look around once in a while because such places can be as fascinating as a Sears Roebuck catalogue. I was in Powers y Cia. one afternoon just before permission to travel finally was granted, and I heard a song — a song that I had first heard many years before in Buenos Aires. It was a tango, "Milonguita."

A clerk was playing an ancient phonograph that must have been on the shelves since the days of the first rubber booms. It was bulky compared with modern machines, but not too heavy — a table model that would have been called a portable if a handle had been attached. It was hand-wound, of course, and the tone was certainly tinny.

On an impulse I bought the machine and the three records Powers had on hand. Telling myself I was crazy, I decided to take it along on the trip because I always liked to take something different from the usual gifts of mirrors, beads, scissors, fishhooks. The old phonograph was it.

When everyone finished eating I got out the phonograph and the records. They all gathered around and watched me, although it was now growing dark and it was not easy to see inside the jivaria.

I put the phonograph on the platform bed, cranked it up, put on "Milonguita," and placed the needle in the groove. There was complete silence in the house until the music of a dance band sprang into the quiet air. Everyone jumped back, and out of the corner of my eye I saw Chumbika sit up and stare at the phonograph.

There was a minute of low talk, embarrassed and uneasy laughs, and then silence again. As the lilting melody unfolded and the steady, rhythmic beat of the tango repeated itself, smiles came to faces here and there. Next came what was bound to come — a rhythmic shake of the head or hand. A few of the women's bodies began to sway, and I fixed my eyes on Chumbika's feet. When the record was half finished, his left foot began to tap in tempo. By the time the record had ended, he was standing and shuffling both feet. And he was almost smiling.

When the Indians were sure the song had ended there was a noisy hubbub of amazement and pleasure. I took the record off and put on another, a Quechua Indian song recorded in Lima. It was strange and weird and haunting, with the rhythm a steady drumbeat. The Jivaros liked it, and most of them were dancing in an unorganized way within a minute. Some of the women dashed back to their quarters and put on the belts of tinkling shells that they wore for their own dances.

I was very uncertain about the third record, but they saw I had a third, so there was no getting out of playing it. They waited quietly, expectantly, happily, as I put it in place. Then I watched their faces to see just how they would like Rudy Vallee singing the "Maine Stein Song."

At first it puzzled them. Nothing could have been much farther from their own music, which is rather monotonous, with very few tones used. But there was a steady beat and that began to move them. They seemed to sense that there was a rousing, inspiriting quality in the song, and it made them dance as if they were marching. Chumbika was particularly pleased with the "Stein Song." He shuffled forward and back rather awkwardly, with an entranced expression on his face.

I had to play those records over many times that evening. I was exhausted and wanted to go to sleep, but the Indians were enjoying themselves too much. I began to get pretty sick even of "Milonguita" and my eyes were closing. It was Chumbika himself who finally noticed my fatigue and ended proceedings. I lay down on the bed by the door next to José and was asleep in minutes. I remember thinking as I fell into oblivion, that I had not yet seen a shrunken head.

I awoke the next morning to the sound of talk among the women, boiling pots, the bark of a dog, a squabble between two children, men moving about — the usual noises of a large and busy household. But the moment I sat up I knew I was in a Jivaro house and nowhere else, and that I had slept on a Jivaro bed. My legs felt as if they had been broken just below the knees. For a Jivaro bed is wide and short — even shorter than the Indians themselves. They average around five feet five inches, I'd guess; but their platform beds are just under five feet long, with a pole at the same height about five inches beyond the foot of the platform. The Jivaro lies on his bed, rests his feet on the horizontal bar, and in chilly weather has them warmed by the embers of a fire that burns on the floor beneath.

I had to put my legs on the crossbar at the bottom, but being somewhat taller than the Indians, it hit me just below the knees. I stamped my legs back to life as I looked around. José and the bearers were already up and eating together. I assumed that most of the Jivaros had already eaten, for they rise with the dawn or before, and it was a little later than that now. I ate some boiled yuca and stepped outside to look for Chumbika. He was talking with some of the other men. In the bright sunlight I could see his many scars easily. They were not old but they were ugly, some having healed badly and irregularly, with black and blue stains under the new skin.

Chumbika turned and saw me, smiled and stretched out an arm as if in greeting. José joined us and I was able to ask, through him, if I might film some of the activities of the day. I was particularly interested in footage of hunting with the blowgun.

Many primitive people dislike cameras. They don't understand them and fear strange and probably magic black boxes with eyes pointed at them. Some that do understand feel that a picture is somehow part of them, and that the man who has taken a picture has taken away some precious soul or life essence. Chumbika and his fellows, however, seemed completely indifferent and perhaps even a little pleased at the idea. I explained that I wanted a shot of them starting off into the jungle carrying their blowguns. José translated well enough for them to understand. Chumbika nodded and went into the jivaria for his blowgun. The others were already armed, with gracefully tapered blowguns about ten feet long, and dart quivers and cotton gourds slung over their shoulders.

As Chumbika stepped from the jivaria, I trained the old camera on him. He walked toward me, straight and serious — a fine shot of a handsome, dignified hunter. Suddenly the camera began to vibrate, with a sound like the death rattle of an ancient alarm clock. I swore to myself. Was it going to give out at my first try? I shook it futilely and turned to take some footage of Chumbika and three companions walking in single file from the clearing toward the jungle edge. No vibration this time.

I hurried along with José to catch up with the hunters. They traveled rapidly at first, knowing that there would probably be no game near the jivaria. After twenty minutes they slowed down, and I had a chance to catch my breath. The hunters stopped and peered ahead through the branches. I looked and saw a small stream and, on the opposite shore, a capybara, the biggest rodent in the world. It resembled a giant guinea pig on thin spindly legs, about four feet long and weighing close to a hundred pounds.

To my surprise the Indians did not even try to shoot it, but stepped through the trees to the shore of the stream and stopped. The capybara dove into the water with scarcely a splash and disappeared. I asked José why they had not shot at the animal, as I knew they ate its flesh. Chumbika explained that it was too near the water. It would take several poison darts and quite some time to kill or even paralyze so large a creature, and it would have been in the water after the first dart. It could stay under water for five or six minutes, and they would never find it.

We crossed the stream and climbed a hill and turned slightly to the north. Suddenly the hunters ahead of me froze in their tracks. I lifted the camera slowly, for a good deal of light filtered through the trees in a few spots ahead. I saw the Indians' heads turn slowly to the left. There, not thirty feet away, stood a jaguar, his yellow coat with black rosettes brilliant in a shaft of sunlight. He was looking at us as if in surprise.

Jivaros need a gun or lance for the jaguar, and then he is not easy to get. For one thing, the big cat usually travels at night when the Indian barricades himself in his jivaria. Even when he is encountered in the daytime, he is usually too fast — the only thing as quick and silent as the Jivaro himself. Consequently a jaguar is quite a prize. Some Jivaros use part of a jaguar's leg bone to make lance points, and a necklace of jaguar teeth is the most splendid decoration a man can wear.

We walked another half hour, up and down hills, across streams, without seeing any game. The Indians halted near a kind of screen or blind of palm leaves, made so skillfully that one could scarcely notice it.

Chumbika turned and spoke to José. He was going to hide behind the blind, which he had constructed two days before, and try to bring the birds to him. The others were going on further in search of monkeys. I could stay with him or go along with the others, as I wished. Much as I wanted to see monkey-hunting I welcomed the chance for a rest. So José and I got behind the blind with Chumbika, and the others went on.

For five minutes we sat without a sound. Then Chumbika leaned forward and let out a throaty whistle. It was a perfect reproduction of a bird sound I had heard several times the afternoon before as we were walking toward the jivaria. At intervals he repeated that sound and others, but I heard no answering calls. After sitting absolutely still for fifteen minutes, I wanted to move, but I tried not to. At the end of half an hour my admiration for the patience of the Jivaro Indian was considerable. Only when I saw Chumbika's hand move slowly to his side did I realize that the sound I had just heard came from a bird and not from him. From the bamboo quiver he withdrew a dart, as slender as a common match and about twelve inches long. Called *tsenac* by the Jivaros, it is made from the ribs of certain palm leaves that are cut at a time when the wood is very hard. I noticed that the sharpened end was brown with curare poison.

Keeping his eye fixed somewhere ahead, Chumbika pulled a tiny wad of cotton from a small gourd attached to the dart quiver, wrapped it around the blunt end of the dart. This would serve to close the space in the barrel of the blowgun enough to allow the full force of air to be exerted against it instead of leaking around the dart. In addition, it took the place of the feather on the usual arrow, to hold the dart on its course.

Before inserting the dart in the gun, Chumbika cut a deep notch in it just behind the poison-covered tip, using the sharp teeth on the jaws of a piranha fish that hung at his waist. With the dart in the barrel, he lifted the blowgun to his mouth, sighted briefly, then puffed out his cheeks. I heard absolutely nothing, but I saw a flash of bright red in the trees ahead of us, as a bird dropped to the ground.

I followed Chumbika to the spot. He picked up a toucan, its ludicrous bills making it look even more out of proportion in death than in life. We returned to the blind and took up our vigil again, with Chumbika repeating his bird calls regularly. At the end of another hour the hunter had four more birds — two pawils, a macaw, and another toucan. He seemed reasonably pleased, and we headed for home.

After walking about twenty minutes, Chumbika, who was in the lead, stopped suddenly. In three quick motions the dart was fixed with cotton, notched, and inserted in the blowgun. A silent puff, and I heard a cry, sharp and almost human, from a tree ahead. Chumbika was already inserting another dart when I saw the spider monkey pull the dart that had stuck in his chest and throw it away. He licked at the wound as three other monkeys swung closer to him, obviously wondering what had happened. There was a second cry and I saw another dart in a monkey on the right, without my realizing that Chumbika had sent it on its way. He was readying a third dart when the other monkeys set up a chattering and scurried off through the trees.

Chumbika replaced the dart as the first monkey fell from the branch, just about two minutes after the dart had struck him. It was almost four minutes before the second monkey fell, and when we found them both we knew why. The first had been struck in the chest and the second in the thigh. In the second case it had taken the poison longer to paralyze the respiratory muscles. Smaller birds can be killed by the force of the dart alone, but in all birds the poison works quickly, because they are small and their body temperature is high, causing the curare to dissolve into the bloodstream faster.

Both monkeys had, of course, pulled the darts out the moment they were struck. But each dart had broken off at the notch, just under the skin, so the poison remained.

Chumbika was obviously very happy over his kills. Monkeys are good to eat and their fur is useful, too, for headdresses, traveling pouches, and for a kind of Sam Browne belt worn by many Jivaros.

As we came out of the jungle into the clearing I saw a pleasant and placid scene — women working in the field of yuca and maize, children playing nearby, a man working earnestly on a blowgun. We approached the jivaria and I saw a woman sitting on a log, nursing her baby. Knowing that mother-and-child shots have appeal, I stepped around in front of her, so the light would be right. I hoped she would not mind.

I was quite startled, for she was nursing not only her baby but a little puppy! Each arm was cuddling a warm and contented creature — baby suckling at the right breast, puppy at the left.

The woman looked up at me without interest or concern and did not change her position. I captured the scene with the camera. Baby and puppy went on nursing. José learned later that the mother dog had been snatched and killed by a jaguar only a few days after her puppies were born. Dogs were valuable, so this Jivaro mother was keeping the puppy alive in the most obvious and natural way.

I felt more at ease inside the jivaria on this second afternoon, because Chumbika was obviously not hostile any more. I wandered about, keeping away from the women's section only, and looked at everything that interested me. The big signal drum, or *tundui*, was suspended from the ridgepole so that it hung about three feet from the floor, not horizontally but at an angle. It was a hollowed-out log, about twenty inches or more in diameter. Both ends were solid, but a zigzag hole was cut in the top, much like the hole in any musical instrument with a resonating box. The drum could be heard for four or five miles, probably reaching a dozen other jivarias of the Huambisa tribe.

Two women sat in the main section of the house making pottery jars. They had no potter's wheel but the jars were remarkably symmetrical. From the piles of clay near at hand, a woman took a big chunk and rolled it out until it made a long thick rope of clay. She then placed this on top of the round structure she had started, pressed and smoothed it into place. Later the jars would be fired in a huge pile of brush until they were baked hard. They were quite brittle and broke easily, so the women were often at the task of pottery-making.

The constant and endless task, however, was the making of the drink nijimanche. I was glad to see that three older women were busy at it, although I wondered if I could drink the beverage again. The three sat cross-legged on the ground, with a large jar of boiled yuca, which had first been peeled and cut in chunks, between them. With their hands they scooped up the warm, thick mass and plopped it into their mouths. Each woman chewed for a while, then spat out a long white stream, of astounding volume, into another jar. Sometimes a woman took some yuca that had already been chewed and masticated it some more, spitting it into another jar. Obviously every bit of the yuca got thoroughly chewed and mixed with saliva. The digestive enzymes in the saliva converted the starch of the yuca into sugar, which would ferment. When a jar was filled, it was covered tightly with leaves and set to one side. There were jars around the wall with nijimanche in various stages of fermentation.

Since most adult Jivaros drink four or five quarts of nijimanche a day, with the children imbibing a good deal, too, it is obvious that several women must keep pretty steadily at the job of masticating yuca.

I never saw anybody really idle for very long, in fact. The Jivaros don't seem to work hard, but they rarely sit and do nothing at all. The men spin cotton thread or weave or make baskets, as well as hunt, fish, or make war, and the women make pottery and nijimanche when they are not busy gardening.

Work is divided according to the sex of the thing worked on, for in the Jivaro view everything is either male or female. Women do the cooking because fire is female, and they make the pots because clay is part of Mother Earth. Yuca, or manioc, is female, like most plants, so the women do the agricultural labor. (The Jivaro word for yuca is *mama*.) Fiber is male, so the men spin and weave. Men weave the baskets, but by some strange quirk, baskets themselves are female, so women must carry them.

It turns out that much of the heaviest labor is concerned with female things. In some accounts of the Jivaros, I have read that women do all the hard work and the men do almost nothing. But that is not what I saw. We had just put in a pretty strenuous day hunting, for instance, and I knew that this was a short and easy hunt, largely on my account. Sometimes the men go out for ten or fifteen days, sleeping in the jungle at night and covering scores of miles. Men chop down all the trees when a new clearing is made — no easy job when they tackle hardwood trees with their primitive tools. And the men fight the wars of extermination, carry on the blood feuds, which are certainly no trivial tasks. Spinning and weaving are as strenuous as pottery-making and nijimanche-chewing. Women do carry the heavy loads, in large baskets supported by lines over their heads, when a family is traveling. But this is natural, for the men must be ready with weapons, against attack or to kill game encountered on the way.

The Jivaro woman is no cringing creature, by any means. She is a person of importance in the family and the clan, even if she doesn't run things. And there is a great deal of affection between husbands and wives.

That evening after eating, I asked Chumbika how many heads he had taken. I saw him stiffen, but he answered with his fingers — four. That was not bad for a young man, I thought. I asked if he had a shrunken head, a *tsantsa*, that I could see. He shook his head violently and looked quite angry. Suddenly he started talking, loudly and venomously, to José. In a few minutes I had the story.

Two months before, just after they had moved to the new jivaria, a white trader had come through. He was looking for tsantsas. Both Peru and Ecuador have passed laws against any buying or bartering of tsantsas. The Jivaros are not expected to know about or pay attention to such laws, but the traders are. Still, unscrupulous traders try to get them, for they bring a good price in what might be called the souvenir black market.

Jivaros don't treasure their tsantsas. After they have shrunk the heads and gone through the long and complicated feast celebrating it, the tsantsa holds little meaning for them. It is not really a trophy like the mounted moosehead of the sports hunter. But when the trader came to Chumbika, the young curaka still had his last head. When the trader offered to exchange a shotgun for the head, Chumbika agreed, especially since a box of ammunition was included in the deal. The chief had long wanted a shotgun.

The trader took his head and went happily on his way. The next day Chumbika loaded and shot his gun. It exploded and burned him badly. The nasty scars I had noticed were black powder burns. I was the next white man Chumbika saw, and his first thought was that I was another trader looking for tsantsas.

When I learned more of the history of the Jivaros' relations with white men, it seemed strange to me that they didn't shoot all whites on sight. But no Jivaro Indian knows much about his tribe's history. He knows what happened to him, his father, uncle, and friends. He may have heard some vague stories about events farther in the past, especially if connected with his immediate clan. The Huambisas, for instance, had a legend about wiping out the town of Borja, although it lacked details or accurate setting in past time. In that case, of course, they had brought back to their jivarias young women and children, some of whom must have lived with the Indians for many years and borne children by them. The story would have been passed along for some time by word of mouth.

There were a few memories of difficulties with the white rubber workers. They were traders rather than workers, for they tried to get the Indians to do all the work of tapping the trees and carrying crude rubber to the rivers for shipment on small boats down to Iquitos. They killed a few thousand Indians in the process. At this time the Jivaros were first introduced to shotguns, not much better than the useless old piece that had burned Chumbika. Special shotguns were made just for trading with the Indians, cheap guns that could not possibly last very long. The idea was to cheat the Indian first with a gun, then be safe from retaliation because the gun would probably blow up and kill him.

No Jivaro I ever met knew anything about his tribe's first troubles with the whites in the sixteenth century. The Spanish conquistadores were as unbelievably courageous in this region as they were everywhere else in the New World — and as cruel. With a handful of men, Juan de Salinas penetrated the Jivaro country, established towns and gave huge grants of land to his followers, with absolute rule over all the natives who happened to live in those lands. The lure that led these men over the Andes and down into the country of the headhunters was, of course, gold. They believed — and experts still agree — that most of the vast store of gold of the Incas came from this region.

By 1599 strongman Salinas was dead. The next governor of the territory was cruel, greedy, and not very intelligent. The feuding Jivaros "buried the lance" temporarily and revolted under the leadership of a curaka named Quiruba. They burned the three sizable Spanish towns that had been built, massacred almost all the whites — the total was between twenty and thirty thousand men, women, and children — taking with them some of the younger women. For the governor they reserved a fitting punishment. When they took him prisoner, they showed him that they had brought along the gold he had been demanding.

As an account by Juan de Velasco tells it:

> He was stripped, his hands and feet tied, and, whilst some of the Indians were upbraiding him, others were melting the gold in crucibles. They opened the governor's mouth with a bone, saying they would now see if he could be satisfied for once with gold. They now poured the melted metal down his throat until his bowels burst within him, when they raised their shout of exultation.

The Spaniards did not try to establish towns in the Jivaro country again.

The next morning the skies were overcast. To the southeast there were black clouds gathering, and I knew that there would be no filming that day.

There was a rumble of thunder; Chumbika came out of the jivaria with the older man who had sat beside him the first evening. He was the witch doctor, called by the Jivaros a *wishinu* or *brujo*. He looked at the black cloud, listened while thunder rolled again, and jumped when he saw a flash of lightning. Suddenly he shouted angrily at the sky, turned, and went inside the jivaria. In a moment I heard the booming sounds of tundui, the big drum, answering the thunder — a crashing boom followed by quick lighter booms, very much like thunder itself. In a few moments the wishinu reappeared, his monkey-fur headpiece on his head, his face painted red and streaked with black. In his hands he held a lance and a round shield made of wood covered with hide.

In a high piercing voice he cried out at the black cloud and shook his lance at it threateningly. He started what seemed to be almost a dance, stepping forward with a hard thrust of the lance, a step back, another attack and blow with the lance. And all the time he chanted a loud series of imprecations at the cloud. Then he blew as hard as he could into the air, blew against the cloud.

I realized that the black cloud might well lie over the land of the Aguarunas to the southeast, and the Aguarunas were the ancient enemies of the Huambisas. The storm, the black cloud with its thunder and lightning, were the work of an Aguaruna wishinu, a threat against the Huambisas, whose wishinu was now exerting his great powers to ward off the danger.

For half an hour he shouted and danced and threatened, but it grew larger and came closer. As the lightning and thunder increased, the old man's shouting grew louder, his lance thrusts and puffings more violent.

Even when the rain began to fall, the wishinu kept on with his defense of his clan, most of whom retired to the jivaria. I did, too, but it was easy to see him at his work through the spaces between the upright poles of the house.

It rained for about ten minutes. The thunder grew louder, the lightning flashed. Then the noise and the black cloud drifted on past us, and gradually the rain diminished, finally stopped. Everyone went outside again. The wishinu sat on a log, exhausted but happy. I was surprised to see him so pleased with himself, for I thought he had failed to keep the storm away. But no. The opposing wishinu was very strong, and the storm had come. But our wishinu had kept the lightning from striking, hadn't he? The clan was safe.

I watched a man making a blowgun and through José learned a good deal about the process. He was not far from the end of the long and painstaking task. His blowgun rested on two forked branches stuck in the ground seven or eight feet apart, as he worked on the final smoothing of the bore.

He had started many weeks before, cutting down a chonta palm, a tree that has not only a hard, straight-grained wood but also strong helpful spirits to make his gun effective. In order to please and placate these spirits the warrior abstains from certain foods during the entire period of manufacture of the blowgun. He cannot have sexual relations with his wife. If he should disobey these injunctions, the wood is likely to warp or crack after the gun is made.

The felled chonta palm dries for a week, after which its sharp thorns are cut off. The Indian splits the trunk in half and where the grain is straightest, cuts out two long strips about three inches square. These are the two halves of his blowgun. Each half is trimmed and shaped carefully so that it is flat on one side and forms a half circle on the other, tapered evenly from one end to the other. When the flat sides are placed together, he has a long, round cylinder, about an inch and a quarter in diameter at one end and three quarters of an inch at the other end.

The Indian places one strip on the rack made by the forked sticks, flat side up. With a sharp bone or shell he cuts a groove down the length of the stick, perfectly straight and right in the middle. The same operation is performed on the flat side of the second stick. Each groove is then gradually enlarged with a bone or sharp tooth until it is just under an eighth of an inch deep. The Indian then puts the two pieces together around a straight round chonta rod he has prepared, somewhat longer than the blowgun. Strips of bark bind together the two halves of the blowgun, that still don't quite meet.

The Jivaro I watched had reached this stage of manufacture. I saw him pour water and fine sand in one end of the blowgun, then work the long rod slowly and carefully back and forth, enlarging and smoothing the bore. More sand, more water, and more careful manipulation of the rod. After a time he tied the bark strips tighter around the two halves and went back to the sand and water routine.

Two days later, he finished the sanding. The two halves of his blowgun fitted snugly together, and the bore was as straight as a plumbline, as shiny as a mirror.

He glued together the two halves with a quick-drying latex and wrapped the outside from one end to the other with long strips of fiber from the ivory nut palm. A coating of latex over this was smoothed with a warm machete blade. A waxy resin was melted with the juice from a small fruit that turned it black, and this was the final coating, polished until it had a high gloss. The Indian carved a bone mouthpiece about two inches long, fitted it tightly to the large end, stuck two small animal teeth on top of the barrel to serve as sights, gave a final polish to the bore with cotton, and his weapon was ready — accurate up to about fifty yards, capable of sending a dart through a half-inch board at ten feet.

It was my last evening with the Huambisas in the jivaria of Chumbika. I wanted Chumbika to tell me about the four heads he had taken, but he had avoided the subject angrily. I didn't know why. Perhaps because of the recent unpleasant experience over his last tsantsa, perhaps because it brought to mind some unpleasant memory. But most Jivaros are not introspective or moody. They spend little time regretting the past or worrying about the future. They live in the present and find it good, most of the time, even though filled with dangers. The worst dangers are, in their minds, largely unseen. They fear the *inguanchi*, the demons or evil spirits, but not the jaguar, the white man, or the Jivaro enemy. The Jivaro world abounds with spirits, some good but most bad. As many things as there are in the world — trees, animals, plants, birds, rivers, fish, butterflies, ants, clouds, earth, and the shining things in the sky — that is how many spirits there are, and more.

I asked Chumbika to explain how he, a relatively young man — around thirty, I guessed — came to be a curaka. He said that a curaka was not a real ruler or chief. He did not dictate to his family, clan, or tribe. He was merely a generally acknowledged leader, respected by others in the clan. Chumbika's father had been a great and brave curaka, but that did not necessarily mean that Chumbika would succeed him. But the sons of curakas, if they were old and experienced enough, were actually chosen quite frequently — not by the clan, but by the wishinu, the witch doctor. He drank the narcotic *nateema*, dreamed dreams, communicated with the spirits of the Old Ones, and learned who should be the new curaka.

Chumbika remarked that if his older brother had lived, he would no doubt have become curaka, because he was a great warrior with eight heads to his credit. The brother had died only a few months before old Cajeke, and Chumbika blamed the wishinu of the Aguarunas for causing a tree to fall on him. Jivaros believe that death is never an accident, that everything that happens has a cause, and death above all, because death is not natural. Life is natural. Life is what we all have, what everything has. When life is taken away, someone must take it, as the enemy wishinu took life from Chumbika's brother. Your own wishinu can always tell you who was responsible for a death, after proper libations of nateema.

"Now I must kill the Aguaruna wishinu and take his head," Chumbika said, matter-of-factly. That would mean a renewal of the war that had never really stopped but had occasional truces. Some time, perhaps months from then, Chumbika would drink nateema to learn if the time was right to strike. If the spirits assured him it was, he would summon as many as possible of his fellow Huambisas, all would fast and go through the ritual required before a raid, and then they would slip through the night to attack the Aguaruna jivaria in which the unknowingly guilty wishinu lived. They would wait outside the clearing until one man was driven out of the jivaria to relieve himself — a necessity resulting from the huge consumption of nijimanche. They would kill him, race through the door that had been opened, cut off as many heads as possible, snatch some of the girls and younger women, and hurry away before other Aguarunas could come to the help of their fellows. In time the heads would be shrunk and a great tsantsa feast celebrated. Then and only then would Chumbika's brother's spirit rest in peace instead of wandering about in torment.

Chumbika believed in the rightness of all this fervently. He did not stop to think that after his raid, Aguaruna brothers and sons would feel obliged, by their deepest religious convictions, to make war on the Huambisas, and especially on Chumbika, to avenge and bring happiness to *their* relatives' souls.

My dreams were not pleasant that night, and I was still rather depressed the next morning when I said good-bye to my Huambisa friends. José and the bearers and I walked back to the Santiago River and met the launch as had been arranged. Downriver about thirty miles we stopped and walked through the jungle to a jivaria belonging to the Aguaruna tribe. I wanted to see these bitter hereditary enemies of the Huambisas.

There are many Jivaro tribes and subtribes, of course, with a total population of about twenty thousand in an area of about twenty-five thousand square miles. There are numerous ancient enmities, and always new ones, rarely a burying of the lance.

The Aguarunas we met were reserved but hospitable, and in a short while quite friendly. Obviously they had suffered no recent unpleasantness at the hands of a white man. To me they looked just like the Huambisas. They wore the same kind of clothes, the same hairdos and adornments. José said their talk was exactly the same. Their jivaria was a duplicate of the one in which I had spent several nights, and their blowguns and lances were identical. The wishinu even wore a monkey-fur headpiece. I wondered how people so similar could come to be such deadly enemies.

The curaka was a different sort from Chumbika. He was about fifty-five, a bit plump, full of smiles, and quite friendly. When I talked to him about headhunting, he was willing to answer any questions I asked. And he had two tsantsas, one of which he traded to me for three machetes.

It was about the size of a big fist, as I had been told. The features were all there in good shape, except that the chin and forehead both receded more than in any Indian I had seen. I looked at the chonta pins through the lips, with chambira fibers hanging from them, put there to keep the hot stones and sand from spilling out when the head was shrunk. The black hair was long and remarkably lustrous.

In the launch going back to Borja, I kept looking at it and asking myself, "Will this be Chumbika next year?" I was so troubled that I scarcely noticed as the launch swept perilously close to the edges of the whirlpools known as Thou Shalt Weep Greatly and Thou Shalt Weep Bitterly.

2

Curaka Peruche

WAR was rumbling close to America's shores when I returned to New York and my business. In a short while the Jivaros seemed like creatures on another planet, except when I got my film back from the processors.

The old Ciné-Kodak had actually taken pictures! Some footage was blurred from the palsy attacks the camera was subject to. Some showed insufficient light — to be expected in pictures taken in the jungle. But there were several hundred feet of very satisfying footage, and they made me determined to go back again with an extra camera and a cameraman to help me.

But the thought was pushed from my mind by our entry into the war, which I spent with Naval Intelligence. With the defeat of Germany, I started planning. It seemed impossible to get plane seats or film, but a few friends and some patience brought both in time. So in 1945 I flew to Panama and on to Quito.

From Quito I flew to Cuenca, a city of about fifty thousand people in which the finest Panama hats are made — not in Panama. Three routes led from Cuenca to the Jivaro country, but I knew little about any of them. I picked the middle route, through the small town of Pan and the village of Méndez.

No one in Cuenca had any ideas about where I could find a guide who had been in the Jivaro country. I heard vague references to a man and his brother, half Spanish and half Indian, who smuggled guns in to the Indians and shrunken heads out. The older of the two was called

Señor Ninguno Nombre — Mr. No Name. The rumor told me that the gunrunners operated out of Méndez.

I hired an ancient Ford truck to take me with my equipment as far as Pan, at which point the road ended. Pan was a true dead-end town, sleepy, dirty, discouraged. There was not even a bad hotel or inn. The truck driver took me to a mestizo family whose adobe hut appeared no better or worse than the others but apparently contained one more room, which could be rented. There I ate a surprisingly good dish of hot beans and baked bananas, which I supplemented with a can of sardines from my supplies — lightweight and nourishing standby of most of my travels.

I asked the truck driver to see if he could find a muleteer with three mules. In fifteen minutes a shouting and gesticulating crowd of a dozen men attacked the hut not just offering their services but demanding that I accept them, threatening me if I didn't.

As I looked the pack over, I saw a solid-looking young man on its rim who did not shout, push, swear, or threaten. He looked solemn and a little sad until I glanced at him, and then he raised one arm like a boy in school and smiled tentatively.

"All right, you there," I called to him. "Come inside and we'll talk. You others can go."

The others grumbled and glared but melted away. Barmio — for that was my man's name — stood inside the door, hat in hand. He was about twenty-five years old, strong and perhaps intelligent. I hoped that he was reliable, too. For he was to take me as far as the mules could go, then come back six weeks later and pick me up. Was it safe to depend on anyone's coming back in six weeks? I had to chance it.

The promptness of Barmio at dawn the next morning made me feel better. He was, I came to believe, much like his mules, but decidedly more pleasant. He was strong and surefooted and dependable. You could not rush him but he would not delay. He knew when to start and when to stop. He knew the steady pace that, despite its irritating slowness at the outset, was best calculated to get you where you were going. His mules knew these things, too, and they possessed his amazing endurance. But Barmio was pleasant and cheerful, whereas his animals were surly and even vicious, bearing a grudge against all other living things.

We met in front of the little adobe church and loaded the equipment on a chunky gray mule that looked to be the strongest of the three. It was a heavy load, but Barmio was an expert at making the burden balance perfectly — an essential when a mule is going to travel on mountain ledges scarcely twelve inches wide. I selected a lean and dark animal for my mount.

We traveled up a narrow trail, then down. Up again, and then down more. At the outset there were few shrubs, and the air was cool, the sun bright, for we were still high in the mountains.

When we plunged down below the vegetation line, the rain began and I hurriedly put on rubber pants and poncho. For much of the time the rain was so thick that I could not see far ahead, and it was fortunate that I could not. The prospect for ten or fifteen feet was frightening enough. Up ahead was Barmio, leading the way. Next came the pack mule. Then I followed. On my right a wall of jagged rock rose up out of sight. On my left an even more jagged wall plunged down into gray mist, how far I could not always see. On the little ledge that looked no wider than a ribbon, my mule gingerly picked his way daintily, casually, sometimes stepping around a fallen rock so that my left leg hung over empty space. But the mule ahead distressed me more often than my own. Because of the packs he carried on each side, he had to walk on the outer edge of the narrow ribbon to keep the equipment from scraping the vertical wall. This meant that the pack on his left side was out in the clear, with nothing above or below it.

Once the narrow trail rounded a bend in the mountain and Barmio disappeared. The pack mule stopped and I caught up with him. I tried imitating Barmio's frenetic cry, "*Carrajo, mula,*" but apparently put too little authority into my tone, for the beast still hesitated. I saw that the trail dropped down a full two feet at this point, like a large step. The mule was very sensible debating whether to make that downward jump, since his starboard pack might strike the cliff and his port pack carry him over the precipice. But we could not sit there forever. I nudged my mule forward a step so that I could strike out with my right foot and kick the pack mule. When I kicked, I thought I would topple all of us into the bottomless pit, but my foot struck home, the mule made the jump safely, and we proceeded on our way.

Barmio and I finally descended below the rocky cliffs and came to mud and clay. Half-set jello would provide as firm a footing as Andean mud, and this mud is usually set at a forty degree angle. Most of the time the mules were all right because they put their hoofs in holes made by scores of mules before them, but there were times when all of us slipped and fell into the muck. Then we had to pull the mules to their feet, slipping and sliding in the process, reload the equipment, and start off again.

As the days passed, my mule and I began to dislike each other more and more, perhaps because I called him Grumpy and he resented it. I concluded that he did not like carrying bulky-looking me instead of neatly balanced packs like those on the back of his friend right ahead of him. At least, he tried hard to get rid of me. When we traveled near rocks, he walked so close that he skinned my knees. In the forest he made sudden dashes toward trees with low-hanging limbs in an effort to knock my head off. When I had helped him up from a mudhole he bit me. When we came to a level stretch and I walked him for a while he tried to kick me. Finally we switched and gave him the packs, while I rode little Chunky. But Grumpy was too angry to be satisfied by then.

I could not help admiring Grumpy, and all other mules, by the end of that trip. No horse could have made it halfway there. I could not have walked those mountain ledges with the assurance and safety of Grumpy. And I came to admire the independent spirit of the mule — a quality I always esteem in human beings. Grumpy would carry me, or packs, and keep on over impossible terrain in rain, cold, heat, with little food. But he would not be nice about it. He would not go faster or slower. And when he was through for the day he was through. Fortunately he always seemed to select a good spot to stop, where there was a clear area without too much mud and with some shelter from the rain afforded by big trees. But it was Grumpy who picked these places, not I.

Maybe Barmio could have exercised some control over his mules, but I have a feeling that the mules just let him pretend he had authority. He shouted "Carrajo, mula!" at them continuously and vehemently, and sometimes after four shouts they would move. I suspect they were going to move at that moment anyway. It was always surprising to see how amiable, if silent, Barmio could be with me just after being so angry with his mules. He never complained of the difficulties of the journey or of the rain. And he never seemed to get tired.

He lived on a kind of corn bread made by his wife for the journey and chewed ceaselessly on coco leaf, which contains a certain amount of natural cocaine. It must have given him a constant lift.

Barmio's poncho was made not of rubber but of llama wool. When it was cold, it warmed him. When it rained, it kept him dry. He rolled up in it at night and slept happily. And he carried spares under the saddles of the mules, to protect their backs.

As the trip progressed, I kept wondering when we would go through the towns shown on my large-scale map — Chontal, Capai, St. Eleno. Finally I asked Barmio and he said we had been through two of them, reminding me of the places where there had been two thatch and adobe huts. So there was no snug dry room with a fire and a hot meal during the trip, as I had hoped when I saw the deceiving map. We camped every night under the dripping trees, often talking for an hour before exhaustion sent us off into a kind of drugged sleep.

One night I asked Barmio if he knew the gunrunner known as Señor Ninguno Nombre. I had hesitated to ask before because the mountain Indians can be very closemouthed. If they don't wish to give information but must say something, they will not hesitate to tell, with an air of conviction, a tale far from the truth. But after five days Barmio and I were close friends and he said that he knew the señor well but that he would tell me who the man was only if I swore never to tell any Spanish people — priests or soldiers. I promised and Barmio said he would take me to the trader in Méndez.

We finally crossed a fragile-looking cable bridge over the Paute River and reached Méndez. It was a pleasant surprise — larger than I had anticipated, clean, with a barracks of Ecuadorian soldiers and a good-sized church and monastery school.

Barmio knocked on the door of my room that evening and said, "Come with me, señor."

We walked down a narrow street lined with adobe huts. He pushed open the door of a hut. We stepped into a room almost as dark as the black night outside.

In a moment I could see — a wide dim circle of light spread from a fire on the floor in the middle of the room; over the fire a large earthenware cauldron bubbled. A low hum of talk started again shortly after we came in. On one side of the darkened room was a table with bottles, cups, and gourds, over which a monstrously fat woman presided. On low benches here and there men sat drinking, smoking and talking quietly.

Barmio pointed to two men sitting on the floor with their backs against the opposite wall. "That is the man you want," he said, and turned back to the door. He disappeared, leaving me alone in a place in which I did not feel very comfortable. But I felt that one rarely got knifed in the back in a place that looked so suitable for such acts. Sinister as all this might appear, these men were poor, half-starved Indians trying to find a little comfort in quiet, companionable drinking. I knew that a fair number of them might be criminals — Señor Ninguno Nombre most certainly was a lawbreaker — but they evaded or broke laws in order to get a little more food or an extra drink or two.

I walked over to the two men leaning against the wall, who looked up at me with no expression. To the older one I spoke in Spanish and he replied. Yes, Barmio the muleteer had spoken to him about me. Yes, we could discuss a trip into the Jivaro country. I sat down on the floor and leaned my back against the wall.

Barmio was an honest man, I felt, and so I trusted his judgment about these men, whose real names turned out to be Pablo and Diego. Pablo was the older brother, the one known as Ninguno Nombre, about twenty-five years old. Diego was almost certainly under twenty. They were both thin, wiry, and strong, half or three-quarters Indian. Pablo told me, when I asked him how well he knew the Jivaro language, that he was part Jivaro. However, he did not claim that he knew the language perfectly, only adequately.

My chief concern was that he might know Jivaro Indians only on the fringes of Jivaro country, where contacts with civilization might have altered the normal Jivaro way of life. But Pablo insisted, when I told him I had six weeks for the visit, that he was on good terms with clans and subtribes far deeper into the jungle than I could hope to penetrate in that time.

"I have heard that you trade guns for heads," I said. "I do not care about what I hear, but on this trip you are to act as my guide — nothing else. You will not carry guns there, nor bring heads back."

Pablo agreed. During all the conversation Diego listened and nodded when Pablo made a statement. I bought them each a drink, which they accepted with dignity and sipped from their half coconut shells while I told them that the party consisted of Barmio and myself, three mules, and equipment. We would leave early in the morning, from the square.

"At seven o'clock in the square," Pablo said, and Diego nodded. I sealed the bargain with part of the fee and left.

The sun was shining brightly, and the path was almost a road, as we set out the next morning from Méndez, lying near the base of the eastern slope of the Ecuadorian Andes. But soon the sun disappeared behind gray clouds. The road shrank to a rocky jungle trail. Two hours later rain began to fall in a steady drizzle, and the trail was narrow, slippery, muddy, and hard to follow. Only one fact minimized these difficulties — we were still going downhill most of the time.

It rained all day and it rained all night. We ate cold food because we could not light a fire. We rolled ourselves in our ponchos and slept only because we were so tired that the rain could not keep us awake. The next morning it was no longer a drizzle. We got hard, driving rain.

At the end of this day we halted, and when I looked ahead through the downpour I snapped out of my numbness and lethargy. There was a river — the Namangoza or the Paute, depending upon which map you look at. They are the same river but some geographers call the upper section Paute and the lower Namangoza, while others name it Paute all the way to its junction with the Santiago.

Across the river, in those thick woods — that was the land of the headhunters. I looked ahead, then to right and to left, searching for the shaky, swinging cable bridge I expected. I could see none. Pablo pointed to a thick rope arching from tree to tree across the river.

He led me close to the big tree and I saw a native-made hemp rope almost as thick as my wrist. There was a cast-iron pulley on it, from which hung two smaller ropes that supported a thick chunk of wood about six inches wide and three feet long. I got the idea quickly enough, but I did not like it. The traveler was supposed to perch on the narrow seat and propel himself across the river by pulling hand-over-hand on the main rope. Just how the traveler was supposed to do all this and carry cameras, tripod, cans of film, bundles of gifts, tent, food, and other equipment I do not know. The bridge was not made for such travelers. It was made for people like Pablo and Diego, who travel light, with a couple of guns slung on the shoulders or a couple of shrunken heads in a sack. But Pablo promised that he and Diego would get us and our equipment across on the rope bridge the next day.

In the morning it was raining, but the sky was considerably brighter and we felt it was safe to hope that the rain might end entirely during the day. And it was light enough to get a picture of the hazardous crossing if I could find a spot from which to take it.

Pablo and Diego were astounded, I know, at my concern about taking a picture. They had thought I was worried about the bridge, and now all I could talk about was a good vantage point for a camera angle! I did find it, a huge boulder that jutted out into the river higher than the bank itself. It was a hard climb to get on top of it, and then one had to lie flat to get a camera view beneath the boughs of the overhanging trees.

Barmio obligingly perched himself on the boulder for a shot of my crossing. I've always been grateful to him for that picture, though the light was bad and it was rather fuzzy. Few pictures have ever been taken under circumstances so precarious to both subject and photographer.

Diego and Pablo held the narrow seat while I slid and squeezed myself into it and practiced the best position. When I was as comfortable as possible, Pablo plunked the cameras and a big box of films into my arms. It was more than I thought I could hold, but I was determined to carry the most important part of my equipment.

Pablo straddled my knees, facing me, although there was precious little space left on my legs to support him. His body pressed against the equipment, however, which pushed it against me so hard that the cargo was held as firmly as if lashed in place.

My arms went around the two supporting ropes. Pablo's naked chest pushed against my nose. And then came a lurching swing as Diego gave us a firm but gentle push and we swung away from the tree, away from the steep embankment, and over the roaring waters below.

The rope looped down at quite an angle over the river, so at first the going was easy, downhill. Pablo's hands above his head grasped the main rope and moved us along without effort. But the seat swayed and tipped with every motion of his arms. I felt myself toppling backward, then tipped forward until I thought Pablo would slide off my knees.

I could tell by our angle that we had probably reached the middle of the river, about seventy-five feet from our starting point. Another seventy-five feet to go — but uphill now. Pablo pulled hard on the rope. I saw the long muscles in his lean, powerful arms bunch themselves into knots. His chest and stomach muscles grew taut and hard as iron, and his knees gripped mine like a vise as he inched the pulley-seat ahead.

I could not see how far away the other shore was. I could see only the throbbing vein in Pablo's neck. I could feel the pounding of his heart, as if it were pounding in my chest as well as his. I never felt so useless, and such a burden.

Pablo gasped for breath. We slipped back along the rope, and Pablo grasped it frantically with both hands. We stopped, swinging gently to and fro. I looked up at the Indian's face and saw that his eyes were almost closed, his mouth slightly open, all the muscles tight, pulled out of place. He looked like a marathon runner on his last lap. We finally reached the other bank. Pablo slid off my knees and held the seat while I fell out of it with my burdens.

In a few minutes Pablo got his breath back and climbed into the seat to pull himself to the other side, where he loaded on Diego and more equipment. I watched their slow progress with anguish but a kind of triumph, knowing I had already gone through it. The crossing took almost two hours. We waved to Barmio and his mules on the other side, and watched them turn away and disappear into the jungle, heading back to Méndez. In exactly forty-five days, I hoped, he would stand at that spot again, waiting for us.

The hazardous river crossing assured me that I was entering Jivaro territory that had scarcely been touched by white civilization. Pablo knew that no good crossing existed for many miles in either direction. Few soldiers, missionaries, or traders would take this route, since there existed numerous simpler routes into other parts of Jivaro-land. Beyond that, we had to walk two days before we reached the first jivaria, over a path barely discernible, through swampy mud hollows, over rocky hills, across numerous streams, with alternate bursts of rain and hot sun.

On the third day after our crossing, Pablo and Diego began to *whedee* at regular and increasingly frequent intervals. After an hour of it, Pablo suddenly stopped. Two Jivaro warriors stood on the trail ahead of us, shotguns slung over their shoulders, lances in their hands. They did not look friendly. They did not look hostile. They just stared. Pablo gave them one minute to look, then spoke in the Jivaro tongue. The Indians did not look at him or Diego, for they doubtless knew these two well. Their eyes were fastened on me.

Pablo was telling the two warriors all about me, in the singsong talk that suggested Chinese. Apparently he told a satisfactory story, for the Jivaros turned and motioned for us to follow. They had been out hunting, Pablo explained, and were about an hour from the jivaria to which they were now leading us. He also told me that they did not bother with their guns when they saw us because they had no ammunition. They always carried guns, ammunition or not, because it made them feel important. They depended upon their lances most of the time, for fighting or hunting.

When we reached the jivaria, I felt as if I were back among the Huambisas. The people looked the same, and so did their clothes. And there on a slight rise of land, in a clearing with fields of manioc, plantain, and other crops, stood the communal hea of vertical chonta poles and sloping thatched roof that I had seen before. Yet I was at least forty miles from Chumbika's territory, with a score of feuding clans in between.

Our welcome was reserved but much less formal than that received from Chumbika. Women and children did not scramble for the backdoor, but stood and looked at us curiously. A half dozen men stared at us, but no one looked angry. They had obviously had no recent unpleasantness with a white man. And Pablo told me they had been at peace for a long time, even with their neighbors.

The surliest Indian of all was the curaka, a persimmon-faced old fellow who talked with Pablo for five minutes before turning and going into the jivaria, leaving the door open. Inside it was dry — the only dry place around, I felt sure. The rain had stopped just before we encountered the warriors on the path, but everything had been saturated before that.

Happily, the greeting ceremony lasted less than ten minutes. I could not have sat there in my wet clothes and soggy boots for a full-scale greeting. The moment it was over I got out gifts for the Indians — mirrors, scissors, a few knives, a length of red cloth — and handed them to Persimmon Face for distribution. Then I stripped off my clothes and wrapped myself in a blanket from a pack that had miraculously kept dry. A woman hung my clothes on a line of fiber running from one pole to another near the front fire and placed my boots nearby. I changed into pajamas and a pair of thin leather slippers. As I sat back on the platform bed, I felt comfortable and relaxed.

Another woman brought me nijimanche, of which I drank a little, and then baked yuca and roast plantain. I dug a can of sardines from my pack and ate ravenously, happily. On the other side of the front door Diego and Pablo were eating, too.

The women were reserved but friendly, the children were wide-eyed and shy and smiling, and the men who entered the jivaria, except for Persimmon Face, seemed at ease and hospitable. I had little need to win them over, and I had no energy to make the effort, anyway. It was dark now and I lay down on the platform bed. I was a primitive man at that moment, happy in the satisfaction of my physical needs, asking no questions about anything.

Most primitives I have met rarely ask for explanations. They do not ask why or how. They are curious about my lighter, my fountain pen, a phonograph, but don't ask how they work. White man's magic, that's all. Since magic is, in effect, their answer to all ultimate questions, they have no need to ask why and how.

The next morning one disadvantage of being a civilized man was apparent to me. My boots were thoroughly dry — stiff dry, in fact. And they were just one size too small for me. This may sound like a minor disaster, but I was immobilized without boots. I could live unarmed among headhunters, tumble down the Andes, or cross turbulent rivers on ropes, but I could not walk barefoot more than fifteen feet in the jivaria and clearing. I was a slave to civilization now.

I sat there swearing softly and glaring at the boots. Then I looked up and saw, across the house, a shrunken head, a tsantsa, hanging from one of the poles. Shrunken head, shrunken boots. Could the process be reversed? Maybe not with a head, but perhaps with my boots. Maybe I could put moisture back in them, first with water which had just come out of them, later with some kind of fat to soften them.

I hobbled to the nearest stream with Pablo. We filled my two boots with small round stones, shoving them down into the toes as tightly as we could. Then we submerged the boots in the stream. I lazed around the hea all day, and welcomed the chance to do so. The sky was still overcast although there was no rain, so I was not tempted to try filming. It was good just to rest. Every two hours I went to the brook and shoved more stones into my boots. And by evening they were my size again. That night I placed them some distance from the fire, with the stones still in them. They dried slowly, and the next morning I rubbed in some fat given me by one of the Jivaro women. It smelled bad but made the leather soft.

As if everything were to be arranged exactly right for me, the morning that I could put on my boots again was also a morning of bright, clear sunshine, ideal for filming. Armed with a camera I walked into the clearing. I started with a shot of old Persimmon Face himself as he sat weaving a huge basket of fiber. When he saw the camera he screamed, dropped the basket, and ran at me violently waving his arms.

The whole clan came running at his scream and gathered behind him, staring at our cameras apprehensively. Pablo and Diego ran to my side, interpreting the old man's outburst.

He would not let us take the souls of his people. He would not let us send evil spirits into them. He would not let us kill the yuca and the plantain in their fields.

I tried to explain what a camera was, showing him pictures of Jivaros on the lower Santiago that I had taken in 1940. He would not even look. Pablo and Diego argued with the Old One. At the end of an hour I knew it was hopeless. I would get no pictures at this jivaria. I consulted with Pablo about the possibility of going on to the next one. He said that the next one would be the same, since they were of the same family, or group, and suggested that we go to the jivaria of a curaka named Peruche.

"Peruche is a great warrior, the leader of many clans," Pablo said. "He's tough, but very smart. A headhunter has to be smart to reach his age, about seventy. He would understand about cameras, I think, and let you take pictures."

So we walked for two days. As we approached the jivaria of Peruche I got the picture I never thought I would get — a full view of a jivaria in its clearing.

Indians usually build their houses on the top of a small hill for the sake of drainage and protection, and I could never get on a higher hill for a picture. Within the clearing itself, it was almost impossible to get a view of the whole house, let alone the house against its background.

But as we came to Peruche's jivaria, we saw it from above — from a hill even higher than the hill on which the house stood. Best of all, there was little foliage between the hilltop and the clearing. I got a clear shot of the whole settlement.

Then I saw a man in the clearing outside the jivaria, and he did what I have rarely seen a Jivaro do. He saw us and waved! It was Peruche.

Peruche was a great and good man, a close friend in a life blessed with many close friends. Even today I remember him with warmth and admiration as a man who lived a full and useful life according to his lights, who possessed understanding, an open heart and an alert mind.

He enjoyed life with zest and vigor. His lined face showed clusters of fine laugh wrinkles around twinkling eyes. At times he would turn to me with the slightest of smiles that warmed my heart, reassured me, and took me into his family. It was a family worth being taken into, for the bonds of love that tied its members together were strong. Never have I seen a more tenderly caressing expression than Peruche's when he looked at his grandchildren.

He was a Jivaro of great repute, a warrior of many heads, a hunter of skill and cunning. But he was a simple man, relaxed and honestly modest. He was so quietly sure of himself that he could forget, when he wished, the customs of the ordinary Jivaro.

The friendly wave was an example of this. It was not the conventional gesture of a headhunter toward strangers who trespassed on his ground. But it was typical of Peruche, who knew no fear, who was the least suspicious of all the Jivaros I have known. Yet he was not uncautious. The Jivaro is intelligent, but Peruche had a singularly facile mind. He looked up and saw Diego and Pablo, two men he knew to be trustworthy. With them was a strange white man, apparently unarmed, who would never have been brought to Peruche's jivaria unless he, too, was trustworthy.

Peruche took in the facts and reached a conclusion instantly. He did not need to look at us threateningly while we stood our ground and he examined us, thought over all contingencies, and fought against his suspicions. He just waved to friends who were bringing a stranger for a visit. And Peruche liked visitors, just as he liked talk and parties.

I learned all these things about Peruche in the course of the three weeks I lived with him and his family, but even at that first meeting I liked him. I liked his informality and the brevity of his greeting. He spoke to Pablo and Pablo answered in a few sentences, and that was all. With a smile he welcomed us to the jivaria and asked one of his wives to bring nijimanche. We drank and were at home.

There were a number of women in the jivaria, of all ages. I soon learned that the old curaka himself had four wives, the oldest around fifty-five, the youngest about twenty. Because of rather unusual circumstances that developed later, I came to know them all rather well — ordinarily a difficult task. I learned at first hand what I had read and heard, that Jivaro wives got along well together. I was unable to sense any indication of jealousy among them, or ill feeling of any kind. Each wife was devoted to Peruche but none felt possessive about him. Only Peruche really possessed Peruche, although he gave of himself freely to wives, children, grandchildren, and friends.

I had always assumed that man was naturally monogamous, but after living with many polygamous tribes I am doubtful. I think that polygamy or monogamy is dependent not upon the nature of man but upon the environment in which he finds himself. In the Jivaro country, polygamy is almost essential because the constant warfare would long ago have wiped out the race without it. Aside from being necessary, it works remarkably well. Peruche's three older wives had helped him select the youngest.

That was the wife he offered me, a day or two after I had set up my tent in his clearing. Abanasa was her name, and she was an attractive young lady by Jivaro standards — robust and strong. She was shy but smiling when Peruche led her to me and put her hand into mine.

When Pablo translated Peruche's offer of his most attractive wife for the duration of my visit, I thanked him warmly but explained that it was taboo for me to take a woman from another tribe. This explanation was satisfactory to Peruche, who could understand taboos, but he insisted that Abanasa should take care of some of my wants if not all of them. No man should perform some tasks, Peruche felt — preparing meals, hauling water, firewood and bundles. Abanasa, with great good spirit and fidelity, performed such tasks as I let her for the rest of my stay with Peruche. She even went along as my "wife" on a hunting trip of several days, to carry supplies.

Jivaro husbands punish infidelity with brutal severity. They do not kill adulterous wives because women are too valuable. But the one who strays may be affixed to the ground with lances for a day or suffer other severe punishment. On the other hand, a Jivaro will offer a wife, as Peruche offered Abanasa to me. Or he will consider a straight business deal with a white man — lending a wife in return for sufficient payment.

Not every Jivaro can easily find as many wives as he wants. Sometimes he gets one from a raid on an enemy jivaria. More often he purchases her from her father or brother. If he is a great warrior and hunter he has little difficulty.

Peruche's three husky sons were all married. The eldest, Juanga, about thirty-five, had three wives. (There had been several older sons, but they had all been killed.) The second son, Peasa, now in his twenties, had two wives, and the youngest, Ambusha, only eighteen, had one. Ambusha was courting a young lady of a neighboring jivaria while I was there. Despite the commercial nature of the transaction, there is a strong element of romance in Jivaro marriages, especially with young couples.

Ambusha had seen the girl when, returning from a hunt, he had stopped at a friendly jivaria. She attracted him at once, and he thought that she regarded him rather favorably, but no words were exchanged. He prepared himself for a visit three days later, painting himself with great care, cutting his hair neatly in front, weaving toucan feathers in his braids, putting small feathers on his ear plugs. The call, however, was not officially a call. Ambusha said he just happened to stop by on his way from a hunt.

He was welcomed into the hea, of course, and was served nijimanche by the women. When the girl of his fancy served him, he took the gourd roughly and acted thoroughly unpleasant. When he tossed the food she served him on the ground, she knew he was strongly interested.

I was at Peruche's at the time of Ambusha's second visit, and saw him bring home the leaves of a plant called *muspa*. He placed them near a fire until they dried, then crumbled them into a powder and added some sweet-smelling herbs. He took this along with him on his next call, together with several gifts — vanilla beans, a comb, and the mirror I had given him only a few days before. Peruche told me that when he entered the girl's jivaria, he would try to rub the powder on her hands and breasts. If she looked upon him with favor, she would let him. That and taking his presents would tell him she would accept him.

Ambusha was very happy when he came home, although he tried to act quite brusque and casual about the whole thing. For the next step he was out of it. He sent a cousin off to negotiate with the girl's father. I never could learn what price he paid, but the deal went through and the girl came to Peruche's jivaria to live. There was no marriage ceremony of any kind. She was obviously very much in love with Ambusha and was warmly welcomed by that young man's other wife.

Peruche seemed pleased that I was so interested in his family. He seemed to understand that I was just curious to learn about their relationships, for he had the same kind of mind himself. He was one of the few Jivaros I knew who asked almost as many questions as he answered — about my country, my clothes, my women. Talking to him was a pleasure not only because Pablo and Diego were both first-class interpreters but because Peruche himself was so quick that much of the customary time lag of conversation through an interpreter was absent.

Peruche was pleased with me because of my gifts and because I was the excuse for a party. The choicest gift was the oddest thing I had even taken with me, even more unusual than the phonograph of my first trip. I bought it on impulse in a Cuenca shop. It was a hat of some kind, although I have never seen such a hat on anyone's head anywhere. It looked like a cross between a fez and an overseas cap, but very fancy. The color attracted me I think — bright red felt, with a white tuft on top. Peruche put it on his head the moment I gave it to him and seldom took it off again. I'm sure he wore it at night, and I know he was wearing it when he died.

He was almost as pleased with another gift I brought — eyebrow pencils. It had seemed like an obvious gift to me after I had seen Indians painting black lines on their faces with sharp sticks dipped in a dye laboriously made from berries of the genipa bush. I should have brought a gross to the Jivaro country, for nothing could have made a bigger hit. I still enjoy running off the film of Peruche wearing the red hat, making himself up as he looks in one of the hand mirrors I brought. He runs the eyebrow pencil smoothly over his cheeks and the bridge of his nose. It makes a fine line so easily and he beams, smiles, adds another line, and then another.

At first Peruche was somewhat skeptical about my taking pictures.

He too had the Jivaro superstition that pictures took away part of a man or a man's soul, but he was willing to be convinced to the contrary. I showed him the prints of pictures I had taken on my trip in 1940 of Chumbika and others in the Huambisa tribe. But first I showed Peruche himself in the little mirror and asked if that took away part of him. No, of course not. Then I showed a picture of Chumbika, almost exactly the size of the mirror, and asked why that should take away soul any more than the mirror. It sounded convincing enough, and I added that Chumbika was still strong and healthy after I had taken many pictures, even pictures that moved.

He was intrigued by the thought of moving pictures but could not understand. I held up the mirror again and told him to talk, laugh, and nod his head. The pictures, I told him, moved just the way he moved in the mirror. He got the idea, but could not understand how it was possible. Still, the how and why were not important once he saw what I meant. But I have never wished so much for a projector and electric current in the jungle. Peruche would have been the perfect audience for almost any movie.

Tuki, the medicine man or wishinu of Peruche's clan, did not really approve of pictures, but once Peruche had made up his mind that they were all right no arguments could change him. Tuki finally allowed me to take some pictures of him, but without very good grace, and I always had the idea that he thought Peruche was too free in his hospitality, too forthright in taking me into his family.

I ate my meals with the Jivaros, often dipping into my limited store of tinned foods. The fish served by the Indians was usually good; the yuca was nourishing, but tiresome after a while; plantains, similar to our bananas, were always cooked and were enjoyable; meat stews were sometimes good, sometimes bad. I could not eat the weevils, ants, bird entrails, and other special delicacies. The chief reason I had to add food of my own, however, was that I drank almost no nijimanche, of which all Jivaros — and Pablo and Diego — consumed several quarts a day. This beverage contains much nutritive value as well as a small quantity of alcohol.

Peruche wanted to start the filming right away but it began to rain again the day after our arrival, and it rained for three days. Then the sun came out and the jungle became as dry as it ever gets. I filmed activities around the jivaria — men weaving, women making pottery and chewing yuca for nijimanche. I had two movie cameras at hand, one loaded for immediate use when the other came to the end of a roll. Peruche hovered around, interested in everything I did, and was happy to appear in as many scenes as possible. We talked about my filming some hunting and fishing scenes, and he was so cooperative that I decided to ask about the sequence I wanted most — the victory dance at a tsantsa festival.

Peruche looked puzzled and explained that no tsantsa feast was planned, as there had been no raids in that region for months. I told him that I wanted to reenact the dance, and asked if he had a tsantsa. He still had the shrunken head from his last feast six months before, and as he came to understand my ideas grew enthusiastic. Here was a chance to have a big party. He would call in people from neighboring jivarias so we would have plenty of fine dancers.

Peruche became my producer. He sent his son Juanga to the signal drum, and a message was drummed out: "Come to Peruche's for a feast." The curaka was particularly pleased that he could have a party without fasting.

"When I come home from killing my enemy," he explained, "I am washed with chicken blood on the legs and painted with black *sua*. The tsantsa is already shrunk, for I have done that on the way. We must be very careful that the spirit of my enemy does not harm me, for his spirit lives in his head, above all in his hair. It tries to get back at me, of course, but we do many things to conquer the spirit and make it obey me, even help me. We stick the tsantsa on a lance in the ground, the lance I killed my enemy with. We dance around it and thrust our lances at it, frightening the spirit, showing how we killed. And the women sing and dance, too. And the other women — the women we have taken from my enemy's jivaria — stand by and weep. If we captured no women, we have some of our own women take their part and weep bitterly. But I must fast, I cannot eat meat or big fish, for my enemy's spirit may enter into them and so enter into me. And I cannot go to any of my wives. For six months I must fast and be continent. Then I can hold the big tsantsa feast and finally conquer my enemy's spirit. Then my sons' spirits see and know that I have killed the enemy who killed them, that I have overcome his spirit. They will be happy and can rest content, and my hunting will be good, my sons will be strong, and I will live long."

He smiled and then chuckled. "Now we will have a victory dance, and I will not have to fast. I can eat good meat and sleep with my wives tonight." Perhaps he wondered why this idea had never occurred to him before.

The guests began to arrive early the next morning, the men decked out in their best finery, feathered headdresses, belts of human hair, necklaces of shells, and jaguar's teeth. The women wore dancing belts of shells, perhaps a necklace or two, but otherwise were dressed the same as usual. A few older children — that is, more than seven years old — came along for the fun.

The formal greetings seemed to last forever, to the accompaniment of the drinking of vast quantities of nijimanche, for Peruche had to greet each man individually, a lengthy procedure even with the old man's shortened version of this ritual. By midafternoon there were about fifty men and women in addition to Peruche's own family group, and everyone was in a festive mood.

Peruche explained the reason for the party. I'm sure that many of his guests did not understand why they should dance a victory dance when there had been no victory, but the curaka's influence was strong enough to make most of them go along with it.

The women entered into the spirit of the idea readily and enjoyed themselves immensely as they formed two lines, through which the victor — enacted by Juanga at Peruche's insistence — strode home with the tsantsa suspended around his neck and hanging against his chest. Juanga thrust his lance into the ground and placed the shrunken head on top of it. He glared at the tsantsa with hatred and venom, supposedly to frighten the spirit that dwelled within it.

Peruche dispensed with the ritual of washing with chicken blood and the dye called sua, made from the genipa berries, feeling that the dance was the important thing. Warriors with lances formed a circle around the tsantsa and started the dance, stepping together forward, then back, forward again, sideways a few steps, back, then forward. A rhythmic chant that may have consisted of words but sounded to me more like a guttural, breathy grunt beat a steady pulse and grew gradually in strength and volume. The forward steps became lunges toward the hated tsantsa on its lance, and next each lunge brought a hard thrust of the lance in each warrior's hand, aimed at the black, shrunken head.

For half an hour the men danced, then broke away, tired and acting as if hypnotized by the scene they had just enacted. Other men took their places, joined hands in a circle and danced around the tsantsa, grunting out a chant about the bravery of the victor, the triumphant killing of the despicable foe, the warnings against the evil spirit to keep away. Three steps in toward the tsantsa, three steps back, then a movement sideways and another closing in on the tsantsa. It was not a complicated dance, nor was it particularly graceful or attractive. So elementary that a child could have learned it in a few minutes, it still carried passion and fierce power because of the chant, the expressions on the men's faces, and because of the presence of the ugly miniature head that had once set proudly on a man's shoulders.

The women next formed a large circle and danced — there were more women than men — but there was none of the same spirit in what they did. I suppose even at a genuine victory dance, the women cannot feel the thrill of the battle, the pride of victory, the venomous hatred of the head. They feel happiness at having their men home again after a war in which all might have been slain, with their heads serving as tsantsas of other tribes. So the women smiled and giggled and danced rather awkwardly.

After more drinking of nijimanche the visitors left for their own jivarias so as to reach them before dark. Peruche was almost jolly, perhaps a little bit intoxicated, happy over the success of his party and my pleasure at having such good pictures. He even had his two younger sons show me how the head of an enemy is cut off. Peasa demonstrated on Ambusha with his hands, emphasizing how important it was to cut just as low as possible, close to the shoulders.

That evening as we sat and talked I asked Peruche how many heads he had taken during his lifetime. He said he had taken five during the preceding year, but some years none at all. He did not tell me how many he had taken all together and I believe he really did not quite know. But he told me of several great curakas who had fifty or sixty heads each. The greatest of all was a curaka named Utitiaja who lived many days' journey to the north.

Peruche named a river near which the famous Utitiaja lived. Pablo told me that he did not know the river but that it was one of the tributaries of the Upano, which joined the Paute, the two becoming eventually the Santiago. I questioned Pablo in some detail, wondering if we might pay a visit to the greatest headhunter of them all, but he said it was impossible — too long a trip. I would have to go into Jivaro country by another route to find Utitiaja.

After my first few days at Peruche's jivaria, I enjoyed each morning a delightful scene. The Jivaros get up early, the men often stirring before dawn. It usually took half an hour of daylight to carry me into full consciousness, until near the end of my stay when I found myself keeping Jivaro hours. Each morning as I pulled back the mosquito netting on the side of my hammock, I saw two wide-eyed children staring at me, waiting for me to make that move. They were Papué, a boy of about ten, and Yangora, a girl of five or six. They were the children of Juanga, grandchildren of Peruche. They were most endearing and they in turn were fascinated by me.

When Papué and Yangora saw that I was awake they ran to me. Yangora slipped her arms around my neck and chattered words I could not understand but did not need to. I almost expected her to kiss me, except for the fact that the kiss is totally unknown to Jivaros. Affection, cuddling, and caressing are *not* unknown, however, and many doting Jivaro parents almost smother their children with demonstrations of love, much to the delight of the children. Yangora liked me and showed it simply, forthrightly. I showed my affection for her, too, wishing that I could do so less self-consciously.

Papué was more reserved, of course. A Jivaro boy of ten is almost a man. He has gone on hunting trips scores of times with his father and is becoming expert with the blowgun. He has accompanied his father on raids, witnessing the slaughter and the decapitations even if not taking an active part yet. There is a certain dignity, therefore, that he must maintain. But Papué admired my pajamas as much as he liked me, I think, for he always sidled up to me smiling, and touched the cloth.

One morning I looked up to see Juanga, his three wives, and Peruche and two of his wives beaming upon us. Jivaro fathers and mothers are devoted to their children and, like devoted parents everywhere, enjoy seeing their children loved and appreciated by others. I know that one of the chief reasons Peruche took me into the heart of his family was the affection between his grandchildren and me.

In the light of these tender scenes, it was shocking one morning a bit later, when I was beginning to get up at the same time as the Indians, to hear Juanga instructing his son Papué in hatred. Early every morning the father with gravity and deep feeling sat his son down before him to teach him, to drill into him, the basic facts upon which a Jivaro's life is built. Diego translated for me.

"Your uncle, my brother, was killed by the wishinu Anguasha of the Achuales of the upper Morana. Another uncle, dead before you were born, was killed in a war with the Achuales, when they attacked in the dead of night and stole two of his young daughters. The Achuales are your enemies, my enemies, your grandfather's enemies. Together we have taken scores of their heads but we have not yet avenged the deaths of my two brothers. When you become a man you must make yourself a brave and clever warrior so you can kill Anguasha and take his head and take his women. Before everything else, that is your sacred duty. Your uncle's spirit is unhappy. You must give him peace. If you do this you will be rewarded with fine wives, with good hunting, with good crops. If you fail you will be cursed — you will get nagging wives who will bear you no children, the game will elude you in the forest, and your crops will fail."

Every morning, day after day, Juanga said these words, or words like them, to his son Papué. He had already been doing this daily, except when he was away on a long hunting trip or raid, for five years. Papué nodded and listened solemnly, with a look of dedication in his eyes.

I walked away from this scene one morning to the other side of the jivaria, and there I found the wishinu, Tuki, going through the same performance with his two young sons. He was bringing home his message with a tsantsa in his hands which he showed to the boys, shaking it in their faces.

Depressing thoughts about the teaching of hate to children stayed with me all day, but by evening, as I sat around the fire with Peruche and Juanga and Papué, I felt better, and I had a glimpse of the sounder and more useful training the Jivaro boys had received. I wanted to learn all I could about the animals, fish, and birds of the region. Many animals and birds I had already seen, and others I hoped to see. The next day, I knew, I would go fishing with a large group from the jivaria. But I sincerely hoped, despite my curiosity, that I would not encounter any snakes. Anaconda and boa run away from man, but the poisonous sankes rarely do. Some of them will attack even when they are not cornered.

Papué told me about the *cascabel*, rattlesnake, its many bright blotches of color, its heaviness, its average length of five or six feet. His eyes darted fire as he told how ferocious the cascabel was, moving forward to attack. "It will never retreat from anyone," he said with admiration. He told me that its striking force was so great that it could break a man's neck.

Papué took the words from Peruche's mouth when the old curaka started to tell me about the largest of the poisonous snakes, the bushmaster, which grows up to eleven or twelve feet long.

"My father killed a bushmaster," Papué said proudly, "with his lance. I saw it. Its fangs were this long." He held up his fingers almost two inches apart. Such fangs can penetrate deep and pour out as much as a teaspoonful of venom.

"My father has killed many *jararacas*," Papué said, "because there are so many of them. They are terrible, even if they are the smallest." From the description I soon realized that Papué was talking about the fer-de-lance, called jararaca in the Amazon basin. It usually grows three or four feet long, but bigger ones have been found. After a bite, if untreated with antitoxin, death occurs in perhaps an hour, sometimes not for several days. But those are miserable days filled with convulsions, excruciating pains, vomiting, and hemorrhages.

We went on to talk about birds, and Peruche, Juanga, and Papué gave me the calls of twenty different birds in the course of fifteen minutes. No one knows the jungle better than the Jivaro Indian, and Papué at the age of ten seemed to know every living creature in it. He would be a great hunter and a great warrior, too.

The next day was festive and gay because community fishing had been planned, which the Indians enjoyed. Almost everyone in the jivaria took part. The women gathered branches of the poisonous barbasco plant. The children had already rushed ahead to the stream when I started out with the men to see if the dam was still all right and perhaps pile more rocks on it. When we came to the stream, about fifteen minutes' walk from the jivaria, I saw what they meant. The stream itself was not large, having a width of about fifteen feet. At one point, where two boulders projected into the water and narrowed the brook, piles of rocks had been heaped up. It was not a complete dam, by any means, for a good deal of water gurgled through and over the rocks. It stopped it sufficiently, however, to back up a spreading body of water for forty or fifty feet.

The women and children, and some of the men, went immediately to the dam, but I wanted to watch the spreading of the narcotic barbasco. Juanga and Tuki and two other Jivaros took the branches, placed them on flat rocks, and pounded them with other rocks until the branches were bruised and oozing sap. When they had a fair quantity prepared, they waded into the water where it spread out in the artificial bay, and tossed the lacerated branches evenly over the surface. The movement of the stream carried the poison slowly toward the other Indians waiting near the dam.

I hurried down there, for I wanted to catch fish, too. In less than ten minutes we saw fish leaping from the water as if trying to get away from it. Others swam frantically near the surface, toward the dam, ahead of the poisoned stream; some slipped through in the little waterfalls that poured over the rocks, but others were trapped and soon turned over on their sides and floated with only feeble movements or none at all.

The Jivaros leaped into the water with joyful shouts, lunging for the stupefied fish. Up came Ambusha with a fish in each hand and one in his mouth; he rushed to the shore and tossed his trophies in a big fiber basket and dashed into the water again. Fascinated, I watched for a few minutes as men and women, boys and girls, snatched at the fish, laughing and shouting uproariously. Without quite realizing it, I was in the midst of them, snatching at feebly swimming fish. I even tucked one in my mouth as I glimpsed another that might get away if I didn't grab it. I think I picked up twenty fish in the next few minutes, and I waded ashore, laughing and tired, to take up my camera and get some footage.

The fish were small, about the size of brook trout, but we had hundreds of them. For many days we had fish to eat.

Later during my visit I had another fishing experience that was not so pleasant. After a downpour of three days, Juanga decided that the water in another river had risen enough to make the fish trap productive. This stream was a good deal larger than the first, and there was no effort to build a dam all the way across. At a spot where there was a natural drop over a rocky ledge of about a foot and a half, the fish trap was set up — a kind of box made of bamboo slats. Most of the water poured onto the bamboo slats and right on through. But the fish were caught. I saw how neatly the trap worked, and then went upstream with some of the men and women, about three hundred feet above the trap. Two women stayed behind to toss the fish into baskets as they were caught.

We waded into the stream with loads of stones in our arms and threw them ahead of us as we walked slowly down the stream toward the trap. About fifty feet above the trap, I looked ahead and saw the women busily tossing fish in baskets. The water grew deeper here, almost up to the waist of some of the short Jivaro women. Suddenly one of them screamed, dropped her stones, and raced for shore, still screaming. I thought of a dozen things — electric eel, stingray, piranha fish, some kind of water snake. But as I hurried ashore behind the others I saw that one hand was clasped tightly against her crotch. The women at the trap forgot their work and came running, too, and all huddled around the young woman, who lay on the ground writhing and screaming. Words were mingled with her cries, but of course I could understand nothing. Suddenly two of the older women seemed to comprehend, cried out in alarm, and gave quick orders. One young man hurried off toward the jivaria on the run, and the two older women knelt beside the young woman in pain and talked to her soothingly as they began to examine her.

In a few minutes the man came running from the jivaria and handed a small object to one of the older women. Behind him came another woman, puffing and muttering to herself, and behind her the witch doctor, carrying several pouches of monkey fur and looking worried.

A piercing scream from the woman on the ground ended in low moans of severe pain, and I saw a good deal of blood on the ground near her. The medicine man stood up. Four Jivaros then picked up the moaning girl and carried her toward the jivaria. The others talked among themselves, shook their heads, as they went to get the baskets of fish and head for home. I went along with them, feeling ignorant and useless.

It was an hour before I learned what had happened to the girl, after Pablo had gathered the information for me.

"Canero," he said, as if that should tell me everything. And in a moment, when the meaning of the word came back to me, it did. The canero is a tiny fish, probably of the catfish family, only about two inches long. It will swim up any orifice — rectum, urethra, or vagina, the only example of a vertebrate human parasite. For many years scientists were convinced that the canero, or dandiru, was only an Amazonian legend, a tall tale of the Indians, but they were puzzled when they saw many Indians in different sections, tribes without any communication with each other, using protective devices when they went in the water. Indians are close observers of nature and are usually great pragmatists in dealing with it. But then the scientists pointed to thousands of natives who wore no protective devices at all.

Finally authenticated cases were observed. A doctor from Pará reported that he had himself handled three cases in one year. In one case amputation of the penis had been necessary. In another he had extracted the fish, but its spiny gills so tore the flesh that a hemorrhage resulted in the death of the victim. The doctor was far from hospital or office and had inadequate equipment. The third patient recovered with no more damage than some loss of blood when the little canero was extracted with a small forceps.

The poor girl in the river had felt the canero dart into her vagina. She screamed and ran to shore. The young man had brought from the jivaria a kind of bamboo forceps with which the canero was removed, the spines clutching at the tender flesh and ripping it. The wishinu had placed medications in the wound to stop the bleeding. The girl recovered, but she was unable to walk for several days and was quite weak from loss of blood.

My own health was in for a serious jolt. I had run out of canned food and lived now entirely on the food of my hosts — baked or boiled yuca, plantains, peanuts, some fish, and occasionally a taste of monkey stew. I carefully boiled all the water that I drank, much to the amazement of the Jivaros as well as Pablo and Diego. Of all the dangers I might encounter in the jungle, drinking water concerned me as much as anything. The Indians had developed immunities over the years which I did not possess, just as I had developed immunities to measles and other "civilized" diseases that would have decimated them.

At the end of my third week with Peruche I began to feel uneasy in the stomach. I thought it was rebelling at getting nothing but food it was unaccustomed to and that in a few days I would feel better. I convinced myself of this because I did not want to miss going on a long hunt with Juanga and two other Jivaros.

Pablo went along with me and the three warriors, as well as two of the warriors' wives, and Abanasa, the women carrying fiber baskets with cooking jars, nijimanche, yuca, plantains. The men painted their faces with *achiote* and fresh markings from my eyebrow pencils. They filled their monkey-fur pouches with toucan feathers and other ornaments they could put on if they should visit another jivaria en route, as well as certain small bones and shells which were good luck charms for the hunt.

The afternoon before the hunt they prepared their poisoned darts. They took small gourds, about three inches in diameter, containing thick, gummy material that looked like dark chocolate. Juanga licked the sharp end of a dart in his mouth, then carefully plastered the dark substance on the point for a distance of a little under an inch, using a small flat stick dipped into the gourd. He stuck the dart in the ground, point up, near the fire. This went on until he had a long row, and still another, of poisoned darts.

The poison was curare, of course, for so many years the favorite of mystery-story writers. It has been built up as a mysterious and malevolent poison of almost supernatural potency, containing unknown ingredients and having no antidote. The facts are that you can take it in your mouth and swallow it without ill effects — Juanga demonstrated this for me smilingly. The essential ingredients of curare are well known. The antidote for it is plain salt.

Curare is an effective poison, all right, but only when introduced into the bloodstream directly; that's why it can be swallowed. And although the Jivaro wishinu who makes curare — he usually has a monopoly — mashes up at least two vines, a pepper, a root, several leaves, and later adds spiders, ants, and other ingredients to the boiling mixture, only one of these items, a vine, makes the poison.

As for the salt antidote, it may not always work, especially if the dose of poison is strong and it has been in the system some time. But the Jivaro may paralyze a monkey with the poisoned dart and then revive it with salt if he wants to give it as a pet to his children. They do not worry about an effective antidote for humans because they never use it on other men and women. They say that the blowgun and curare were given to them for hunting and if they use them to kill men they will lose all effectiveness on animals and birds. The fact is they would probably make poor weapons in war. A man would have to be filled with darts before the poison would have much effect. And of course he could always take salt.

The next morning we were on our way as the sun rose. The Jivaros were making no effort to be quiet for the first hour or two, but I could not hear a sound as they walked through the jungle. Once when Pablo and I were at the rear of the column, I halted him for a moment. We listened. Although six Indians were still in sight of us, we could hear absolutely nothing. Even the women made no sound as they trudged along carrying the heavy baskets.

The hunters were always on the alert, but we saw no game before we stopped for a midday meal. During the afternoon the hunters bagged three monkeys, which they wrapped in leaves and stuffed in the women's baskets. That night we ate another meal like the one we had before and slept on the ground. Strangely, I did not feel at all uneasy, although I heard sounds in the jungle around me that might have been jaguars. I knew that as long as the Jivaros slept peacefully all was well. Except for my stomach, that is. It complained bitterly, and made me get up three times during the night.

On the third day we visited a friendly jivaria for a couple of hours, and had our midday meal there. Juanga's friends regarded me curiously for a few moments, and that was all. They accepted the strange sight of a white man with an amazing casualness despite the fact that, as Juanga told me, they had seen only four white men before.

The next day we caught a three-toed sloth. I think I could have passed within ten feet of it without seeing it, but the Indians spotted it. Even when we stopped and stared at it, scarcely four feet away, it did not move, other than to turn its head slowly and look at us with a vacant, absentminded expression.

The longer I looked at it the sorrier I felt for it. I have seen many silly-looking creatures, including the anteater, but the sloth is a caricature of what an animal ought to be. It lives its life upside down, for one thing. There was this creature, its four curved paws hooked around a branch of a tree, its long thin legs reaching down to a body about the size of a small dog's. At one end of the body was tucked a tiny head, at the other end nothing.

Juanga thrust his lance at the sloth and brought him to earth. The sloth was determined not to die, it seemed, for it kept moving its legs even after Juanga pierced its heart with his lance.

I had a question in my mind and finally asked it after the sloth had been stowed away in one of the large baskets. Did Juanga plan to eat this sloth or make a tsantsa from it? Juanga intended to eat it, for its meat was delicious. He told me that tsantsas were made from sloths' heads only as substitutes for human heads. Sometimes in war an Indian may kill his enemy but be unable to take his head. A counterattack may drive him away until the dead man's friends retrieve the body. Or the victim may be a relative of one of the attacking party, in which case it is unethical to cut off the head. But the warrior who kills his man is entitled to a tsantsa and a tsantsa feast if he wants. So he kills a sloth, shrinks its head, and goes through the whole ritual with this substitute, which serves all supernatural purposes just as well as the real thing.

On the next day I felt weak. There was no doubt now that I had a bad case of dysentery. When Juanga saw that I was quite ill, he showed deep concern and discussed with his fellows the best procedure to follow. We were far from Peruche's jivaria, I knew, even if we went back by the most direct route.

Juanga finally decided that the best thing to do was to visit a jivaria nearby, the clanhouse of a friendly group although not of the same subtribe as Peruche's. We could reach the jivaria, he said, in an hour's walk, and there I could rest more comfortably for a day or so, get better food for my ailing stomach.

We heard the boom of the big signal drum in a short while. Juanga and the others stopped and talked excitedly with each other. From Pablo I learned that the signal was a signal of war, war being launched by the men of the jivaria we planned to visit! I wanted to turn right around and go back that instant, but Juanga finally decided that all would be well. Peruche's group and this clan of Asapi had always been at peace. Asapi had an age-old enemy farther to the east, on the tributaries of the Morona River. They had buried the lance many times but had always dug it up to fight again. Although I did not like to barge in on preparations for a war, Juanga insisted that we would be received as friends.

I followed in his wake, listening somewhat fearfully but lethargically to the louder rumble of the drum as we approached. If I had felt better, I would have been more frightened, I think. I did not have energy to expend on fright. And Pablo seemed unconcerned. He knew Asapi, he told me.

We approached the war jivaria cautiously, with many *whe-dee's*, and were challenged by fierce-looking warriors. But they accepted

Juanga and his fellows; they knew Pablo. I was the only suspect, but Juanga's vouching for me and my own too obvious sickness calmed their suspicions.

Inside the jivaria there were about twenty-five warriors, tense, excited, overstimulated. They had been drinking *nateema* or *maikoa*, narcotic drinks — probably for several days. Before a raid many warriors drink the narcotics, and the leader of an expedition always does, to learn from the spirits what success will be achieved. The dreams had been very propitious, it was obvious, for this group was exuding fury and smelling triumph already.

I sat on a platform bed at one side of the jivaria and, after a short ritual greeting, was brought nijimanche, which I refused, and boiled yuca. I asked for plantain and boiled water, nothing else. When the water came it was scarcely warm, and I had to insist that it be taken back and put on the fire until it boiled. When this was done I lay back wearily. Juanga and the others ate and joined me to keep out of the way of the preparations for the war expedition.

I got almost no rest that night. At about midnight the warriors lined up in two rows, facing each other, and danced the loud lance dance. They chanted at the top of their voices, lunged forward threateningly, waved their lances, acting as if they were about to kill each other. Pablo explained to me that the shouts were chiefly exhortations to each other. "How brave we are! Tomorrow we kill! I kill my enemy this way! He will not kill me! We shall make tsantsas!"

Despite the noise and the rare spectacle I was witnessing, I drifted off to half-sleep occasionally, to be roused by a new burst of blood-curdling cries from the warriors. I looked at Asapi, the curaka, and saw that his eyes were glazed from the effects of the nateema he had been drinking. How could a man in this condition carry out a raid successfully? Then I learned that the Indians would have to travel three days before reaching the jivarias of their enemies. By that time they would be sober and alert.

Shortly before dawn the war party prepared to leave. The women, who had remained in their section of the house most of this time, came out and said good-bye. I saw then that fully a dozen of them were also prepared for traveling, with heavy fiber baskets on their backs. They would accompany the warriors, carrying food and nijimanche. I saw, too, that four boys, about ten or eleven, were preparing to go along.

The women who were staying formed in a circle to dance a dance and chant a song that would bring victory to their men. It was not nearly so loud or disturbing as the warriors' dance and song. I watched them for a few moments and could detect no sign of fear or sadness in any of them. Across the room I saw a very old man on a bed nodding his head in time to their chant, perhaps wishing he were not too old to go to war. In the women's section the wives of our party lay on a bed resting, and half a dozen young children were there, too. I lay back again and went to sleep. It was some time later that I heard the story of the attack. For three days Asapi led his party over hills and across rivers toward the jivaria of his enemies. On the night of the third day they cautiously approached the clearing, keeping off the paths, which were probably set with traps. For this was not a secret sneak attack, as are many Jivaro raids. The lance had been formally buried between these two warring groups and when Asapi, through injuries he felt he must have suffered at the hands of the enemy wishinu's spirits, wanted to make war again he had to dig up the lance and announce it to the enemy himself. The enemy was prepared, waiting behind the stout chonta walls of his jivaria.

The barking of dogs told the enemy that Asapi and his warriors had arrived. Inside the house the warriors at once went into a victory dance similar to that I had witnessed, shouting defiant insults at Asapi's men, who listened on the fringes of the jungle and hurled back louder insults and fired off the few guns they had. Those inside fired guns, but no one was hurt.

As dawn was breaking the defiant noise inside the house rose to a screaming crescendo, and a particularly loud volley of shots poured out. Asapi quickly gave orders for a noisy retreat. A quarter of a mile away they circled back as silently as jaguars and waited in the jungle on the side of the jivaria nearest the women's door. The house was silent.

In fifteen minutes the women's door opened and an old woman slipped out, looking about in fright. She heard nothing and walked a little further around the side of the hea. Then Asapi and his men rushed from the jungle, crashed through the open door, and attacked the defenders. Guns were thrown aside and only lances used in this fierce hand-to-hand battle. Asapi shrieked with gloating triumph when he saw that despite the warning of attack his enemy had assembled only about eighteen warriors in the hea. With the fury of jaguars the men attacked each other, thrusting lances, lunging, dodging, parrying. One man was caught as he dashed for the door, but another succeeded in getting through the front door just as a lance pierced the wall in the spot where he had stood a second before. The one thrusting the lance was immediately impaled on a lance himself, and crumpled to the ground, oozing blood.

Children screamed and got in the way; they were lanced at once. So were the old women. In fifteen minutes Asapi and nineteen of his men stood bloody and triumphant in the midst of bodies. Somewhere in the fight three more of the enemy had managed to escape. At one side of the house huddled five young women, two of them little more than girls. Four young women had been lanced because they fought against the invaders.

Five of the slain men were recognized as relatives by some of Asapi's fighters, and those bodies were shoved aside. Their heads could not be taken. The little children were kicked aside, too, for no Jivaro is interested in a child's head, or a woman's. A woman has no soul in the Jivaro world. That left nine heads, and the warriors went quickly about the business of severing those nine heads from the bodies. Two of the defeated men were not yet dead, but that made no difference. With the sharp lance points the skin was cut on the chest and rolled back. The muscles were cut through, and then the lance pushed expertly between two vertebrae low on the neck.

Rounding up the women captives, the warriors went outside. They pulled long strips of palm leaves and strung the heads upon them, leading the strips through the mouth and out through the hole in the neck. Then hurling insults and looking fearfully back to see if perhaps the escaped enemies had found reinforcements, they went swiftly into the jungle toward the camp where they had left their own women.

They marched hard and fast for a full day, until they were out of the territory of the enemy, although not yet close to their own. On a sandy beach by a small stream they made camp, and the women prepared food while the men prepared their tsantsas.

Asapi took a sharp bamboo knife from his monkey-fur pouch and parted the hair of the enemy wishinu carefully up the back. Then he cut through the scalp neatly, from the bottom of the bloody neck to the top of the skull. Next he peeled back the skin away from the skull, using the bamboo knife where necessary to free the flesh from the bone. In fifteen minutes he had removed the skin from the skull, which he tossed aside. Asapi then sewed the eyelids shut from the inside, after which he turned the skin right side out.

From his pouch the tired but happy curaka took three short, pointed pins of chonta wood which he thrust through the lips. He wound long chambira fibers around the pins to make certain the lips remained shut.

He then went to a jar of water that had been placed over a fire. Into it he dropped the juice of a vine that he knew would keep the hair from falling from his tsantsa. Holding the head by the end of the hair, he lowered it into the water. While the head cooked, Asapi went to the water's edge looking for stones, round stones of certain sizes. When he found two or three he returned to the fire and put them in the ashes to become hot. He lifted the head from the water to see how it was coming along and noted with satisfaction that it had already begun to grow smaller.

Asapi had to wander far up and down the stream to find enough of the stones he wanted, for there were eight other warriors going through the same process and all searched for stones. The boys who had come along helped, of course, and watched closely every operation performed by the fighters.

After about two hours of boiling the head was about a third the size it had been originally. Asapi took it from the water, holding it by the hair and waving it so it would cool off enough for him to handle it. It did not look much like a human face, for many of the features were out of shape and the skin was a dirty yellow. But Asapi knew he could take care of those things. He had done all this many times before.

Holding the head in his left hand he made holes with a chonta pin along the sides of the incision, then neatly sewed them together with fiber. He now had a kind of hollow sack that had only a few hours before been scowling at him and hurling insults at him. With a forked stick, Asapi reached into the fire and found a round stone that would fit into the neck opening of his tsantsa. As he dropped it in, there was a loud sizzling and a cloud of steam arose. Holding the head in both hands he rotated it rapidly so that the hot stone rolled around inside, searing away all loose flesh and drying out the skin.

When the sizzling stopped that meant the stone was cool, so Asapi

One of Africa's most dangerous and unpredictable animals is the irascible rhino. I was filming the charges of a rhino against an elusive jeep driven by Ace DuPreez, with cameraman Johnny Coquillon beside him. Suddenly the rhino saw me and started for me (top picture). I ran for my truck as DuPreez tried to divert the surprisingly speedy rhino (middle picture). But the rhino kept after me and was perilously close (bottom picture) when I reached the truck, which sped away to safety.

ABOVE: These two young men of the Masai tribe, of Tanganyika and Kenya, have only memories of the days when they were fearless lion-hunters and fearsome warriors, but they have kept their pride, their beauty, and their ceremonial finery. BELOW: I visited these plate-lipped women of the Babira tribe on my 1937 trip to Africa. Babira men considered them attractive, but lip-stretching died out, and by 1964 only a few old women were still this "beautiful."

ABOVE: Rudahigwa, then king of the aristocratic, seven-feet-tall Watusi, in Ruanda, enjoys the amazing high jumping of his athletic subjects. BELOW: His even-taller father, Msinga, deposed by the Belgians for his cruelty, posed for me with some of his wives and children in 1937. By 1964 both kings were dead and many of the Watusi had been killed or driven from the land by their former serfs, the normal-sized Bahutu.

ABOVE: On one of my visits to the Pygmies I approached the Ituri Forest, seen in the background, by way of the Ituri River, in a dugout propelled by some Bantu villagers. BELOW: Chief Ekibondo of the Mangbetu tribe in northeastern Congo, with four of his many wives. Each stool on which we sat was beautifully carved from a single block of hardwood. I had to use two in order to sit at a comfortable height.

A Mangbetu mother binds her baby's head to make it grow in the elongated shape favored by the generally attractive women of this tribe. Her own elaborate hairdo accentuates the length of her head. In recent years, head-binding has almost disappeared, although it caused no damage to the brain.

The Pygmies of the Ituri Forest, in the northeastern Congo, hunt elephants by smearing themselves with elephant dung to cover their human scent, smoking some hemp to give them courage, creeping silently up behind their chosen prey, and hamstringing it. As the huge beast tries to drag itself away, the hunters dart in with repeated thrusts of their slender, sharp spears. ABOVE: Four Pygmies carve up an elephant that has finally fallen. BELOW: The whole village celebrates the successful hunt with a dance that lasts most of the night.

Although I am of average height, I felt like a giant with these Bambuti Pygmy women. Most of them were scarcely over four feet tall, while a few were even shorter, like the two on the right in the front row. Men average two or three inches taller than the women.

On Mt. Bugalamisa, in the Congo, I found gorillas with the help of some Pygmy guides. When none of the gorillas moved into a good light for pictures, I jumped down a ledge to get closer. As I readied my camera, this gorilla expressed its anger by uttering a piercing shriek and racing toward me. So the one shot I took was photographically disappointing, but it still serves as a reminder of one of the most dangerous encounters of my life.

The Bororo Indians of Brazil's Mato Grosso have many ceremonial dances, but their favorite is the funeral dance, for which they put on their finest headdresses and make their bodies up in a great variety of ways. ABOVE: I discuss the filming of the funeral dance with the Bororo chief. BELOW: Some of the dancers line up for inspection.

dumped it out and chose another hot stone, this one a little smaller, for the head had shrunk a bit more.

During the second whirling, Asapi took up a small unheated stone with a smooth flat surface and began to rub it over the outside of the face, pushing here, pressing there, to form the features as they should be. So with stone after stone he seared the inside of the head, the heat shrinking it more all the time. And he shaped the features carefully, plucking eyebrows and eyelashes occasionally but being careful not to burn them off or pull too many out. There must be just enough to look in proportion to the small head.

Finally Asapi scooped up hot sand from under the fire and poured it into the head. He whirled it vigorously, poured it out when it had cooled, put more hot sand in. The hot sand reached every crack inside the tsantsa, drying and shrinking it. When Asapi concluded that the process had gone far enough, he bound the neck opening with fiber, poked a hole through the top of the head, and pushed a long cord of fiber through, the fiber having been doubled over a pin to hold it inside. Then he stuck his lance into the sand at an angle, hung the tsantsa in the smoke over the fire, and lay down to contemplate his handiwork.

Within half an hour all the men had finished their work and lay on the sand by the fires, warming their feet and watching the heads turn hard and black. They talked of their great triumphs, of the vengeance they had wrought, of the peace their deeds would bring to the souls of their ancestors.

The next day they sent the youngest of the warriors ahead to announce the victory and have the women prepare the bowls of chicken blood and sua, to get everything ready for the victory dance. After the dance, Asapi and the other winners of heads would fast for months and then hold a great tsantsa feast lasting four or five days. And perhaps in another few months their enemies would attack them.

I learned of the success of Asapi's raid a good many days later, and at that time I did not care. For on the day after the warriors set out I headed back for Peruche's jivaria. As I was weak and feverish, I remember little of that long and arduous trip, except that Juanga and his friends were kind and helpful at all times.

Peruche was worried about me and insisted that I move into the jivaria at once, where I could be cared for by his wives. But I knew I would never get well unless I got back to civilization. I sent Diego off as fast as he could go to Méndez, to bring Barmio to the cable bridge earlier than the appointed day.

Papué and Yangora stood beside my hard bed and stroked my arm gently, talked to me quietly in words I could not understand but in feelings that told me they were sorry I was sick and that I must get well. Peruche stamped around and muttered orders to his wives and then countermanded them, trying to do something to make me well. He brought in Tuki, the wishinu, and ordered him to make me well, but Tuki, I am happy to say, insisted that his powers could do nothing against a white man's sickness.

Peruche lost patience and said that the wishinu of his friend Nakata had once made a white man well. He would go and fetch Nakata's wishinu. I begged him not to go, told him that in another day I must get up and travel to the bridge.

He said flatly that I was too weak to go. He would get the fine wishinu who could cure me. He would go at once, for Nakata's jivaria was just a short day's journey away. There was no arguing with him, especially when I knew that he wanted so much to help me in the only way he could think of. When he called me "my son," I thanked him. He left almost at once with one of his wives.

The next morning I felt a little stronger, probably because of the good rest I had enjoyed. But I knew I was not strong enough to make a trip of four days through the jungle. Encouraged, I thought that in a day or two I could start. If only the new wishinu did not make me sick again.

Late that afternoon I heard a loud wailing in the clearing, coming closer and closer to the jivaria. Juanga, who sat beside me, jumped up and ran outside. The women streamed from their work. All I could do was to lie there and wonder. In a few minutes Pablo dashed in to me.

"Peruche is dead!" he cried.

Peruche dead! I could not believe it. The wail I had heard came from Peruche's wife, who had accompanied him to Nakata's jivaria. The wishinu Peruche had gone to fetch was away for two days. Peruche, worried about me, did not want to delay his return, so he left word with Nakata to send his wishinu when he came back. Then he set out for home once more. Less than an hour away from the jivaria he was struck in the leg by a bushmaster snake. In five minutes he was dead.

Peruche's wife had run as fast as she could to the jivaria, but she knew Peruche was dead. Juanga and Ambusha and Peasa followed her back to the spot where their father lay. They picked him up and brought him home, not forgetting the funny red cap he liked so much.

I felt I had lost a real friend, but I could not tell his sons, his wives, how I felt. I think they knew, though, for they acted more sympathetic to me than ever. The jivaria was a silent place.

That was not the end, of course. For no Jivaro could believe that Peruche had just been killed by a snake. An enemy had sent the snake to kill him. Who was the enemy? It was up to Tuki the wishinu to find out.

I was too sick to know all the ritual Tuki put himself through. He went into the woods to drink nateema and dream the dreams that would give him the answer, the name of the slayer of Peruche, who would then have to be slain by Peruche's sons.

I was a bit stronger the next day, when Tuki went into the woods to drink nateema. One more day, I thought, and I could leave. Suddenly a frightening idea hit me. Tuki had never cared much for me. Tuki might feel that my sickness had really caused Peruche's death, because it had sent the grand old man on the trip that proved fatal to him. Would Tuki's dream tell him I was the enemy who had sent the snake to kill Peruche?

I told myself that Tuki would not believe that I had the power to send spirits through a snake — only a Jivaro had such power. But the thought kept creeping back into my mind and I did not sleep well that night. I was awake when, shortly before dawn, Tuki plunged into the hea, crying that he knew the enemy, the Old Ones had shown him.

The wishinu's pupils were dilated and he could not focus his sight on anything. He was wild-eyed but triumphant, and I thought he kept staring at me. And when he announced his discovery it seemed almost as horrible as if he had really named me.

He named Nakata, the old friend Peruche had gone to visit.

Everyone in the jivaria was thunderstruck. Nakata was related to Peruche by blood. He looked upon Peruche as his own head curaka. They had been friends for fifty years, and their families had never fought, had never engaged in a feud.

No one doubted his guilt, of course, except me and possibly Pablo. And we could say nothing. Juanga stood up straight and said "Nakata" several times. And I knew he was vowing to take Nakata's life.

He would not take the head, not in a case of personal family feud like this. A life for a life, that was all. And then, of course, someone in Nakata's family would have to avenge Nakata's death. And so another feud, another endless series of assassinations had begun.

Pablo and I left the next day. Juanga and Peasa and one each of their wives went with us for much of the way, carrying our equipment and some food. I had to travel slowly and rest often. Many times I decided it was not worth the effort. It would solve all problems best if I could just lie down and die.

And that was when my most hated enemies of the jungle saved my life. I lay down, hoping not to get up again. Then came mosquitoes, flies, gnats of a hundred kinds, biting, stinging, making me slap at my hands and face to keep them away. They would not let me sit still and rest, would not let me lie down and die. They drove me on despite weakness and exhaustion. I kept on going, knowing that even if I could make it to the river I could never get across. And even if I could get across I could never climb the mighty Andes again.

One day's journey from the bridge Juanga said good-bye. As he walked away into the jungle with his brother and their wives, I knew that he would soon go out to kill and be killed. I had slept next to him. I had hunted with him. I had admired his father. But he was a Jivaro and I was not. I didn't like to think about it. I still don't.

I reached the bridge and saw Barmio and his mules on the other side waving to me. Pablo helped me into the seat and pulled me across without equipment, going back for it afterward. After a rest I climbed on the back of a mule and let him take me up the Andes.

We reached Méndez and I went to the Salesian mission there. The good padres took me in, fed me, bucked up my spirits. After three days I felt strong enough to go on to Pan and then to Cuenca where I could have medical attention. Luckily my dysentery turned out to be of the bacillary rather than the amoebic variety. In two weeks I was on my feet again, none the worse for wear but ten pounds lighter.

Soon after returning to New York, my film came back from the lab, and half of it — several thousand feet — was no good. The lens of one camera had been jarred out of focus somehow, probably by one of the falls I took going down the Andes. From the other camera I got enough first-class film for a lecture. Warner Brothers made a two-reeler out of it, but I had dreamed of having the first full-length feature film in color to come out of the jungles of South America, and nothing less would really satisfy me.

I made up my mind to go back again, but it was four years before I could make it.

3

Colorados and Camayuras

IN THE course of my four trips to South America, I visited many Indian tribes in different regions, including two short trips each to the idyllic San Blas Islands off the Atlantic coast of Panama and to the Choco Indians in the interior of Darien. Both tribes were interesting but even then were beginning to emerge from their primitive state. The San Blas Indians are a not uncommon — and certainly worthwhile — tourist stop. The Chocos have regular contact with civilization, though they still live much as they have for generations.

On the other hand, the Yaguas, who live about eight hundred miles east of Jivaro territory, are so isolated in a dense jungle that civilization will never reach them before they die out, as they will in another decade or two. I wanted to see and film them because of their skill with the blowgun and their costumes of bushy fiber skirts and headdresses. These outfits were responsible for the Amazon River getting its name, for when Francisco de Orellana sailed down the river, he was attacked by many tribes, but the most ferocious were a group he took to be women. The king of Spain decided they must be the Amazons he had read about in Herodotus.

On my 1940 trip, I persuaded Lieutenant Benavides to fly me from Iquitos to the tiny post of Pifuyal, nearest to Yagua territory. There we found a guide and two bearers and bought salt and machetes for the Yaguas. Benavides and I started the next morning. Mechanic Serafio stayed with the plane, and in a short time Benavides wished he had done the same. For we walked on a path through a jungle so impenetrable that the bearers had to keep hacking at it with their machetes to make a passageway. Heavy dampness filled the air and turned the ground beneath us into deep mud. In fifteen minutes our shirts were clinging to our backs and sweat was pouring down our foreheads, burning our eyes. In an hour we were exhausted and had to stop for a rest.

As I sat on a log, Pedro, the guide, called attention to ants crawling over my hand. I shook them off with difficulty, and Pedro told me about the big ants many Indians use to heal cuts. They put an ant down carefully on the cut and its pincers, which are about half an inch long, dig into the skin. Then they snip off the ant's head, but the pincers stay in place, just like stitches. For a long cut, use several ants.

We hauled ourselves to our feet and went on. For three hours we slogged through the tenacious mud and rotting vegetation. By the time we got to the Yagua clearing Benavides and I were numb with fatigue, heat, and thirst. I saw a beehive house and, happily, no Indians. I did not have the strength to meet and greet and give presents to anybody.

Pedro explained that the whole village must be working on the raft they were building, to move to another territory. They had hunted out the area in which they had been living. He would go to look for them. One of the Indian bearers cut off a stalk of sugarcane and handed pieces to me and Benavides, and we sucked thirstily at the juice inside. The lieutenant found a small thatched hut at the edge of the clearing, crawled in and went to sleep. Slapping mosquitoes at every step, I wandered toward the house, an oblong of about twenty by thirty feet.

I lifted up a thatched door from a small entrance and felt a cool draft on my face. It was dark inside, but I crawled in, found a mat, lay down on it, and fell asleep. I don't know how much later it was that something woke me, but I looked up and vaguely saw two women with spears, who smiled and said something that sounded like "TV." This startled me so that I sat up, shook myself awake, and realized that I was in a Yagua clanhouse, and that the two figures were men with blowguns. But I could not make sense of the "TV."

Outside in the clearing, I found a crowd of men, women, and children who looked at me with smiles of anticipation, and I knew Pedro had already told them about the gifts we had brought. I went to look for him when I heard a roar of laughter from the edge of the clearing where Benavides had found his little hut. I joined the Yaguas to see what had happened. There was the lieutenant crawling out, dirty, tired, and embarrassed. But the laughter of the Indians was friendly and contagious, and in a few moments he was laughing, too.

Then I found Pedro, who was laughing as hard as the rest. He explained that Benavides had crawled into a hut that had been specially made for an expectant mother to give birth to her baby, which had occurred the day before. It struck the Yaguas as hilarious to see the Peruvian lieutenant emerge from this place. One of the women thrust a baby in his arms and everyone laughed again. Benavides grinned sheepishly, the baby started to cry, and the mother took her child back.

Pedro was pleased, because the Yaguas have a great sense of fun, and this incident got us off to a good start with them. I asked Pedro what the Yagua word for salt was. "Tivi," he said, and I understood what the Indians were so eager for.

We got out the packs and distributed a block of salt and a machete to each family. Then came a bolt of red cloth for the women; they do not wear the more feminine fiber skirts of the men. Some of the Yagua men went into the clanhouse for a huge pottery jar and several gourds. This was *masato*, their equivalent of the Jivaros' nijimanche. Soon the party was gay and noisy. The men began to play odd-sounding melodies on panpipes, one of them playing a two-note flute-like instrument with a gourd on the end. Others started singing and dancing, and I got some good shots of the scene.

I asked Benavides to film me talking to the dignified chief, who brightened up when I gave him a package of cigarettes. He lit one of them, took a long drink of masato, and laughed when one of the dancers tripped and fell down. As the dancer was about to sit down on a log for a rest, the chief reached out and kicked the log away, so the dancer sprawled on the ground. Everyone laughed, the chief and the dancer loudest of all.

I got my share of the Yaguas' love of practical joking a little later, when the light had grown too dim for filming. I sat on the end of a bench, really a long log laid across two other supporting logs, trying to make friends with three boys on the other end of the log. They began giggling and whispering together, and gesturing. I caught on the fact that they were planning on jumping off the log suddenly, up-ending it so I would spill to the ground. So I looked away to give them their chance. They jumped, and I sprawled on the ground with arms akimbo and legs outstretched, acting quite astonished and laughing. A roar of laughter went up from the whole crowd, and I was the Ya-guas' friend.

As the women began to prepare the evening meal, the insect hordes increased in number and viciousness. By the time we had finished eat-ing, they were unbearable. I spoke to Benavides, Pedro, and the two bearers. There would not be room for us in the clanhouse, and we had not brought mosquito netting. I could not conceive of suffering the night in the open, so suggested that we go back to Pifuyal. We had a kerosene lantern and two flashlights.

The trip back was worse than the one out, although it was cooler and the insects disappeared when the rain came. But the rain was a deluge that turned the path into a fast-flowing river. Dawn was light-ing the eastern sky as we staggered into Pifuayal after a hike that had taken four hours longer than it should have. The commandante of the post saw that we had warm water to wash, dry clothes, and comfort-able cots to sleep on. After eight hours of dreamless sleep, Benavides and I felt refreshed but full of aches.

We took off from the water, circled, climbed, and headed for Iqui-tos. The upper Amazon twists and curves continuously. We were fly-ing rather low over a long stretch of jungle between big bends in the river. Suddenly the engine coughed, backfired, and died. Benavides's face went white. The treetops were rushing past as we glided down toward them. I realized we could not make the river. Benavides gripped the controls as if he were trying to lift the plane by his own efforts. I braced myself for the crash, but then, when it seemed that nothing could save us, the engine roared into life again. The pilot tilted the plane's nose upward and we surged forward for about three minutes. Then the engine died again, this time with a note of finality.

But the river was close ahead, and in a few minutes we splashed to a safe landing. As the plane floated toward shore, we sat as if stupefied. Then Benavides turned and threw his arms around me.

"This is a miracle!" he said. "We have been born again."

"And I know it is true," I said, "a remark I have often heard — that God is good to Peruvian pilots."

We crawled out onto the pontoons and the mechanic Serafio got to work on the engine. He found dirt in the gas line and carburetor. After the motor stopped the first time, enough gasoline had trickled through to run the engine for those precious minutes that carried us past a crack-up to a safe landing. In an hour we took off and flew the rest of the way to Iquitos without incident. It took longer than usual, however, for Benavides followed the river all the way.

A few hundred miles west of Jivaro territory lives another fiercely independent and individualistic tribe. They have handled civilization not by knuckling under to it, not by fighting it, but by retreating from it. These are the Colorado Indians, living in the jungle on the western slopes of the Andes. There are only a few hundred of them left. They live as they have lived for hundreds of years, except for three items — red-white-and-blue striped cloth for skirts, machetes, and matches. They have forgotten how to make fire without matches.

Most important, from the point of view of color photography, the Colorados are the only really *red* men among the Indians of the world, for they cover themselves from head to foot with a thick bright-red paste — and that includes the hair, cut in bangs with the stiff paste on it so that it looks like a cap. When the red rubs off or gets dirty, they add more. They spend all their lives coated with the stuff, which is almost unbelievable to me, having once had it on for a few hours, when I was made a blood brother.

I visited the Colorados first in 1940, when I met André Roosevelt in Quito. His daughter Leila had married Armand Denis, with whom I was later to co-produce the African film *Savage Splendor*. Roosevelt told me about the Colorados, said they had never been photographed in color, and agreed to go with me to visit them. We stayed several days, shot some good sequences, and came to know well the chief, Alejandro, who also served as *shaman*, or medicine man. I returned nine years later, while I was looking for sequences of interesting tribes for incorporation in the film *Jungle Headhunters*. Photographer Jules Bucher and I found a guide and set off for a Colorado clearing I had visited before. I wondered if shaman Alejandro was still alive. He had been about fifty when I had known him in 1940. Unlikely, I thought. After a few hours we went through a clearing that looked vaguely familiar to me. The guide led us on, and in about ten minutes there was a bright flash of red against the green background of the forest. Two Colorados stood in the path before us. We all stood stock still for a minute. The guide spoke, and Bucher and I held out our hands to show *No weapons*. The Indians carried machetes.

I pulled two small mirrors and two fishhooks from my pocket and handed them to the Indians. Then I reached into my breast pocket for an envelope containing some color prints of pictures I had taken in 1940. I picked out one shot of two Indians playing the marimba and handed it to one of the men. He recognized himself! His eyes opened wide under his stiff red bangs, and his lips broke open in a smile that revealed every one of his *empo*-blackened teeth. He pointed to himself in the picture, telling his friend to look.

Suddenly the man turned and stared hard at me. I took off my hat so he could get a better look. Could he possibly recognize me after nine years? Maybe I had given him a present he especially cherished. Anyway, he thought he recognized me, and that was what counted. I was his old friend.

He talked and gestured to explain that he would run ahead to the clearing at once, while his friend would guide us the rest of the way. He set off at a trot, the picture still in his red hand.

We came to the first fields in about ten minutes. They were small clearings hewn out of the jungle by machete and planted with banana, yuca, yams, maize, pineapples, and chonta palms, which supply not only hard wood but succulent palm cabbage. We forded a shallow brook and headed up a gentle slope, so I knew we were coming to the big house and clearing. Just as I saw the glare of light that meant an opening in the jungle ahead, a group of glowing red figures came toward us along the path. I saw my friend of the picture, and with him Alejandro himself, the shaman! The chief had thrown a kind of toga over his shoulders for the occasion and walked with great dignity, followed by eight or nine other men and as many children ranging from three to twelve years of age.

In a moment, Alejandro was beside me holding out his hand and smiling broadly. I produced the pictures and gave him one of himself standing beside me. Then I showed the *pièce de résistance:* a copy of *Life* magazine with a few pictures I had taken of the Colorados on my 1940 trip. The men were delighted and wanted to keep the magazine, but I had to take it back. I had only one copy, and there were pictures of Jivaros there, too. In view of the effect it would have on them later, I was glad I kept it.

I took out scissors, mirrors, and more fishhooks and handed some to Alejandro and the other men who gathered round. In five minutes we were a happy, chattering group, walking together toward the clan-house, which was about thirty by fifteen feet in size. The front is not so much a room as a veranda. Behind it is the enclosed portion of the house, with walls of split palm trees stuck in the ground and held close together with lianas.

Two women were quickly sweeping the already clean and hard-packed earth floor of the open veranda as we approached, but they melted away as we came near. They cover only the face and neck and sometimes the breasts with red dye. On festive occasions they may plaster a small blob of the red paste on the crown of the head, but they never cover the whole head. From the women you can see that the natural hair color of the Indian is black, the skin a light coppery brown. We sat down and Alejandro called to one of the women to bring food. We were served outside, squatting around huge banana leaves that served as plates. There was banana, or plantain, cooked and mashed and reshaped like banana, that was delicious; boiled yuca and — special delicacy for the occasion — large palm weevils. I refused them politely but ate a bit of the monkey stew. I did not lick the common block of rock salt that the other men took up occasionally, stroking it with their tongues with great relish.

After the meal my cigarettes brought pleasure to all. It was the cig-arette, I believe, that finally determined for Alejandro his next sugges-tion. He wished to make me a blood brother of the Colorados.

I protested as politely as I could. That was too much, I was not worthy, and so on. I was gratified, but in truth I didn't know exactly what I would have to go through to become a blood brother. It was not a trivial rite offered to any casual visitor, obviously. So I finally agreed to become a blood brother if Bucher could film the whole process.

Alejandro agreed, and said that a festival should be made of this occasion. He sent some of the young men running to other houses in the neighborhood to tell everyone to come to a party. It made me think of my old friend Peruche.

For a party there had to be *malakachisa*, the Colorados' nijimanche.

There is a difference, however — the addition of sugar cane sap to the masticated yuca, giving it an apple-ciderish flavor. And I noted another difference: the Colorado women do not spew the chewed mass of yuca into a pot in an astonishing stream, but take it daintily with their fingers and place it on a huge leaf. It is prettier to watch. The Colorados, incidentally, have an equivalent of nateema, too, called *nepe*, drunk primarily by the shaman for serious matters. We drank malakachisa from large gourds, but after the first sip Bucher got busy setting up both cameras.

Friends from neighboring families began to troop in, expectant looks on their faces. I had no more gifts, but they were content with the malakachisa and my cigarettes, of which I had plenty. Finally there were about seventy-five men, women and children gathered.

Alejandro and his friends were tugging at my shirt. I turned around to find them trying to take my clothes off. I protested, but they just laughed happily and told me that the ceremony of making me a blood brother was about to begin. I was to be stripped, covered with red dye and zebra stripes, and dressed in a native skirt. I could not back out now, of course.

I took off all my clothes except my underpants and put on a skirt of the inevitable Colorado white with red and blue stripes, with a red sash to top it off. Alejandro then prepared to do the job.

He reached into a hollowed tree trunk and brought out some pods from the achiote tree, opened them and removed the small vermilion seeds. Then he crushed the seeds between his two palms, spat on them, crushed and kneaded some more, spat again, until he had a thick red paste on his hands. He applied both red-smeared hands to my bare white chest. Chatting happily with the men around us, he wiped his hands on my chest until they were almost clean, then reached for more achiote seeds. Crush, spit, knead, and smear — the process went on until my chest and belly, my back and neck were done a nice vivid red. The stuff went on rather easily, for there is a waxy substance in the seeds that makes it something like theatrical greasepaint.

Bucher, busy shooting this scene, was enjoying himself hugely. He kept telling me to look as if I were happy and pleased about the whole thing — not an easy task when I saw my old friend Alejandro spit in his hands and then wipe them on my hair.

It was not too bad, however, until he started to work on my face and over my mouth. Then I wanted to call the whole thing off. But it was impossible. I endured it and let him finish the job.

When my hair was thick and stiff with the red paste, Alejandro called for his bowl — a gourd that fitted nicely over my head so that the bangs could be cut. After the hairdo was completed, a cloth crown was placed on my head. Finally, the zebra stripes were painted across my chest and face with a little stick dipped in dye from the genipa berry. Then Alejandro stood back to judge his handiwork. He and everyone else admired it immensely, and I began to be curious as to how I looked.

The drinking of malakachisa had continued off and on during this time and the men — about thirty of them — felt very gay. Someone called for music and two men went to the marimba which hung from the rafters of the open veranda. Chonta wood bars make the tones, covering about two octaves and in rather good pitch. Below each tone bar hangs a tube of thick, hollow bamboo to give resonance — long tubes for the deeper tones, gradually getting shorter as they go up the scale. The Colorados borrowed the idea for the instrument originally from the Negroes who were brought to the coastal regions of Ecuador as slaves back in the seventeenth century.

With music and malakachisa there was bound to be dancing, an important scene to round out the sequence. But it was a sorry disappointment. There was no form, not much movement, and little grace to the dancing. The men hopped and shuffled about in a childish imitation of the foxtrot. They loved it and grabbed me to make me dance with them. This was one native dance in which I felt as graceful as the savages themselves. I defy anyone looking at the film of this scene, to select the civilized white man from among his many "brothers."

One young Colorado had a sudden brilliant idea which he tried to tell me about in many words and happy gestures. I understood that he wanted me to come and live in his house, but there was more I couldn't get. I called our guide to translate just as the young Indian strode toward a group of women and came back with a girl about eighteen years old. She was quite attractive but did not like being pulled around this way.

Proudly he showed her to me and explained. The guide interpreted, and I knew that I was being offered the young Indian's sister as my wife. I was a true Colorado, he insisted. I must stay and live with them forever, and for that I needed a wife. Here she was!

The girl glared at her big brother. Without words or gestures she told me that while she had nothing against me, she was angry at her brother for trying to push her around and dictate to her.

It was even simpler for me to bow out of this offer gracefully than it had been when Peruche offered me a wife, for the Colorados are monogamous. I just said that I was already committed in my own tribe and could not possibly take another wife, attractive as the prospect might be.

Two men passed out on the ground. I knew it was time for us to be going back toward Quito. I could not try to remove the red and black dyes until after I had left my blood brothers, so I decided to wait until I got to the city. I found my clothes on a bench on the clanhouse veranda, everything but my hat and boots. I looked around for them and saw them walking across the clearing to me, containing a very young Colorado boy. He had tried them on and had been tramping about for some time in them. Bucher got a good shot of him.

I wondered if my clothes had been rifled. There was money, a knife, a watch, cigarettes, and other items an Indian might find tempting. Not a thing had been touched. These people, like most genuine primitives, are scrupulously honest. I learned later from the authorities, for instance, that there had been no crime among the Colorados for decades.

I dressed and went through half an hour of affectionate farewells before starting off. It was past midnight when we came to the city, after a hair-raising ride that would have frightened the wits out of me if I had not been so tired.

As we entered the hotel, Bucher chuckled and said, "You are probably the first Colorado Indian to put up at the Metropolitano."

I had to do something about my red dye and zebra stripes right away. I walked into the hotel rather hesitantly, pulling my hat brim down as far as possible. Luckily there was no one in the lobby at that late hour to take fright at the sight of me. The hotel clerk was startled and agreed to get me hot water right away.

When I looked at myself in the mirror I did not wonder why he turned pale and agreed to my request at once. That line of black running across my cheekbones and over the bridge of my nose made me look sinister and tough as an assassin.

I climbed into a long full tub of warm water that started to turn pink at once. In five minutes I felt that I was sitting in a tub of blood.

Still, just the outer layer of red dye had come off. I had to scrub hard with soap and brush to get it all off.

My hair was the biggest problem — I thought. It took half an hour to bring back the natural color, and there was still plenty of pink around the roots. I finally gave up, dried myself, and looked in the mirror. I still looked sinister!

Most of the red was gone, but the black lines were as strong as ever. I did not worry about the stripes on my chest, but the face lines were terrible. I took a washcloth, more soap, and stood in front of the mirror scrubbing. The lower lines finally faded a bit, but the bar under my eyes and over my nose stood out prominently. I tried scouring powder, but to no avail.

I went to bed, determined to get up early in the morning and find someone who could make me presentable before an eleven o'clock appointment at the American embassy.

In the morning I went to a large drugstore and asked a startled girl clerk for the "doctor." Six girl clerks gathered around me and stared, asking questions. The pharmacist sympathized, assured me he could find something that would remove the black line.

He tried alcohol and rubbed hard with cotton. No good. He tried something else I did not bother to identify. Then something else. Each time there was vigorous rubbing, of course.

The line was not so pronounced, but it was still visible. No one would have noticed it, however, for now I had two beautiful black eyes. I had apparently rubbed so hard that I had broken the tiny blood vessels in the skin under the eyes, which is just what happens when you bump into that open door in the dark, the proverbial cause of so many black eyes in the civilized world.

I did not look quite as sinister. I just looked beaten up. It took a good deal of explaining, which few people put much stock in, and I became accustomed to having people look askance at me during the next few days. It was another week before I stopped being, at least in part, a Colorado Indian.

Despite a good deal of exploration in the past twenty years, the Mato Grosso remains the largest unknown territory in the world, an area of about two million square miles in the heart of Brazil. Scores of different Indian tribes live in this region, many of whom have had their first contact with white men since 1942, while some have seen no white men at all. I had looked at intriguing pictures of some of these tribes in a book about the Indians of Brazil by Candido Rondon, who had led Teddy Roosevelt to the River of Doubt in 1913. Part Bororo Indian, Rondon had founded the government's Service for the Protection of the Indians (SPI) and had made its program the official policy in dealing with the primitive peoples of the Mato Grosso, best summed up in the phrase "pacification through love." Rondon's men were forbidden to shoot at an Indian, even in self-defense.

The SPI had kept out traders, gold-seekers, and other potential troublemakers, while slowly and patiently opening up area after area of the Mato Grosso. I wanted to visit and film some of these tribes during my 1949 *Jungle Headhunters* expedition, but I knew that few outsiders were granted this privilege. After ten days in Rio fighting red tape, however, I received permission to visit the Bororos in the south central section of the Mato Grosso. With a fine Brazilian cameraman, Pedro Neves, I flew to Cuyaba, capital of the province of Mato Grosso, then took a bruising truck trip to some Bororo villages. An SPI man accompanied us as interpreter.

The Bororos were fine-looking people. Taller than any natives I had seen in South America, though not so tall as the Watusi of equatorial Africa, most of the Bororo men stood about six feet. I did not tower over them as I had among the Yaguas and Colorados and even Jivaros. The women, although shorter, possessed erect trim figures. They wore very little, which caused some difficulty in getting film that could be released for theatrical distribution. In the villages that were farthest from outposts the men discarded skirts and wore, except for festive occasions, nothing but a few ornaments around the neck and a penis sheath — a small stiff palm leaf designed to emphasize rather than conceal the sexual organ.

I had never seen such curious people. They loved to handle, turn upside down, poke and prod everything that was strange to them. They asked innumerable questions and were especially interested in the black boxes in our hands and suspended from our necks. When we began filming they wanted to stop everything and look at the camera I held, listen to the whirring noise it made, then watch me wind it up again. We took a half hour off to let them satisfy their curiosity. Once when I was opening a can of sardines, so many heads came close to watch the operation that I could hardly use the opener.

Like so many primitive people, the Bororos proved to be fine actors,

as I filmed some of the men weaving, making necklaces, smoothing arrows, and the women making pottery, cooking, carrying huge loads of
corn from the fields. These were interesting but undramatic shots, but
I wanted the Indians to get used to the cameras before attempting more
action. One day I asked about the vicious piranha fish, which is common in the rivers of South America and strikes terror to everyone's
heart, although it is only ten or eleven inches long. But it looks as if it
is all jaw, plentifully supplied with sharp, triangular teeth. The Bororos
told me of a favorite spot for piranha up the river, so, with a tapir's leg
for bait, we got our cameras ready and tossed the leg in the water.
Nothing happened. If piranha had been around, all the flesh would
have been stripped from the bones in two or three minutes.

My disappointment was overcome that evening, however, when two
excited hunters brought the news that they had seen a herd of peccaries
about seven miles upstream, twenty or twenty-five animals in the
group. These wild pigs are favorite food of the Bororos, who laid plans
for a hunt at once. This is a community affair, for a herd of peccaries
can be dangerous. They rarely attack men without provocation, but
killing some of them is provocative. Since peccaries weigh around a
hundred pounds each and have razor-sharp tusks for teeth, they are
not to be trifled with.

The hunt was to start before dawn, for peccaries often feed in the
first hours of morning. I went along, but did not take my cameras
because I felt sure there would be insufficient light at that hour. Several women, children and dogs were given instructions to act as beaters, driving the herd of peccaries toward the hunters. I did not at first
understand why several men, with bows and arrows, clubs, and harpoons, entered canoes and headed upstream by water.

When we approached the peccaries' feeding place I saw how carefully the Indians planned the hunt. They had taken into consideration
the wind, for one thing, for peccaries have an acute sense of smell,
although their sight and hearing are poor. The women, children, and
dogs were guided in a wide circle by two of the men to approach the
animals on the windward side. Meanwhile the hunters disposed themselves and me, putting me on a low branch of a tree at the bank of the
river. A few Indians also climbed trees, and others hid behind tree
trunks so that they could shoot at the onrushing peccaries without
being trampled. They were so positioned, also, to drive the surviving
animals toward the stream. Then I realized the purpose of the men in

canoes. Peccaries are slow and clumsy in the water, although they can swim. Some of those driven into the river would be killed by the water-borne Indians.

It was light enough to see as we got into position, and we still had to wait some time. I began to wish I had brought a camera, although I probably could not have handled it without falling off the branch. As it was, I almost fell off from excitement when the peccaries came rushing toward us at a speed that was amazing for such fat creatures with such spindly legs. As they ran they gnashed their tusks rapidly, making sounds that were at once ludicrous and menacing. I was happy to be in the tree, not just because of the peccaries but because of the arrows that flew from the Indians' bows. Several of them found their marks, and the beasts stumbled and fell. The others swerved under my branch and headed for the river. I watched as the first one plunged into the water, an arrow sticking from its hind leg. But before the Indians could close in to finish him off, he turned for shore. He never made it. Suddenly the water around him seethed and percolated as hundreds of fish swarmed around, flopping out of the water in their efforts to get at the flesh of the big creature.

Piranha! Here were the fish I had been searching for — and I had no camera!

The Indians in the canoes saw their prey going to the voracious piranha. The remaining peccaries smelled or saw, and turned from the water, preferring the arrows to the teeth of the piranha fish. One, however, plunged into the river. An Indian in the closest canoe harpooned him at once, then leaped to shore at the foot of my tree and tugged on the harpoon rope to pull the peccary on land before the piranha devoured it. But what he landed was a head, neck and skeleton, with a dozen wriggling fish hanging on for one more bite. Most of them flopped back into the water, but the Indian clubbed one. He reached down for the fish, which lay still until the hand came close. Then with a sudden flip it actually lunged at the nearest finger. The Bororo was just quick enough and gave the fish two more blows. Finally it was dead.

Seeing the other Indians coming from behind the trees, I knew the hunt was over, so climbed down. I looked at the piranha closely, and felt as if I never wanted to go into water again. Nothing can look more ferocious and thoroughly mean than that carnivorous fish.

The Bororos were annoyed. Although they had shot eight peccaries, they had expected to get another four or five in the water. Nevertheless their spirits rose as they carried home the slain animals. They would feast for days. My spirits, however, were sagging. I had witnessed two of the most exciting scenes of an entire trip without getting a single shot of them.

But I was able to film a dramatic reenactment of the Bororo funeral dance. It is a great pageant, one of the most exciting events in a Bororo's life. Everyone takes part; all the men dress in spectacular costumes, and some act the part of spirits, jaguars, and tapirs. It had to be reenacted because the dance usually takes place at night. But the Bororos were in the right spirit, for they had just finished, the day before we arrived, the eight-day funeral ritual for an eleven-year-old boy. They told me about it with zest and even enjoyment.

The ritual began when the boy's body was wrapped in the mat on which he had slept, while his close relatives stood over him and wailed in loud and piercing tones, reciting the great virtues of the dead one. Mother and father lacerated their flesh with sharp shells until blood dropped on the wrapped corpse. More blood was smeared over their bodies. Relatives and close friends joined in the chant, inflicting pain and punishment on themselves. A friend pulled out the mother's hair in small bunches as she knelt over the body of her son.

Meanwhile the chief and most of the men of the village decked themselves in startling costumes. One man wore a shroud of green leaves. Another covered his entire body with a sticky black resin, then stuck on white polka dots of duck feathers. Some wore fiber skirts, others wore belts with brilliantly colored feathers hanging from them. And all placed on their heads magnificent sunburst crowns of bright feathers. The men then surrounded the mourners and added their wails to the cries of the dead boy's family, their bodies moving slightly in tempo as gourd rattles, a trumpet and hoarse flutes contributed to the din.

There was at first a temporary burial in the shallowest of graves, where for seven nights the mourners gathered and wailed, extolling the dead one. Then on the eighth day, the *bope*, or evil spirits, were summoned by the chief's shrill bamboo whistle. They were slow to appear. In the ritual drama which followed, a spirit-representative of the dead boy and his bodyguards — all elaborately costumed — called upon the bope to arrive and disinter the body. The bope appeared as tapirs, jaguars, and horses and were urged to perform their work of digging up the body, which at last they did — but only symbolically. It was not until early the next morning, before everyone was awake, that one of the bope representatives stole from the clanhouse, dug up the body and took it to the river, where he scraped and washed all the flesh away from the bones. No one, supposedly, knew who did this. The village awoke to find the bones in a basket, skull on top.

This ritual had just ended when I arrived. The basket of bones, newly decorated, was still in the woods nearby, where the bope would find and dispose of the remains. I asked what happened to the soul of the boy after all this, and learned that it wandered around unhappily, sometimes living in the body of a frog, a bird, or at best a deer.

The Bororos seemed to be preoccupied with death. In their opinion man is essentially bad. There are only evil spirits; no good ones prevail. For them the life of the soul after death is an endless, unhappy wandering.

There was considerable evidence that the Bororos were committing race suicide. There were remarkably few children in the villages. Like many other primitive people the Bororos kill those who do not seem healthy and sound at birth. Moreover, the medicine men have the power of life and death. When one of the group becomes sick, for instance, he predicts whether the person will live or die and actually names the time of death. If the patient still lives on that day, the medicine man fulfills his own prophecy by killing him. In a community in which sickness and death are common among children, the medicine man can hasten the decline of the tribe.

A few decades ago the Bororos were a brave warrior tribe numbering over five thousand. By my 1949 trip they had dwindled to about two thousand, and in 1963 there were only a hundred twelve left. In a few years they will be gone. I cannot explain fully this defeat of the Bororos in confronting civilization, which has treated them with kindness and respect. But I suspect that it lies in their preoccupation with death and its rituals, and in their belief that man is essentially bad, doomed to unhappiness even after death.

When I returned to Rio after the trip to the Bororo country, I met Major Luis Sampaio of the Brazilian Air Force. Oxford-educated and handsome, he was the first man to fly directly across the Mato Grosso from Rio to Manáos on the Amazon; he had also made more than fifty survey flights for the Roncador-Xingu expedition, searching out routes to follow, reporting the location of Indian villages and trails, and acting as the farseeing eye of the entire project. Within two days I was sitting in a Beechcraft piloted by Major Sampaio as it took off from the military airport in Rio. We came down at Aragarças, then headquarters of the expedition, and the first settlement and airstrip established.

The Roncador-Xingu expedition was cutting a straight line thirteen hundred miles in length across the Mato Grosso. Against greater obstacles than ever confronted any exploring group, they moved forward and established the first links across that thirteen-hundred-mile stretch in less than ten years. One purpose of the trek was to link places more closely by air. More important was the future opening up and colonization of two million square miles of land that has great and valuable timber reserves, and possibly gold, diamonds, rubber, and other resources of incalculable value. The Brazilian government backed the Central Brazil Foundation when it proposed the venture back in 1942, but the success of the expedition becomes all the more remarkable when it is realized that at no time were more than twenty-four men working with the expedition and often only ten.

Colonel Floriana de Mattos Vanique, one of the world's great explorers, was the first chief of the expedition heading for the Roncador (Thundering) Mountain and the Xingu River on the road to Manáos. But old Candido Rondon had a good deal to say about the relations with the Indians, although he was not connected with the expedition itself.

General Candido Rondon was fearful when the Roncador-Xingu expedition set out to cut right through the territory of the Indians, encountering among others that most persistently and ruthlessly hostile of all tribes, the Chavantes. Rondon insisted that the members of the expedition abide by his rules: no shooting of Indians, even in self-defense. Somewhat to his surprise, Colonel Vanique agreed. So did the three Villas Boas brothers, who served under Vanique.

There was a long halt when the expedition came to Chavante territory. Planes were shot at by the warlike Indians, who even tried to throw their war clubs at the flying machines. I had been fascinated by pictures of the Chavantes, taken from the air, showing their fierce attacks on low-flying planes with tiny bows and arrows. I asked Major Sampaio if we might visit this tribe. He assured me that understanding and patience had already won over the Chavantes.

"Why, we even have a settlement there called Chavantina," the major said. "Anyway, we are way past them now. I'm taking you to the real spearhead of the expedition." I asked if the Indians there were hostile.

"Far from it," the major laughed. "Just wait till you meet them. They are the friendliest and happiest people in the world. You see, until we came along I don't think there had been more than a handful of white men in the Camayura territory in all history. The Chavantes lived to the south of them and kept everyone away. And there was about five hundred miles of jungle to the north. So they were never bothered at all, and they rarely made war themselves. They just go on living as they've lived since — well, since the Stone Age."

We stayed at Aragarças that day only to refuel, and then took off for the next airstrip in the interior. In just forty-five minutes we landed on a strip near the Rio das Mortes. It had taken the expedition two years to make that journey! From the small field at Rio das Mortes we flew about two hours to the Kuluene River and landed.

The next morning we hiked to the Camayura village. I had just caught a glimpse of the top of their thatched houses when some of the Indians came to greet us. I have never seen such a sight.

Not one of the Indians wore any clothing at all. Yes, on closer inspection I saw that each woman wore a thin fiber strand around her waist. Another strand went from this down to the crotch. (Later, I obtained one of these complete wardrobes — an *uluri* — and found that at the end of the dangling thread there was a piece of dried fiber about half an inch square; this was tucked in the crotch.) The men also wore fiber belts, but nothing else.

The men and women were both superb-looking specimens. They were statuesque and well proportioned and appeared taller than they actually were. The women were about the size of the average American woman, five feet four. All held themselves erect. Shoulders were broad, hips narrow, legs strong but gracefully shaped, with narrow ankles. The breasts of the younger women were firm and round. And on neither men nor women was there any body hair. They pluck all hair — on face, under arms, and in the pubic region — with tweezers made from shells. Except for the bangs in front, the women let their dark hair grow long; the men cut theirs even all around.

They were rather light-skinned people, not white but scarcely darker than a European who has spent the summer at the beach. Their features were not like those of any other Indians I had encountered, being less Mongoloid. In fact, they looked a great deal like us, except that the women were generally more beautiful, the men more handsome. Even the older women, whose figures had sagged a bit, looked attractive. I decided it was largely because of the expressions on their faces.

There were no lines on any face, no slightest sign of concern or worry or suspicion or hostility. Complete ease and relaxation of mind and heart and body were obvious in every one of them. Eyes sparkled and smiles almost continually turned their lips upward at the corners. The girls laughed readily, but softly. They sang little snatches of a song, warbling notes that just bubbled out because there was so much happy song inside that some was continually spilling over.

They were very obviously happy to see us. I realized that I had no gifts for them, but the major said they never expected gifts. As they approached, I expected them to stop a few feet in front of us and speak. I stopped but they did not. A lovely girl of about seventeen came up to me, snuggled close to me, her breasts pressing against my body, and rubbed her nose over my ear and cheek. On the other side another girl, perhaps a bit older, did the same thing and then wriggled happily. She took my hand and obviously wanted me to stroke her just as I would an affectionate pet.

Then the two girls threw their arms around each other and rubbed noses against ears, ears against cheeks, and smiled happily. I was still feeling bewildered when a young Indian man threw his arm around me and hugged me vigorously, smiling happily. Major Sampaio was enjoying the same kind of greeting, but he was not as surprised as I. He had gone through this before. I saw that he was smiling happily, too, and I realized that I was beaming. How contagious happiness is, I thought.

In the midst of this twittering and laughing throng the major and I went into their village. There were six large houses in a circle, each house about fifty feet long and completely thatched from top to the ground. About thirty people lived in each house, made up of three or four families that were closely related. The men lived on one side, the women and children on the other. Everyone slept in hammocks. The place was clean, as were the Indians themselves. They went swimming at least twice a day.

I was in the midst of close to two hundred Indians, but I did not hear an unpleasant word or even see an unpleasant expression on a face all day long. They never had to worry about food because there was plenty of fish in the rivers and manioc tubers in the woods. They did not have to work very hard to procure and prepare these. They fought with no one. Their only weapon was the bow and arrow, which they used only for fishing and hunting. They knew nothing of blowguns, white men's guns, or fermented drinks. They possessed not even the primitive loom, which caused no difficulty because they wore no clothes. What religion or superstition they believed in, and there did not seem to be much, troubled them little. They had medicine men who could successfully dispel evil spirits when they needed to be dispelled. These people really fitted the old romantic picture of a primitive paradise, but I feel sure that their lives could not have been as perfect as they seemed to be. There must have been sickness and accidents sometimes, and little knowledge of how to cope with them. I doubt that there was much unrequited love, because these people had no inhibitions whatsoever, and everyone gave so much love to everyone else that each person felt secure. As in many primitive tribes, there was no insistence on chastity in girls before marriage. There was no marriage ceremony. A boy asked a girl's father if he could have her; if he said yes, the girl went to his hammock and the marriage was consummated. Among the Camayuras a chief may take more than one wife, and any man may marry two sisters. There is a wide use of contraceptives or abortives, so the birth rate is low.

Although the camera captured the forthright affection and the all-enveloping happiness of the Camayuras, regretfully little of the film could be used in a motion picture for theatrical release.

A few days later we flew less than half an hour to the next airstrip, on the Xingu River. At that time it was the farthermost field, but since then a strip has been completed farther along, on the Tapajós River, only an hour and a half by air from Manáos. The strip at Kuikuru was finished by Claudio Villas Boas in 1958.

From the field on the Xingu, we visited the Calapalos Indians, whose village was almost exactly like that of the Camayuras. While not so attractive, they looked very much like their happy neighbors, and the tribes were good friends. Many marriages have taken place between men and women of the two tribes.

The Calapalos, however, are considerably more hostile than the Camayuras. Never a warlike tribe like the Chavantes, they still go in for fighting now and then. They make and own war clubs shaped like baseball bats. They have been a bit more resentful of the approach of the white man, too, or rather more suspicious; they have not actually caused any difficulty to the men of the Roncador-Xingu expedition.

The Calapalos were the Indians who reputedly killed the famous English explorer Colonel Percy Fawcett back in 1925. Fawcett's disappearance was one of the great mysteries of the twenties; with his son and a friend, he went into the South American jungle in search of a fabled "lost city" and vanished. Every now and then, someone else comes up with the tale that Fawcett has been seen or that his death is now certain.

When the rescue expedition reached Calapalo and Camayura territory, two Indians confessed to having killed Fawcett. One of them actually took the white men and showed them where he had buried the body. A human skeleton was uncovered and for a time everyone believed that the mystery of Colonel Fawcett had at last been solved. But when the bones were shipped back to England, it was proved that they could not have been those of the explorer. An exact copy of his denture would not come anywhere near fitting the jaw that had been dug up. And measurements of the bones proved the corpse to have been a man fully six inches shorter than Fawcett.

Major Sampaio and I flew back to the airstrip at the Rio das Mortes to find Orlando Villas Boas waiting for us. He and his two younger brothers, Claudio and Leonardo, had volunteered for the first Roncador-Xingu expedition in 1943 and had been in the interior ever since. When Colonel Vanique retired as head of the expedition because of ill health, Orlando was appointed in his place. I had heard many great tales about his work with the Indians, which rivaled that of Rondon.

So I was surprised to find a short, slight man about five feet six. He wore no clothes except a faded pair of pants and a battered cloth hat, and he was tanned as dark as his Indian friends. His slight stature and nondescript appearance were forgotten the moment I looked at his face — a hawklike face with a short fierce beard, both contradicted by gentle eyes. Two young Indian children were clinging to his legs and, as he spoke to me, he reached down and patted them on the head occasionally.

We ate rice and beans for dinner, and talked late into the night. And the next morning we ate rice and beans for breakfast, then talked some more. I learned how at the beginning of the expedition he had developed Rondon's technique for making contact with the Indians. Those that were suspicious but not openly hostile were easy to meet, although Orlando stressed the need for patience and a slow pace in getting to the business of making an airstrip. He had to have the Indians' enthusiastic cooperation, not just their consent, for he never had enough men with him to do all the work. The Indians had to help clear the land, smooth it, and burn off the brush.

Because he was learning to think and feel like the Indians, Orlando learned patience. In the past they had been killed and enslaved by white men, so white men were to be killed on sight. How could the Indians know that the temper and policy of the Brazilian people and government had changed — *really* changed? They could learn only from men like Rondon, like Villas Boas and his brothers, men who had limitless understanding and patience.

Orlando never pressed on to an Indian village after making friendly contact along the trail. He always waited until the Indians asked him to come. Then he went, a small unarmed man, often alone, walking into the stronghold of a warlike tribe. There were times when he had to flee for his life, and only a seeming miracle allowed him to escape from the arrows shot after him. But most of the time his patience brought rewards. It took him six months to get through Chavante territory and make two airstrips, but he did it without losing a man. And those airstrips were never attacked by neighboring Chavantes, who had come to trust Orlando Villas Boas.

Although I learned a great deal about the early years of the expedition, just a few short years before my arrival, I saw that Orlando was really more interested in talking about today and tomorrow — the airstrips still to be built, to be followed later by small strips that would be offshoots from the main line, enabling him to reach out to still more tribes, pacific or belligerent. He had learned many of their languages.

He had learned to walk off into the jungle, barefoot, at a moment's notice. He could live off the jungle as the Indians did.

When I went back to the Xingu in the fall of 1963, Orlando Villas Boas met me at the airstrip at the Leonardo Villas Boas Post, named for one of his brothers, who had been killed only a year or two before. Even though fourteen years had passed, Orlando remembered me, perhaps because after our first meeting I had been one of his sponsors for membership in the Explorers Club.

He had good news for me. In a few days, several friendly tribes of the upper Xingu were to meet for a yearly "Ceremony of the Dead," called a Guarúp. Orlando asked me to go along with him to the meeting.

There were Indians of several tribes around the post, some of them former enemies. But they worked and slept and ate side by side without any difficulty. There was a good deal of coming and going at the post, too. An Indian and his family would appear on a trail leading into the clearing. When they saw Orlando, they rushed to him, and there was much smiling and talking and back-patting. If there were two small children, Orlando would have one in each arm.

Later in the day another group would arrive in a dugout canoe and the happy scene would take place again. The Indians were particularly glad to find Orlando at the post, for often he was away in the jungle for weeks or even months at a time, going into new areas to make contact with tribes he had never visited, or rushing to a village where an epidemic of measles or flu had broken out. There was little he could do in these situations, for there was no doctor or medical officer within hundreds of miles and Orlando's supply of medicines was pitifully inadequate.

Finally the day of the Guarúp came. Orlando and I boarded a small plane, a Helio-Courier, specially built for tiny and rough airstrips. It was on loan to Orlando from the University of Brasilia, to whom it had been given by a wealthy Philadelphian. After a short flight we landed at a small airstrip near the host village for this year's Guarúp. The tribes rotate as hosts, and it was now the turn of the Kuikuro tribe, who welcomed Orlando joyously. A few members of other tribes had already arrived, but most of the guests were on their way — Camayuras, Calapalos, and Mehinacos. They traveled from several hours to two days to reach the village, and I was able to film the arrival of many of them. Most of them stopped to bathe in the river before entering the center of the village, and some had to cross the river to get there. I was filming the approach of some Camayuras in dugouts when I got my first shock. Here came the people I had thought the happiest in the world, the people who had laughed and twittered on my first visit to them. Now they glowered at me as I took pictures of them, and one young man even tried to splash water on me with his paddle. I was dumbfounded, but I kept the camera going.

In the village, greeting friends, the Camayuras smiled again and were more animated. And they looked almost like their old selves when they saw Orlando. The Camayura women were still as lovely as I remembered them, and they still dressed only in the miniscule uluri, but they were certainly not as effusively affectionate as they had been fourteen years before. The men were still fine physical specimens, but there was a lackluster air about many of them.

My disappointment over this change in one of my favorite peoples was thrust aside by the activities of the Guarúp. The men, who had been busy in the forest for some time, came trooping into the open square of the village carrying big logs six to eight feet long and up to a foot and a half in diameter. There was one such log for each member of the tribes who had died since the last Guarúp the year before.

Each post was buried upright with about four feet showing above ground. This part was then decorated with black genipa and red urucu paints, with cotton waistband and feather headdress. Some of the men were decorating themselves with black and red paints, feather headdresses, arm and ankle bands. Orlando told me they were getting ready for the dance called urúa.

Many watched as the two dancers appeared with their flutes. These instruments were double-tubed bamboo reeds, one tube about seven feet long, the other about five feet long, bound together with fiber strands. A kind of quartet floated out of the throaty but pleasant-sounding flutes. It was a lively melody, as it had to be to accompany the dance, which was a spirited trot with a rapid emphatic beat given by the right foot.

The dancers circled the open area of the village, suddenly lowered their flutes and ducked through the low door of a hut. In a few seconds they emerged, still playing their flutes, trotted, and ducked into another hut. After a while two young ladies joined the dancers. Each girl put her right hand on the right shoulder of the male dancer in front of her and trotted behind him in perfect tempo, went into the huts and came out again.

That night I slept in a half-finished hut. I strung my hammock between two poles and looked out at the entire village, for there were no walls. Near the base of each half-buried log, the female relatives of the dead person it represented kindled a fire, then sat down to weep. They wailed, they sobbed, they called out the name of the departed one. All night long the wake continued. I slept fitfully, roused to consciousness occasionally by a touching crescendo of lamentation.

At dawn the fires died down and the women left their posts. Now the souls of the dead ones had risen from the logs and were free. The logs had served their purpose.

I was sleepy and tired, but the action of the day made me alert enough to take pictures. The wrestling teams of the four tribes attending the Guarúp met in a fierce but happy competition. Wrestling is the favorite sport of most Indians of the upper Xingu and a champion has great prestige. The style of wrestling is closer to the Greco-Roman, and bears little resemblance to the rough-and-tumble spectacle now seen in America. Pinning an opponent's back to the ground is not the objective, but grabbing his buttock. The match starts with the two men facing each other kneeling, while each one places his left hand at the back of the neck of the other. Then as they lunge, grasp and whirl about, they keep grunting, "Hooka, hooka, hooka." Although the legs do most of the work, the hands are the winners of victory.

During the day I saw only one man thrown on his back. He was a brash youngster who challenged the champion of champions. It was so presumptuous that the champion felt the upstart needed humiliating. And in Mato Grosso wrestling, nothing can be more humiliating than to be thrown to the ground by your opponent.

When the Guarúp ended, Orlando and I flew back to the post. The next day I found that a Camayura chief and his wife were returning to their village and I asked if I could go along — it was only about an eight-mile walk through the forest. The chief, magnificently built, insisted on carrying all my gear, because I was a friend of Orlando's. It was a big load, including hammock, blankets, cameras, tripod and film.

About halfway to his village, I saw him stagger a little. I ran ahead of him and made him stop, put down the packs. He was having a malaria attack, sweating profusely, unable to stand. Almost everyone in the jungle has such attacks, including Orlando.

After a rest, we redistributed the gear and went on to the village, which consisted of five large huts. We dined on hot soup, beans, rice, and some powdered milk I had brought along.

The night was getting chilly when I hung up my hammock-tent in a small unused hut on the edge of the village square. It became colder as the night wore on, and I ended sleeping in pajamas, a sweater, two blankets and a groundsheet. In all the other huts, the Indians were sleeping naked. And all night long I heard them coughing and hacking and spitting. Pneumonia, influenza, smallpox and tuberculosis are taking terrible tolls on the gentle Camayuras. The thought that I was witnessing the probable end of a wonderful people saddened me as I lay awake that night.

Not only did the Indians lack immunity to white men's diseases; when they became ill with a high fever they did everything that was wrong. They did not lie quietly, but ran around, jumped into a cold stream or lake to cool off. So they are dying off.

When I saw the tribes of the upper Mato Grosso around the Xingu River, in 1949, I felt that the fate of the Bororos would never befall them. They were among the happiest people I had ever met. Yet when I returned in 1963 the Camayuras numbered a hundred and ten; they formerly had four villages, now one. The Calapalos were down to about the same number. The Trumai tribe had been wiped out almost to a man, not by disease alone, but by an enemy tribe. Ten survived and found homes among friendly tribes. Another group, the Yawilapiti, were now down to twenty.

Why was it, I asked myself, that the contented, peaceful peoples were the first to go? The tougher, warlike tribes seemed to survive better. Or was it just a matter of time for them, too? I remembered what Orlando Villas Boas had told me. He was giving his life to the Indians of the Mato Grosso.

"They are all doomed," he said. "Civilization will inevitably come here, one of the last fortresses of primitive man, and there will be no place for them. But maybe we can make the change a little slower, a little easier. At least we can try."

4

Curaka Utitiaja

ON MY 1949 trip, filming *Jungle Headhunters* for RKO, I finally got back to the Jivaros. After visiting the Yaguas again, and the tribes in the Mato Grosso, I took off from Quito, with Jules Bucher as extra cameraman, in search of the greatest headhunter of them all, Utitiaja.

I had picked up a copy of *El Commercio* in Quito and read an article about the Jivaro Indians by a Salesian missionary. In the section around the Upano River, where I planned to go, the newspaper said that there had been a recent increase in the number of wars and assassinations for revenge. One man held responsible was a chief named Utitiaja, who was said to have taken fifty-eight heads. He was the most feared warrior the Jivaros had produced in many years.

In Quito I had also found another good cameraman named Bodoworth, who agreed to go along. With three cameras in good hands, I could not miss. This time, too, there would be no chance of banging a camera out of focus while lugging it down the Andes on the back of a mule. We were going most of the way by plane.

Since my last trip two small jungle airstrips had been cut out of the forest on the edge of Jivaro country. The one at Macas had been the scene of numerous crack-ups because of the soggy ground, but the one at Sucua, where there were two missions, was satisfactory if weather, wind, and luck were all favorable. Sucua was north of my last portal of entry, at Méndez, but south of Macas, just about where I wished to go.

Colonel Winstead, head of the U.S. Air Force Mission in Quito, very kindly loaded Bucher, Bodoworth, and me, with all our equipment, into a DC–3 one sunny morning and took off for Sucua.

We were met at the Sucua airstrip by the two competing missionaries, Padre Natali of the Salesian Mission and Michael J. Ficke of the Protestant Evangelical Mission. They were friendly, of course, but they were after the same thing: the souls of young Jivaros.

Colonel Winstead was eager to take off for Quito again while wind and weather were still right. We arranged to meet at this spot in exactly thirty days and, he wished me luck and took off, his wheels brushing the tops of the trees as he fought for altitude. Suddenly, with the plane gone, I felt a very long way from civilization.

Both missionaries offered their help and hospitality. We stayed at the Salesian mission because it was larger and had more room. There were about seventy-five Jivaro boys and fifty Jivaro girls going to school there, ranging in age from five to twelve. In almost every case the children were there because their families had been wiped out. They were happy, good workers, good students, but even after a few years in the mission their traditions and the indoctrination of their early years held them bound. Some children would not speak to or play with children of clans that had been enemies of their clans. Even with both families wiped out, the bitterness remained. I was told of one boy who graduated from the mission and, wearing the cross and a Catholic medal, went back into the jungle and killed four men to avenge the death of his father and brothers.

We spent two days at the missions preparing for our journey. As guide, the missionaries recommended a young Jivaro of about twenty-three name Shuara. Now, Shuara is the name the Jivaro Indians call themselves, meaning "the people." Shuara was called that name because when he ran out of the jungle as a tot, that was the only word the missionaries could understand. It had been his name ever since, although the Jivaros of the jungle thought it was no name at all. Shuara had become a good Christian, but he had kept up many contacts in this section of the Jivaro country. Since his family were all dead, he was no one's enemy, and since he had become a good Christian he had no desire to seek vengeance. He was one of the few true neutrals who could travel safely anywhere in the headhunter country. He knew both Spanish and the Jivaro tongue equally well. Above all he was intelligent. Without him I could never have accomplished the unprecedented feat that in time caused a stir as far away as Quito.

I was also offered the services of a mestizo named Don Bodillo, a burly tough trader from the mountains who had settled down on a little ranch not far from the mission. Thinking that his brute strength might prove useful, I took him on as a second guide.

Shuara and Don Bodillo both knew a great deal about the location of different clans and the relations between them. The article in the newspaper had been correct: there was much war, many raids, and almost every group was feuding with another. But Shuara assured me that they would all welcome me. He was particularly impressed with a copy of *Life* magazine with colored pictures from my 1945 trip, showing Peruche and others from the Paute region, and he said all his friends in the jungle would be impressed, too.

We borrowed four horses and five mestizo bearers from the mission and set out for the river. That night we camped near the banks of the Upano. The next morning, when I looked at the river, I almost wished that there was a cable bridge. The Upano was four hundred yards wide here — four hundred yards of rushing, turbulent waters that poured down from the Andes with such force as to carry huge boulders, often as far as the Pongo de Menseriche a couple of hundred miles away. I could see no boat or canoe, and I doubted that we could paddle a raft across such a stream.

Shuara was not worried. He pointed out to me a jivaria high on a cliff on the other side of the river. The Cuticu Mountains rise up abruptly from the river edge at this point, and one Jivaro clan had chosen a ledge about a thousand feet high for its home. It certainly would have been a difficult place to attack.

Shuara cupped his hands and shouted up at the jivaria. Don Bodillo did the same in a booming voice that sounded like a Jivaro signal drum. The rushing of the waters smothered the sounds. For five minutes we all shouted and waved our arms, and finally two headhunters happened to look down and see us. They waved back and started down a long winding path to the river edge.

They appeared on the opposite shore, near a twenty-foot dugout canoe tied there. They recognized Shuara, and stepped into the canoe, paddling furiously toward us. The force of the current carried them downstream a couple of hundred yards, but they pulled the canoe up to our little beach.

Bodoworth and I elected to go first and carry some of the cameras and equipment. Bucher was going to film the crossing from our side, then we could film his crossing. We went upstream about three hundred yards. There, while Bodoworth and I settled ourselves on our knees, an Indian held the stern fairly quiet by standing and grasping a liana that hung from a tree at the river's bank. The Indian in the bow got himself set and called. The liana was released and we shot down the stream like a jet plane. The Indians paddled with all their force for the opposite shore. Bodoworth and I clung to the gunwales for dear life as it bobbed and bucked on the rough water.

We reached the other shore only ten feet below our goal. After unloading us, the Jivaros started back for the others without waiting to rest. It took three more trips to bring everyone and everything to the eastern bank.

Then we started the climb for the jivaria on the cliff, almost straight up. The jungle path was rocky in places but muddy most of the way, and I slipped and fell three or four times in five minutes. About three-quarters of the way up my heart began to pound like a pneumatic drill.

I edged over to the side of the path and wedged myself securely against the trunk of a tree. I fell asleep and slept soundly for about fifteen minutes. When I woke up I felt quite refreshed and made my way up to the jivaria without too much difficulty.

The jivaria of Take had one of the most magnificent views in the world, and Take knew it. He was proud of his house and its location, but more from the point of view of its defensive position than its scenic values. After going through a proper amount of formality and eating some food, we set out for the interior.

For the next two weeks we visited two jivarias, one with just six men, the other with five. I didn't get fifty feet of film I could use. Good documentary stuff, yes, but no big dramatic climax essential for a feature-length true-life film. I needed more than eleven men for such a scene and asked Shuara if we could not bring in more people from jivarias nearby. He explained that these two were all that remained of a once powerful clan. They were surrounded by enemies, not friends who could come to help them make pictures. So we turned north, visiting briefly in two jivarias that showed little pictorial promise, and finally came to a large jivaria of the Sepa group, Jivaros who lived along the Sepa River, a tributary of the Upano.

It was a wonderful spot for taking the scene I wanted — a level clearing larger than that around most Jivaro houses, good light, little hills here and there about the edges of the clearing that would serve as good vantage points from which to film long shots. Nayapi, curaka of the Sepa group, was friendly but very reserved. Still, he wanted to be helpful, to cooperate. He brought in men and women from several other jivarias in his group, so that I had twenty-eight men assembled.

We tried to reenact the tsantsa dance with them. They were willing, dressed themselves in bright feathers, necklaces, headdresses. They performed the dance and we filmed it, but I knew it was not right. There was a lethargy in the dancers, and it showed too plainly. They went through the motions almost automatically and that's all. I knew it would look like that in the film, too.

Bodoworth and Bucher agreed with me but had no suggestions. Even Shuara and Don Bodillo seemed to understand.

"What I need most of all is a dynamic character, a real leader like Peruche who can get some spirit into these people, an actor like Juanga who looks as if he were really the victor at a tsantsa feast. Everybody else catches fire from a person like that, and you get a great performance, something that has an air of reality because the dancers begin to feel the same feelings they have had at real tsantsa dances. The dance itself is simple, rather dull. Its effect depends entirely upon the emotions of the dancers."

My thoughts turned again to the champion headhunter Utitiaja, and I asked Shuara if we could visit his jivaria. He said we probably could, but he had another idea.

"I do not know if you can take the pictures you want at his jivaria. The clearing is small. And even though he is a great warrior and curaka, he has only about twenty-five men. Let me take the copy of that magazine with pictures of the Jivaros of the Paute. I will go to several clans in this region and ask them to come here, which is the best place for taking pictures, and help you make the film."

"You mean friendly clans?" I asked.

"No, there are not many friendly clans," Shuara said. "I mean clans that are now at war with each other but that will bury the lance to come and do this."

"Why should they bury the lance for me? Why, it's unheard of — getting several clans to stop a hot war. It hasn't happened, probably, since 1599 when the clans gathered under Quiruba to massacre the Spanish."

"Perhaps not," Shuara said, "'but I think they will do it. They will do it for you because of the things I will tell them about you. I will show them the magazine and tell them that you have visited Jivaros of the Santiago and of the Paute and taken their pictures so that people all over the world, far beyond the seas, have seen them, read about them. I will tell them you have come back again to take pictures of the Upanos because you know they are the greatest warriors of all the Jivaros. You want to tell your people about the Indians because you admire them so much. I will tell them that it was you who came on the big bird the last time it flew over the jungle. I will tell them that you have many gifts and a great feast for them. And I will tell them about the magic tricks you showed me at the mission. Every wishinu of every clan will want your kind of magic."

In accordance with my custom of finding something unusual, in addition to regular gifts to take to the Indians I had bought some gadgets in a store specializing in magic tricks. I knew little about such things but by a great stroke of luck ran into the noted performing magician Russell Swann. He was an old friend and had dropped into the store to pick up a few things himself. He helped me make my selections and, more important, showed me how to work them with some deftness. I had not yet used them except at the mission in Sucua one evening. I had grave doubts about their drawing power in the South American jungle and was afraid they might annoy the medicine men.

And I wondered about the great feast Shuara would promise the feuding Jivaros. I had plenty of small gifts, but no feast. Shuara had already figured everything out. I could send two bearers back to the mission to buy three swine — the meat Jivaros always ate at a feast. They would return in a week, by which time he would have visited the different clans.

The next morning he started out with a copy of *Life* magazine, and the bearers headed back for the mission. The days passed, with Bodoworth, Bucher, and I loafing or going fishing and hunting with some of the men of the Sepa clan, on whose clearing we had set up camp.

By the fifth day after Shuara's departure, I was becoming very restless and concerned. So were the Sepa headhunters, I thought; they had agreed to Shuara's plan before he left, provided they had sufficient warning of the approach of any other clan.

Shortly after dawn on the sixth day Shuara burst into the clearing after a few loud *whe-dee*'s. He was tired but elated, for he had succeeded. He had run ahead to give us the news and to notify the Sepa Indians.

I could not quite believe it, and even today I find my story greeted with raised eyebrows in some quarters that know the Jivaros. That is why I treasure my copy of a letter that Michael Ficke, of the Evangical Mission at Sucua, wrote to President Galo Plaza of Ecuador (later U.N. Arbitrator on Cyprus) at the end of my third Jivaro trip. Mr. Ficke wrote:

> The expedition proved singularly successful for several reasons. One of the unprecedented things accomplished was the bringing together of four distinct groups of Jivaros that had been noted enemies since time immemorial. The four tribes are as follows:
> 1. Utitiaja's group from the Chupientsa territory.
> 2. The Cambanaca group.
> 3. The Tutanangosa group.
> 4. The Sepa group.

Our hosts the Sepas seemed as incredulous as I was, and readily agreed to welcome the other clans in peace. Shuara raced back into the jungle to tell the Tutanangosa group, with which he had traveled. The Cambanaca group would arrive about noon, he said, and Utitiaja's around two o'clock.

"How did you manage to get Utitiaja?" I asked.

Shuara smiled. "I told him you could not have a successful film without the greatest warrior of the Jivaros," he said.

The bearers with the meat had arrived, and the Sepa women agreed to prepare it for that evening's meal. Bodoworth and Bucher and I got our cameras and tripods ready in time to catch Shuara entering the clearing with about twenty-five warriors of the Tutanangosa group, followed by as many women and children.

I waited until the icily formal greeting of the Sepas and Tutanangosas was completed before I welcomed the curaka of this clan. Bodoworth and Bucher were filming as I handed out presents to the men and then watched them file into the forest a short way, where they cleared a small space for temporary shelter. The women were heavily loaded with big baskets of food and nijimanche.

I took Shuara to one side. "Are you sure there will be no trouble?" I asked. "These two groups looked daggers at each other during the greeting."

"I know," Shuara said, "And they may be fighting when you leave in a few days. But they will keep their word. The lance has been buried, and no Jivaro would dream of violating a truce, no mattter how much he would like to stick his lance into the man he drinks nijimanche with."

It was just noon when the Cambanacas, with nineteen warriors and their women, arrived. This time the Sepa greeting and the Cambanaca reply was so stiffly formal that I felt cold shivers run down my spine. I could see the Cambanacas figuring very quickly that they had the smallest number of men there.

They had received their gifts and retired to the forest in another direction to build a shelter when Utitiaja appeared, shortly before two. He entered the clearing from a path close to our little camp. While there could be no question as to who was Utitiaja, the curaka of this group, he was totally unlike my image of him. I realized that no one had ever described him to me, but many had talked about his great feats of war. So I had imagined a man big, strong and fierce-looking. Instead he was a trifle shorter than the average Jivaro, and of rather slight build, though compact and effortless in his movements. Most striking, however, was his face — mild, placid, even somewhat gentle. No lines marked his forehead or cheeks and there was not the slightest suggestion of fierceness or cruelty in his expression. His simple *itipi* did not even have the human-hair belt so loved by most Jivaros. He did not wear a necklace of jaguar's teeth, but a simple one of plain white beads. Nevertheless, despite his mild appearance and his simplicity, he moved with authority, with an inner assurance and dignity that marked him unmistakably as a leader.

There were two younger men on either side of Utitiaja who came much closer to looking their part: bodyguard to the great chief. I have never seen two more murderous-looking characters. They were tense and alert. Their eyes darted around them ceaselessly.

Utitiaja saw me standing by my tent and came to me, holding out a hand. I had not expected this, for it was good etiquette for him to be welcomed by the Sepa curaka first. I felt that in Utitiaja I had another unconventional soul, like Peruche.

With Shuara by my side to translate, I thanked Utitiaja for coming to help me make a film that would tell the world about the Jivaro Indians, and above all about the greatest Jivaro warrior. He nodded and smiled and said he was glad to come. It should be interesting.

I asked him where his jivaria was. At the confluence of the Chupientsa and Upano Rivers. How far away? Seven hours' walk; they had left very early in the morning.

Since Utitiaja seemed willing to talk, I invited him to sit down on our camp benches. He did, with his two-man bodyguard standing close behind him, and the rest of his twenty-four warriors and their women and children squatting and making themselves comfortable at the edge of the clearing.

Utitiaja mentioned the pictures in *Life* magazine. They had fascinated him, and I felt sure they were what had brought him to my camp. I brought the magazine out and we looked at it together — Bodoworth and Bucher were shooting the scene — and then we looked at other still pictures I had of the 1945 trip. Utitiaja said he did not know Peruche but he knew three other men in my pictures, those I had taken on my long hunting trip with Juanga and his friends. Utitiaja pointed them out to me — they were not people I remembered well — and told me what had happened to them. This one was killed and his head taken. That one had drowned. The other had disappeared completely and no one had any idea what had happened to him. Perhaps a snake had killed him and no one had discovered the body.

Utitiaja spoke to one of his bodyguards and showed him the pictures. I learned that the fierce young warrior was Utitiaja's son-in-law. He sat down, too, upon Utitiaja's insistence, and so did an older man the curaka called to. He was Tubushi, the wishinu of Utitiaja's clan, with a most photogenic face. He remained very aloof.

I asked Utitiaja how many heads he had taken in his life, and he held up his ten fingers five times, then held up eight — fifty-eight! Then I asked Juantinga, his son-in-law, and Juantinga gestured twenty-eight. I asked how it happened that Utitiaja had so many more. Juantinga replied, seriously, that he had not lived as long as Utitiaja.

Utitiaja then asked me just what pictures I wanted to take, and I told him about my desire to film the tsantsa dance with as much realism and feeling as possible. He nodded and said he would try to help me.

The conversation ended and Utitiaja arose to pay his respects to the Sepa curaka and the others. I watched him approach the jivaria of Nayapi, followed by his warriors. I saw the men of the Cambanaca and the Tutanangosa groups had returned to the clearing and were standing at the outskirts staring at Utitiaja. Every pair of eyes followed him, and many of the eyes were filled with fear. I knew there might well be a dozen young men in the clearing who had been told almost daily from boyhood that this man was their greatest enemy.

The tension mounted as Utitiaja approached Nayapi — in everyone, apparently, but Utitiaja. He walked with perfectly relaxed steps and without any apparent reaction to the unprecedented scene. If he thought of the fact that about seventy men surrounding him would like to kill him, he gave no sign of it. All the rest were frightened, at least to some degree, even Utitiaja's own men. But Utitiaja was not. I made up my mind to try to get to know him better, to learn the source of such amazing confidence and inner assurance.

When the greeting was ended, Utitiaja did not lead his people out of the clearing to make their shelter, but directed that it be put up at the edge of the clearing, next to my camp. And then he returned to me and suggested that we get down to business.

With Shuara beside me I went to the different groups to explain what I wanted. They all understood, as Shuara had already briefed them pretty thoroughly. For the first time I saw them begin to think of something besides Utitiaja, as they looked forward to the dance. I picked the men I wanted from each group, enough to make a total of about thirty or thirty-five men. I wanted strong, individual types, trying to select particularly those who looked sensitive or deeply emotional. You can't always tell, of course, with just a glance or two, but I was able to get an impressive crowd together. I had already decided that Juantinga should play the part of the victor with the tsantsa.

The men selected made themselves up at once, taking different materials from monkey-fur pouches or bamboo makeup kits which they carried. They drew black lines on their faces, braided extra toucan feathers in their hair, put on necklaces, inserted earplugs, and then placed on their heads a brilliant array of headdresses. Some were made of red feathers, others of yellow down. Some had monkey fur and feathers combined, and many had long muticolored feathers stuck in the round headpiece so they stood up tall and sparkling.

The men all assembled in the large flat area we had chosen for the dances. And then I thought of the tsantsa. I asked Nayapi if he happened to have a tsantsa we could use, and he produced a shrunken head immediately. It occurred to me that this might be the brother or father or son of someone now present, but apparently the thought did not enter the heads of the Jivaros themselves. The tsantsa, by the time it was shrunk, had little human connection in their minds.

First I wanted some footage of the victory dance with lances, the scene I had shot at Peruche's jivaria. Juantinga therefore drove his lance into the ground in the center of the circle of men and placed the tsantsa on top.

The participating dancers were ready with their lances, and a group of musicians had gathered close by with small drums and long flutes. I explained that we would have a short rehearsal first, to be sure of what we were doing. Then I stepped back and gave the signal, the music began, and the men began to move.

The spectacle was wonderful, but at first the dancing was crude. The men were stiff and self-conscious and moved without vigor or conviction. In a few moments it improved as they got into the spirit of it, but the whole thing still lacked conviction. I called a halt and stepped into the middle of the circle, taking one of the lances with me. I told the dancers that I wanted them to act just the way they did in the victory dance.

"Everyone of you has come home with a tsantsa!" I cried. "Remember how you danced *then*, how you felt *then*. Dance that way now. Thrust your lance hard, as if you were facing an enemy."

Shuara translated as fast as I spoke. Then I demonstrated what I meant, leaping forward energetically and pushing the lance with what I hoped was a dramatic and vital movement of the whole body.

They all burst out laughing! It caught me off balance, for just a moment, and then I realized how ludicrous it was for me to be telling these men how to thrust a chonta lance, how to do a victory dance around a shrunken head. I laughed, too, and retired somewhat abashed, but pleased to see this mixed group of enemies laughing together.

And my instructions helped. The men got the idea of what I wanted, in any event, and when the dance started again it had zest and earnestness and life to it. Bucher was shooting long shots, Bodoworth close-ups, and I at one point crawled inside the circle to get more striking views, showing the men lunging directly toward the camera.

At the end of half an hour, when I knew that we had plenty of superb shots, I had a hard time stopping the dancers. But I wanted to get footage of the dance that is performed over and over again during the tsantsa feast, the *hantsemata*. In this dance the men join hands and dance around in a circle, with queer, shuffling side steps that carry them forward and then back. The victor is one of the dancers, and wears the tsantsa hanging from his neck.

I handed the tsantsa to Utitiaja, a fascinated spectator of the performance, and took the lance from the ground. After a brief talk about what I wanted, we started the whole scene. Utitiaja handed the tsantsa to his wishinu, who then hung it around the neck of Juantinga. The men formed the circle, the strange rhythmic music started, and the dance began. The low guttural huffing of the men began, too, gradually rising in volume until it sounded threatening and ominous.

Shuara pulled at my sleeve. "See those two there — the one with the yellow feathers and next to him the man with the jaguar necklace? Well, the man with the yellow headdress killed the brother of the man with the necklace of jaguar teeth. And look — they are holding hands and dancing together!"

As the dance continued, I could see that the men were being stirred by the memory of other tsantsa dances, by the feelings of exultation and triumph and mysticism that had seized them then. Faces were tense and body movements became more sharply defined, more true in rhythm. I grabbed my own camera to get some dramatic close-ups of faces that the others might have missed. And finally, after about twenty minutes, I called a halt. Stepping into the circle of men, who still held hands, breathing deeply, I took the hands of two of the warriors while I thanked them for the fine dancing that would make the sequence so true. Without warning, the music started up again and the men took up the dance, still holding me by the hands. I did the only thing there was to do — I joined in.

It was not difficult, of course, and in a moment I was following their rhythmic steps: sideways forward, sideways back, in a shuffle. I found myself emitting a hoarse grunt along with the others, and being a part of that movement, a contributor to that weird sound, made me share their feelings, somehow. A steady rhythm can do strange things to people and for a few minutes it almost made a Jivaro out of me. Across the circle I watched the shrunken head as it bobbed against Juantinga's chest. I looked at Juantinga's face and saw a rapt, dedicated expression that welled up from the depths of his soul. And I felt something of that emotion myself. For a little while I was very close to experiencing the feelings of a man who has cut off another man's head, has shrunk it, and now dances around it.

When the dance ended I was a little dazed, but I remembered I had obligations to fulfill. There was not sufficient light for any more filming that day, but it was time for the feast itself.

I supervised the cutting and handing out of the meat, at which all the men looked hungrily. I hoped they would stay together and eat together, but the suspicions were too great, the fears too deep. After the dancing was over, there was nothing to bind them together, and each group took its meat and went off to its own shelter. I ate only a little, for I suddenly felt extremely tired.

I could not sleep well. Every time I heard a sound of movement during the night, I was afraid that one clan was trying to make a sneak attack on the other. I should have believed what Shuara told me about the Jivaros living up to an agreement, for nothing at all happened.

But the next morning the Cambanaca group did not appear, and a visit to their shelter proved that they had left to return to their own area. Their fear had been too great. They were outnumbered by every other group. I suppose they could not sleep either.

I was sorry, of course, but their departure did not upset my filming plans. Since Juantinga was now the principal character in my dance sequence, as the victor who had taken a head, I wanted very much to re-create some scenes in which he would appear so that they could be used to build up to the final scene.

I spoke to Juantinga and Utitiaja about the idea that morning, and they were enthusiastic. I think that Juantinga was beginning to like the idea of being an actor. He certainly proved himself an able one.

During the next day we staged many scenes that might lead up to the tsantsa dance. Juantinga and other warriors were preparing for a raid, then saying good-bye to their wives and leaving the clearing.

Our company moved out on location — that is, to a path through the jungle where there was just enough light to shoot some footage of Juantinga and his fellow warriors moving swiftly and silently, and later crossing a rushing stream.

In the afternoon we took other scenes, including one of a man being struck by a chonta-spike trap across a path, followed by a shot of him lying on the ground and being found dead by his fellows, a long shot of Juantinga supposedly cutting the head from a fallen men, then rising and wrapping something in a big leaf.

Back at the jivaria I suggested one scene that I wanted very much but which I hesitated to ask for. This was an assault of Juantinga's group on a jivaria, and a battle. It could be taken from a distance, but I wondered what might happen when some of these lifelong enemies pretended to fight each other. Might they not suddenly get caught up with their emotions and fight in earnest? I asked Shuara and Utitiaja about it and they thought it would be all right, and very interesting. So with some misgivings I gave directions and then the go-ahead signal. All went well, and we obtained excellent shots without a casualty.

But that night the Tutanangosa group left for their homes without saying another word.

Utitiaja was so fascinated by the filming that he wanted to continue the next day. So we made some scenes of Juantinga preparing the tsantsa. Another scene showed Shuara and me coming along a forest path, a chonta lance being thrown across the path about three inches in front of Shuara and embedding itself in a tree; we stopped, of course, and saw Juantinga and others peering through the trees at us. Then we were taken to the clearing, where Utitiaja sat in state with his wishinu and another warrior. A kind of trial of me and my motives in visiting the Indians was played with gestures.

Suddenly I had an idea. I had never got around to showing the magic tricks Shuara liked so much. This would be a good chance to show them to everyone. I went to my tent and got the tricks. One was an old-timer, a beautiful red silk scarf which was pushed into one fist only to emerge as a blue handkerchief. Everyone seemed pleased with this, though not particularly startled. The favorites were the collapsible plastic items that could be held in a tiny space in my hand but would blossom out into something big when released.

I put my hand under the itipi of one warrior and came out with a small bunch of bananas. Next I produced a bouquet of flowers and finally a human skull. There were gasps from everyone and great appreciation as well as mystification. If I really had been trying to get myself into the good graces of these headhunters I would surely have succeeded with those tricks, although as usual my cigarette lighter proved the biggest attraction of all.

As I anticipated, old Tubushi, the wishinu, was the only one who did not look favorably upon my magic. Competition, of course. He wanted to get close to my skull and flowers and bananas. While these objects look real from a distance of about ten feet, they cannot stand closer inspection or handling. So I kept them away from Tubushi, which annoyed him further. Later when Utitiaja asked about them, I gave them to him. I always like the idea of Utitiaja's mystifying his own wishinu with my magic tricks.

I was sorry when the day came to an end. Utitiaja was to leave the next day. After the evening meal I asked him if he would like to come to my tent to talk for a while, since this was our last evening together. He brought along the wife who had accompanied him on this strange journey, a woman in her fifties and probably his first wife. Juantinga stayed outside the tent. I offered a campstool to Utitiaja's wife, but Utitiaja sat down on it and his wife sat on the ground at his feet.

The great headhunter seemed to be happy. He spoke of the pictures we had taken, of the scenes we had enacted, with genuine pleasure. He hoped he would be able to see some of the pictures some day.

He stopped talking, as if he had finished saying what he wanted to say and had no other thoughts on his mind at the moment. He looked down at his wife and smiled, and she gazed at him with adulation.

"How old are you, Utitiaja?" I asked. I did not think he was the man to be offended at this question. He would just answer or not answer as he wished. But on this subject he was a little vague. He held up his ten fingers five times and then added a few more whose number I could not see.

Shuara translated his mumbled words. "He is not certain. Fifty-six or fifty-seven."

I asked how old he was when he went on his first raid. The answer was ten. He went with his father for training, but did not fight.

"Were you afraid?" I asked.

"Yes, I was very frightened, but not as frightened as when I took my first head. I was seventeen then."

"Who taught you to be a great hunter and warrior?" I asked.

"My father, as all Jivaro boys are taught, if their fathers are alive. My father lived until I was thirteen, so he taught me much. He showed me how to hunt, how to aim the blowgun, handle the lance, move through the forest like the jaguar. When I was seven I started going on hunts with him. I listened and watched him and so I learned. And every morning since before I can remember, he sat me down in front of him, even before we ate food, and told me what I must do when I grew up. He told me who our enemies were, who had killed my brother, his father, his brother. Each time he told me exactly how they died and who had caused their deaths. He had avenged his father by killing the man. Really the man had killed himself by doing what he did to my grandfather.

"But there was more than my father's talk in training to be a warrior. When I first accompanied him on a raid, at ten, he kept me close to him through the fighting. When he had killed his enemy with the lance, he called me to his side and gave me the lance. Then he told me to plunge it in the dead man's body so that I would come to know the feel of it and learn how hard I must thrust. He wanted me to do this, also, so I would not be afraid, so I would become accustomed to blood."

He looked at his wife with a twinkle in his eyes. "My father also told me that I would become weak if I had anything to do with women" — he paused a moment — "before puberty." His wife smiled. "When my hair was grown and I reached the time to become a man, my father and mother had a great feast for me. It lasted three days. The wishinu blew tobacco water up my nose to strengthen me, and then I went into the woods with a jar of maikoa to make me dream fine dreams.

"I built a lean-to in the forest, a dream house. For five days I fasted and drank only maikoa, which makes you dizzy and then brings the *arutuma*, the Old Ones, your ancestors, back to talk to you and give advice. In my dreams the spirits of the Old Ones came and told me of my future, told me whether I would really become a great hunter and warrior or would get myself killed at an early age. I had many dreams but one kept coming back to me day after day. In this dream I was lying alone in the forest resting, my lance at my side. Suddenly a jaguar charged and leaped at me. I sprang up in time to grab my lance and speared the jaguar through the heart."

"How did you know what that dream meant?"

"I did not know then. I went to the wishinu and told him my dream. I knew from his expression and the happiness of my father and mother that I had dreamed a good dream indeed. The wishinu said the dream of killing a jaguar was the most significant dream anyone could have. It meant that I would grow up to become a strong and brave warrior, a great hunter. If I could kill the jaguar I could kill anything and would have no troubles. When I dreamed that I jumped up so quickly that the jaguar could not kill me, that meant I would be cleverer and faster than my enemies. They could never trick me or ambush me. Once, later, I thought the dream was wrong — enemies jumped out on me as I and my sons were hunting. I had a great hole in my chest and they thought I was dead. But I got well and lived to kill those that ambushed me."

"When you were a boy and learned all that the dream meant, how did you feel?" I asked.

Utitiaja looked at me in amazement. "I felt exalted, of course, as anyone would who knew that he would be successful in achieving the most important thing in life."

"But still you were frightened when you went on your first raid?"

"Yes, I was frightened because it was my first. Doing something the first time is always hard, even when you feel you will succeed. Because the enemy has spirits, too, spirits that are sometimes as strong as yours. But after the first time I learned that my good spirits were stronger than my enemies'. And I would always win. You see, I had drunk nateema before the first raid, and the Old Ones had told me I would kill my enemy and take his head. So it had to be that way.

"On my first raid," Utitiaja went on, "I killed the man who had killed my father. I had sworn to him that I would avenge his death so his soul could rest in peace. I was thirteen when he died. It was four long years that his soul was restless and unhappy because I could not take blood revenge. When I killed him I could say, 'See, my father, I have brought your soul peace.' "

"Utitiaja, you have killed fifty-eight men," I said. "Now that you are getting older, don't you worry about it sometimes? Do you think it is right to kill men like that?"

"It is right to kill your enemies, who would kill you if they could. Even you people know that, for I have heard of your wars."

"But do you think it is right for you to take the law in your own hands and execute the man?"

"Who else would kill him?" Utitiaja asked. "I hear that you pay certain people to do that for you, in your country. I think that is wrong. I am the one who has the right and the duty to kill him. And I have always fulfilled my duties, not tried to get someone else to take care of them for me."

"What is the tsantsa feast like, Utitiaja, when you are the victor celebrating the destruction of your enemy and the overpowering of his spirit?"

"It is a wonderful thing," Utitiaja said. "You feel that you are good, that you have done what you are supposed to do in this world. You have triumphed over your enemy by killing him. You now triumph over his evil spirit and make it a good spirit to help you more. And you tell the souls of the people you loved that they can stop wandering unhappily. Those are all splendid things to feel. It seems as if you are soaring high like the condor. I wish I could have had more tsantsa feasts."

"More then fifty-eight?" I cried.

Utitiaja laughed. "Oh, I have not had fifty-eight. Only nine or ten, I believe. Sometimes I was too busy fighting to celebrate the feast. Usually I did not have enough swine and chickens to give a big feast. It is too bad."

I was glad to know that there were some things even the greatest headhunter of them all could not afford. It suddenly made him more human, at least from my point of view, to see him figuring up the cost of a tsantsa feast with his wives and reluctantly concluding that they just could not afford it this year. Next year, maybe.

I asked Utitiaja what qualities he thought were most responsible for his great success as a warrior.

"My father was strong and smart," he said, "and he gave me some of his strength and brains. He trained me well. But the main reason is that before any war or raid I always drank nateema or maikoa and through my dreams learned from the Old Ones whether my plans would succeed or not. If they said no, I postponed the raid. If they said yes, I went ahead, knowing that I was absolutely certain to win."

There was the secret of his supreme confidence, the deep inner assurance I had sensed in him from the moment I first saw him. It was a feeling of confidence that had been confirmed fifty-eight times, at least. Nothing could shake it now. I asked Utitiaja what caused the terrible wars.

"Sometimes the clans have always been enemies and no one knows how it started," he said. "Aside from that, witch doctors and women cause the wars. Men need several wives to be happy and if they cannot find them in friendly clans, they will make war to get women. I can think of so many raids made just for that reason — to steal a woman."

I heard a low sob from Utitiaja's wife and looked at her. I was amazed, because Jivaro women rarely show much emotion openly. She was trying to stifle her sobs, but could not. Utitiaja was not perturbed. He reached over and patted her head gently, comfortingly.

I looked up at Shuara with a question in my eyes, but he shook his head. He had no idea what was wrong. Utitiaja saw my look and turned to me.

"I'll tell you why she weeps," he said. "Our daughter married a brave young warrior who lived in a friendly jivaria. They had been married only a few months. Recently an enemy clan raided his jivaria and killed him. They stole my daughter. We don't know for sure where she is, because we do not know who made the raid and took her. I have been trying to find out so I can kill the man, and bring my daughter back to us. I believe I know who the man is. And I must thank you for that. I am quite sure he was here. I will make sure before I kill him. Thank you."

It was quite late when Utitiaja and his wife returned to their shelter. I went to bed right away, but when I woke up in the morning I saw that Utitiaja's camp was deserted. They had probably left in the dark, just before dawn.

About two months after I returned to New York I received a newspaper clipping from Quito, sent by a friend who knew of my visit with the greatest of all headhunters. The paper reported that the notorious Jivaro chief Utitiaja had murdered a man of the Tutanangosa tribe. As he was returning to his own home he fell into the hands of a small detachment of soldiers who had been flown into Sucua to see if the recent wave of murders could not be put down.

Some authorities insisted that the "gangster" Utitiaja be flown to

Quito to stand trial for murder. But the government cited a law providing that no savage could be punished for crimes against another savage, on the theory that such primitive peoples can best get along by following their own codes of justice. Utitiaja was released and returned to his home.

So Utitiaja had number fifty-nine now! And perhaps he had his daughter back. In any event his daughter's husband's soul could now rest in peace.

I could not picture Utitiaja in the hands of uniformed soldiers or in a prison cell. Well, he wasn't. His dreams were still correct and he was still ranging the forest, dispensing justice, and living the good life of a competent and dedicated human being. I found myself hoping that he could afford a tsantsa feast that year.

I heard little about the Jivaros for a number of years. Startling changes were coming to primitive tribes all over the world, even among many tribes I had visited in other parts of South America. But I had a feeling that the Jivaros were still isolated in their vast jungle. The revolution over most of the world would scarcely touch them.

But I heard one final word about Utitiaja, the greatest headhunter of them all. In January, 1964, I had a letter from missionary Mike Ficke in Sucua. It read, "In regard to Utitiaja, he quit fighting and killing after his arrest, due also to his son's influence, who is a Christian schoolteacher in Chupientsa. A tree fell on him, breaking his leg, and as he was so far in the forest at the time, they had quite a time trying to take care of him. He died from the broken leg, and possibly from the infection, although the missionaries cared for him as much as they could."

I don't think I'll go back to South America again. It is too sad to see tribe after tribe dying out. Despite the most enlightened protection of primitive tribes by Brazil, the diseases of civilizations are wiping out some of the most admirable groups. A kind of death-wish fatalism, as, for example, among the Bororos, hastens this trend. Even the Yaguas, isolated as they are, are down to barely a hundred, compared with a thousand when I first visited them in 1940. Only the Jivaros maintain themselves and continue their old, warlike ways, despite the excruciatingly slow reforms of the government and, chiefly, the missionaries. The never-ending wars and feuds of the Jivaros may kill them off before civilization reaches them.

But the Jivaros have courage, and maybe they will endure. Must I believe that only the cruel and belligerent can survive in this world? Africa makes me think this may be so, but I don't like the idea. I wish the happy and loving Camayuras might prevail.

III

NEW GUINEA

1

Sepik

THE LAST stronghold of the Stone Age lies in New Guinea, and it is crumbling so fast that within my lifetime there may remain nothing but a few pockets — chiefly in the western half of the island — of truly primitive culture. Within a few decades, hundreds of thousands of men and women may have made a leap of ten thousand years of social, scientific, and moral development.

These people have been subjected to more new situations and pressures than man soaring into outer space, and their experience proves better than any astronaut's the flexibility and capacity for rapid change of the human mind and emotions, if not always the human body. To the highland natives of New Guinea, beaten bark or fiber was cloth, pointed sticks and stone axes were the only tools, and war was a way of life.

In 1933, only twenty-five years before my first expedition, more than half a million primitives were discovered in the central highlands of New Guinea. They knew nothing of metal, the wheel, pottery, or the sea. Five years later, in 1938, several hundred thousand more were found in what was then Dutch New Guinea and is now Indonesian West Irian.

What sort of island is this last outpost of the truly primitive, and why was it the last to become known? New Guinea is the second largest island in the world, a long, ragged, jagged mass of earth and stone thrusting up out of the Pacific Ocean north of Australia. Seen from the air, it almost looks like an unfinished work, a leftover mass of sand and stone and rivers (some with gold in them) and Adams and Eves and very few animals and many, many mountains. The mountains proved to be the barrier preserving this stronghold of the Stone Age, until the airplane flew over them, which was done although it took — and in many areas still takes — the most daring and skillful flying to avoid mountain-filled clouds and to land on narrow, tilted runways. In New Guinea there are more mountains crowded into less space than anywhere else in the world, and several of these mountains are more than fourteen thousand feet high.

This corrugated mass of rock more than a thousand miles long is fringed with some narrow strips of humid lowland and some sandy beaches; it is penetrated by a few rivers, many of whose headwaters lie within a few miles of each other. Politically, it is divided into three sections. The western half, where the island is broadest, is West Irian, covering about 150,000 square miles and with an estimated 775,000 aborigines (but this is the roughest of rough estimates, since there are hundreds of square miles that have not been visited). The southeastern section is called Papua and belongs to Australia; it contains about 88,000 square miles and half a million natives. The northeastern area belonged to Germany until 1920, when it was mandated to Australia under the League of Nations and later under the United Nations; its area is about 90,000 square miles and its population over a million. It is, therefore, the most densely populated part of the island.

Mountains are the greatest barriers to the penetration of any unknown country, and the island of New Guinea is one huge mass of rugged peaks and lofty ranges hiding a few lush and lovely valleys. On the other hand, rivers have always been the avenues of easy travel into new lands, and New Guinea has its share of rivers. They proved less helpful to exploration, however, than did the rivers of Africa or South America. Cutting through such mountainous country, many of them offered treacherous rapids and impassable waterfalls. And their banks are lined with hostile natives. It is easy to understand why for several decades white settlements were almost entirely confined to the narrow coastal regions. In some places, the coastal area is so narrow as to be little more than a thin line along the shore; the Rai Coast, for example, southeast of the town of Madang, rises so abruptly that a peak of thirteen thousand feet is reached only eighteen miles from the sea.

In spite of their dangers and difficulties, a few of the rivers of New Guinea have served as the entering wedges for explorers and prospectors and missionaries. On the Papuan side of the island, the chief of these is the Fly River. In the mandated territory of northeastern New Guinea, the Sepik has long been known as that area's Amazon or Congo. The land through which it flows and the natives who live along its banks are in sharp contrast to other terrains and peoples of the island.

I went to the Sepik in a small cruiser accompanied by cameraman Bede Whiteman and Curly Fraser, my assistant producer, both Australian. Running close to the shore, we saw row upon row of coconut trees on the plantations producing copra, New Guinea's chief export. We also saw the twisted and rusting wrecks of ships and landing craft from World War II, looking particularly out of place on this beautiful tropical shore.

When the boat slid from clear blue into yellow, muddy waters, we knew we were approaching the Sepik, which spews quantities of New Guinea earth into the sea in a widening arc extending fifteen miles from its mouth. With such obvious evidence of its existence, I wondered why the Sepik had not been discovered until 1885. Two years later, a German expedition traveled by launch three hundred eighty miles up the seven-hundred-mile river, but they did not learn much about the country. The natives were so hostile that the explorers had to stick to the middle of the stream during the entire journey, except for two quick and dangerous stops. A few subsequent trips told them that most of the natives were headhunters and cannibals; they were also tall and strong.

It was a long time before the villages along the Sepik came under the influence of white men, and then progress was slow. Traders were among the early civilizing pioneers, followed by labor-recruiters looking for workmen for the big copra plantations. Government posts and missions were established on the lower Sepik, but no determined effort was made to wipe out headhunting until the Australians took over from the Germans after World War I. And, after twenty years, the old practice of looking for heads revived in some areas during World War II. There had been a time when a man could not get married or wear a flying-fox apron until he had taken a head, and such customs die hard.

Soon after entering the mile-wide mouth of the mighty Sepik, we pulled up to a village, alongside a strange-looking craft on which we were to travel further up the river. It consisted of two long, narrow dugouts, each with a carved crocodile prow. They were joined by planking upon which sat a small, boxlike, screened room. At the stern, between the two dugouts, was an outboard motor. We boarded this craft along with a government medical assistant, Eric Roy, and a police boy named Kapok, plus a small crew. Then at a more leisurely pace we pushed upriver. One of the crew stationed himself as a lookout at the bow to watch for partially submerged logs that might damage the boat — huge hardwood logs that travel hundreds of miles from the forests of the Torricelli Range. They are treasured by the natives of the lower river, who depend upon the Sepik floods for the only sound hardwood they have, wood for dugouts and the piles on which their houses are built.

In a short time, we passed some of these villages, clusters of thatch-roofed huts built high above the flat banks of the river, and we caught our first glimpse of the tall, well-built natives. The most striking sight on the lower river, however, was the vegetation along the shore — a thick tangle of pit-pit grass, reeds, vines, nipa palms, pandanus, and sago palms. Thousands of birds flew in and above the tangle of green, but at that time we had not yet made the acquaintance of the chief flying population of the Sepik.

We saw an occasional crocodile slither into the water, an occasional native in his dugout hugging the shore where the current was not so strong, a white trader haggling in midstream with an old native whose dugout was full of crocodile skins. We came around a bend and saw a small village ahead. There was an immediate scurrying about of women in the village as they heard the *putt-putt* of our outboard motor.

"What's going on?" I asked Eric Roy.

"You'll see in a minute," he said with a grin. "I'm not stopping here on this trip, since I made my inspection just last week. I found the village pretty dirty and gave the women a lecture. I think you'll see the result now."

The riverboat slowed down and turned closer to shore. As we passed the village, we saw all the women busily sweeping the ground around and between their stilted huts. With proud smiles they looked at the boat as they swept, and Eric Roy smiled back and waved his approval of their display of cleanliness.

"Where are all the men?" I asked. All I could see were a few old fellows.

"Some of them may be fishing or hunting crocodiles," Roy said. "But most of them are off working on the copra plantations along the coast. They don't grow or catch anything around here — except a few crocodiles — that they can trade for goods they want. So they go away to work. Just wait till the next village — there'll be hardly a man in sight."

There was one man at the next village — the chief. It was beneath the dignity of a chief to go off working as a laborer on the plantations, for one thing. For another, male authority had to be upheld by someone; he did it, single-handed, in the midst of dozens of strong and spirited women, most of whom came in long dugouts to greet us as we approached.

They made an impressive sight — about twenty nearly naked and finely formed women standing upright in a dugout about forty feet long, each one wielding a twelve-foot paddle with a leaflike blade. Their vigorous strokes, in unison, shot the slim craft through the water much faster than our outboard could have moved it. And there was not just one of these female-laden dugouts but a fleet of them to escort us to the village.

This town had given up the fight against the torrential spring floods, and built its houses on stilts in the water. The result was a kind of primitive Venice, where all travel was by dugout, and the village square was a group of floating docks. Here Eric Roy set up shop. One by one the women and children came to be examined, willingly letting the medical man peer down their throats and into their ears and eyes — and not quite so willingly taking the medicines he gave to those who needed them. Even the chief came for his checkup, his face and torso painted blue and white, and his head and body adorned with shells, feathers, and bands of flying-fox fur. The visit of the *lik-lik* doctor was obviously an occasion of considerable importance to him, as to the others of his village. In their attitude toward Eric Roy, and their acceptance of his inspections and prescriptions, I could see why medical officers had proved such effective promoters of goodwill from the outside world. These people had seen medical officers cure their friends and relatives of once dread diseases such as yaws. Perhaps they thought the medical officer was no more than a particularly potent medicine man, but they respected him and listened to him; and because they trusted him they were inclined to trust other white men.

When the medical work was done, we set off upriver again in our double-crocodile of a boat. I sat on the platform in front of the screened box and relaxed, watching the luxuriant growth along the banks, wondering what might be around each new bend of the wide river. And the Sepik did nothing but bend and twist and turn upon itself. There were times that I thought we must have made a complete circle; when I spoke about this to Roy, he said we had almost done just that. The serpentine Sepik has so many loops that they almost form islands. I understood why, on its seven-hundred-mile course, the Sepik covers a plane's flight of only two hundred miles. Another unusual feature is that in those places where New Guinea is not rugged mountains, the terrain goes to the other extreme, giving the Sepik, in its lower reaches, a broad, flat swampland to flow through. In many places the land is only a few feet — or a few inches — above the level of the river, and almost as wet.

Then came the sunset, so gaudy it was not quite real. Far, far away to the south there was what looked like a purple-black cloud hovering over the earth, but it was really a series of towering mountain ranges, invisible during the day this far down the river, but becoming black as night before the night was there. There were blotches and streaks of deep purple and red, and above them huge white billowy clouds turning pink on their westward slopes. And all these colors were reflected in the broad river, where they were shattered into merging kaleidoscopes by the ripples and waves.

I heard a kind of singing whine and, as I wondered what the sound could be, slapped at my forearm, where I felt a bite. Then at the back of my hand, at my forehead, at the back of my neck. The whining sound increased in intensity, and I saw in the fading light shimmering dark clouds coming over the surface of the water from the thick reeds and grasses of the shore.

"Time to get inside!" Eric Roy called. "Here they come!"

We scurried inside that blessed little box of a room on the stern of the platform and hid behind the screens from the hordes of mosquitoes that awoke at dusk and went out searching for prey — like leopards. Within half an hour I knew that I would have preferred meeting the leopards of Africa or the jaguars of South America to those voracious hordes of stinging insects. Most wild beasts will avoid man if they can, but these mosquitoes sought him out. And for every ten you destroyed, thousands more attacked.

A few of them had managed to slip into the screened section with us, of course, so even behind our protective barrier we had to slap and wave and brush them away. But when I looked at the black patches on the screens, I knew that we had to endure only a slight annoyance in comparison with the torture that would greet us outside. The whining, singing sound had become a blatant siren reminiscent of the frightening wail of air-raid signals. I never heard of any creature's being killed by Sepik mosquitoes, as I knew of animals being killed and stripped of flesh by ants in Africa, but they could certainly drive a man crazy. I decided that some of the stories I had heard about Sepik mosquitoes were not such wild exaggerations as I had thought. Except, of course, for the one that every newcomer to the Sepik hears, about the two mosquitoes that swooped down on a native boy and picked him up. As they flew away with him, the first mosquito said, "Where shall we take him to eat him?" The second said, "How about going up to Angoram?" The first replied, "Oh, no! If we go there the big mosquitoes will take him away from us."

The natives along the Sepik make their own kind of netting to sleep in, each family having a big sausage-like bag of woven grass and reeds supported at intervals by arches of bamboo. One by one the members of the family crawl into the bag through the narrow opening. The last one fastens it tight and they all go to sleep. Some air can filter in and out of the close mesh, but no mosquitoes can get in. The quarters are cramped, the odors strong, the heat stifling, but anything is preferable to a Sepik mosquito.

I found myself looking for the really "big" mosquitoes at Angoram, but during the day they were sleeping in the marshes. There was plenty to do, however. We filmed some Sepik women making sac-sac, the starchy sago which is the basic diet in the river country, made from the pith of the big sago palm. The fundamentals of day-to-day living had changed little despite several decades of white man's influence. Food and its preparation represent, apparently, more deeply rooted traditions than even such semireligious customs as headhunting. Women put the sago pith into wooden troughs and pounded it rhythmically with heavy wooden beaters as water was periodically poured over it. The pounding separated the starch from the stringy fibers. Mixed with the water, the starch formed a pink, gelatinous mass which was nutritious but tasteless. The Sepik peoples lived principally on this sac-sac, although their diet was sometimes supplemented by yams, sugarcane, bananas, fish, pigs, and crocodiles. But pigs were rare, and crocodiles had to be caught. If possible, they had to be caught alive, for the meat of a dead animal goes bad quickly in this climate. In several villages I saw pens of live crocodiles being kept until the natives were ready to eat them, and I heard of some places in which as many as a hundred crocs might occupy a well-stocked pantry.

At Angoram I met Sepik Robbie — Eric D. Robinson — one of the legendary men who have frequented the region of the Sepik River. Robbie first came to New Guinea shortly after World War I. He worked there first as a medical assistant, then as a patrol officer, with time out as a coast watcher behind Japanese lines at Bougainville during World War II. During his first years as a patrol officer, headhunting was still a common practice along the Sepik. It was a most difficult custom to stamp out because it bore a considerable religious and social significance. Like many religious and social customs the world over, it had lost much of its true meaning but none of its force. Originally, I suppose, the Sepik natives looked upon headhunting in much the same way as the Jivaro Indians of South America. They felt a sacred duty to kill and behead any enemy who had killed any member of their family or clan. If they did not meet his obligation, the spirits of these relatives would be unhappy and would bother them. And in turn, after death, *their* spirits would find no peace. This concern for spirits and the hereafter was not so deep nowadays, but taking a head still brought prestige to a Sepik warrior, made him obviously brave and strong, a whole man.

Getting more than one head added to one's social status, of course — and there were emblems to make this plain. One head meant a flying-fox — or black *bockis* — apron. Two heads enabled a man to wear a possum-fur headband. Each additional head put a tassel on the stick he used when chewing betel nut. With both religion and status involved, it is small wonder that headhunting was such a hard practice to stamp out. But it had been done, with the exception of some tribes far up the river, or between patrol posts or back in the little-known areas away from the river.

I was dozing when I saw one of the huge floating islands of the Sepik gliding past us. It is a startling sight to see a few acres of ground, complete with reeds, grass, and even trees — with birds in them — moving serenely down the river. Along the Sepik, much of the land is so undermined by water that big chunks of it break away at times and move along with the strong current. They may be trapped at a sharp bend in the river and moor themselves for a long or short time. Or they may float clear out to sea, where they eventually break up. Sepik Robbie told me of one huge island that was captured by the men of a village downstream and secured to their own land. But the original owners came down and, after a brief battle, took it back. As I watched a big island go past, I could not understand how men in dugouts could possibly pull that unwieldy mass against the current, but they had done it.

I saw several clumps of land and pit-pit grass follow the first large one toward the ocean. Then came another, larger than the first — and we were heading right towards it. The wind had blown it across our channel, the route we were following to go up the river to the village of Kambaramba.

"I think we can get through it all right," Eric Roy said. "There's what appears to be a fairly wide barrat up there that should take us through."

Barrats are narrow channels cutting through the swampy land around the Sepik, like little tributaries of the mighty river. Sometimes they offer shortcuts across a big loop of the Sepik, and small craft can usually manage to get through them. But they shift and change, especially when they are on floating islands. Still, I could see that the barrat ahead was our best chance. The island was so large, and our boat so slow against the current, that we would have a hard time skirting around the edge of it.

So we putt-putted into the barrat which at the edge of the floating island was about twenty feet wide. For a few minutes we moved ahead easily, but the barrat gradually narrowed until it was no wider than our craft and finally not quite as wide. Still we made headway for a while; then the barrat made a turn and we faced a dead end. By this time it was impossible to turn around. There we were, trapped in the middle of a floating island which was taking us back to the sea at a considerable speed.

But were we in the middle? We could not see, surrounded by the tall grass as we were. Perhaps we were only a third across. Perhaps the other side was only a few hundred feet away. Meanwhile we were hot and getting hotter, for the air around us was moving with the island and we felt no breeze as we had in the boat. Mosquitoes, aware of something new in their midst, swarmed out from the tall grasses and attacked us.

The outboard motor had been stopped to avoid its being fouled by the reeds. There was only one thing to do — try to pole our way through to open water. Everyone turned to with a pole, pushing against the oozing bottom. Some of the crew jumped out and pushed. It was startling to think that a floating island had an earth bottom on which men could walk; actually, this sea-going piece of acreage may well have been twenty-five or thirty feet thick.

Luckily there was still a remnant of the barrat ahead of us, though it was narrow and choked with grass and reeds. With the most strenuous poling and pushing, we inched ahead and, after half an hour, caught a glimpse of open Sepik water ahead. In another ten minutes we had reached it, feeling as if we had escaped from the clutches of a huge octopus of vegetation. We started the motor and were on our way to Kambaramba.

Kambaramba has been called the Brothel of the Sepik. It is a well-known stopping-off place for traders and for natives going up or down river, for here the favors of any of the married women may be bought. Kambaramba women are known to be more attractive than many others along the great river, so the community is especially inviting. But why did prostitution ever become the chief business of this small community in the first place?

Ralph Ormsby, a former district officer on the Sepik and later a magistrate, explained it to me. The land around Kambaramba — if such a swamp can be called land — is poor for gardening. The village does own a patch of solid ground about five miles away, but it is small and not very productive, at least not productive enough to feed the village's five or six hundred people. They had few pigs, and the land was so inundated that even the animals had to live in houses on stilts.

The people of Kambaramba caught catfish in the river. They made sac-sac from the few palms they could find on their land. But still there was not enough to eat.

People from other villages on higher land, people with fine gardens, brought food to Kambaramba to sell it. But the villagers had nothing with which to pay for food. So they offered their wives. They obtained food.

When the government came into the region matters were actually made worse. Medicine and pacification were welcomed, but not the ten-shilling head tax. Small as this amount was, it was more than the natives of Kambaramba had. So, in order to pay taxes and buy food, the practice of prostitution was actually extended. Patrol Officer George Ellis tried to stop it some time before World War II, but he could make no progress. He had no answer for the Kambarambans, who argued, "The government makes us pay taxes, and now it wants us to stop the only thing we can do to get the money to pay the taxes."

In many ways, Ormsby told me, Kambaramba is a most moral town. The women must be chaste until they are married. After marriage, their husbands allow them to sleep with other men, as do Eskimos, but no woman dreams of doing this without the arrangement first having been made with her husband. She would never give away free the one source of wealth for her family.

"It's strange," Ormsby said. "Not fifty miles away from Kambaramba, on the Yuat River, there is another village where morals are quite different. A single girl may be as promiscuous as she pleases, but as soon as she is married she may never have anything to do with another man."

Did Kambaramba look different from any other village along the Sepik? Did its people seem different? Of course not. The houses were on stilts in the midst of marshy land. The men and women were tall and well-formed, proud and self-confident, as were most of the natives along the Sepik. Their wood carving on dugouts and stools was as good as that of villages on either side of them. And they seemed not the least bit worried about being called the Brothel of the Sepik.

Further up the Sepik was the village and patrol post of Ambunti, where Sepik Robbie was stationed for some time. He told me the story of the murder of another government man, Assistant District Officer

Edward Colin McDonald, at that post in 1935. The story seemed familiar to me, although I knew that I had never heard it before.

McDonald had a native policeman on his staff who became very attached to a dog that followed him everywhere he went. When the policeman had to go on a fairly long trip down the river, the dog was left behind and became attached to another policeman on the post at Ambunti. When the first policeman returned, the second would not give up the dog. The aggrieved dog-lover appealed to the *kiap*, headman McDonald, who sent each man to a different corner of the room, and had them both call to the dog. The dog ran to policemen number two, and McDonald declared that the dog was his.

The first policeman was outraged but said nothing. That night he took his rifle and shot McDonald as he slept beneath his mosquito netting. Then he did a death dance, climbed a tree, and tried to commit suicide by jumping from it. He succeeded only in breaking both ankles, was captured, tried, and hanged.

The village of Maprik is thirty miles from the Sepik River, but it is part of the Sepik culture. Its people are tall and well-built, obviously of the same general group as those along the river. But they do not build their houses on stilts, nor do they move about chiefly in dugouts; for they are in the uplands that rise toward the Torricelli Mountains west of the river.

There was a road leading from the river to Maprik — narrow, rough, and often a morass of mud. Since we had to do a lot of traveling over such roads in New Guinea, we welcomed the chance to reach Maprik by plane. The flight in the little single-engined plane was short, but as we climbed over ridge after ridge of higher land, I saw more different shades of green than I could have imagined. And flying low as we did, I saw clearly several man-made notches along the tops of ridges where natives had cut down trees to make traps for the huge fruit bats, or flying foxes, some of which have a wingspan of five feet. The meat of the black bockis, to give it its pidgin name, is considered a great delicacy.

In this part of New Guinea there were thousands of these bats, the largest of all flying mammals. After sleeping in the deep forests during the day, they took off as darkness suddenly descended at six o'clock — there is no long lingering dusk in that part of the world — and apparently followed regular flight patterns over the ridges. The natives learned just where a large group of bats regularly flew and at that spot along a ridgetop they cut down all trees for a space of twenty to thirty feet, as if to make an easy avenue for the bats. The bats would then take the path made for them until one evening the natives assembled with huge nets on poles, which they erected to fill the gap in the trees. The bats struck the nets and fell to the ground or became entangled in the vine netting. They were clubbed by the natives, who, according to Father Wiltgen, "bite their fingers for joy" when the catch is a good one.

Maprik was little more than a small cluster of houses near a tiny airstrip, but it was located in the middle of an area with many native villages. We were greeted at the airstrip by Assistant District Officer Bill Brown, who put us up at his house during our stay. The chief object of my visit to this area was to see and photograph a house-tamberan, the men's house and house of spirits. While all the villages along the Sepik once possessed fine examples of the house-tamberan and of the strikingly beautiful art without and within, most of them had been pretty well stripped of their painted and carved figures long ago, before the Australian authorities took steps to preserve native structures and art. At Maprik, however, there were several house-tamberans completely unspoiled. And those in this area had always been more beautiful than the ones along the Sepik.

Bill Brown took me and my crew to the native village of Bobemugen. We could see the towering peak of the house-tamberan long before we reached the village itself. Soaring high above the other houses and above the tallest palm trees, even this first glimpse made me hurry along faster. I found myself becoming somewhat impatient with the always necessary talk between the kiap and the *luluai* of the village. These district officers never ordered the headman to show us around and help with our filming. They politely and respectfully requested that we be allowed to shoot some film of what was to them a sacred place, the home of their tribal gods, the scene of all initiations, and the center of their religious life.

In a short time, arrangements were made, and the tall, dignified luluai, accompanied by his assistant, or *tultul*, and several other old dignitaries of the village, led us to the house-tamberan. It was set in the center of an open, grass-covered kind of park, at the edge of which we stopped to stare at the soaring, graceful lines of the most beautiful man-made structure I saw in all of New Guinea. Somehow these natives had managed to endow a building of logs, poles, bark, and grass with a spiritual feeling comparable to that of a tall church spire reaching for the heavens. The house-tamberan was one perfect symbol of such reaching, such upward striving. Shaped like a sharply angled inverted V, its walls climbed steeply to a ridge almost a hundred feet above the ground. The effect of soaring was heightened by the fact that the front edges of these walls, and the recessed front of the building itself, sloped outward in a graceful overhang. I felt as if the house-tamberan were almost animate, for this overhang gave me the feeling that the structure was on the verge of toppling forward. But then, as I became accustomed to this unusual feature, I saw that there was no imbalance, no insecurity in the outward thrust of the walls. The building grew firmly out of the ground, and all of its lines swept swiftly upward to converge at the peak.

It was an awesomely lovely sight from a distance, but when I came near the house-tamberan I was more interested in the details of its decoration. These were chiefly on the woven-rattan front wall, which was recessed eight or ten feet under the eaves of the steep roofs. There was a small door at the bottom, so small that anyone but a child would have to get on all fours to pass through it. At either side of the door, the woven wall was decorated in bright pigments that were little more than abstract designs, but at a height of about ten feet from the ground there was a row of weird faces painted in blacks and reds and yellows on large pieces of palm bark. The eyes were round targets, the noses were long and flaring, merging into a mouth within dark parentheses of facial lines.

I knew that inside the house there were works of art surpassing by far those decorations on the facade, but how could we film them? Bill Brown obtained permission of the luluai for me to enter, so I got on my hands and knees and crept through the little door into the sacred building. There I found a darkness that seemed even more dark in contrast to the thin shafts of light that filtered through small spaces where roofs met walls. In a few minutes, however, I could make out above me a complicated network of beams, poles, and fine fastenings.

When my eyes had become accustomed to the darkness, I could see dimly huge face-masks three or four feet high, and many carved and painted wooden figures, large and small. Even with so little light, I knew that I was looking at unusual primitive art.

Some flashlight pictures had been taken inside the house-tamberans, but I was most anxious to film many of these rare objects outside in the sunlight. I crawled out and had a little talk with Bill Brown, who was very skeptical about my chances. He spoke to the luluai, who looked around almost fearfully and shook his head. Bill respectfully asked again, and this time the tultul and all the elders joined the chief in saying no. To these men, I understood, these carvings and paintings were not just carvings and paintings. They were ancestors, the founders and heroes of the tribe, the spirits that brought good crops and health and even a good life after death. I was asking them to disturb and move their most sacred objects of reverence — and fear.

I decided to make a brief speech, which was translated into pidgin as I went along.

"I have traveled all over the world making pictures with this camera that makes things move as in life. I have taken pictures of many beautiful things, but never of a building as beautiful as your house-tamberan, never of artwork as beautiful as your cherished masks and figures inside the house-tamberan. But I cannot take pictures of those inside for I must have light, bright light. I want to film them not only to show the rest of the world how wonderfully you carve and paint, but to show them your revered spirits, your honored ancestors — the things that mean more to you than anything else."

At the end of this, there was no immediate headshaking, but a consultation. And finally they agreed to bring some of the carved masks and figures from the house-tamberan into the sunlight. But there had to be considerable preparation. Two of the natives went into the house and got some large, gourd-shaped whistles, the sacred flutes. And before anyone made a move to bring the precious figures from the house-tamberan, the two men started to play on the flutes. They continued their shrill, plaintive and (to me) tuneless playing all the time the figures and masks were outside the building. It was a warning to the women and uninitiated children to keep away from the house-tamberan. If their eyes had looked upon the sacred tamberans it would have meant their death.

Finally the tamberans were brought from the spirit house, along with some huge masks painted on sheets of bark similar to those decorating the facade of the building. And there were several *maselais*, small figures representing evil spirits — their purpose was to frighten away the real spirits they portrayed. The tamberans, however, were the most striking and unusual — full man-sized figures, most of them, carved from wood and painted in vivid red and yellow, with strong accents of black and white. They were the "gods" of the tribe, the protectors of its well-being, the insurers of big yams. They suggested human beings, but they were certainly oddly proportioned. On one the nose might extend down beyond the face, beyond the bulbous belly, to become the male organ. On another, there might be a second belly below the first, between the legs.

Most house-tamberans had to be completely rebuilt about every seven years because of the destruction to main beams brought on by high humidity and insects. Every time a new house-tamberan was built, the crossbeams had to be carved and painted, as well as many of the beams and supports inside. And after every initiation of boys — which took place every few years — a completely new set of tamberans had to be made. The old ones had no power or worth in the eyes of the natives once they had been used at an initiation. But still women could not look upon them. So they were wrapped in bark and taken into some deep spot in the jungle, where they soon rotted.

Bill Brown took us to several other villages around Maprik. In his Land Rover we crossed the Amugu River, fording it easily, and then not so easily climbing a narrow road of mud and rocks that had been cut into the side of a cliff. When we were on the other side of the river, Brown mentioned that sometimes after a rain the Amugu rose ten feet overnight. Sometimes he was stranded on the other side, away from Maprik. But there was no rain, and we returned safely, in time to see and film the dancing at a sing-sing in one of the villages.

The dance was slow and uncomplicated. The drums thumped out a steady rhythm, and the first dancers chanted to accentuate the beat. From somewhere out of sight I could hear the whistling of the sacred flutes. Since women and children could witness the dance, the flutes could not be brought into view, but they could be heard.

When I visited my first native village near the Maprik patrol post, I had heard the big *garamut*, or log-gong, announce the event to other villages about, and had heard their reply. I have heard similar drums among primitive people in other parts of the world, but rarely has the drum communication system been so efficient and well-organized as I found it around Maprik and the middle reaches of the Sepik. The relaying stations in various villages could pick up a message and send it along — north, east, south, and west — for scores of miles in only a few minutes.

The garamuts were made from big logs, the largest twelve to fourteen feet long and two to three feet in diameter. A long slit was cut down one side of the log, which was then hollowed out through the slit. When the big drum was hit with the butt end of a smaller log used as a massive drumstick, it emitted a deep resonant boom that suggested thunder. And like thunder, it rolled through the valleys and over the hills as far as five miles. Smaller garamuts had a shorter range, of course, and several big ones struck in unison could be heard more than five miles. But it was really not necessary to send messages farther, for there were usually several villages within that range, where the announcements or requests would be relayed if necessary.

Father Wiltgen, who spent some years in this region, told me later that each native had his own "percussion number" similar to a telephone number for us. The system worked somewhat like our direct distance dialing, for if a native had a message for a specific person in another village, he first beat out on the garamut the percussion number of the village in question whether or not the other village was within range, for he could depend upon a relay station to pick it up. Next he pounded the percussion number of the person in the village he wanted to communicate with, followed by the message itself. There were, of course, standard combinations of long and short beats representing all the fundamental items of native communication. Father Wiltgen was present when a father beat out on the garamut a message to his son to come home right away. The son had been visiting a friend in the next village.

My friend the late Thomas Gilliard of the American Museum of Natural History put the garamut telegraphic system to good use on one of his expeditions to New Guinea. He had come to study and photograph the rarer species of birds of paradise. On the evening of his arrival at a village not far from the Sepik River, he was with most of the male natives in the men's house and noticed that they were listening to the beating of drums to the north and south, and he was told that word of his arrival and his purposes had reached scores of miles.

Since he wanted to enlist the support of natives in finding the rare birds, he decided he could use the garamuts to spread the word quickly. He asked for and received permission to talk in pidgin to the assembled natives, so he explained exactly what he wanted and what prices he would pay for the different specimens he was seeking to study. And he made it plain that he wanted no specimens brought to him but that he must be taken to the spot, so that he could photograph them in their natural habitats. It was a long talk, filled with the necessary amount of polite speech and appreciation for help received and about to be received. But the results were gratifying, for, as he told me, "before long the jungle's Associated Press was knocking off bulletins, followed by price quotations, to all subscribers."

2

The Central Highlands

FROM THE Sepik, one of the first areas of New Guinea to feel the impact of civilization, I went to the barren mountains of the Kukukuku country, on the edge of the central highlands, one of the most recent to see the white man. There I saw no great art, no art at all, but a group of truculent warriors — and some weird sights that I will never forget.

It was at a Kukukuku village that I saw a bent woman carry a burden from her thatched hut and place it carefully on the ground where it could lean against one wall. I looked down at the gruesome caricature of a human body, the smoked remains of the warrior who had been this woman's husband. It looked rather like a human skeleton that had been untidily wrapped in a bluish-gray parchment, and it sat there in a natural, relaxed position, its back against the thatched wall, its knees bent, its arms lying in its lap. Its head was bent forward slightly, as if the warrior were staring contemplatively at the ground.

The woman brushed a fly from the "mummy's" forehead and adjusted a woven cane mat behind its back as if she thought the rough wall might be uncomfortable. But these were tiny expressions of solicitude compared to her actions every day during the preceding month. This woman, of a tribe almost as primitive as any I have ever encountered, had gone through a great deal to show her love and respect. I had heard of the process of smoking humans, had had it described to me vividly, but the sight of this body made me realize what tender, loving care had gone into the task.

A second, younger wife of the dead man came from the hut with a small boy and girl. The second wife stood beside the first, while the boy and girl sat down on either side of the thing that had been their father. The boy patted one bony knee affectionately and smiled up at the women. In a short time the dead Kukukuku warrior would take his last journey, to a rocky ledge in the mountains where he could sit and gaze down on the small part of primitive New Guinea in which he had lived and fought and loved and died.

A month before, he had been killed by a blow from a stone club that crushed his skull, during a dawn attack on his ridgetop village. I learned that the raiding party came from a neighboring Kukukuku group that had been his tribe's enemies since his great-grandfather's time — perhaps longer, but the verbal tradition carried him back only that far. When the warrior's body was brought to his hut, there was loud wailing, a chant of mourning carried on by the dead man's wives and children, his relatives and close friends, some of whom came from distant villages to pay their last loud and mournful respects. Those closest to the departed worked themselves into paroxysms of grief, groveling on the ground, pulling out their hair, and even beating their foreheads with clubs to draw blood. Such extreme demonstrations of sorrow seem strange in a people to whom violent death is a commonplace, even casual, event, a people brought up to kill and expecting to be killed. I suspect that these visible evidences of sorrow are engaged in for their effect on the spirit of the departed. Since such spirits can, according to most primitive societies, help or hurt the living, it is a good idea to prove how highly they were regarded and how much they are missed.

After four days of mourning, the body of our warrior had been placed upon a specially built platform above the hearth inside the hut. Here he was fixed in a sitting position, and the smoking fire was started beneath him. The first wife — sometimes aided by the second — tended the fire constantly so that a steady cloud of warm smoke rose up to envelope the body before filtering out through the thatched roof. The heat soon raised blisters on the man's skin; these were carefully wiped off by the wife until the entire skin had disappeared. A length of hollow bamboo drained the body liquids from the abdomen, but the process of dehydration was very slow. After a month of such care — and inconceivable stench — the body was completely dehydrated and weighed only about thirty pounds. This was the "mummy" we filmed, ready for his last journey to the mountains.

Sometimes the dehydrated bodies are kept near at hand for some time before their final trip. Since the spirit of the dead person stays near the body after death, it can be helpful to the living members of the family if so inclined. The tender care of the body during the smoking process is thought to influence the spirit to be kind, to make the sweet potato crops plentiful, and to ward off enemy attacks.

One man was killed from ambush while preparing his garden for planting. After his body was smoked, it was taken to the garden by his family, placed on the ground, and told, in effect, "Look — now we are planting your garden. Please see that it grows well." At another time, during a long dry spell, a smoked body was brought from the house and placed in the open. Precious water was brought in a bamboo (the only method of carrying it known to these people), and sprinkled on the corpse and all those standing about, with a request to the spirit to bring rain.

The dead warrior being given even longer life on the film of my cameras was fortunate to have had two devoted wives to preserve his body. And he had many friends who came to say a last farewell before the wives carried him up to the mountain ledge, where his body might resist disintegration as long as a tough piece of leather. I looked at the assembled men and women, and tried to realize that this shriveled and shrunken corpse had once worn the fierce and challenging look of some of the warriors near me.

Even on this occasion the men looked angry, truculent, belligerent. I soon learned that this was the normal, natural expression of the male Kukukuku, although on rare occasions one may smile broadly and warmly. They look angry in the way they stand, the way they hold their clubs, the way they shoot arrows from their short but strong bows. The nosepieces that many of them wear through their septums, at least on important occasions, enhance the defiant expression, for they are short, thick pieces of bone from the cassowary or the tusks of a pig.

I looked above and beyond the group of men and women toward the gray, corrugated mountains. They made the same impression as the Kukukuku men, angry and forbidding, inhospitable and cold. Their upper reaches are, in fact, too cold to live in and cannot be cultivated. Even in the village where I stood, at about five thousand feet above sea level, the nights were sometimes bitterly cold. There were no lush valleys in the Kukukuku country, as there are in many other parts of New Guinea. Indeed there was almost no land flat enough to make an easily tended garden. Even if there were, the Kukukuku would not plant there, for a flat area surrounded by hills would be too vulnerable in case of attack.

It took a good deal of aerial surveying to find the sizable flat area where the Menyama patrol post, mission, and airstrip were established, and there was not a single Kukukuku living on it. They lived on the tops of ridges, usually in little clusters of eight or ten huts to a village. They made their sweet potato gardens on steep slopes, breaking up the soil with long pointed sticks. When the rains washed the good soil away, they moved to another steep slope and planted another garden. If they lived on a wooded mountain slope, they cleared a patch by burning the undergrowth, which killed the trees; they did not bother to remove the trees or stumps that were left standing. This was too long and arduous a task for their stone adzes.

It was not easy for the Kukukuku to get enough food out of this hard land. Sweet potatoes and more sweet potatoes made up most of their meals day after day, with some sugarcane and bananas for a little variety. There were few animals to hunt in this forbidding land. There were some wild pigs, and small birds, and fish in the streams. The big cassowary could supply meat for a week, but these birds were rare and so fast that they could kick a hunter's brains out with one blow if he got too close.

Why do the Kukukuku live in such a harsh country? It is believed that long ago they were driven from the more fertile areas by larger and stronger tribes in a series of wars. They fought all the way up into the mountains, they had to fight to get enough food, they fought each other for the highest and safest ridges. Fighting — killing — became a way of life, the basis of life, almost the reason for life. And when the white men came, the Kukukuku fought them as if these rugged, windswept mountains were the last place on earth — there was no other place to go. They killed the white men who came to tell them that they must stop killing each other. Ever since civilization first came in contact with them, the Kukukuku have had the reputation — and earned it — of being the fiercest of all the primitive tribes of New Guinea.

Gold prospectors, always ready to penetrate new territory despite all dangers, eventually met the Kukukuku, with sometimes fatal results. Government patrols into the interior ran into showers of arrows or came upon villages deserted only a few minutes before. Practices that had worked well in so many contacts with primitive tribes — friendliness, gifts, trade goods — failed more often than not because it was so difficult to make any kind of contact with the Kukukuku, who either fought fiercely or just disappeared.

In 1909, two Germans made their way up the Markham River and a tributary, where they found rich deposits of gold. They were not even in Kukukuku territory, but in the valleys below the homes of the mountain men. Still, the Kukukukus hated the idea of anyone coming within reaching distance of their country. They swept down from the mountains into the valleys. They sent ten arrows into the body of one German prospector, seven into the other. The latter managed to get away. He kept talking about going back, so he refused to tell anyone the location of his strike. But he never went back.

The next year, 1910, an Australian prospector followed the same route, reached the Bulolo River, and found gold. Again the Kukukukus, watching from their mountains, attacked, killing many carriers and sending five arrows into the prospector.

The 1926 discovery of rich gold deposits on Edie Creek, a tributary of the Bulolo, brought another swarm of prospectors, among them Michael J. (Mick) Leahy. Mick, with his three brothers, was later to play a most prominent role in the discovery and development of the New Guinea highlands, but on his first trip he arrived too late to stake out a very rewarding claim. He figured, however, that the gold deposits in Edie Creek must have come from some source further inland. He started searching for it in 1930 with a partner Mick Dwyer.

The two men headed west. They climbed mountains and searched out small valleys. They were looking for the headwaters of the Ramu River which eventually found its way to the sea on the north side of the island. They found a stream that seemed to be headed in that direction, so they followed it. Even when it turned south they continued to follow it, panning at every likely place in their search for gold.

The encountered natives who had never seen white men before, belligerent natives who did not like trespassers. But Mick Leahy found out that they were, above all, curious. Their interest in clothes, utensils, weapons, overcame their animosity. So they accepted the newcomers, for a few hours at least, and passed them along to the next tribe if it was friendly. If not, they left the explorers at the edge of a no-man's-land, on the other side of which waited hostile natives armed with clubs and bows and arrows, but filled with curiosity.

The natives that the two Micks met were not all Kukukukus, for this trip skirted the edge of the mountain men's territory. But the men they met were certainly not friendly. There was a time when a belligerent crowd surrounded them, and Mick Leahy took off his hat, an old weather-beaten fedora. The natives moaned and ran away. They thought the hat was part of Mick's head.

Later they were confronted by a particularly pugnacious group that responded to none of the usual overtures. As they wondered what to do, Mick Dwyer, who had been chewing on some sugarcane and got a fiber caught in his teeth, removed his upper plate to get rid of it. The warlike natives scattered!

The time came when the two Micks knew that they were irrevocably headed south. They could not turn back, because they had no more gifts to win the temporary friendship of the native tribes whose territory they had passed through. They clambered through gorges in the Owen Stanley Range of mountains, which had been considered the continental divide of the island. They came upon a river from the west that brought down the dead bodies of warriors. Mick Leahy was puzzled, because the river came from a territory that all maps marked mountainous and uninhabited. He stored this bit of information in the back of his mind for future exploration.

Eventually the two Micks came to the sea on the southern coast of the island, hundreds of miles from their goal. They had cut a path through a big blank space on the map.

Within a year, Leahy headed back again, this time with his brother Pat and with fourteen native carriers. They decided to head straight for the Kukukuku country, because so few white men had been there to look for gold. Even though the Leahy brothers had heard hair-raising tales about the ferocity of the Kukukukus, Mick felt sure that he could handle them as he had handled scores of unfriendly natives on his long trek.

After two weeks of fruitless but relatively safe travel, the Leahy group camped, late one afternoon, near a stream. They had seen smoke from a Kukukuku village atop a nearby ridge, but they thought it was too late in the day to try to establish contact. They would wait until morning. They expected, however, that the villagers would come to the edge of the ridge to look them over, as was their usual practice; but not a native was to be seen until about dusk.

Just before dawn the Kukukukus attacked. Mick heard the warning cries of his carriers, grabbed his revolver, and darted out the back of the tent. There he saw another figure and asked, "Where are they?" At that moment he made out one of the attacking Kukukukus crossing the stream, his bark-cloth cape streaming out behind him. The man saw Leahy at the same time and raised his bow and arrow to shoot. Then several things happened at the same instant. Leahy fired his revolver at the Kukukuku, felt the attacker's arrow slice his cheek, and was knocked down by a crushing blow from a stone club in the hands of the man he had mistaken for one of his own group, behind the tent.

Mick dragged himself inside his tent as one of his carriers shot an arrow into the club-wielding Kukukuku. Mick heard a bedlam of scream, war cries, and shooting outside, and collapsed across his cot. Even then he realized that his brother Pat would be needing more ammunition. He reached under the cot and dragged out the pack contining cartridges. As he opened it, Pat rushed into the tent pulling an arrow from his arm and calling for ammunition. He snatched the cartridges that Mick held out to him, took one horrified look at his brother's battered skull and blood-covered face, cried, "My God, they've brained you!" and dashed out to carry on the fight.

Mick pushed himself erect, found his rifle, and went outside, stumbling over the body of a Kukukuku at the entrance to his tent. In the faint light of the rising sun, he saw two Kukukukus chasing one of his carriers up a hill. He tried to shoot, but his eyes could not focus. So he handed his rifle to one of his boys who had reached his side, and the boy dropped one pursuing Kukukuku with his first shot. The other ran away, and the carrier came back into camp, which was suddenly quiet.

Five dead Kukukukus lay about the camp, but not one member of the Leahy party had been killed. There were casualties, however. Pat Leahy had received, in addition to the arrow in his arm, another arrow deep into his shoulder, which Mick thought might have cut into his lung. One boy had an arrow so deep in one knee that Mick needed pliers to pull it out.

Mick Leahy knew that the Kukukukus would attack again, so he dressed all wounds as well as he could with a raging pain in his head, eyes that went out of focus regularly, and the sound of a roaring waterfall in his ears. Pat was obviously in bad shape, and needed medical attention as soon as possible. But first they had to climb high mountains, avoid all Kukukuku villages that might have heard of the fight, and yet find food on the march.

They made it, after five agonizing days of marching and several more floating down rivers on rafts. All wounds were healed, although Mick Leahy still has three permanent dents in his skull and a left ear that can hear nothing but the perpetual roar of a waterfall. And he still is convinced that the Kukukukus are the most determined killers to be found anywhere, with the least respect for human life and the greatest resistance to civilizing influences.

The Kukukukus were inexplicable. They traded with the German Helmuth Baum for years and then bashed his head in just before he was going home. In the establishment of a government airstrip, they were sometimes helpful, sometimes deadly. And then there was Miss Blackwood.

How can one account for the experiences of Miss Beatrice Blackwood, ethnologist with the Pitt Rivers Museum, Oxford University? For nine months, in 1936 and 1937, she lived, unarmed and unharmed, with the Kukukukus. I visited her at Oxford on my way back from New Guinea.

The village in which Miss Blackwood lived was only about six hours' walk from the Otibanda patrol post and had been under government "influence" for some time, but the officer in charge called the village only "temporarily safe." He knew the Kukukukus were still too unpredictable for him to think of safety in other than temporary terms. At any rate, this particular group had not attacked any white men for some time, and their intertribal warfare had either stopped or been well hidden. And there had been no evidence of cannibalism.

So much for that village, but Miss Blackwood did not stay there. She went wandering, in the company of some of her Kukukuku friends, to other villages which the patrol officer considered not even temporarily safe. Yet she was never attacked, never threatened, never caught in the middle of an intertribal war.

Was she safe because she felt and showed no fear? This cannot be the explanation, for Mick Leahy and many others had shown no fear before they were attacked. Was she safe because she was a woman? While the Kukukukus would fight courageously against great odds for their own women, and were certainly not afraid of other women, they would wipe out women and children in a raid against an enemy village. They would bash in the head of a woman they happened to meet along the trail, if they felt like it and the woman was of another tribe. They would kill their own wives for just nagging too much. No, the Kukukukus had no special respect for womanhood when it came to killing.

From Miss Blackwood I got one clue that might explain, at least in part, her safe sojourn among the Kukukukus. That one clue was her kitten, which accompanied her into the dangerous land. The Kukuku-kus had never seen a kitten, or anything like it, and they loved it. Some of the usually belligerent men would spend hours pulling a string for the kitten to chase and pounce upon. They smiled broadly and their eyes filled with warmth and happiness when the kitten climbed upon their shoulders or purred affectionately.

But most of the time they were taciturn, uncommunicative, and distant. I know from my own experiences with primitive peoples that this is unusual. If a friendly person stays with a primitive group long enough to overcome the initial suspicion and fear, its members are likely to be most outgoing. They may hide some of their most secret rituals; they may be reluctant to talk about religion or evil spirits; but they will happily and volubly demonstrate and talk about their activi-ties and their feelings. The Pygmies of Africa's Ituri Forest had, with effervescent enthusiasm, reenacted the dance of the elephant hunt for me. The Bororos of the Mato Grosso had done the funeral dance, with-out a corpse. The Jivaro headhunters had performed the tsantsa dance. And I had almost been killed by some Masai warriors in Africa trying to show me how they had attacked the enemy in the old days. Every-where I had found that most primitive people were great hams who would act out their glorious deeds at the drop of a hat. They would talk about their hunting and their wars endlessly.

But the Kukukukus were different. In my short time with them, I could understand why Miss Blackwood ran into stone walls trying to probe their innermost thoughts and feelings. They were cooperative in demonstrating to her how they made their adzes, stone clubs, bows and arrows, bark cloth, and string bags. She learned something of their legends, got a glimpse of their religion, but the heart and soul of the Kukukuku were kept secret. And she could never understand the greatest mystery of all — her complete safety during her stay with the unpredictable killers, who kill "just for the hell of it."

Sixteen years after Miss Blackwood's entry into Kukukuku country, the University of Pennsylvania Museum considered sending an expedition there for study, but concluded that the area was unsafe for any but a strongly armed party.

It is frightening to think of what might have happened if gold *had* been discovered in Kukukuku country. The pressure on the Australian authorities to open it up and make it safe would have been almost overwhelming. This problem has caused trouble enough among peoples far less belligerent than the Kukukukus. With their resistance, much blood would have been spilled.

You can condemn the gold prospectors, if you will, but such greed seems to be almost universal; it is found even among the Kukukukus, who direct their acquisitiveness toward knives and shells and beads only because they do not know the value of gold. And the gold prospectors have, in the main, shown not only great courage, but also great curiosity about the lands and the peoples they have found. Many of them, like Mick Leahy, realized that they were "invaders," and tried to deal with the native peoples with honesty and patience and justice. There have been bad ones, of course, but the fact remains that gold prospectors have often been the first to push into new and unknown territories.

And what about governments? Sometimes they have gone into newly discovered lands to protect and help the prospectors who got there first; in New Guinea, at any rate, they have restrained and restricted those prospectors in the interests of the natives. Sometimes they penetrate the unknown merely because it is there, like a vacuum that must be filled.

The world found out the truth about the New Guinea interior only a few minutes ago, in the terms of history's clock. The man chiefly responsible for revealing the truth was Mick Leahy, who was nearly brained by the Kukukukus. He was not looking for a lost world, but he found it. He *was* looking for gold. He did not find much of it. But then, many explorers have found things better than what they were looking for. Columbus searched for a short route to the Orient, which would have meant gold to him and his backers; he found half a world. And much of the northern hemisphere was revealed in countless probings for a northwest passage. If you think it is farfetched to compare the discovery of the highlands of New Guinea with the American discoveries, remember this — in the early 1930's Michael J. Leahy found a land with a hitherto unsuspected population about as large as the Indian populations of the United States at the time Columbus first touched America's shores.

Nor was this just an ordinary world, with run-of-the-mill people. It was, and is, one of the most beautiful and salubrious valleys on earth, occupied by a strikingly colorful people. It still startles me to realize that this discovery was made only a few years before I made my first expedition to Africa, that I have had long talks with the discoverer and his colleagues. It's as if I had been able to talk to Livingston and Stanley on my trip to Tanganyika and the Congo, or to Orellana when I travelled down the Amazon.

Mick Leahy and his three brothers were chiefly interested in finding gold in New Guinea, but they handled all kinds of jobs to bring in money for their prospecting. On one trip Mick reached the Bena-Bena River, where there were fair but not too promising traces of gold. He returned the following year with his youngest brother, Danny, and pushed further into the interior, meeting thousands of natives who had never seen white men before.

Mick and Danny got some natives to help them clear a little airstrip near Bena-Bena so small planes could bring in supplies. One boy, who had attached himself to Mick, rode back to the coast in the plane. The boy returned with some hairs from a horse's tail to prove to his friends that there was an animal bigger than a pig. He had a bottle of salt water from the sea, for he knew that none of his relatives would believe his story of such a vast expanse of water, all of it tasting of precious salt. He could bring back no evidence of the electric light he had turned on and off a hundred times, or of the ice that turned into water. He was least impressed by the plane that carried him to the coast and back, for he had already accepted the idea that it was just a big bird that carried men and boxes. In Salamaua he was disappointed in automobiles because they could not fly. The most fantastic tale he told when he came home was his description of a dump heap containing uncountable bottles and tin cans.

One day Mick Leahy climbed a hill west of Bena-Bena and studied the clouds to the southwest. "People said only mountains were out there," Mick told me, "but these were not the kind of clouds you see over mountains. They were the hazy clouds you see over grassy plains. As I looked at them, I remembered the bodies floating down that unknown river from an unknown region in the mountains. They must have come from the same area that made those grassland clouds. Since I had already found many people and villages where no one thought they would be, it was easy for me to think that there might be more people out there under those clouds, enough people to have wars which would send dead bodies floating down a long river. So I told myself I'd have to go in and have a look."

In February, 1933, Mick and Danny Leahy, with a mining company surveyor, climbed up the mountains they had seen only from a distance. On the second day they encountered natives quite different from those they knew in the Bena-Bena region. They were taller, more proud and erect; their faces were tattooed, and they wore more decorations — shells and gaudy feathers, wings and beaks of birds. They were friendly and traded food for shells, and they were insatiably curious. The rope cordon around Mick's camp was bordered by natives several layers deep. They wanted to touch every strange thing they saw. They wanted clippings of hair from Mick's dog Snowy. (They had never seen a dog before.) And when Danny went into the bush to relieve himself, some natives quickly snatched up his excrement.

Many natives accompanied the explorers the next day as they marched on — or rather up, always up. At one point they were stopped by a new group shouting menacingly, waving their bows and arrows and wooden shields. But Mick's companions, who were friendly with the new tribe, assured the belligerent ones that the strangers were peaceful, so the party was allowed to proceed.

They came to the top of a ridge, expecting, as usual, to see another and higher wall of mountains beyond. But this time it was different. Through a corridor in the forest they saw a long, narrow valley stretching out below them, bright in the sunshine, lushly green, with neat squares of garden marked off by drainage ditches. A quarter of a century later, Mick Leahy telling me about this first sight of the Wahgi Valley could not keep from his voice a tone of awe and wonder. How many men have enjoyed an experience comparable with finding a beautiful lost world — and the Wahgi is one of the most beautiful valleys on the face of the earth — with half a million people in it?

After a long look, Mick and his companions turned back to Bena-Bena to plan and organize their exploration of the valley. He ran into a good friend, James L. Taylor, who was an assistant district officer and the sole, though occasional, government official in the eastern part of the New Guinea highlands. Taylor had just come to the conclusion that there must be people where the maps showed only mountains, but for reasons different from Mick's. He had served on the Sepik, near the western end of Australian New Guinea; in Salamaua at the eastern end; and at Bena-Bena in between, but near the east. He knew that some goldlip pearl shell had been traded from tribe to tribe clear across the island. There had to be people in the interior to complete this trading chain.

Now Mick Leahy had found a 60-mile-long link in the chain. He and Jim Taylor planned to explore it together. They got support and supplies from both the government and a mining company. They would survey from the air, then go in on foot, build an airstrip, and get needed supplies by plane.

On the first flight they flew the length of the valley and back, noted the oblong, rather than round, houses, the carefully cultivated gardens, the mighty Wahgi River, the towering limestone cliff that served as the northern wall of the valley. And they saw not a single native.

"They were probably terrified by the appearance of the plane," Mick explained.

After a second aerial look, the party moved in on foot — Mick and Dan Leahy, Jim Taylor, a surveyor, a small detachment of armed native police from the coast, plus a horde of carriers. They passed through the mountain corridor and walked down into the valley. They encountered natives — awed, curious, and frightened at the same time — different from those Mick and Danny had met on their first trip to the rim of the valley. They were even taller, almost the height of the explorers themselves, and their height was accentuated by long, waving plumes on their headdresses, red, blue, black, and gold. Women as well as men decorated themselves beautifully and, as Mick said, "the marys were good-looking wenches."

Jim Taylor noted that there were many woven articles, uncommon in New Guinea, and even a clay whistle, surprising among a people that had no other pottery. They met one obviously important man with a new kind of decoration through the septum of his nose — a long, gracefully looped, thin feather of blue from one of the rarest of all birds of paradise, the "King of Saxony."

They ran into no hostility. They found it easy to trade shells for sweet potatoes, pigs, and sugarcane. Mick Leahy began to think that perhaps they had come to a peaceful valley, a peaceful new world. This incredible idea was fortified when through sign language the explorers learned that the natives of the Wahgi were as horrified at the thought of eating human flesh as the white men themselves.

But Mick's hope that he had found a peaceful valley was short-lived. Even before his party ran into any difficulty, he learned that the tribes of the Wahgi Valley followed the pattern of many other primitive peoples all over the world, with ancient feuds and wars that were the chief activity and glory of life for the men. In one small area, there were tribes called the Womkama, the Golgome, the Minga, the Barengigl, the Inau, the Denglagu, and many others. Some were allied, some bitter enemies. And they were lumped together as the Chimbu, the name given them by white men, taken from a call with which the natives greeted them. Later they learned that *"Chimbu! Chimbu!"* meant something like "Hurrah!" But Chimbu became the name of the tribes living in that region, of the river that flowed through it, and of its gorge-like valley.

When the Leahy party first went in, there were no real villages. Houses were not clustered together, with garden areas farther away. Each family had a kind of homestead, with an oblong house — perhaps more than one house if the man was important and had several wives — and its own garden, usually fenced in. A homesteading plan is not often used in densely populated areas, where people usually crowd into villages and towns. But white men found the Chimbu to represent the most heavily concentrated population of the highlands, perhaps of all New Guinea. The estimate, a few years after its discovery, was 160,000 people in the small mountainous region at the eastern end of the Wahgi Valley. With such crowding, the borderline between one tribe and the next was not a vague no-man's-land a mile or so wide. There was not enough land to waste such space. Each square foot of earth, no matter how steeply angled, was treasured and fought for.

The Leahy party moved farther down the valley, crossed rivers on frail, swaying vine bridges, and in the main fared well with the natives they met. The people in the valley had seen the plane, and hidden from it, during its two reconnaissance flights, so the entire party was considered supernatural, creatures who had come back to earth from the hereafter. Some women snatched at a few of the native carriers and wept, insisting that they were the spirits of long-dead fathers or brothers or sons.

When the first supply plane came in, locating the rough airstrip through smoke signals Mick and his group had made, the natives groveled on the ground. The motor was cut off, and the Stone Age men and women raised their heads. At that moment, Ian Grabowski, the pilot, climbed from the cockpit. He was a tall man, dressed in white flying suit, white helmet, and green goggles. The hundreds of natives witnessing this miracle groaned and moaned, and threw themselves on the ground once more.

In time, of course, they became used to planes, but for a while all aircraft were awe-inspiring, along with the men connected with them. The Leahys and Jim Taylor knew how quickly New Guinea natives could get over that feeling of awe and curiosity. So they were on their guard at all times as they walked to the end of the valley, near Mt. Hagen, lead out another airstrip, prospected here and there, met natives of different types and of even more impressive character, and who spoke about 150 different languages or dialects. They occasionally ran into suspicion, fear, and some belligerence, but they were able to convince the natives of their peaceful intentions and to carry on some trade and communication with them.

But there was always danger in too much familiarity. Mick Leahy told me, "On your first trip into a new country, the natives will probably be too much in awe of you and too curious to be hostile. On your second trip they begin to size you up more closely, to lose their fear since you have not harmed them, and to covet the steel axes and shells in your packs. On your third trip — watch out!"

In the Wahgi Valley this process took place quickly. Jim Taylor, with the surveyor and some carriers, walked back through the valley to Bena-Bena. All the way they encountered truculence, threats, ambush, and attack. Taylor finally had to shoot the leader of an attacking band, an act he resorted to only in the most extreme emergency. He went right back in again, of course. The Leahys went in and out many times, airstrips were built, missionary posts established. But it took a long time for the natives to learn about the strange and sometimes wonderful ways of the white man.

3

The Wahgi Valley

TWENTY-FIVE years after Mick Leahy discovered the Wahgi Valley, I flew into the area on the first of two expeditions to make the full-length color film *Primitive Paradise*. As we ducked down a narrow pass, flew straight toward an overwhelming range covered with clouds, then turned at a sharp angle to follow another valley, I could see why for so long everyone had thought interior New Guinea consisted of nothing but mountains. But we landed at a fine airstrip near the town of Goroka, a town that did not exist when Mick Leahy first went there. It was a small town, but there was a pleasant hotel, a bank, a nine-hole golf course, a sawmill, and even a jail. And there was a road stretching out east and west.

The town was so neat and orderly, such a perfect picture of a brand-new village, that I wondered if I could find any genuine primitive people in the neighborhood. My doubts were ended when I saw a dignified warrior with bow and arrows in hand walking down the street. He was dressed in his best finery for what was obviously, to him, an important occasion — plumed headdress, white tusk through the septum of his nose, a large goldlip shell on his chest, with many smaller cowrie shells on headband and armband. His hair, done in greasy ringlets, fell to his shoulders. He went into the bank to deposit some money. He did not even glance up when a DC-3 swooped down for a landing.

The incident was a revealing introduction to the New Guinea highlands, a glimpse of the primitive and civilized side by side and an indication of those features of civilization most readily accepted by the natives of this area. The *balus* (pidgin for *bird*, and meaning airplane) was a common sight, bringing in goods and men, taking highlands products to the outside world. A motor car, on the other hand, attracted more attention. There were few of them in the highlands, since they and the gasoline to run them had to be flown in. The gaudily dressed native I saw may have ridden in a plane, but had doubtless never been in an automobile.

The natives around Goroka had obviously accepted money and banks as a good feature of civilization. Before these came to the highlands, the native's wealth had been in the form of shells (with pigs in a secondary role), and his bank had been his body, on which he wore his fortune. Shells were, of course, personal decoration as well, and since he was proud of them, he would not give them up entirely. Still, he quickly took to the idea of getting money for work on the road or for surplus *kau-kau* grown by his wives. With that money he could buy steel axes or shovels or cloth or other miracle goods from outside. And meanwhile his money would be far safer in the bank than it had ever been on his body.

There was another innovation of the white man that made selling and banking and buying possible — the road, the road that could lead him to Goroka easily and along which he could walk without fear of attack. That law had been among the first and most rigidly enforced of all the white man's regulations — no fighting on the roads or airstrips. The road was thus the greatest single pacifying and civilizing influence in the highlands. Later I was to talk to the two Australians chiefly responsible for building the first roads — without machinery, without dynamite for blasting, with only the simplest hand tools when there were tools at all. Meanwhile I traveled over some of these roads by Land Rover to reach areas around Goroka in which I could film Stone Age man.

They were scarcely roads in the sense that a traveler in America uses the word, and there were places where they ended and we had to continue on foot. And it was striking to note that when one went beyond the end of the road, he usually found himself in an area marked "under partial control" rather than "controlled." And if one went a bit further — with a special permit and accompanied by a government patrol — he was in "uncontrolled" territory, an area that was shrinking rapidly on the maps of New Guinea.

In the "uncontrolled" areas there was still intertribal war, and there were still feuds and murders within tribes; a man rarely dared go more than a few miles from his own village, except to a village allied with his own. In "partially controlled" regions, intertribal wars, called *rova*, had been reduced to occasional flare-ups, but feuds and killings within tribes, called *hina*, continued, and were more difficult to stop. But where the roads had penetrated, and for a short distance around other posts, there was control, which meant that patrol officers could go on their rounds with only moderate precautions against attack; intertribal wars were ended because tribes took their major differences before the patrol officer, or *kiap*, for settlement. But a man might kill his wife if she annoyed him or was unfaithful; a woman accused of sorcery might be put to death. But the natives knew that the *gom-man*, or government, would come and punish those who killed.

Somewhat reluctantly, then, the various tribes around Goroka had accepted one more idea of civilization — that warfare and murder are not a way of life. The weaker tribes and clans welcomed this strange regulation, and the weaker men within all tribes did, too. People in general were happy to be able to walk along a road in safety, without fear gnawing at their innards every moment. Everyone was glad to know that a former enemy was probably not going to kill him; the difficult time came when a man was angry and wanted to kill. Then the law of the white man seemed unreasonable and contrary to every natural instinct.

Cannibalism apparently never flourished in the main Wahgi Valley, but in the eastern highlands between Goroka and Bena-Bena and as far east as Kainantu, it was a not uncommon practice. In 1933 some people of the Bena-Bena groups readily admitted to Mick Leahy that they had eaten human flesh. The reason for cannibalism is sometimes hard to determine. Even in as small an area as the eastern highlands, there seemed to be several motivations. In some tribes, cannibalism was largely ritualistic, with each person taking no more than a bite or two of the flesh. Some tribes ate only their enemies, while others expressed great disgust at this practice, for they ate only their loved ones and friends.

In some cases, it was gastronomic; it was clear that these tribes ate human flesh because it was meat and was considered good food. The Australian anthropologist R. M. Berndt told of the women of a tribe fighting over the best cuts of a body brought back from a raid, hacking at it sometimes while there was still life. He also recorded an instance of a man having intercourse with a dead female enemy while he was dismembering the body.

Some of these particularly violent and repugnant actions are associated not only with cannibalism, however. They are rather expressions of the temperaments and personalities of these people. Even in the controlled areas, I sometimes sensed the violent tempers of the people. Some groups appeared to me tense and nervous; even their walk was jerky, unlike the smooth and easy movement of most primitives. They went about their day-to-day work as if they were holding back an inner explosion only with the greatest difficulty.

This was not true of all people in the area, of course. It is always difficult to stereotype the natives in a region where many basic languages are spoken, with innumerable dialects of each, and where differing — and contradictory — customs are practiced just a few miles apart. In the Bena-Bena area, for example, I found the natives relaxed and smiling. But this friendly attitude was comparatively new. Mick Leahy, while able to trade with them, had not found them so friendly when he was first prospecting on the Bena-Bena River. He always kept an all-day-and-all-night watch around his camp.

It was natural, of course, for even "good" people like the Bena-Bena to resent and resist the invaders. For centuries "invaders" had meant enemy tribes that wanted to steal their pigs and women, burn their villages, destroy their gardens, and eat the most edible things among them. The white invader was at first even more frightening because of his appearance, his weapons, his planes, his clothes, and above all his aims. These aims were almost incomprehensible to all natives of New Guinea, for they were, at the beginning, the few shiny particles that might be found in some streams. The New Guinea native would not have traded a goldlip shell for a sack full of the stuff. Beyond that, the chief goal in life for the native — killing without getting killed — was to the white man the worst thing one could do. That wanton murder is not to be allowed was a concept calculated to create only disbelief, resentment, and rebellion among the natives. But when the man who lays down this new law has a giant balus that roars through the air and brings what he wants, and fire-sticks that put holes in things, and white skin, and sometimes red hair, and knives and axes that cut ten times as fast as anything you have ever known, and more shells than you have ever dreamed of — then you begin to believe that you should obey his law, no matter how contrary to your nature it may be.

Then when you see that he does not kill even when he *can* kill all of those trying to kill him, you are deeply confused. Finally, when he does not take your pigs unless he gives you shells or axes in return, when he does not take your women even when you offer them to him, when he does not burn your house, uproot your garden, or eat the captives he has taken from you — then you know you have met a new kind of human being. It takes a long time for you to believe all this, but in time you believe. And if you give up killing and being killed, and eating man, then you will live peaceably with the new giver of laws and take his medicine to cure diseases, his security, his taxes, and the new food plants that he brings. The tribes around Bena-Bena had reached that state, and were seemingly happy in it.

With my cameraman Bede Whiteman, I drove from Goroka to Bena-Bena in a borrowed Land Rover. For a short distance from town, the road was relatively flat, and we had time to enjoy the views of towering mountains ringing the green plateau. But then we began to climb, twisting and turning along a narrow road cut into the sides of the steep hills, then dropping down into a valley only to climb a taller hill in sweeping curves that reduced the angle of ascent.

As we neared Bena-Bena, about thirty miles from Goroka, we saw groups of natives working on the road, some with shovels, some with long poles like the digging sticks used in their gardens. Some were clearing away earth and stones that had slid into the roadway. Others were widening the road at sharp curves. They stared at us and smiled as we passed. We came to a stream and, as we approached the bridge, saw rows of red flowers long both sides of the road. Later I saw more examples of roadside planting and learned that this was done by the natives without even a suggestion from the white men. They were so proud of their road that they wanted to beautify it.

The natives of the highlands were good agriculturists. Their gardens were laid out in neat, orderly squares bounded by drainage ditches. At that time, most of the turning and digging of earth and the making of ditches was done with the one native agricultural tool, a long, pointed stick. They had welcomed the introduction of new plants by government officers, especially coffee, one of the most successful. Some of the pioneer district officers and pilots had planted coffee in the highlands. Right alongside their plantations were those of natives, tended mainly by women, the chief gardeners.

We took many other trips to outlying villages, using Goroka as our base for a time, although on several occasions we stayed at "Snowy" McFarlane's plantation at the top of the Asaro Valley, not far from Goroka. At a village behind his place we filmed the native "mud-men" dancing. While all New Guinea natives decorated themselves elaborately on festive occasions, only this tribe made the amazing masks of hardened and baked mud that we saw along the Asaro River. They were really more than masks, for they covered the entire head, and were so heavy that the men wearing them had to dance in a slow and cautious way.

The masks were like nothing I have ever seen anywhere else — big, hollow heads of roughly sculptured mud, with weird Picasso-esque eyes and one or two long snouts. The eyes usually bulged, and were painted white, with red rims; the snouts, too, were often outlined in red. Each mask differed from the next, indicating a good deal of freedom of individual expression. While they did not compare artistically with the carved wooden figures and faces of the Sepik River, they had a similar distortion of human features. Most surprising, these people who had learned to bake mud into masks had no pottery, like all other tribes of the highlands. One might think it would be a natural step from baked mud masks to dishes and jars, but it seems never to have occurred to the mud-men to use their skill for anything but decoration.

In most of the villages we visited in the eastern highlands, the natives were pleasant and cooperative. Of course, we had the invaluable help of District Commissioner Seale, his assistant, and two patrol officers. But it was interesting to note that they never gave orders to the natives, only suggestions. They dealt with the village luluais, headmen who proudly wore the metal badge of office on their headdresses, or their assistants, the tultuls. But when one group did not want us to do any filming, as in the village of Kori-Koritoe, the government men just accepted their decision.

I always paid, in tobacco and other goods valued by the natives, for any work they did for us, such as the reenactment of scenes for our cameras. Many of the shots we took were, of course, of current events taking place anyway. But the mud-men danced specially for us, and were paid.

In one village the natives built us a small house while we filmed the operation, a primitive version of prefabrication. One group wove big rattan mats about six feet wide and eight or ten feet long, while another made straight posts from the branches of casuarina trees, and a third gathered tall kunai grass in bundles. Then the three materials were assembled.

Posts were driven into the ground to serve as the framework of the building. The mats were stretched around them to serve as walls, fastened in place with vines. Smaller posts served as the base of the roof, rising to a peak to form a kind of cone. Over these were laid the big bundles of kunai grass, overlapping and in several layers. It made a good roof, absolutely rainproof and quite cool. In less than an hour my assistant, my cameraman, and I were sitting in front of our new house having tea.

We visited the natives south of Goroka, the ones who I had been told were nervous and jittery. Physically, and in matters of decoration, food, houses, and such, they were like all other tribes nearby. But the Gahuku-Gama group, consisting of several tribes, had a high incidence of ulcers. Among primitive peoples in Africa and South America, ulcers are unknown, so I had concluded that they were a disease of civilization — and many authorities agreed with me. Why were the Gahuku-Gama tribes an exception?

Dr. K. E. Read, an Australian anthropologist, lived among the Gahuku-Gama and studied them for two years. Some of the tribes making up the group had been allies, some bitter enemies warring with each other until the white man brought pacification. Had this enforced thwarting of an age-old urge brought on the tensions? Dr. Read concluded that it had not: the same results had not occurred among other tribes that had had to give up war as a way of life. That change had brought difficulties of many kinds, but not neuroses or ulcers.

Dr. Read found one significant difference in the lives of the Gahuku-Gama, and this, he suggested, was probably at the origin of the ulcers — the relationship between men and women. Now, in all tribes of the highlands, man considers himself more or less superior to woman. Women exist for the pleasure of men, to bear children, to till the gardens, do the cooking; but their influence is considered debilitating. Initiation rites for boys invariably involve some symbolism representing the cutting of ties with the mother.

Among the Gahuku-Gama, however, the antagonism between men and women was *always* strongly in evidence. Women were not only inferior, they were nothing — mere vessels for the nurturing of young, useless without the male. Beyond that, women were actually dangerous! The Gahuku-Gama man believed that all women hated bearing children and tried to avoid it, a belief with some foundation according to Dr. Read, who found that most Gahuku-Gama women did indeed hate to have children, saying that the pain was almost unbearable and they were afraid they would die. They ate plants that they thought would cause sterility, and when these failed they often tried to induce abortion.

Since men were eager to have children, here was one reason for the men to hate the women. Males could not fulfill this desire without some contact with women, but they tried to have as little to do with them as possible. They slept apart, and did not allow their wives to touch their hair, weapons, clothing, or decorations. After intercourse, and especially after a wife bore a child, the husband went through special rites to cleanse himself.

When boys were six or seven years old, they were taken away from their mothers for a preliminary initiation, the primary purpose of which was to get the terrible woman's influence out of and away from the boy. His tongue and his penis were cut with bamboo knives to rid him of the blood of his mother. He was strenuously washed in a cold stream. Long slivers of bamboo were thrust down his throat to make him vomit — more cleansing action. Sharp sticks were pushed up his nostrils to cause more bleeding. (Some of these purifying rites were carried on even in adulthood, when some association with women made a man feel the need of cleansing. I filmed one example — the swallowing of a four-foot length of flexible bamboo. The man warmed it, bent it double, and forced it down his throat, inch by inch, until the doubled end reached his stomach and the two ends protruded a few inches from his mouth. The secret of the performance — utter relaxation of throat muscles, and an empty stomach. But it was obviously painful and made me gag just to watch it.)

After his preliminary initiation, the Gahuku-Gama boy was kept away from women, not allowed to eat food prepared by women. But

Among the Jivaro Indians, near the headwaters of the Amazon, one of life's greatest rewards comes from cutting off an enemy's head, shrinking it to the size of a fist, then dancing around it. Here a headhunter is shrinking the head by slow boiling, after having removed the skull bones. The process takes many hours.

ABOVE: With the shrunken head, or *tsantsa*, atop a lance, Jivaro headhunters dance their victory dance, lunging and thrusting their lances at the head to frighten the enemy's spirit that may still reside in the hair. BELOW: A witch doctor holds a *tsantsa* and instructs his two sons in the sacred duties of all Jivaros — to avenge the death of any member of family or clan. Such teaching is drilled into youngsters almost daily for years.

ABOVE: Dogs are so valuable to the Jivaros that, when this puppy's mother was killed by a jaguar, an Indian mother took it to nurse along with her own baby. BELOW: The mild-looking man taking one of my cigarettes is Utitiaja, the greatest headhunter of them all, with fifty-eight *tsantsas* to his credit when I talked to him.

ABOVE: One of the greatest and most unconventional Jivaro chiefs was Peruche, killed near the end of my long visit with him. On the right is Peruche's *jivaria*, where he and his sons and their families lived together. BELOW: Warriors of the Kukukuku tribe, the most feared in all of New Guinea, always look truculent, but especially so on this occasion when we all viewed the smoked body of one of their leaders, shown in the color section.

ABOVE: Australian Patrol Officer Craig Symons conducts a "hearing" in the Wahgi Valley to settle a dispute over a girl. Betrothed as a child by her parents, she preferred another man when she reached the ripe age of fourteen. Since payments had been made for her, the issue became economic as well as romantic. BELOW: This huge New Guinea signal drum, near Maprik, carries messages for many miles. Drums in other villages form a great network and pass messages along until they reach the people concerned.

ABOVE: All agricultural work in the Baliem Valley of western New Guinea is done by the women, as in most primitive societies. Despite the simple Stone Age implements like the digging stick used here, the Baliem gardens are neat and quite productive. BELOW: Transportation is equally primitive. This craft crossing the swiftly-flowing waters of the Baliem River consists of two big logs lashed together. The smiling man in the bow is the witch doctor Waganogo, called "Weepy" by the missionaries.

At one of the most northerly settlements in the world, on Ellesmere Island, I bring the sounds of New York, over three thousand miles away, to Ouisa, daughter of the Eskimo leader at Grise Fiord.

This Eskimo mother carries her baby in her *amoutik*, the hood of her parka. Most Eskimo clothing and food comes from the animals hunted and trapped by the men. Without a Hudson's Bay Post or a missionary station, the seventy-two Eskimos at Grise Fiord live almost the way their ancestors did centuries ago.

ABOVE: Akpaliapik, leader of the Ellesmere Island Eskimos, examines a soapstone carving he has just finished, a figure of a walrus hunter with his harpoon. Using knives and files, these untutored primitives carve sculptures so striking that they are eagerly sought by museums and collectors. BELOW: Eskimo hunters drag the body of a 3000-pound bull walrus they have just slain across the snow-covered ice to their hunting village. Its tusk ivory will be fashioned into needles and other implements, and its flesh will feed the indispensable dogs.

then at puberty there was an interesting development. In spite of the low opinion men had of women, there was a good deal of envy in them. They reluctantly admitted that, in a ritual sense, women are constructed better than men. A girl, for example, shows unmistakable physical evidence of attaining maturity, in the swelling of her breasts and above all in the beginning of menstruation. This regular flow of blood was imitated in some fashion by the boys, since they could not let the women get away with this evidence of superiority. At this time, the nose-bleeding rite was engaged in once a month — a rough stick being sawed up and down in the nostrils till the blood flowed freely. But no woman was allowed to see this, or the cane swallowing.

When a boy was about fifteen years old, he became engaged to a girl who had been chosen by his father or other relatives. But for eight years before that time he had been living in the men's house, where he was filled with the "truths" about the inferiority, weakness, and danger of women — *all* women. So it was not difficult for him to follow the rule of the tribe to avoid his betrothed above all other women.

Intercourse was considered weakening and dangerous, although essential for the production of children. So when a young man's sexual urge was at its peak, it could find no satisfaction. The misery that resulted was one more thing to be blamed on women, one more thing to hate them for.

Betrothals among the Gahuku-Gama were tenuous affairs, despite the many rigid rules. Dr. Read found that a majority of them were broken off at some point, and that some young men were "engaged" several times before they were finally married. Finally, however, there came a period of "courtship," when the young man and woman lay side by side for hours, rubbing their foreheads, noses, and cheeks against each other until the skin broke and bled. But no sexual intercourse was allowed.

The marriage ceremony showed more evidence of the antagonism between men and women, for the husband's first act in this should-be happy event was to shoot an arrow into his bride's thigh — and a particularly painful, four-pronged arrow, at that. This set the tone for the marriage, which continued to be one of antagonism and pain. Even the sex act had to be violent and painful. The man had to go through it for his physical satisfaction and to produce children, but he hated this very necessity, even while it was taking place.

Since the bride came from a different (though friendly) tribe, her mate was always a little distrustful of her. Moreover, she was probably a sorceress — women are the only witchcraft practitioners among the Gahuku-Gama. If she wished, she might get some of his semen and cast a spell over it to make him sick or weak. If a Gahuku-Gama man became ill, he always looked around for someone to blame it on, as do many primitives. But a Gahuku-Gama's suspicions were always directed first at his wife.

So among the Gahuku-Gama there was continual antagonism between men and women; there was envy and jealousy and pain and worry. Dr. Read found that it was not easy to live among such people, that their villages were never for even one whole day quiet and peaceful. He said, "To the outsider they seem to be continually on the verge of some more or less violent and unexpected outburst."

Learning about the Gahuku-Gama taught me a good deal. I realized that much of the antagonism to white men shown by the natives of New Guinea, and by some primitive groups in other parts of the world, stemmed not just from their suspicion of the alien white man himself, but from a deep suspicion of almost everyone.

I encountered another strange disease, farther south and a bit to the east, among several clans of a tribe called the Forei. Formerly they had been almost as belligerent and resistant to pacification as the Kukukukus, who live next to the Forei on the south. When I was there, the area was still under only partial control, and had been so classified since the time of the establishment of the first patrol post at Okapa.

The Forei people suffered from a strange "laughing sickness," a sickness known nowhere else in New Guinea, and in only one or two spots elsewhere. It was first noted in 1951 by early patrols going into the area, but the natives said that it had been among them for a long time. It began with a kind of spasmodic trembling, with occasional outbursts of giggling or loud laughter. Then came, inevitably it seemed, increased trembling, loss of balance, inability to walk without support, and more and more laughing, which continued to the point of exhaustion. What was particularly shocking was that in the midst of this loud laughter, there was no joy — only a kind of resigned despair. Once the disease started, the victim knew that he was going to die — and die he did within a year, unable to move, emaciated, and still laughing feebly.

The laughing death struck people of all ages, but it was more common among women than men. The two doctors who had been studying *kuru,* as the Forei people call the disease, knew little more about it than the natives themselves, and their treatments were no more effective than those of witchcraft. These people believed that one who contracted the disease was the victim of sorcery. The enemy managed to obtain something belonging to the victim — part of a skirt, spittle, excreta, or whatever. This was wrapped in leaves, pounded, cursed, and hidden in a swamp. That was when the trembling began.

The relatives of the sufferer first tried to find who the sorcerer was, and then to discover the object in the swamp; if it was retrieved, a cure could be effected. While that never seemed to happen, it was not uncommon for these relatives to find one whom they called the sorcerer, who was then subjected to unspeakable tortures before death. The muscles and genitals were mercilessly pounded to a pulp between stones and the trachea was actually bitten until broken and crushed.

As government control of the area is extended, this kind of cruelty is being stopped, or reduced. But it is a difficult task, so long as the white doctors, who have studied and tested for years now, can offer no hope. The most puzzling question of all — why should this strange ailment strike only this one small tribe, which lives and nourishes itself in the same way as all other tribes around, tribes whose members seem to be immune?

While some doctors tried to discover the secret of the laughing sickness, others were busy curing yaws and other ailments that afflicted the natives of all the highland regions. The result was, of course, an increase in the population. This accentuated the problems of the district commissioners and their patrol officers, but fortunately the administration did not try to change the marriage customs, habits, or religious ideas of the natives under their supervision. (Missionaries have been busy in these fields, however.) The civil authorities stopped much of the killing, brought justice, and offered opportunities for the natives to improve their crops, their health, and general well-being. And they tried hard to find substitutes for the outlet of energies formerly expended on killing — with most tribes a lot of energy went into this activity. The officials know that when war is taken away, something must fill the vacuum.

I saw many attempts to fill the huge gap made by peace, and many were successful, more and more successful as time went on. The best substitute was work, of course, work that brought good material rewards to the natives. Those who owned their own coffee plantations, for example, had a good deal of work to do — even the men — and they reaped considerable benefits. In some areas of New Guinea sheep and cattle have been introduced, with modest success. And for the less enterprising natives, there were jobs to be had.

But work alone can never be a substitute for war, which was not only a way of life and glory but in many cases almost a game. At least, the excitement it engendered was similar to that brought out in big sporting events. So the administration even tried sports. I filmed a football game, of the rugby type, between teams of two tribes that had been busy killing each other not long before. The first step was to gather up all the spears and bows and arrows of the contestants, the next to explain the game, which was not easy in pidgin. But they would accept rules, especially when their headman agreed to them, for they were used to certain rules and regulations in war and in all human relationships.

They were wonderfully quick at catching on and, to no one's real surprise, very adept at the game after a short while. They did not seem to mind admonitions and warnings when they broke the rules. And there was even more loud shouting than at an American game — from both players and spectators. The patrol officers were a bit worried about the outcome of the game, and they soon heard that the losing team's tribe was discussing an old-fashioned raid on the winning tribe. This came after I left the area, but I heard that the officers stepped in quickly with a suggestion for a return match, which was arranged. I never did learn how this turned out, but I know there was no flare-up of killing in the Goroka region, so I must assume that the first losers won the second game. The loss of face in losing two games in a row would have been a big incentive toward a resumption of the old ways of settling differences.

The natives pick up some games themselves. I mentioned that there was a golf course at Goroka. It was a pleasant nine-hole course greatly enjoyed by administration officials, plantation owners, and other settlers near the town. On my first trip to New Guinea, I saw some men playing, with natives acting as caddies — natives in full regalia, as for a *sing-sing*. Nowhere else in the world would one find caddies with headdresses of flaming plumes of the bird of paradise, with curved bones through the nose, with decorations of seashells, and with bodies painted in red, white, and black.

One day a golfer missed an easy putt and became so angry, as golfers often do, that he blamed everything on his putter and gave it away to his caddie. The caddie went back to his nearby village and decided to make his own golf course, or at least part of one. He had found some golf balls on the Goroka course; he had a putter. All he needed was a green. With the enthusiastic help of his friends, he cut an area of grass as close as possible, sunk a hole in it, and even put into the hole a pole with a piece of cloth on top.

He was obviously enjoying himself so much that some of his friends improvised putters, and the entire village was soon betting on the putting matches that were held regularly. I saw the native putting green on my second visit, less than a year after the first putter had been given away. The men were quite good. But there were some changes. The caddies on the Goroka course no longer dressed in full regalia. They wore white shirts. As soon as they had earned a little money, they had rushed to the trading store for shirts.

For a select few, the problem of finding a new outlet for old energies offered no serious problems. These were the men accepted as members of the native police, whose chief training post and barracks for the highlands was not far from Goroka. It is not an easy task for a native to learn the military discipline of the white man, to learn that he must never use his gun, a weapon few other natives have, in haste or anger, but only under order of his superiors. It is not easy for him, on patrol in a new territory, to be fired upon by natives of his own kind without firing a shot in return. Certainly it is amazing that these men, who drank in pay-back killing and revenge and war with their mother's milk, can learn that killing must stop, that wars must end, that despite all kinds of provocations and even at the risk of one's own life, a shot must not be fired until ordered by the white officer in charge of the party.

Native police usually served as interpreters on new patrols. They were of great help because they could say to a belligerent group, "Look, we fought the white men at first, too, but we learned that they do not steal our pigs or women, do not burn our houses, do not take our food without paying. They help us get well when we are sick. They send our children to school. They bring new crops to plant. And they stop the killing."

The record of the native police is a remarkable one, as comes home when one hears from the lips of Keith McCarthy, for example, how his life was saved by a native policeman who lost his own life in the rescue. Every patrol officer from the early days has similar stories to tell. During World War II, many native police became soldiers, many serving behind Japanese lines. One of the most famous was Sergeant Simogen, who was attached to a group of Australian "Coast Watchers" in New Britain, and whose ruses and stratagems proved brilliant. Even in those days he was called "old Simogen," but he was still active years later, when I was in New Guinea. Simogen became a member — the only native member then — of the Legislative Council, created in 1951.

One of the white men *elected* by the natives to serve on that first council was Ian F. G. Downs, an early district officer in the highlands. I visited him at his plantation at the head of the Asaro Valley outside of Goroka, which had for many years been his headquarters. (It is significant that a number of the first officers and explorers in New Guinea had settled there — the Leahys, Jim Taylor, George Greathead, and Downs, among others.) Ian Downs is a man of positive opinions and forcefulness in translating them into action. Mick Leahy had called him "a man and a half." He joined District Services as a patrol officer when he was only nineteen years old. At twenty-four he was sent into the Chimbu, for many years the most difficult subdistrict in the highlands. During World War II Downs was in the Australian navy, but returned to New Guinea at the end of hostilities. At thirty-seven he was made district commissioner for the eastern highlands.

Downs is a remarkable man in many ways, but without doubt the building of the road was his greatest single achievement. He started building roads when he was a patrol officer in the Chimbu, at the eastern end of the Wahgi Valley. Greathead was then assistant district officer at Mt. Hagen, at the western end of the valley, and between them they decided to make a road through the entire valley, connecting their two posts. Downs asked the headmen of the villages under his direction to find out if their people really wanted a road. They wanted it, and badly, and Downs made it plain that they would have it if they worked for it. Within a few months, there were thousands of natives pushing a road toward the other end of the valley, bridging streams, working with almost no tools but their pointed sticks. They worked hard, must of the time with no supervision at all, and they got their road.

But when Downs moved east to Goroka in 1952, he faced more difficult problems — rushing rivers and tall mountains in the way. At the time there were roads out of Goroka for only eight miles toward the west and six miles east. He envisioned a road going west, climbing the ridges that had kept men out of the central highlands for centuries; and another road going east to Lae on the coast; still another connecting with Madang on the northern coast. He knew that the highlands would develop very slowly if everything from the outside had to be flown in.

He had the support of the Administrator of Papua-New Guinea, Brigadier D. M. Cleland, and of the Australian Minister of Territories, Paul Hasluck, but there was no money available until later, and Downs wanted to start work at once. Downs had no engineer, not even a surveyor to help him lay out the road. He had no road-building or earth-moving equipment of any kind, not even dynamite for blasting. It was estimated that the road west from Goroka and over the divide to the Wahgi Valley and east to Kainantu would take about three years to build, at a cost of around one hundred and fifty thousand dollars. Downs built it in one year at a total cost of less than thirty thousand dollars. There were many bridges to be built, large and small; on one section there were seventeen more than eighty feet long, and the bridge over a branch of the Asaro River was of the wire suspension type — 165 feet long. When he could not get the administration to issue him enough wire cable, he managed to get hold of enough old elevator cable to do the job, and for just ten per cent of the cost an expert had estimated.

He got enough shovels by the same kind of maneuvering. The authorities issued him very few, but he wound up with seven thousand of them. He obtained most of these by collecting wartime scrap and swapping it to traders for shovels. Since they were not, then, listed on his books, he let the native workers know that they could keep their shovels when the road-building was completed — a good work incentive.

He *had* to give them incentive, too, for at the outset he explained that he could not always pay them for work they did, that such pay would come only when the job was finished. How did he get them to work then? First, he explained what the road would mean to them; many of them had friends who lived along the short stretches of existing road, and they knew the truth of what Downs said. And they worked for him, secondly, because they saw that Downs kept every promise he made to them.

Meanwhile Downs had the job of feeding thousands of natives working at some distance from their villages and gardens, so he sent his patrol officers out in advance to see that gardens were planted along the route of the road. As the road was pushed ahead, east and west, it was cut into land growing food for the men making the road.

There were great rewards and great problems during the year of road-building. When the bridge over the Bena-Bena river was completed, the reaction of the local natives was, as Downs told me, "terrific." They could bring produce into Goroka to sell it, could get to town to buy things, could visit friends on the other side of the river.

Sometimes the road came up against a giant outcropping of solid rock, with no way to go around or over it. Without explosives, Downs turned to the method called, in pidgin, "cookim stone." Natives picked away at the base of the rock, making niches in which fires were kept burning all day. At night when the temperature dropped sharply, as it does at altitudes of six or eight thousand feet, the rock cracked. So a way was made, and small rock for surfacing was obtained at the same time. The road climbed over rocky ridges seven thousand feet high at the eastern end of Downs's district, more than eight thousand feet high at the western end.

Downs encountered human problems, too, the most difficult involving a native named Kamindo. In ordinary times Kamindo might have been no more than a minor nuisance, but the building of a bridge over the Asaro River made for very unusual times in that region. And it was an absolute essential for the success of the road-building project; Goroka and the Wahgi Valley could never be connected without the bridge. Kamindo threatened not only the bridge itself but the years of progress that the Australian administration had made in dealing with the natives of the eastern highlands.

Kamindo was a tall man for his tribe, and a fine orator — two things that gave him position in the eyes of the natives. He was strong and agile and might well have been the war-leader of his group in the days of wars. But there was no more fighting, and Kamindo was almost crazy with frustration, unable to find any outlet for his talents. Those talents did not mean that he was appointed luluai or tultul of his tribe, so he had no standing at all except for what he could create for himself. He decided that he could create stature only by defying white authority, the government. The building of the bridge in his territory gave him the opportunity.

The bridge over the Asaro called for heavy hardwood timbers, from trees that grew high up on the mountains. The luluais of the tribes of that area were told how many trees, of what size, would be needed, and they agreed to have them brought down to the bridge site. The price was not fixed because no one knew at that time just how much time and labor were involved. But until Kamindo started his campaign, the luluais knew from experience that they could trust Downs to be fair.

The trees were felled and brought to the bridge site, and Downs decided that 359 Australian pounds was a fair price for them. But when this amount was offered, Kamindo rounded up the luluais and many of the workmen — he already had considerable following because of his oratory, height, and general belligerence — and told them they were being cheated. They should get three thousand pounds before they let the kiap touch the logs. Downs knew that these people, who had been introduced to money instead of shells as pay only a few years before, had little idea of what three thousand pounds meant, but when Kamindo talked as if *he* knew, they listened.

Kamindo persuaded enough of the luluais to prevent delivery of the logs and the building of the bridge. But they were not breaking any laws, and Downs was never one to take the law into his own hands. He knew, as did the other officers of the administration, that the only way one can ever instill respect for laws not always understood is to respect them more than anyone else.

So the bridge was held up for a time. And Kamindo, heady with temporary victory, talked more and louder. He talked about running all white men out of the valley; he scoffed at the medical help they gave. But Downs knew that such an ambitious blusterer was bound to trip himself up in time.

He did not have to wait long. Kamindo had decided that no one from his area should take produce into Goroka for sale until the price for the bridge logs was settled as he wanted it settled. Moreover he declared that no one from another region could pass along the road that had been completed to sell his labor or produce in Goroka. When a man from the Chimbu tried to walk along the road to Goroka, Kamindo beat him up. Now at last he had actually broken a law. Downs knew that he could arrest him for assault and put him away for a month or so.

But would this be wise? Downs understood the native psychology well enough to guess that Kamindo might gain great prestige, might wield even greater authority than ever before. Even if he arrested Kamindo, he could not force the luluais to sell him the hardwood logs if they did not want to. Somehow he had to undercut Kamindo's influence. To do this he had to make the man lose face in front of his followers. It was risky, it was dangerous, but it had to be done.

So word was sent out to the Asaro Valley that the kiap wanted to talk to the tribes that had brought the logs from the mountains. In planning this meeting, Downs reversed a technique he had always used in the Chimbu with great success — assembling a thousand or more friendly natives to accompany him on a visit to a troublesome group. But different problems call for different answers, and in this case Downs wanted to face — almost alone — as large a crowd of Kamindo's followers as possible.

"There were about eight thousand of them there when I arrived," Downs told me, "and I wondered if I hadn't gone at this wrong. I had with me only a couple of patrol officers and a handful of native police, not one of whom was armed. I didn't want any shooting, no matter how things turned out. And I carried no weapon."

Downs talked to the great assemblage of natives, none of whom greeted him in friendly fashion. He saw Kamindo among them, but did not even look in his direction. He would not speak until they had all sat on the ground, an old technique of his, but when they were seated he launched into a lengthy oration. Downs is ordinarily terse and to the point, but he knew that the natives had no respect for short speeches and he was dealing, in the case of Kamindo, with a great orator. He repeated, in as flowery language as possible, all the things he had told them before about the many advantages the road would bring to them. He spoke of the bridge and the timbers for the bridge, and the price he had offered. The natives leaned forward slightly, for they knew that he was coming to the crux of the matter.

Suddenly he mentioned Kamindo, saying that he had been hearing a great deal about this man Kamindo, about how he had insisted three thousand pounds was a good price for the logs, how he had said he would chase all white men out of the valley, and how he had beat up a man who wanted to work on the road. Downs said that this Kamindo must be a very big man, a very important man, to do and say all these things. He said he would like to meet such a man and pay him in a way befitting such a big, important personage.

Everyone turned to look at Kamindo, and Downs then looked at him for the first time. Kamindo was obviously pleased at the attention given him in front of such a large assemblage but at the same time he was a little suspicious, a little uncertain at this turn of events, which he had obviously not expected.

Downs asked that this big man, Kamindo, step forward to receive his very special pay. And Kamindo, suspicious though he was, could do nothing but step forward. When he stood in front of Downs, the district commissioner asked Kamindo to hold up both hands to receive his special pay. Kamindo did so, and Downs slipped a pair of hand-cuffs on his wrists, saying loudly, "This is the kind of pay we give to a big talker like Kamindo."

Kamindo was so thunderstruck that he could not say a word — and an outburst from him might have turned the tide. The assembled natives seemed to hold their breath for a full minute, then let it out in one big sigh. Downs turned and took Kamindo away with him, to his jeep and then to jail in Goroka. No one had been hurt, but the issue was still not resolved. The first step had been made, however, with the removal of Kamindo and the expected loss of Kamindo's influence through his having been taken in such a fashion. Downs knew that all the natives greatly admired slick stratagems, and he felt they would admire what he had done, while they would have nothing to admire in Kamindo's actions at the meeting.

Then, that night, the unexpected happened. Kamindo in jail committed suicide by hanging himself with his loincloth. His loss of face had been so great he could not endure the humiliation. Downs was deeply troubled. For one thing, his conscience bothered him since he had brought about this loss of face which caused Kamindo to take his own life. It did little good to tell himself that far more lives might have been lost, plus an entire program of progress, had Kamindo kept gaining more influence. But there was a more immediate and practical aspect of the matter that troubled Downs — Kamindo was likely to become a martyr in the eyes of his tribe as a result of this act. Would the natives believe he had actually taken his own life? And even so, would he still not be a martyr, a man who died for them?

Downs had Kamindo buried in the hospital cemetery in Goroka. And he was not surprised when the next day a group of Kamindo's relatives came to ask for his body. They wanted to bury him with great honors, to hold a long and emotional wake for the dead hero of his people. Downs knew that if he allowed this to happen, Kamindo would indeed become a martyr, and it might be years before there would be a bridge over the Asaro and a road two hundred miles long in the highlands of New Guinea.

So he told Kamindo's relatives briefly — this was no time for oratory — "No." And he added the greatest insult that anyone can give to a native: "Kamindo — rubbish man."

The relatives turned without a word and walked away. And within a week there was no more talk about Kamindo, even among his tribe. The luluais accepted the price of three hundred fifty-odd pounds for the logs. The bridge was built, and the road climbed beyond it to a height of over eight thousand feet, to dip down in gentle curves to the floor of the Wahgi Valley.

Now Ian Downs has retired from government service and lives on his own plantation in that same Asaro River valley. Some of his neighbors are those who once listened, for a while, to Kamindo. A few of them have their own coffee plantations, and others are growing new crops brought in by the agricultural officer over the bridge and the road that Ian Downs built.

One strong influence in the development of the central highlands of New Guinea has been that of the missionaries, of various nationalities and denominations. They were never far behind the searchers for gold and the government officers. Father Alphons Schaefer, of the Society of the Divine Word, first suspected there *was* a Wahgi Valley at about the time Mick Leahy looked at the grassland clouds and decided to investigate some day. He heard from the natives around his station at Bundi, just north of the divide between the Ramu and Chimbu Rivers, that they had friends on the other side of the mountain. Without having heard of the Leahys' discovery, he went in from the north with some colleagues and a group of carriers. They walked through the Chimbu gorge and halfway up the Wahgi Valley without encountering any trouble from the natives. Then they returned to plan the setting up of missions.

Meanwhile the world had learned about the Leahy discoveries, and other Catholic missionaries in New Guinea decided to move into the Wahgi to establish posts. In 1934 an American, Father William Ross, S.V.D., with two colleagues and seventy-two carriers, traveled to Bundi, over the divide to the Chimbu River, and into the main Wahgi Valley. They, too, had no trouble with the natives and were able to build a mission at Mingende, about midway up the valley. Later Father Schaefer took charge at Mingende, and Father Ross and Brother Eugene marched to the end of the valley and built a post at Mt. Hagen. (Father Ross was still there in 1958 and 1959, when I had several long talks with him.) He is a remarkable man, a devout and good man, but he had no illusions about the dangers he was facing. He had with him six dogs, of which the natives were frightened, and he never walked two steps in those days without a revolver. By the end of 1934, he had built houses, stores, a church, and a school. Other missionaries had created several new stations in the Chimbu area, and some along the Wahgi Valley.

But the first missionaries were put off their guard somewhat by the initial friendliness of the natives, and they forgot or did not know that with familiarity their awe and fear departed. At Christmas time, 1934, three missionaries, with carriers, set out from the Wahgi Valley for Bundi, north of the Chimbu divide. One tribe in the Chimbu Gorge, the Womkama, attacked them. Two missionaries were killed and one badly wounded, saved by faithful carriers who did not run away.

Within a remarkably short time, the Chimbu welcomed the Leahys, the District Commissioner from Salamaua, Keith McCarthy, Jim Taylor, Alan Roberts, and George Greathead. This was too formidable a team for any tribe or group of tribes to face. Fortunately for future relationships, not one of these men believed in punitive expeditions, but they were also convinced that even one killing of a white man, if allowed to go unpunished, might result in subsequent deaths for tens, hundreds, or more.

Roberts built a large jail, or compound, without a single nail. Jim Taylor, with the help of Dan Leahy and others, rounded up a total of more than eighty prisoners among the Womkama in surprise raids. He dismissed and freed the old and the sick, flew sixty-seven down to Salamaua, among them many men who had been identified by the carriers as leading the attacks on the missionaries.

The prisoners were not tried, for Jim Taylor convinced his superiors that such a trial would be only a farce, with the accused understanding nothing of the language, laws, procedures, or even the moral concepts of the accusers. The men were put to work building houses in which they could live while they were prisoners of the government. They worked in and near Salamaua, witnessed the amicable relationship between white men and the natives of the coast, saw the wonders of civilization, and learned some pidgin so they could talk to white men. Then they were taken back to the Chimbu, where most of them told their relatives and fellow tribesmen that it would be wiser for the natives to work with the white man than to fight him.

There were still some "uncontrolled" regions, even in the Chimbu area, when I was there. The newest patrol post in the district was to the south, in the foothills of Mt. Karimui, so I decided to visit it. From the post at Kundiawa I flew in a little Cessna to a tilted hillside strip near the village of Omkalai, a few miles below Gumine, the site of the government post and the almost inevitable mission. My cameraman Bede Whiteman and I were met by Bob Greaney, senior patrol officer in charge of the Gumine post, who proudly showed us his new Land Rover and told us about the road that had just been built from Omkalai to Gumine, pointing almost skyward as he mentioned it.

"The road has been finished just a week," Greaney said. "You'll be the first visitors to travel over it."

After the bouncing landing of the plane on the slanting airstrip, I welcomed the idea of traveling over a road — until I found myself on that particular road. We loaded our cameras and equipment in the back, so Whiteman and I sat in the front seat with Greaney — a tight fit. At first the road was not too bad, although it climbed so steeply that I could understand Greaney's pointing upward as he spoke about it. As we drove higher into the mountains, however, the twists and turns became sharper and narrower. We struggled up, cut around a boulder on a gravel shelf hacked out of the mountainside, then dipped as if to get up steam for the next, steeper climb. I was wedged in the middle, finding it a bit difficult to breathe, looking up occasionally at the forested slope above, down at the forested valley far below, and listening to Bob Greaney chat happily about the building of the road. Suddenly we topped a crest, turned sharply to the left, and dipped down as the hairpin curve continued.

"It's a little tricky here," Greaney said, braking the Land Rover to a stop with the right front wheel almost hanging over the edge of a precipice. "The turn is too sharp or the road is too narrow or both. I always have to back up and take another shot at it to get around."

He put the car in reverse, backed up about four feet so that it was the right rear wheel on the edge of space. I felt like jumping, but was wedged in too tight. Whiteman actually opened the door on his side, ready to bail out. Greaney had stopped talking in his concentration. He cramped the steering wheel sharply to the left and took his foot off the brake. Down went the car, completing the curve with no more than a few inches to spare on either side.

Whiteman and I started breathing again, as Greaney continued his conversation. "I'll have to get a crew up here some day to widen that stretch a bit," he said.

Although the road continued to dip and climb, we were soon at Greaney's headquarters in Gumine. The next day the patrol officer drove us on an extension of the road, and we soon came upon a group of about twenty natives building a bridge over a thirty-foot gorge cut by a mountain stream. Since the light was good, we set up our cameras and filmed the completion of the construction — the natives serving as willing actors in close-ups showing the tying of the bridge floor in place. This flooring was quite uneven, since it consisted of small round tree trunks lashed with vines, to larger carrying beams. Not a nail was used in the bridge, which was strong enough to carry the Land Rover without difficulty.

With Greaney's help, we filmed several other interesting sequences in and around Gumine, including some shots of the tree-climbing kangaroo, which is rarely found outside of New Guinea, of natives weaving pit-pit for the walls of their houses, of a mock battle staged for us with almost frightening realism by a large group of shouting warriors.

And in the evening I had a good talk with Father Fisher, S.V.D., of the mission at Gumine, who thought the natives throughout the Chimbu were unusually bright and adaptable. "They are basically no different from most people," he said. "You could take an average native and — providing he got over his homesickness soon — put him down anywhere and he would get along all right. He would have just about the same weaknesses the rest of us have, but he strikes us as almost savage because he has so few inhibitions. He felt — until the white man came — few curbs except those induced by fear, and fear is the basis of his religion really. When he got angry, he struck out in anger; if he was angry enough he killed. And there was nothing in his society to condemn this. He soon learns, however, the great advantage of some restraint. For one thing, he is not so likely to get killed by someone who gets angry at *him*."

Like most of the missionaries I talked to, Father Fisher expected to perform no miracles in the way of converting great numbers of natives. "There are so many difficulties," he said, "that no one can foresee. For instance, we believe in giving last rites to a native who is dying. But since the natives believe that death is an unnatural thing, a result of witchcraft or sorcery, they are apt to conclude that the last rites were what actually caused the man's death. Wasn't it the last act performed before his death — up to that time he had been alive, even if ailing? Many missionaries have been so discouraged by this reaction that they have in some cases given up last rites. But I do not believe in this. I believe in carrying out the act and doing my utmost to make the natives understand. They *must* be made to understand."

He sighed. "But it is not easy. Even after you learn their language well, you find that they do not even have words to express some of the basic things we try to teach, very few words to indicate abstractions. For example, they have no word for *hope* and there is no word for *love*. How can we teach Christian ideas without these two words? The closest approach to the word love is the phrase, *I do good to you*. It is not the same, of course, but it gets across at least one part of the idea of loving."

During other jaunts in the Chimbu region in the course of my two trips to New Guinea, I met many natives who helped me understand both the difficulties and the successes of the white man in bringing the concepts of civilization to Stone Age man. Two of these were outstanding leaders of their people. Kondon Agaundo and Kavagl were alike in many ways, but there were some startling contrasts.

Kavagl was a man famous throughout the Chimbu country and even beyond its borders. He was about sixty, no longer young, but his personality still carried a strong impact. He was taller than most Chimbus, and age could not hide the great strength that had once been his. He was relaxed and pleasant as I talked to him. I sat on a camp chair and he sat cross-legged on the ground at my feet. As we talked, he leaned forward occasionally to touch and stroke the soft leather of my boots. And each time, he looked up at me and smiled.

For decades Kavagl had been the leader of the Korugus, and of other neighboring tribes. He had killed hundreds of enemies in war and in personal combat, and his method of fighting, his terrible temper, and the fear he inspired in his enemies were still great legends among the people of the Chimbu. One of his nicknames was *togl kumba yagl*, the man with the fence-pole club. This came about because when a sudden fight flared up or Kavagl lost his weapon, he would pull up one of the big fence poles around the gardens and lash out with it until he killed his enemies or chased them away. Later he bought or traded to get himself an axe — not just a hatchet but a heavy axe, the biggest axe in the entire Wahgi Valley. In his hands it was a terrible weapon.

When I talked to Kavagl I saw that one eye was blind and that there were numerous other scars on his body, so I inquired about his wounds. Almost proudly he reported that he had received an arrow through his eye, a spear through his leg, another spear through his arm — and so many more lesser wounds that he could not count or remember them. Then the interpreter gave me his next words: "I have fought many battles, taken many women and pigs, burned many houses, ruined many gardens."

I asked Kavagl about his wives.

"For my first wife," he said, "I paid five pigs, four red bird of paradise feathers, ten stone axes, two goldlip pearl shells, and one string of small shells. She was called Gaglm and was from the Vaugla tribe. She gave me a son, called Kutne. But once, when we were fighting the Vauglas, I told her to tie the pigs up well so they would not be stolen. One pig got away, so I spoke angrily to her. She spoke back to me and I did not like that. I picked up a club and hit her on the head. She fell down dead. I did not really want to kill her, but she called me bad names. I was sorry she was dead and I cried a long time."

For the second wife, Duruagl from the Narugu tribe, he paid six pigs, five shells, three knives, five bird of paradise feathers, and four iron hatchets. She bore him three children, one of whom so enraged Kavagl that one day he killed the boy. And later he and Duruagl had such a terrible fight that he picked up a hatchet and killed her. He did not really mean this, either, but he was so angry he could not control himself. He grieved so deeply that he cut off part of his ear to show his sorrow.

Kavagl's third wife died a natural death after giving birth to a child. His next two were from the Vaugla tribe. One, named Uare, provoked him just once, and was so beaten that she never tried it again, but was always obedient. The other, however, named Chivikor, was a high-spirited woman and, although this enraged Kavagl part of the time, he was really very proud of her. Once he struck her on the head with an axe, but she did not die, and Kavagl was very solicitous in bandaging the wound and caring for her.

And Kavagl had considerable respect for the white man and his ways, although he found it difficult to follow his rules. He used to attend church services with regularity, although he never became converted. And he used to give his own harangue to the natives when services were over, urging them to accept the missionary's words.

Kavagl could urge his fellows to follow the rules even though he did not obey them himself because he considered himself so far superior to the rest of his tribe and neighboring tribes. Rules just did not apply to him, that's all. For example, when he was in Bundi he saw the sort of breechclout the natives there wore, and he took a fancy to it. It was a piece of cloth pulled through the legs tightly. In his own country such dress was considered indecent, but that did not bother Kavagl, nor did the rather hesitant joshing he got about it. He won another nickname, *dem joyo yagl*, meaning "the man with the naked buttocks," but he went on wearing the breechclout unperturbed.

While most Chimbus save their fanciest dress — shells and plumes — for festive or solemn occasions, they wear every day more shells and decorations than the natives further west in the valley. But not Kavagl. For everyday wear he was unadorned, although he had a magnificent headdress and several fine goldlip pearl shells for special occasions. And he alone decided when the occasion was special enough.

All other men slept at night in the men's house, but not Kavagl. He always slept in the house of one of his wives, and paid no attention to the jokes made about it. He never took as many wives as his wealth and prowess might have called for, and he explained this by saying that he did not much like to work, and if he had many wives he would have to build a separate house and garden for each one. He knew that he was the acknowledged leader of his tribe and did not have to prove it by many wives, many pigs, many shells.

Probably the most striking example of Kavagl's disdain of the rules of his people was seen in his attitude toward his daughter Ninmongo. When she was little he carried her around in his arms a great deal of the time. When he sat down, Ninmongo slept in his lap, until she woke up and began to pull at his beard and crawl over him. No matter what this daughter did, Kavagl never lost his temper or patience. When she cried he tried to learn what she wanted so he could satisfy her. Once when she reached for his bamboo pipe, he let her smoke it. She liked it and continued to smoke it frequently. She was certainly the only child — and a female child at that! — to see and play with the sacred flutes. This meant death to any child or any female of any age — but not to the daughter of Kavagl, who merely laughed at the warnings of what the spirits would do to him and Ninmongo.

Another chief I met in the Chimbu was Kondon Agaundo, the leader and government-appointed luluai of the Naruga clan. We filmed him before a sing-sing, as the vivid paints were applied to his face and body, and the magnificent headdress of bird of paradise plumes was put on his head; big goldlip pearl shells hung from his neck and other strings of shells adorned his arms and legs, and a belt covered with green beetle shells went around his waist.

He was a tall, proud man, and he was something to behold in his native dress. But a few days later I might have seen him in Lae or Port Moresby or Melbourne or Canberra dressed in a white shirt, necktie, and suit. For Kondon was a chief who had not only accepted the ways of civilization but was fighting to bring the best of it to his own people. He once had ten, and still had eight wives, and by them many children, the oldest of whom was a schoolteacher. Kondon's father was Akau'undo, leader of the Narugas before him; Akau'undo had known Jim Taylor and Ian Downs in the early days of white penetration of the Wahgi Valley. Now Kondon was pleading with the Australian authorities to teach the younger generation of natives to read and write English, to look after their health properly. To him it was not enough that the fighting and much of the murdering had stopped. His people had to be led away from their superstitions and fears, taught how to improve the soil, diversify their crops, improve their standard of living. And he insisted it could be done without taking away from the people their colorful culture, their art, their cherished customs.

When I talked to Kondon, I spoke through an interpreter who talked pidgin. I could catch a word or a phrase now and then, for I had heard enough pidgin to have grown familiar with it. But I thought I noted in Kondon an irritation, a smoldering anger, at the language itself. And later when I read a speech he made as a delegate from New Guinea to a conference on South Pacific problems, I understood why I had had this feeling. To him, pidgin was a lingua franca that had enabled whites and natives to communicate about essentials, but it was a bastard language of no breath or depth and should be supplanted by a true tongue, such as English. Here is the English translation of what Kondon said to the assembled delegates from many nations:

"I am from Kundiawa in the Chimbu. There are many people in Chimbu — as the white man calls the number, half a million. When I came here I did not know there were people living in the Pacific, such as Fiji, Samoa, and all the other places, for it is only twenty-five years ago since my country, the highlands, was found by the white man.

"At that time we were living as primitive people and fighting one another. We had very little of the good things of life — poor houses, no roads, and we were sometimes very short of food.

"That is only twenty-five years ago. Now we are on the way to civilization, we have medical services and schools, and my people are greatly improved, although there are yet very few white men or civilization among us.

"Perhaps you will laugh at me because I speak pidgin and cannot read or write, but soon I will die and pidgin will die with me, and my children will be able to speak English and so understand you all."

Kondon was elected head of his local council and then to the New Guinea Legislative Council as the representative of New Guinea's largest constituency — about 160,000 natives. He continued to urge the building of schools, the sending in of more teachers, the establishment of medical centers, and the rapid extension of civilization's worthwhile features to his people.

He once pointed out that the slow growth of schools actually increased the incidence of crime in his area, for the ambitious young men had learned that if they were arrested they might be taken to a town on the coast where, even in jail, they had a good chance to learn English and a trade. When they returned to the Chimbu they had a decided advantage over their fellow tribesmen.

When the Council was changed to a genuine parliamentary assembly in 1964, Kondon was defeated for the post of representative. A younger man, even more impatient than he, was elected in his place. The demand for more rapid change has grown to a roar, and the tempo of that change is accelerating every day.

In New Guinea, the Stone Age and the Atomic Age occasionally meet and mingle in one person. To my surprise, the best amalgam of the two cultures that I encountered was in a girl I met at Minj, in the middle Wahgi Valley.

Danga was a girl who in the old days would have been married before she was twenty and would have spent her life bearing children, tending pigs and the garden, and living as a virtual slave to her husband, perhaps even sharing that slavery with one or more other wives. And she would have made a good marriage, for she was the daughter of a subchief of a sizable clan.

When I met her she was wearing a neat blue cotton dress without ornament; her face was unpainted and she wore no shells. She sat at a table in the government Malarial Control Center at Minj peering through a microscope at slides she had prepared, searching for the larvae of the dread malaria carrier, the anopheles mosquito. She was serious, clean, neat, and efficient. She was not self-conscious and obviously did not feel out of place doing such work. The doctor who had trained her told me that she was quite capable. And for this work she received more money than most of the men who hired themselves out for labor, more money than most of the government-appointed officials, the luluais and tultuls of the tribes in the area.

I saw Danga again a few hours later, after she had left the thatched-hut laboratory. The blue cotton dress had been discarded. Her face was painted — red on the forehead, black and yellow stripes on the cheeks and chin. Through the septum of her nose there was a curved sliver of shell, and on her head there was a band of cane inset with small shells and green beetles, surmounted by an array of red bird of paradise plumes. From her neck several big goldlip shells were suspended just above her bare, firm breasts. Around her waist was the wide belt of woven cane worn only by unmarried women, and she wore armlets of the same woven cane and other armlets of opposum fur. A skimpy skirt of fibers hung from a band around her waist.

I do not mean to suggest that Danga, after leaving work each day, went home and dressed herself in all this finery. She went home and dressed as other native women dressed on ordinary days, without all the painting and headdresses and fur and shells. No, I had asked her to dress as she would for a sing-sing or a pig festival. So she was wearing the same things she had actually worn at a magnificent pig festival only a few years before, when she had killed her own pigs just like the chiefs and subchiefs of the other clans. And that is the way I filmed her.

I tried to figure out which way she was most at home, but I could see no difference. She was thoroughly at ease and comfortable in the laboratory, at work. She was thoroughly at ease and comfortable in her native dress, eating sweet potato and pig fat with her old father. There seemed to be no conflict within her over her seemingly double life.

There was other and stronger evidence of this lack of conflict, for Danga had denied the traditional role of woman completely. Here she was, in her middle twenties, a strong and comely girl, without a husband. In a culture where wives were bought and paid for, she had not been bought. She worked, but not at the menial labor that women were supposed to do. And by this time she was worth considerably more than any native man that might want to buy her. She was a "career" woman who had cut the age-old ties of dependence upon the male.

Perhaps she wanted a husband and children, but she seemed to be a relatively happy human being. She had adopted a small boy, and I had a feeling that she would find a husband before long among other government-trained natives, some young man who would not expect her to go back to the serfdom of primitive woman. (She did.)

How had Danga happened to make this great leap from the Stone Age to the present so satisfactorily? There had been a great crisis and tragedy in her life when she was quite young, and this had helped her to break with the old ways. Her small clan had lived for many years in an area along the shores of the Wahgi River, where the ground was for many months of the year damp and even swampy. Most native groups avoided such land, but the weaker tribes had been forced to live there after more warlike tribes took all the good land. There was malaria in the swampy lands, despite previously held theories that the anopheles mosquito did not breed at altitudes of over 5000 feet — and Danga's clan had been wiped out by the disease, all but herself and her father, the little boy she had adopted, and a few others. They might have gone to live with a friendly tribe and been accepted completely by the new group. But Danga found another way out, a way that meant for her not only an undreamed-of independence but a chance to help eradicate the disease that had killed off her own people.

I saw and filmed many of the rituals of courtship and marriage that Danga had escaped. They were colorful and unusual, but not always calculated to bring much happiness or satisfaction to the women involved, except for about three years of freedom and pleasure between betrothal and marriage. When marriage came, that was almost the end of life for many native women.

As in most primitive societies, brides were bought, but I found great variety of detail even in a small area such as the Wahgi Valley. In some tribes, brides were "marked" for a particular boy, with a kind of down payment by the boys' parents, when the children were only a few years old. A further payment would be made at the official betrothal ceremonies, sometime when the boy and girl were in their teens; another payment came at the time of marriage, but even that might not be the end. The natives of New Guinea invented installment buying long before western civilization conceived of it, for some wives were not fully paid for before they had grown old.

In many New Guinea tribes — and most of those I visited in the Middle Wahgi — brides were not purchased in early childhood, and there was a little more freedom of choice than in the more rigid primitive societies. The *kanana* was the ceremony through which this partial freedom of choice was exercised; it was also a means to a good deal of lovemaking without serious purpose. The kanana was originally, it seems, a device for enabling young girls and men to get acquainted with each other rather intimately so that they might find mates, not unlike dancing parties and other social events in our society. But it is considerably more colorful and the purpose more evident.

Although they may vary in small detail as to number of couples present and the time of day and the degree of supervision, most kananas are about the same. I saw one held in a long low thatched hut. Down the center several fires burned, giving a soft and flickering light, fires tended and kept alive by youngsters who looked curiously and perhaps enviously at the teen-agers, and a few older men, lined up along the walls.

There were about a dozen couples in the long hut, ranged along both sides, with their feet toward the fires and their backs against the walls. And they were busy with what is called, in pidgin, "turnim head and carry leg." A girl placed both of her legs over the thigh of her escort and he then crossed his other leg over both of hers, a position of some intimacy which allowed for and suggested a good deal of love play between the two partners. But in most cases this did not start until the kanana had been going on for some time and emotions had been aroused. At the outset, couples might confine themselves to "turnim head," which meant putting forehead against forehead, nose against nose, cheek against cheek, and then turning the head slowly from side to side. There was no kissing of lips, but there was almost constant contact between the faces of the two lovers, who, as they became more and more aroused, pressed against each other with increasing force. Sometimes the skin of forehead or nose became so raw that blood flowed, but neither girl nor man seemed to be aware of this.

As the couples pressed their heads together in mounting tension, they closed their eyes and sang little songs that seemed to have no words, although I was told that in some groups there were love songs sung only during the kanana. All I heard was a kind of low crooning and musical sighing.

This sort of thing usually goes on for hours. There may be one or more older women present, as chaperones, but they often get tired and go home before the party is over or pay little attention to what is going on. It is not surprising that an older woman refrains from restricting activities — she recalls her own kananas as one of the few happy times of her life. During the early hours, a man looks in occasionally and youngsters build up the fires. But by midnight the fires have died down, the light is feeble and the onlookers have disappeared. If a couple is really attracted to each other — or rather, if the girl is really attracted to the man — lovemaking that is the equivalent of "petting" begins. And this, in turn, may go on for a long time. Sometimes a couple gets up and goes off somewhere to have intercourse. Often both parties are so exhausted that they cannot go on to that climax even if they want to. (They report this themselves, especially the men.) If the party is a small one and the fires have almost died, a couple may have intercourse on the spot.

New Guinea natives generally approve of sexual promiscuity for girls between betrothal and marriage. Even the fiancé does not object to his prospective bride's having sexual activities with many other men, though she will have nothing to do with him during this period. As the women say, "There is plenty of time for that sort of thing with you after we're married." Both know that sexual fidelity is demanded of a woman after marriage. The only time a fiancé becomes upset is when he finds his betrothed having intercourse with one man time after time. Then he is worried that she may become too attached to him. But if she sleeps with a different man every night he is not at all concerned.

The women are, at least before marriage, the aggressors in all sexual matters. It is always the girl who invites a man to a kanana for "turnim head and carry leg," although she may not do this directly unless they are "going steady." A girl who is attracted to a man — and he may be an older married man if she is more interested in sexual pleasure than in finding a mate — usually tells a friend in the tribe to let the man know she will be waiting for him at the next kanana. And no man ever refuses such an invitiation. He appears, even if he is really more interested in some other woman. If after a short period of "turnim head and carry leg" the girl does not find the man attractive, she merely fails to respond with any warmth, and the session soon ends. She may dismiss him and take on another man. But in many cases, if she is led to believe that he has worked some love sorcery or used some magic potion, she will suddenly become inflamed and succumb to him. Auto-suggestion is a powerful force, and many Wahgi Valley natives still believe in sorcery.

If a couple leaves the party to have intercourse, the girl is still the aggressor throughout the sexual act, according to all reports. If she is aroused sufficiently to indulge in intercourse at all, she will be violent about it, with much biting and scratching. And on the day after a kanana, the man with long fingernail slashes across his skin will be the object of some envious joshing, and he will laugh with pride. There are some older men who, on such occasions, proudly show the scars left by severe bites from girls many years before.

The kanana does serve its original purpose by mating many young men and women who come to know and like each other through such parties. When they have decided that they want to be married, there is the traditional business to be conducted — consultation of parents, haggling over the bride-price, and making the down payment when the price is agreed upon. Then follows the period of the girl's greatest freedom, which may last for several years. By the time the marriage comes around, she may no longer be so enthusiastic about the idea. But the deal has been made and, no matter how much she may resist, her own parents, her tribe, and the groom and his family or tribe will insist that she carry through her part of the bargain, even if it means taking her by force. On such occasions she is no longer the sexual aggressor, and the husband may have to subdue her by repeated raping until she learns that he is her master and owner and that her life of pleasure is ended forever.

In the controlled areas of New Guinea, there is less and less of this sort of thing as the years go by. The girl who has decided that she does not want to marry the man to whom she is betrothed, the man who has paid a considerable amount of shells and pigs and axes for her — such a girl knows that there is now a kiap, the white patrol officer, to whom she can appeal for justice. And the man knows that the kiap will listen to his plea for the return of the bride-price, even if not of the girl herself. Always the families of both parties are involved, for the man's family has really paid the price for the young man's bride, and the bride's family has taken and used most of it.

When he is appealed to by the natives on any matter, the kiap listens and judges. We heard and filmed a trial, held in the open, concerning a girl who did not want to fulfill her obligation to marry a certain man because she had found another she loved and wanted to marry. It was a well-attended hearing, with the kiap, Craig Symons, and his native soldiers and interpreters, plus the girl, her promised husband, her desired husband, and the families and many clan members of each party involved.

I heard some fine oratory, especially from the men; there is nothing more admired among the tribes of New Guinea than resonant and sustained oratory. The kiap heard the girl, the fiancé, the lover, the parents. He asked a few questions. And he made his decision. If the girl's family returned to the fiancé's family the bride-price, she would be freed from her obligation to marry the man she no longer liked. At this, there was a loud wail from the girl's family. *But,* the kiap continued, if the new man whom the girl now wanted to marry wished to have her, he or his family had to pay the same bride-price. At this, there was a great sigh of relief from the girl's family; they would really lose nothing.

Even the family of the newly chosen bridegroom were satisfied, for they had always expected to pay a bride-price on behalf of the young man. The girl was happy. The new lover was happy. The original fiancé looked glum, but for only one person to feel sad in such a situation was the best that could be expected. Thirty years before there might have been several killings and the beginning of an endless tribal feud over this matter.

While it may not be too difficult for an engagement to be broken, divorce is complicated and relatively rare, for after marriage numerous large installments of the bride-price have been paid and distributed among the members of the bride's family or subclan. Wives may run away from their husbands and go back to their parents, but the parents usually make them return to the husband. Even the bride's brother will insist upon her return — and the attachment between brother and sister is far closer than any other in the New Guinea highlands.

Another factor strengthening the pressure to continue a marriage is the strong family or clan feeling, the idea that the welfare of the group is paramount. When a clan member buys a wife, the clan is strengthened because she will tend more gardens, take care of pigs, and have children. Although she is never really accepted as a member of her husband's clan, and never gives it her full loyalty, a wife is a valuable piece of property for the clan to possess. Moreover, in many cases the family or clan has exchanged a woman in order to gain one. Sometimes the exchange of brides is complicated by involving several clans in a multiple deal. If even one of these wives is content with her marriage, untying the complicated knot is impossible.

So reluctant is a clan to give up a woman bought by or for one of its young men that even if the husband is discontented he will turn over his wife to another member of his clan rather than send her back home.

There are, of course, exceptions to this general pattern. There are many happy marriages. Sometimes girls are actually allowed to choose the men they want, especially if they are the daughters of clan leaders, powerful men of authority. And there are some divorces — but perhaps more suicides on the part of wives who, after repeated failures to escape from an unhappy marriage, take death as the only way out.

Then there is the "wandering woman," who has, for any of a variety of reasons, left both husband and her own clan, which would insist upon returning her to her husband. She has thus broken all the ties that are really meaningful to her, and she goes from one group to another, living with one man after another. Such women are, in a sense, prostitutes. And they do not appear to like the life any more than most prostitutes of civilized societies do. They want to find husbands and settle down, and once they have achieved this goal, although it is difficult, they are not looked down upon for once having been wanderers.

It is not the sexual promiscuity of the wandering woman that makes men doubtful about taking her as a wife, for all wives have spent several years of sexual promiscuity before marriage. Men are likely to feel that a wandering woman cannot make a good wife because she, judging by her past, cannot settle down and do the work a wife is supposed to do. She has run away from one husband many times, and has even broken relations with her own clan. She *must* be unstable and unreliable — untamable. So they take her in for a few days or weeks, then pass her along to others. Occasionally, however, a man who needs a wife badly may keep her and, if she does her work well, take her as his wife. In such cases, he may then make a small payment to her brother or father, in which case the woman resumes good relations with her own clan.

There are numerous reasons for a wife's becoming a wandering woman, but one that is worth mentioning is the enmity of an older and earlier wife. According to most investigators — Father Ross is an exception, as will be shown later — most native women in the central highlands dislike polygamy as much as the men like it. Sometimes a new wife is accepted without too much fuss by a number one wife; if she comes from the same clan as the first wife she may even be welcomed warmly, as the two women probably were friends during childhood and the glorious days of the kananas. But more commonly the first wife feels deep resentment and makes life as miserable as possible for the new woman. If she happens to come from a clan that is a longtime enemy of her own group, the resentment is heightened to hatred and perhaps fear. She takes every opportunity, especially when the husband is not around, to scold, nag, berate, insult, and even beat the new wife. She is clever at finding ways of blaming things on the most recent member of the household, so the husband becomes angry, too.

Sometimes the new wife can weather this storm; if not, she is likely to run away to her own family, only to be sent back by them to the husband, who has paid a price which would be difficult to return. If the situation remains unbearable, the woman has only two ways out — suicide or becoming a wandering woman.

I was surprised to hear suicide mentioned at all, as I had rarely encountered it among the primitive tribes I lived with in Africa and South America. But from Father Schaefer and others I learned that until recent years suicide had been not uncommon, especially among women. A wife badly abused by her husband might throw herself in the river. A girl forced into a marriage she did not want might hang herself. Witches committed suicide by being forced or driven with spears to do so. (And it is strange to think that witches are always women; men with supposedly supernatural powers become respected medicine men.)

I was assured that suicides had diminished drastically since the coming of the white man. Much of this improvement has no doubt resulted from the fact that the kiap is usually on hand, in controlled areas, to settle disputes fairly. Just as the highlands natives are learning, with difficulty, that taking other lives is not right, so they are also learning that taking one's own life is taboo.

The work of missionaries, of various denominations, contributes strongly to the inculcation of such new ideas as the sanctity of life and the worth of the individual. But the results of some Christian teaching are sometimes unpredictable — and quite the reverse of the missionaries' intention. For example, missions of all faiths try to get the natives to abandon polygamy and put aside all but one wife. (This is not divorce, in the eyes of most missionaries, because there was never true Christian marriage.) Sometimes, however, a chief may throw out *all* his wives and take a new one. But even if he only dismisses three out of his four mates, there may be a serious problem about the fate of these discarded women. Some may be so old as to find it impossible to get another husband, and in any event there is considerable reluctance among the male natives to marry a woman who has been cast off by another man, no matter what the reason.

Some of the rejected wives may find husbands, since no bride-price need be paid, and men thus gain more wives at no cost. But then polygamy is continued and even increased, among men who might not otherwise be able to afford more than one wife. And prostitution is increased, as the women without men turn to that trade in order to gain a livelihood. I was told that a number of the wandering women in the highlands were once wives who had been put aside by men who had been convinced of the sinfulness of polygamy.

At Minj, in the middle Wahgi, I showed my New Guinea films to natives for the first time. This was during my second expedition, in 1959, when I had brought along several thousand feet of film from my first trip. I had shown them in Australia, on the way in, and in Moresby. A large group of patrol officers and district officers gathered in Goroka to look at them, and their comments were heartening and helpful.

At Minj, Craig Symons, the patrol officer, thought it would be interesting to show the films to the natives and get their reactions. So he arranged for a projector to be flown down from Goroka, and his native police sent out word that pictures would be shown that evening.

The natives began to gather early — men, women, and children. I do not believe that many of them had any idea what they were about to witness. Some of them knew about still pictures, of course, but I was curious to see their reaction to lifelike motion, especially since they might recognize themselves. (It was a good thing that I had not heard at that time about the violent and almost disastrous reaction of natives in Dutch New Guinea when they saw pictures of men who had been killed since the filming.)

We took from Symons's house the biggest white sheet we could find and stretched it over one outside wall to serve as a screen. There was a generator for electric current, and a long extension leading to the projector. As it became dark Symons explained what was going to happen, reminded the people that I had visited them the year before. He also told them that I had visited many other places in New Guinea, and had taken pictures of many other tribes.

There was no sound track on my film at that time, so I usually made a running commentary when I showed it. For this screening, however, I decided to keep my words to a minimum, saying only enough to explain what and where we were in the film. This would allow time for an interpreter to translate my words into pidgin and, most important, give periods of silence during which I hoped to gain some idea of my audience's reaction. Craig Symons stood beside me so that he could translate and pass on to me any pertinent comments he might overhear.

The film at that time opened with some shots of the planes that took me to Australia and then on to New Guinea. The natives were not very interested as they saw airplanes all the time. But the moment the screen showed actual shots, in full color, of natives, there was immediate and obvious response. As might be expected, the sequences that I had taken in and around Minj were favorites. They cried out and laughed and clapped their hands. They pointed and called to one another, "There you are! There you are!" They were delighted with the prominent part played by Danga, considered one of their own.

The sequences I had taken at Mt. Hagen brought a different reaction entirely. Here I got comments chiefly from the old men, who had fought the Hagen tribes in many battles before the coming of the white man. There were derisive, taunting cries, but without anger in them. Almost twenty years of comparative peace with Hagen, and the sharing of a road, had taken the fight out of even the old warriors. The young men did not even cry out. Perhaps some of their best friends were Hagen men — or girls.

I was startled when a moan, a kind of groan of fear, swelled up from the audience. They were looking at the dance of the mud-men of the Asara Valley, too far away for any of them to have seen or heard of this strange group. The huge clay heads, distorted and painted, made them afraid. They kept muttering about evil spirits, Symons told me and many turned their heads aside, refusing to look.

Then came shots of several sing-sings in different parts of New

Guinea. The women of the audience were particularly delighted with one rather long sequence of a Hagen girl being painted and decorated for the festival. They giggled and laughed and exclaimed admiringly over the beautiful headdress that was finally put on the girl's head. And when the crowds of dancers came on the screen, moving in perfect rhythm and beating their small drums, the people in the audience began to sway in time to the dancing, even though they could hear no music or drums.

It was one of the most successful showings my film ever had.

Mount Hagen, over twelve thousand feet high, stands as a sentinel at the western end of the Wahgi Valley. I had good luck at Mt. Hagen for soon after my arrival I found that a really big sing-sing was planned, had indeed been planned for months, and would take place while I was there with my cameraman. People from friendly tribes all around — and there were more of them after the road went through — were coming in for a gigantic feast and for dancing. With the co-operation of the district officer and the headmen of the Hagen tribes, I would be able to film all that went on in daylight. The only thing for me to do was to pray for clear skies and good light.

I looked over the dancing park that was to be the focal point of the sing-sing. It was beautiful, more formal than similar parks I had seen in other parts of the valley, with tall casuarina trees lining it on both sides in exact and even rows, and with plantings of smaller, flowering shrubs between the trees. The open space was large enough so that the trees would not cut off much light from the sun, *if* there was any sun.

There was an air of excitement throughout the area, of course. Men were chopping wood for the fires, and more were bringing wood down from the mountains and from far away. "The lack of firewood is one of our great probelms," Father Ross told me in one of our many talks at Mt. Hagen. And I could see that it was a serious problem for the natives planning the sing-sing. Gathering enough wood to cook a few hundred pigs, along with the pyramids of sweet potatoes and other vegetables, was a big problem.

We were able to film a good deal before the sing-sing began, for the process of making up and decorating oneself for such an occasion takes many hours. Some shots of a girl being decorated were particularly good, and showed how an ordinary creature could be transformed into something vibrant and colorful. Heavy thick pigments were applied to face, neck, and arms in patterns of red, yellow, and black and perhaps other colors I did not notice. I do know that there was a definite pattern, rather than a hit-and-miss application of color, for there were triangles, squares, and other symmetrical designs. Even the girl's eyelids were coated, so heavily that she could barely keep her eyes open.

She had possum-fur armlets and wristlets, feathers through the septum in her nose, earrings, necklaces, and shells hanging from her neck. But the *pièce de résistance* was her headdress, made of the plumes of many cassowaries and birds of paradise, a towering structure that waved in the slightest breeze, undulated when she walked.

Hundreds of girls and thousands of men were being made up in similar fashion. I saw men in full regalia applying headdresses to men who were only three-quarters dressed for the occasion. And the men's paints and plumes were even more spectacular then the women's, as might be expected in a society so close to nature. The plumes were more plentiful, more brilliantly colored, and taller. The septum pieces were longer; one was made of the thin tail feathers of the King of Saxony bird of paradise, one of the rarest of these rare birds.

The drums were exciting — scores of them, mostly the small drums shaped like hourglasses, all with different pitches. The pitch was not important, the beat was what counted. It was steady, and it seemed to intoxicate the first men who came into the dancing park. The different groups of dancers formed outside the dancing park, waiting for their entrances. When one group had reached the end of the park, another one entered. They usually came four abreast, with some space between each man in the row. My cameraman and I were both trying to be in several places at once, for the light was perfect and the colors and movements spectacular.

As one group came into the park with a particularly spirited beat of the drums, I decided that it would be a good a idea if I could film them coming straight at me. I ran into the middle of the park and aimed my camera at the column of dancers coming toward me. It was a superb shot, and I was so pleased with what I was getting that I did not even stop to wonder if my close-up position would bother the dancers.

But they danced past me without seeming to notice, two men on my right, two men on my left. Although I did not upset the dancers, there was one old diehard who became incensed. I did not see him at first, but they told me later that from the moment he spotted me among the dancers, he started shouting angrily and waving his arms in one of which was a beautiful Hagen axe. In the midst of the danc-ers I could neither hear nor see him.

Then he started for me; I caught a glimpse of him as I took the camera away from my eye for a moment to look at the next group coming in. He was on the far side, near the end of the park where the dancers came in, but he started diagonally across towards me, bran-dishing that big axe and looking as if he meant business. He was about thirty feet from me when I decided to get out of there. And at that moment the oncoming dancers cut him off. He tried to scurry around the end of the group, but by that time I had lost myself in the crowd on the other side.

The sing-sing went on for days, and for some time the light was so good that we got adequate coverage. But the sky clouded over some-what, and at the same time I began to get physically sick of the sight and smell of pigs being killed. When I found I could get a little plane to Wabag, about an hour and a half's flight west of Mt. Hagen, I de-cided to visit it. Since Wabag was over the mountains in the next val-ley it might offer some different kinds of people and sights from the Wahgi Valley. It did, as I discovered even in the short time I was there.

Chief among them were the Wigmen, so called because of their truly amazing, spectacular hairdos. They are tough, good-looking men, somewhat shorter than the natives of Mt. Hagen, and they lack the dignity and poise of those fine specimens. The wigs make up for a good deal of this, however. They are large dome-shaped wigs, made carefully of their own hair-clippings, plus clippings from their wives, children, and even from the corpses of dead relatives or friends. The clippings are very carefully and laboriously poked and punched into a kind of felt, then shaped into semicircular wigs that are sometimes two feet across.

While at Wabag, I went on a little further to a village called Lia-gam, where the people were much the same. But in the areas surround-ing Wabag the wigs take different shapes and forms. In one tribe they are made like big thick horns spreading out sideways from the head. In another, they are diamond-shaped.

Back at Mt. Hagen I had a chance to talk at some length with Father Ross, who has been at the Mt. Hagen Mission since 1934, shortly after Mick Leahy discovered the valley.

"Yes, the natives here are changing rapidly," Father Ross said. "For example, just think what the introduction of steel axes has meant. A man can cut down a tree in one-tenth the time it used to take him with a stone axe. He can now do in three months what used to be a year's work. What does he do with the rest of his time, especially since there are no wars any more? That has been one of the problems, but the making of the road helped, giving many men work to do. The introduction of new crops has been another boon to them. But at the same time the population has trebled since I came here, as is bound to happen when medicines and medical men are around, when we have a little hospital as we do now, when wars and at least a good deal of the murdering has stopped.

"To show you how modern we are here," Father Ross continued, "we have been suffering from inflation — that is, the young men of this area have been suffering. You see, the bride-price had increased about ten times since I came here. That means that only the rich men, who already have several wives anyway, can afford to buy new ones.

"This makes for a great deal of unhappiness, chiefly among the young men, but also among the girls, many of whom cannot find husbands and who cannot marry the young men to whom they may be attracted. The situation encourages prostitution, of course, because there are so many unmarried girls and young men around."

There were so many complaints that finally the district commissioner had to call a meeting, although ordinarily he kept entirely out of such tribal matters. Thousands of people attended and expressed themselves volubly and at length. The most powerful men — who were also the richest — wanted to keep things just as they were, so they could continue to have the pick of the crop of young beauties, without much competition from younger and more attractive men. But the great majority of the people was against them, and a new scale of prices for brides was finally set up. It was a revolutionary action, and everyone knew it. But the results were good. Inflationary spirals were halted.

Among the scores of fascinating things Father Ross told me about Mt. Hagen life, one gave me a different attitude toward polygamy. Almost everyone I had talked to said that native women did not like the institution at all, but Father Ross said just the opposite. I suspect that most missionaries and even some government officials allow their wishes to control their thinking sometimes, but Father Ross, while a most devout man, is a realist.

"I've never seen the different wives of a man acting jealous of each other," he said. "Each wife has her own pigs, her own gardens to tend. They rotate the job of cooking and other tasks. If a woman were the only wife she would be at her husband's beck and call all of the time and would have much more work to do. The women around here definitely prefer polygamy."

At Mt. Hagen, and one or two other places in New Guinea, I had seen women nursing piglets at the breast. I had taken pictures of this, just as on previous expeditions I had filmed a Jivaro woman nursing a puppy, an African woman nursing a lion cub. I knew that all over the world primitive women nursed baby animals whose mothers had died. But this sort of thing was most common in New Guinea, because the pig was such a highly prized creature. Father Ross added to my knowledge about this custom.

"Many times during services in my church," he told me, "I have seen women take piglets from a basket and start to nurse them. I know of one woman who refused to let her husband kill a pig that she had nursed when it was little. The most extreme case, however, was that of a mother of twins. While she was nursing them, a mother sow belonging to her was killed, leaving one nursing piglet behind. The woman killed one of her own babies so she could nurse the piglet along with her remaining child.

I have corresponded with Father Ross regularly since my visits to New Guinea, and from his letters I know that I really did just get in under the wire in my search for the primitive there. In 1963 he wrote me about the great Mount Hagen Agricultural Show held in May of that year. Such a thing would have been inconceivable just four years before, at the time of my second New Guinea expedition, for at that time pigs and sweet potatoes were still the chief agricultural products of the natives. Government officials and the few white settlers had introduced coffee and other crops, but only a few natives were trying to grow them. By 1963, however, there were scores of products on display, and seventy-five thousand natives attended the show, some from hundreds of miles away. When I was there, you couldn't have found seventy-five thousand natives that would not fight with each other, yet most of these visitors were housed together in specially built dormitories about two thousand feet long, beside the main road into Hagen. The governor-general of Australia was there, and the American ambassador. Dan Leahy was the honored sponsor and made the speech opening the show.

In December, 1963, Father Ross wrote me of various happenings in his area. He told of the recent death of the paramount chief in the Hagen area. Although he had attended Father Ross's church for over twenty years, he did not become converted until shortly before his death. At that time he freed his eight wives. When he died the Australian radio broadcast a eulogy and the prime minister sent a telegram of condolence to the natives.

"What may be the last of the big feasts is being held right now," Father Ross wrote. "Over a thousand pigs were killed. Sing-sings and dances are still going on. Some ten thousand natives were involved in the big barbecue and picnic."

But he was wrong about the last of the big sings-sings. Only three months later he wrote me:

A few days after Christmas the local natives killed 2430 pigs. At this time they are hard to understand; they have trucks, tractors and jeeps; have coffee holdings and money in the bank; want all their kids put into school from an early age; have their own bar and beer garden; many run their own trade stores; are now voting for a member to represent them in the House of Assembly at Port Moresby; are wearing more and more European clothes; buy a lot of bread, sugar, rice, tea, milk, in local stores . . . and yet they can turn primitive overnight and stage an old-time sing-sing where pig grease and shells and feathers, red paint and blue paint, make them unrecognizable even to their best friends, and put on a feast where 15,000 pounds of pork turns into a present for visiting friends and relatives. Independence? Some day, but we hope not before 25 years. It is only 25 years since these highlanders climbed out of the trees to tolerate the presence of strange white people who must have come out of the sky. You saw it all when you were here, yet the tempo of so-called progress has been stepped up to a furious pace, and you would be amazed to see Mt. Hagen now.

Back in 1958, I left Mt. Hagen to fly to Madang, on the north coast, and from there took a single-engined plane to the little airstrip at

Aiome. I wanted to see the pygmies who lived near there. Ever since my African expeditions, when I lived with the Pygmies of the Ituri Forest for long periods and came to like them so much, I had been interested in small people anywhere. Scientists have set up standards by which they determine whether to apply the term "pygmy" or even "dwarf people" to any group. The Kukukukus, for example, are not considered to be either, although they average little more than five feet in height. But I knew that the natives near Aiome were no taller than the Ituri Pygmies — around four feet nine — so to me they were pygmies and I wanted to see them.

I was unable to go into the country in which they lived. For one thing, it was so mountainous that clambering up the precipitous sides of their homeland was almost impossible. Father Martin Gusinde, an American anthropologist, has said that the Alps are a smooth, broad avenue compared to the country inhabited by the Aiome pygmies.

Aside from the ruggedness of the terrain, however, the area was not under complete control. I thought that I might get permission to accompany a government patrol, but there was no patrol going in at the time. So I had to be content with a visit to Aiome itself, a post on the edge of the Schrader Mountains, where some pygmies had come down for a visit. This was not much, but it was better than nothing.

At Aiome, I met Professor R. Ruggles Gates of London and his charming wife. He was engaged in a study of the "dwarf people," as he preferred to call them, reserving the term "pygmy" for the inhabitants of the Ituri Forest. Since he had also studied these people, my favorites among primitives, we immediately found a great deal to talk about. Having the Aiome natives come down from their mountain homes — sometimes a march of three days — worked out satisfactorily for the professor, since he was interested primarily in measurements of heights, heads and such. But in such circumstances I could not really get to know them as I wished.

They were attractive, however, on first meeting. I thought they were stockier and better muscled than the Ituri Pygmies, probably from climbing up and down those steep mountain slopes. They looked rather dour to me, without the impishness of my Ituri friends, but this may have been because they were visiting the area of the taller natives, whose ancestors had driven *their* ancestors up into the inaccessible mountains.

We took many pictures of them, adorned with the bright yellow leaves of the croton bush, standing and posing helpfully, which was very nice, but nothing for a moving-picture camera. Finally we went outside the village some distance, where the land began to climb up toward the mountains in a series of small precipices. Here we got some good shots of them clambering up the hills, scooting along ledges, and swarming up cliffs without apparent difficulty. They seemed to enjoy this activity, and laughed, talked to each other, smiled at me as they passed my camera. This was more like home to them — which was exactly what I wanted to film.

Father Gusinde, who was able to go up into the real pygmy country for a while, found these small people amazingly happy and contented considering the terrible difficulties of living in the mountains where food was scarce. He learned that they were not at all warlike, and committed few if any murders. In the end, he concluded that their pleasant temperament came from one of the principal items in their diet, a very large beetle and its larvae. These insects, he said, contained a large amount of Vitamin T, which produces a generally agreeable feeling. If this theory is substantiated, it might be a good idea to have this vitamin introduced to the people of the civilized world.

Before leaving Australian New Guinea, I must mention the Cargo Cult. This strange phenomenon has occurred in several places in Oceania, but it is more common in New Guinea than anywhere else. This is understandable when one realizes that the Cargo Cult is a reaction to the sudden impact of modern civilization on Stone Age peoples. And nowhere has this confrontation been more sudden, affecting larger numbers of people, than in New Guinea.

There are certain requisites for the development of Cargo Cult ideas. First, primitive people must believe in sorcery, the existence of ever-present good and evil spirits, and the great power of their ancestors. Second, they must be ignorant of the civilized world, its goods, how they are made and shipped and sold and bought.

When the natives of New Guinea first saw white men they believed them to be supernatural and the planes that brought them to be supernatural birds. Before long, they knew that neither was supernatural, of course. But white men seemed to come from some place different from this world as the natives knew it. From this far-off place came more shells than they had ever seen before, axes sharper and longer-lasting than any they could conceive of, cloth finer than the finest bark cloth, foods different from anything they had ever tasted, salt in such profusion as they had never dreamed of, and weapons which roared and killed. The men who brought all these things talked in a strange tongue, and wrote things down on paper, considered by many to be an act of witchcraft. They had boxes from which talk and music came, and they spoke into little round things to their friends far, far away. One could go on ad infinitum listing the everyday actions of civilized men which could only seem miraculous to the natives of New Guinea.

After enjoying some of the products of civilization, some natives wanted more and more. Fear and awe sometimes changed to envy. Why shouldn't *they* have such things? With this situation, the ground work was laid for the growth of a Cargo Cult movement. Just what actually starts it off in a particular area is hard to determine. Perhaps some spell of drought, or too much rain, that has ruined the sweet potato crops; sickness that has wiped out many pigs or people; or anything that has brought hardship of some kind. If in such a situation there is an ambitious leader, a demagogue like Kamindo, he can turn dissatisfaction into a mystical movement that reaches amazing proportions.

The movement may sometimes be directed against the white people, in thought and theory if not in action. The tale is told that all these wonderful goods — cargo — really belong to the ancestors of the natives. But the white men stole them while they were being shipped to New Guinea. The ancestors' spirits are angry and soon they will put a stop to the stealing, will see that the cargo reaches the people for whom it is intended. Then the natives will have all the things the white men have, and will *be* like the white men themselves. The leader of the movement urges everyone to prepare for the great day. There is no use laboring in the gardens, for the cargo will have mountains of huge sweet potatoes. No use tending the pigs or saving them for a festival — the cargo will bring a profusion of pigs, bigger and fatter then any ever seen.

In a tribe where the Cargo Cult idea has taken hold, almost all work stops. Men walk around with sticks supposed to resemble the guns of the white men and their police. Poles are set up on tops of houses, with vine "wires" extending from then, to represent radio antennae. Men sit down at improvised desks and pretend to read and write all day. And everyone waits for the Great Day when the cargo will arrive.

If the tribe lives inland, the cargo is expected to arrive in a fleet of big airplanes. If it lives on the sea, the cargo will come by ship, so a big wharf may be built out into the water to receive it.

In some cases the white man is not the villain of the piece. The natives merely believe that at some specific time in the near future their ancestors and the good spirits will bring to them all the wonderful things of the white man's world. Or things of their own world, but far, far superior to anything they know. The natives may cut down their banana trees, for instance, because the cargo will contain much larger trees producing much better bananas. This sort of thing is one of the saddest results of the Cargo Cult — the actual destruction of food and pigs, the neglect of gardens and all other work. Sometimes terrible hardship is created before the natives finally realize, as they must, that the cargo is *not* going to arrive. It usually takes a long time for them to believe this. They kept clinging to the dream weeks after the announced Great Day.

What happens? The idea just peters out, slowly and painfully, and the tribe that has been seized by this hallucination gradually goes back to its old life, its old ways, its old thoughts — but under worse difficulties than they ever experienced before.

What can be done to stop Cargo Cult? Government officials have gone so far as to take the leaders of a cargo movement to Australia, to show them factories where goods are made, to stores where people pay money to buy these goods. But to a people unused to a money economy, the handing over of a piece of paper for something is not buying and selling as the natives know it. It is just one more magical act. So these efforts have not been very convincing. It will take time and patience and education — education in the workings of the civilized world. That is a slow process.

As New Guinea natives received more and more of the gadgets and benefits of western civilization, the Cargo Cult movements died down. But the election of 1964 for a genuine House of Assembly — a major step toward independence — revived Cargo Cult ideas all over New Guinea. Father J. Nilles, a missionary at Mingende in the Wahgi Valley, wrote me just before the election, "The striving for independence becomes more and more pressing, though the average native does not know what it actually means. Strange how the election for the parliamentary representation has inflamed anew the blaze of old Cargo Cult ideas! When we have a parliament, they fancy, then their ancestors will finally send us the long awaited cargo, and we shall like like Europeans in wealth and prosperity."

The elections had other strange results, too. As the *New York Times* reported on August 23, 1964, some months after the election: "Officials are building a special jail on New Hanover Island in New Guinea to contain 'President Johnson' cultists. Since June, administration officers, aided by armed police, have been steadily arresting islanders who refuse to pay taxes. Instead, they want to use the money to buy President Johnson as a ruler for their tiny island. The cult started during the territory's first general election in February, when about 2000 of the island's 7000 population refused to vote for the official candidates and attempted to write in Mr. Johnson's name. When they were prevented from doing so, they withheld the tax money."

The election of 1964 was a fantastic thing. In 1962 a United Nations mission had recommended two actions for New Guinea — a thorough economic survey to plan development of the country with the help of the World Bank, and the election of a genuine parliament. While Australia held northeastern New Guinea under a United Nations mandate, the southern part, Papua, was an outright colony, but both were administered together so the United Nations recommendation applied to both. In October of 1963, the advisory Legislative Council decided upon elections, to be held by April of 1964, for an Assembly consisting of ten public servants nominated by the Australian administrator, ten elected white residents, and forty-four openly contested seats which, it was assumed, would be filled by natives. The Australian government retained, however, the right to veto.

There had been great pressure for such an election, as a step toward independence. It was part of the worldwide condemnation of all colonialism and the movement toward independence for new nations everywhere. While Australian authorities did not believe that the time was ripe for such elections, they agreed to go ahead with United Nations recommendation. Once committed, they went all out to make the elections as truly representative of the natives' desires as possible. Starting in May, 1963, more than four hundred government patrols went out to put together a voter roll of 1,030,000 natives, most of whom were completely illiterate, and who spoke, all told, more than seven hundred dialects. The patrols had to explain the meanings of such essential words as "election," "legislative assembly," and even "New Guinea." They used filmstrips, tape recorders, and loudspeakers in their educational work, and after a few months many natives began to understand what it was all about.

Enemy tribes agreed on a month's truce at the time of the election to allow safe movement to ballot boxes, all of which were within one day's walk of every voting native. Local councils held elections to decide on their candidates for the Assembly, and in most areas there were rival candidates. More than a million natives voted, using cards with pictures of the candidates since they could not read. Surprisingly, six of the openly contested seats were won by white residents, among them Ian Downs, against native leaders. Downs, incidentally, has long believed that New Guinea-Papua should be made a state in the Australian Commonwealth and that all natives become Australian citizens.

Many changes have come about as a result of the election. Among other things, the Department of Native Affairs has ceased to exist, as those affairs are now the natives' affairs. Among the native members of the Assembly, and they are in the majority, some press for immediate independence while others want statehood, and still others want independence, but after a while. Most white men are agreeable to the idea of independence, but after about twenty-five more years. While the natives have made almost unbelievable strides in a quarter of a century, it takes longer than that to leave primitivism behind. There are trained native medical assistants, for example, who still believe that certain illnesses and deaths are caused by sorcery. There are natives attending schools who won't eat the food when it is prepared by members of a tribe that was once hostile. They fear poisoning.

As in the Congo, there is little sense of nationalism, almost no awareness of what a nation means. Chief loyalties are to tribes rather than to any vague concept of "New Guinea." Although I have much admiration for the intelligence and adaptability of the New Guinea natives, I know that if independence were granted them within the next few years, they would go through a period of anarchy and civil war that could become more chaotic than that of the Congo.

4

West Irian

ABOUT four hundred miles west of the Wahgi Valley, in the towering mountains of what was Dutch New Guinea and is now Indonesian West Irian, lies another "hidden" valley, discovered even more recently than the Wahgi and far less influenced by civilization. Somewhat smaller than its counterpart in northeastern New Guinea — it is ten miles wide by forty miles long — the Grand Valley of the Baliem contains about sixty thousand Stone Age inhabitants, many of whom have not, to this day, seen a white man.

On my second expedition to New Guinea, in 1959, I was determined to see the Baliem and its people. But it was not an easy place to reach. After making the necessary arrangements, I flew to Hollandia, the capital of the then Dutch colony. But despite the cooperation of officials there, I was unable to fly to the "hidden" valley in the two-engined plane that had been arranged for. Once I found myself in the little Cessna 180 of the Missionary Aviation Service, I began to figure out why the larger plane had been "unable to take off," as officials explained it to me. After a short period of pleasant flying on the 150-mile trip, I saw looming ahead jagged mountain peaks 1600 feet high. As we approached they disappeared one by one in the gathering clouds hiding the pass through which we must fly. I became tense but the pilot seemed relaxed.

I crossed my fingers and watched the first wisps of cloud streak by the windows of the plane. We flew steadily ahead, into brief squalls of rain, into thicker clouds. But there was still some visibility. We could still see, though vaguely, the mountain on either side.

"Maybe we'll make it," the pilot said. "Of course, we can always turn back if it looks too bad. That is, if it hasn't closed in behind us."

It did not help my confidence to recall, at that moment, that only three years before, A. J. Lewis, pilot of a plane for the Christian and Missionary Alliance, had crashed into a mountainside at more than ten thousand feet and been killed. The theory was that *he* had decided to turn back but everything had closed in behind him.

Between the pilot's skill and my crossed fingers we made it through a narrow mountain pass at a height of about nine thousand feet. Suddenly the Grand Valley of the Baliem lay clear as crystal below us, a long, narrow corridor between steeply slanting mountains. A broad river snaked its way through the valley floor.

"Here is something you might like to see," the pilot said, veering a bit to one side. "If you look below and to the left in a minute or two you will see the wreckage of the DC-3 that crashed back in 1945, near the end of the war. You remember — the attractive WAC who had been to Shangri-La."

I recalled. Near the end of World War II, some American servicemen and women had gone off on a sight-seeing flight out of Hollandia over the exciting "hidden" valley. The plane crashed against a mountain and twenty-one were killed. Three survived, a lieutenant, a sergeant, and a WAC corporal, but they were badly injured. They were too high in the mountains to encounter any natives, but undoubtedly hundreds of men, women, and children in the valley below had seen the plane, heard it crash, and caught a glimpse of the flames from it. And it is reasonable to assume that those natives were frightened, that they considered the whole incident a supernatural event of the greatest magnitude.

The three survivors of the crash knew little about primitive men. So they were fearful of meeting bloodthirsty savages, probably cannibals, as they made their way slowly down the mountain looking for a clearing where search planes might spot them. After two days they met their savages — a hundred men armed with stone axes, long spears, bows and arrows. There were no women or children around, a sure sign that the men were prepared for battle.

This is the kind of situation that has always fascinated me — and I have been through it a number of times, without the tragedy of a plane crash and the death of friends — the sudden, unexpected, unplanned meeting of people from the twentieth century A.D. with those living as if in the eightieth (or more) century B.C. On both sides, they are human beings; only the civilized men are absolutely certain of this fact, but they are filled with bits of knowledge and tall tales about primitive savages, and the savages themselves are full of superstitions about returning ancestors, gods, and evil spirits.

In a confrontation such as this, there is always that "moment of truth" when neither side knows what will happen. In this case, the three crash survivors showed that they were unarmed and they smiled, smiled, smiled until the smiles seemed frozen on their faces. Then the native who was obviously the leader of the group of warriors smiled, too, and the tension ended. In a short while the three white people realized that the savages had been just as frightened as they had. The natives brought food and showed endless curiosity but never animosity, even when planes appeared and dropped supplies, shells for trading with the natives, and finally medical corspmen to aid the injured three. It was six weeks before they were well enough to travel out of what by that time had come to be known as Shangri-La in the newspapers of the world.

Their method of departure was unusual and spectacular, even by modern standards; to the natives it certainly must have made the whole incident even more supernatural. A large glider towed by a C-47 plane cut loose and landed gracefully in the clearing. Half an hour later the C-47 swooped low, caught the towrope of the glider, and snatched it off the ground, scraping the treetops as it gained altitude. Before that, there had been much wailing among the natives at the news that their friends were to leave them, and not a few tears were shed by the three Americans who realized, as Corporal Margaret Hastings put it, that they were leaving "some of the best and kindest friends I would ever have." They had become particularly fond of the chief, whom they called "Pete."

When these same natives next saw white men, many years later, they were violently angry and aggressive. It was eventually learned that after the rescue of the DC-3's survivors, an epidemic had killed most of the clan's pigs. The sickness was attributed to white people and the metal of their airplane.

Circling around the wreck we flew on, and soon began to see the amazing patterns of gardens and villages that cover the Baliem Valley.

On either side of the river and its many tributaries, we saw acres upon acres of neat, small garden plots. Some were edged with stone walls or wooden fences, but most were lined and intersected by ditches, straight or curved according to the contour of the land — ditches used for drainage, sometimes for irrigation, and always to keep out the pigs. As the plane lost altitude and we dropped closer to the valley floor, we saw that many of the small plots were in cultivation, as carefully tended as any gardens in the world. Others, grouped together, were overgrown, being allowed to lie fallow for a number of years to restore the soil.

Specialists who know more about these things than I do have told me that the agricultural attainments of the Stone Age people of the Baliem are most impressive, showing an understanding of soil erosion and depletion that is remarkable in such a primitive group. My admiration was the more profound knowing that these hundreds of acres — and more hundreds that I could not see — had been cleared of forest growth with nothing more than stone adzes; and that the garden plots and deep ditches had been prepared with long, pointed wooden digging sticks, the only agricultural tool of the Baliem.

The government airstrip at which I landed, large enough to take two-engined planes, had been completed only the year before my visit, although some missionary stations had for years had small strips for single-engined craft. The Dutch district officer, Gonsalves, who greeted me there, had arrived in the valley just when the long strip was completed.

"This airstrip has, in more ways than one, been the start of our work here," Gonsalves said. "Not just for getting men and supplies into the valley, but for our biggest job — bringing peace to the warring factions. You see, we established the airstrip as a kind of sanctuary, a sacred ground on which no fighting or killing could take place. And the natives learned quickly — most of them — that the airstrip and the land near it are off limits. They can come here, but they cannot fight here. It makes sense to them, because the airstrip is needed to bring in supplies, including shells and other goods they want in exchange for food and labor."

Gonsalves talked to me about the causes of the never-ending warfare. "There are many reasons, of course. War is the greatest glory, and a man is not really a man, in his own eyes or anyone's else's, until he has killed another man. Killing seems to be a necessity of their society, and there must be some drastic changes in their social structure, their fundamental beliefs, before it can be stopped. Most of the fighting is over pigs or women, and is perpetuated by the need for revenge.

"The groups live too close together here," the district officer continued. "There is a big population in this small valley, and just about every inch of good ground is cultivated. There is very little space for a no-man's-land between feuding groups. Then, too, there are clans living up in the hills and on the mountain slopes where there is little cultivable land and living conditions are hard. They make raids on those lower down, to steal pigs and food and women. The river people have to retaliate, and so it goes on and on."

Gonsalves explained that there were really two kinds of warfare. "In the more formal kind of war, there are long preparations on both sides, and big armies are gathered. Some restless braves from one group will go to the edge of their territory and shout until some of the enemy people hear them. This is likely to be across a gully, which serves as a good boundary between the groups. The first warriors will announce that they want to have a battle in, say, three days, and the others agree. The warriors on both sides paint themselves and dress in their best finery to march out on the appointed day. It is rare that all the men in both armies fight at once. One contingent will rush down into the gully shouting and brandishing weapons. A crowd from the opposing side will rush down to attack them. Those remaining on the ridges yell encouragement to their fellows and insults at the enemy. After a skirmish, there is a withdrawal, then another attack, and so on. Actually, very few people are killed in this kind of war. It is more like a game with rules. Often when just one warrior is killed, his side is considered defeated and will probably withdraw."

The same sort of formalized war is conducted in parts of the Wahgi Valley. There the battle may end when one man is wounded; or combatants may shoot only at the enemies' legs.

"The other kind of war," Gonsalves went on, "is just ambushing, and it kills many more people. For here there are more than armed warriors involved. The ambushed party may consist chiefly of women, children, and old people — it makes no difference to the killers.

"This ambush type of warfare is most difficult to stop. But we're making good progress, faster than I expected. Probably because these

Dani are intelligent people. They are industrious and they work hard. You saw what good gardeners they are. They also have quite a sense of humor. But the main characteristic that helps us is their keenness. They are smart enough to learn quickly that constant warfare is costly and harmful. They probably knew it all along but didn't know how to stop it — like some modern nations I can think of. But now they have had a taste of peace they like it — most of the time.

"They revert to their old ways occasionally, and they often seem unpredictable to us. That's because we don't always understand what makes them angry or fearful or shocked or ashamed. For example, they look upon stealing as an art, an accomplishment of which one should be proud if he is successful. Missionary Gerald Rose says they can steal the cream out of your coffee if you don't stir it quickly. The unknown frightens them — and there is much that is unknown to them. Like the rest of us, they want to find an explanation for everything, but they have no idea of what causes sickness or death — except death in war — and they often find quite erroneous and, for us, dangerous explanations. I'm sure they often find us just as unpredictable as we find them."

I said something about how dangerous and strenuous his life must be, and Gonsalves agreed. "But that's all right," he added. "The Baliem Valley is the most wonderful place in all of Dutch New Guinea — or the whole world." I often wonder what has happened to him. He left his favorite spot even before the Indonesians came in.

The largest and strongest group in the valley was led by a chief named Ukumhearik, with the power of life and death over about ten thousand Dani in the valley. I heard a good deal about him from Gonsalves.

"How does it happen," I asked Gonsalves, "that this man has such power? You've told me about other powerful chiefs, but you speak of Ukumhearik in a different way, in a different tone of voice."

"You're right," he said. "There is a difference. There are others in the valley, of lesser stature, but still of great power and influence. But Ukumhearik is above all these in every way. He is a big man, taller than the average. He is a strong man physically. In his day — he is now five or six years past his prime — he was a great warrior, fearless, high-spirited, indomitable. But the big difference is probably Ukumhearik's intelligence — a curious and eager intelligence. But no, it's not just that. There is a force of personality within the man that is immediately dominating."

"Is he as awe-inspiring as all that?" I asked.

"Not most of the time," Gonsalves said. "But when he is aroused there is no man more imposing. Normally he is friendly; he smiles, he jokes, he is gracious and polite. He is usually the most reasonable of men, far more reasonable than any other chiefs here. His anger — well, that is something awesome and frightening, indeed."

Ukumhearik, I gathered, had overwhelming self-confidence. He was the chief, and he knew that he was worthy to be chief. He was convinced that he was superior to the government officials and to the missionaries. He accepted them and helped them. Certainly the missionaries could not have been there without his help and permission, and the government would not have followed. But he was helpful not out of fear like most chiefs. Ukumhearik felt fear of nothing, in this world or the next. He really acknowledged the authority of no one over him and his people. He was told that his land was Dutch —and he just smiled. He was a realist, and he took care of his people, with vigor and with justice as he saw it.

Ukumhearik was flown to Hollandia to see what a European town was like. He visited the governor's house, and was dignified and gracious the whole time. But when he saw the picture of the queen of the Netherlands and learned that *she* was the ruler of the great governor-general, he had a quizzical expression on his face. Could such a thing have happened in his land? He went back to the Baliem and carried on in his old ways.

Not entirely. He liked the steel axes for his people, the medical care, the bringing of peace — except when *he* wanted to fight. He was smart enough to know that it would be a long time before more white men came into the valley, or at least into a good part of it, unless he agreed to their coming. He could drive every white man out in a few days, if he wanted. He didn't do it. But it was *his* decision.

"I've told Ukumhearik about your visit," Gonzales told me, "and he is looking forward to meeting you. You'll find him and his people cooperative about filming. But they do not dress and decorate themselves flamboyantly, as so many primitive people do. You may be surprised, however, when you meet Ukumhearik, for he dresses more simply than any of his subchiefs. In most of the valley, the sure sign of a chief — at least on important occasions — is a big white shell on the chest. Most of the time Ukumhearik doesn't bother with it, although he has plenty of shells. And where lesser chiefs put a dozen feathers on their heads, he wears just a single, small feather." Ukumhearik didn't need the usual trappings of a chief to prove he was chief, any more than Kavagl did. "His personality," said Gonsalves, "is more than any decoration or badge of office."

Gonsalves told me that I would meet Ukumhearik under particularly fortunate circumstances. "There is going to be a great pig feast. That happens only every two or three years."

I climbed into the small government motor launch with Gonsalves, heading downstream for Ukumhearik's village. The current was so strong that the boat lurched and churned with great effort in the water, and I was glad that Gonsalves had made me put on a life jacket. After a rough trip of about half an hour, we came to a small landing near Ukumhearik's village. No one was there.

"Everyone is busy preparing things for the big feast," Gonsalves explained, as we started down a path through woods and reeds that were soon supplanted by gardens. I saw the village, which looked to be considerably larger than most of those I had seen from the air. It was surrounded by a low fence, over which a kind of stile served as the entrance.Hundreds of people inside the enclosure were working at a dozen different tasks, meanwhile talking, shouting, and laughing. The air of excitement and celebration was unmistakable, a bit contagious even at a distance. We stood by the stile, waiting to be seen and invited in. In a moment, one of the young men spotted us and called out to the others, and there arose a general cry of welcome, "Najak! Najak!"

A group of obviously important men — they wore big white shells on their breasts and many feathers in their headdresses — started toward us, followed by numerous strong young warriors and then by old men, women, and children. Among those in the lead was one man about half a head taller than his fellows, and I knew this was Ukumhearik. He was a big-chested man who moved with an easy, loping grace. His long, muscular legs carried many ugly scars, and I recalled that Gonsalves had told me the chief had once been incapacitated for months as a result of a leg wound from an enemy spear.

Ukumhearik wore no bailer shell on his chest, only a wide strand of very small cowrie shells. On his head there was a woven, netlike cap from which one small curved white feather stood up. A narrow fur armlet circled his right biceps. And, of course, he wore a long and upright orange penis gourd, as did all the men and all but the smallest boys. Each gourd, except those of the pre-adolescent boys, was held upright by a thin fiber strand going from the end of the gourd around the waist.

I have met many primitive men, such as the Calapalo Indians of Brazil, who wore no covering over the genitals; and others who used only a few fiber strands or leaves. The Bororo Indians of the Mato Grosso wore small palm-leaf penis sheaths that served to accentuate the organ somewhat, but the Dani of the Baliem were the first men I had seen who went to considerable lengths to call immediate attention to the penis, and to convince everyone that it was in perpetual erection.

The gourds are cultivated in small garden plots, where the vines are trained to grow on racks so they hang without touching the ground, which might rot or discolor them. When ripe, they are hollowed out skillfully, and are prized by all men in the valley. After the age of three or four, little boys begin to wear small penis gourds fashioned by their fathers, but for some years they are allowed to hang down. At manhood, the gourd is longer and held erect. And as the young man grows taller and older he wears longer and more brightly colored gourds — and the orange color is striking indeed in this generally green-and-brown environment.

A Dani man is undressed without his penis sheath. He might leave off feathers, shells, and armlet, but he would never dream of being seen by his neighbor without his gourd. If a man is walking a trail and a snapping branch breaks his gourd, he dives into the bush and hides, calling out to his companion for help. The friend gets another gourd as soon as possible. It occurred to me that this extreme shame of being without a penis covering might arise from having others see what has been hidden by a gourd twelve to twenty inches long.

As the villagers approached, I saw that Ukumhearik was such a self-confident chief that he did not even have to have the longest gourd. Everyone was in a jovial mood but his smile was more easygoing than any of them. He had a rather long, flaring nose, and deepset eyes that darted fire. And he shook my hand with a warmth and vigor that left no question about his feelings. (Handshaking is the most common greeting between men in the valley, although in some areas the wrists are grasped rather than he hands.)

I was also introduced to Ukumhearik's chief medicine man, Waganogo, affectionately called "Weepy" by the missionaries of the valley. He was smiling, too, although it seemed to pain him somewhat. Waganogo's beard was a little longer and curlier than those of the other men, although they all wore exactly the same type — wispy sideburns leading into a circular growth under the chin. The rest of the face was kept clean-shaven by plucking with split twigs. The short beards, framing the men's faces as they did, were attractive. And the faces themselves were striking — expressive, intelligent, strong reflectors of the personalities behind them. The skin was brown, the cheekbones high, the noses generally long and aquiline, the foreheads high over deep-set eyes.

The women looked like the women of almost all primitive groups, considerably shorter than the men, and possessed of a kind of resigned listlessness. The girls were full of the bounce of youth, but some women no more than thirty had sagging breasts, protruding stomachs. All women wore short skirts and net bags suspended from their heads and falling down the back.

Most of the natives returned to their work. And what a bustle of activity there was! Big stones were heating over several fires. From one of them some men were taking up hot stones in long saplings split at one end so they acted as a kind of huge tongs. The hot stones were carried to a big pit and placed so that they lined the hole. Then women brought bunches of green leaves and shoots to put over the stones. We got our cameras ready to film the steps of the cooking process. There was a stack of pigs that had been cleaned and split down the middle, and several of these were taken to the pit. From a huge pile of sweet potatoes — there were many such, as well as mounds of other vegetables — the largest were added to the pit, and then there were more leaves, more hot stones, and still more leaves piled up into a mound of steaming green. This was bound around with ropelike vines, and the men and women turned their attention to the next pit. Several had already been started before my arrival, and the aroma of roasting pork filled the air. Occasionally the men and women paused in their work to breathe in the wonderful smell, pleasantly exchanging a few words with those nearby.

Ukumhearik returned to *his* work, too — the killing of the pigs.

This is always the task of the chief of a group — and he had already been busy with his ceremonial chore for some time, judging by the scores of pigs. Some were being cooked, some cleaned, and others were piled up waiting for the next pit to be prepared. But there were still more to be sacrificed, so two strong men held up in the air a squealing pig. Ukumhearik fixed an arrow to his bow and, from about six feet, shot the pig in the chest. Pigs must always be dispatched by an arrow through the lungs.

While my cameraman and I were busy filming as many activities as possible, Ukumhearik finished his slaughtering and came to see how we were getting along. He immediately became a kind of assistant director, ordering his people about when I indicated that I wanted a particular shot or angle. Then he rushed off to see about something else. He was everywhere, supervising the placing of the hot stones, examining the sweet potatoes to make sure they were large and firm, flattering the women, fondling the littlest children, jesting with his medicine man, Waganogo, and yet seeing to it that his white guests were enjoying themselves. He was an ebullient, gracious host, never the backward and awestruck Stone Age native trying to make an impression on superior white men. No, he was royalty entertaining the emissaries of other royalty. There could have been no doubt in anyone's mind that this was *his* village, and — in large measure —*his* valley, *his* world.

Finally the first cooking pit was opened and the pork and sweet potatoes brought to Ukumhearik.With a bamboo knife he carved one of the pig halves, selecting the choicest morsels for me, his honored guest. As on many previous occasions among primitive peoples, I wished that I might forgo the choicest bits for more common fare. Of course, I did not have to drink nijimanche, the spittle-fermented brew I had gulped down when visiting the headhunting Jivaros, or eat the elephant meat so relished by the Pygmies of the Ituri Forest in Africa. But the choicest bit of a pig, in the opinion of the Dani of the Baliem Valley, is the fat around the stomach, the oozing liver, or perhaps an eyeball. And for the special guest, the delicious sweet potato must cradle a monstrous chunk of fatty pork. Thanks to Gonsalves's dog I was able to dispose of much of the greasiest portion of my meal without being noticed by Ukumhearik (or anyone else). But I would have preferred a meaty slice from the leg of that pig, which was given to the common folk because it lacked the prized fat of the other cuts.

A few days later I visited Gerald Rose and his wife, Darlene, in their home in the village of Hepubah, in the Baliem; and I learned that I had really fared quite well. As the first white woman to enter the Baliem, Darlene Rose has had some amazing experiences, one of the most gruesome of which was at a special pig feast that Ukumhearik gave in her honor. He was particularly attentive to Mrs. Rose, who thus had no chance to slip a piece surreptitiously to a dog even if there had been one around. "There was a big crowd of Dani men and women gathered when the government plane landed," Mrs. Rose told me. "They wanted to give a royal welcome to the first white woman they had ever seen, and they were terribly curious. When I stepped from the plane they all shouted, 'Mama! Mama Horosee!' (That's the way the name Rose came out when they pronounced it.) The shouts grew louder and louder when I waved. 'Mama, mama Horosee! Waaaaa! Mama Horosee! Waaaaa! Waaaaa!'

"Men and women were streaming in from all over," Mrs. Rose went on. "And the men were dressed in all their finery as if for a victory dance. Most of them had feathered headdresses, some had pig tusks in their noses, and they were painted with red clay, gray clay, and black pig fat mixed with charred castor beans.

"The Dani women pushed forward, feeling that they had the prerogative to greet a woman from the outside world. They wanted me to join them to eat some sweet potatoes they had brought along. So we sat down in a big circle, and one by one the women came up to look at me closely. They seemed particularly interested in my hair, gently pulling it out to its full length, smiling, talking to each other. Mr. Bromley, the missionary who is our linguistic expert in the Baliem, stayed nearby so he could tell me what they were saying. The men were more interested in the whiteness of my skin. When the women gave them a chance, they touched my arm, then pushed up my sleeve to make sure the skin was white underneath.

"Then Mr. Bromley told me that Ukumhearik was coming," Mrs. Rose continued. "I had already heard about him, of course, and knew what an important chief he was. When I got up to greet him I felt sure I was seeing a man who in every way was superior to his fellows and it was easy to understand why he was not only feared, but respected by all. He has great poise, and welcomed me with warmth and graciousness. Then he invited me to his village the next day, with the missionaries and government men. He said that he was going to kill a pig in my honor. And I knew that there was nothing more that a Dani chief could do to show his friendliness.

"The next day, when we came to the fence surrounding the men's roundhouses, I stopped, for I knew that it was not customary for women to walk into this male sanctum sanctorum. The men of our party climbed over the stile, but I stayed outside. Ukumhearik came up at once and invited me in. Then in front of one of the houses, I saw a row of men — and it was obvious that these were the most important subchiefs, medicine men, warriors, and such, lined up as a kind of receiving line. I had to say a formal hello to each VIP.

"Ukumhearik was beaming and smiling as he gestured us to sit down in a semicircle on the ground. Then they brought the pig, and Ukumhearik killed it with an arrow. They burned off the hair over a hot fire and then cut it up for cooking. Most of it went into the pit with the hot rocks, of course, but they kept out what we call preacher's meat at home, and the ribs. These were roasted over a fire while the rest was cooking in a pit.

"Ukumhearik sat down right in front of me, and after a while a man came with the ribs. Ukumhearik cut them into portions for everyone in our party — two or three ribs each. They were really delicious, and I was enjoying my meal, when I noticed that every time I or anyone else put a bone down, Ukumhearik picked it up. He cleaned each one off thoroughly and effectively with his finger nail, getting every particle of meat or gristle. When he finished cleaning a bone, he cleaned the meat out from under his nails and put it carefully on his bare thigh. When he collected enough for a good bite, he picked it up and popped it into my mouth! And I ate it!

"Well, there was a gasp from everyone in our party, and one of the government officials, an older man, suddenly stood up whispered a few words to Mr. Bromley, and walked around to the other side of the enclosure and stayed there quite a while. When he came back he did not eat any more. Later, on the way back to our house in Hepubah, Mr. Bromley asked me how I had managed to eat that special scrap of meat. I answered that I had seen him go through the same thing. Ukumhearik had put the second bite, gathered in the same way, into Mr. Bromley's mouth. But Mr. Bromley showed me that he had it in his pocket. He had managed to slip it out of his mouth without Ukumhearik's noticing.

"Even if it was a rather unpleasant experience," Mrs. Rose said, "I wasn't sick from it. I couldn't show that I was an unappreciative guest. You know, I've lived among these people a long time now, and I've eaten with them many times. They serve foods we'd never dream of eating at home, and some of them are delicious."

I told Mrs. Rose about nijimanche and weevils, locusts and elephant meat, which I didn't like but had to confess that I *had* eaten some very unusual and tasty foods when visiting primitive people.

"Well, at this first meal with Ukumhearik," she continued, "I kept getting the special delicacies, such as the lower jaw with the tongue still resting between the teeth. The teeth didn't look very clean, and I found myself swallowing a little hard, too. But then I thought, well, this is a new experience. I've never eaten this particular portion before and I might find it delicious. But before I started, each of us was given a little bundle of the intestines wrapped in sweet potato leaves. It began to look as if I'd never get a piece of that nice lean ham.

"Suddenly it started to drizzle," Mrs. Rose said. "These Danis hate to get their fancy headdresses or even their hair wet, so they suggested that perhaps I might like to take that lower jaw, with the tongue still resting between the teeth, and my bundle of intestines, and eat them later at home. I thought this was a very good suggestion.

"But before we left, Ukumhearik told Mr. Bromley that he wanted me to know that he had taken me into his clan, the clan of the Ahsoes. Then he turned to me with a smile and said, '*Naha-logo,*' which I knew meant *my daughter.* I had been studying Dani on the coast while waiting for permission to come into the valley, but I didn't know a great deal at that time. Well, when Ukumhearik said that to me I was flattered and replied in the way I thought I should, calling him *no pase*, meaning *my father.* He looked startled, and Mr. Bromley explained that Ukumhearik did not feel that he was *that* much older than I. You know, the men in the Baliem are just like men all over the world. When they get a little older they are sensitive about their age. So I quickly corrected myself and called Ukumhearik *Hehrouk,* which means *beloved fellow-clansman of the same age level, opposite sex.* Ukumhearik beamed with pleasure, and we have always called each other by these terms since that time."

Gerry Rose was the first of the missionaries to see the Baliem Valley, although he did not enter it at the time. In 1952, he set out on a trek overland from the Wissel Lakes mission with some government officials and fifty carriers. They reached Lake Habbema, but they did not go down into the valley itself.

When Mrs. Rose and her young son came to the valley, the natives were almost as excited about seeing a white baby as a white woman. "And Bruce made a big hit right away," Gerry Rose said, "even though he was just under two years of age. When we got out of the boat at the little pier in Hepubah, an old woman came running up with a big sweet potato for him. He'd never seen one before, but even in this strange and perhaps frightening moment, with hundreds of eager faces staring at him, he just grabbed it with both hands, dived in, and started gobbling it. Well, the natives shouted happily. The men flipped their penis gourds and snapped their fingers, as they do when they are delighted, and they all shouted, 'He's one of us! He's one of us. He loves potatoes!' "

So things started out well for the Rose family in the Baliem. But then an epidemic of measles struck the native children, and the Danis decided that the aluminum of the Rose house was the cause of the sickness.

"The metal was so entirely new to them," Gerald Rose told me, "that it was an obvious thing for them to pick on."

"Do you think some of the older men might have remembered the big pig sickness after the DC-3 crash?" I asked. "The plane was made of aluminum."

"Well, it was in the mountains at the other end of the valley," Rose replied. "But such tales travel, of course. In any event, Ukumhearik's people took measures to counter the evil influence of the aluminum house. Led by the witch doctor, Weepy, they smeared pig's blood on the sides of the house and put a bundle of pig fat on the roof to drive away the blight.

"Then our little Bruce came down with a bad case of measles, and that changed everything. There was no more blood or fat, no more angry looks at our house. The natives decided that our aluminum would not cause the sickness of our own child. They came to inquire about Bruce and to comfort us. Ukumhearik himself was particularly concerned. During the worst part of Bruce's sickness, when he had a bad rash, fever, and was crying a lot, Ukumhearik came every after-noon, walking ten miles each way from his village, to stay with Bruce for an hour or two. He entertained the baby, singing songs and danc-ing and doing everything he could think of to take Bruce's mind off his itching and fever.

"Well, that's one side of Ukumhearik," Rose continued. "But on the other hand he can be immensely cruel. He was actually proud of having speared a woman — of an enemy group, of course — and her nursing baby with one thrust. There was a big victory dance for that feat. Then there is Ukumhearik the diplomat. You realize that within his territory there are clans, subclans, and submoieties. The alliance among these is kept in good repair because of Ukumhearik's work. Almost every day he goes from village to village; and he's the only man who dares walk about unarmed. I've seen him sit down and talk to the leader in a village, asking about his pigs, his children, what prob-lems he may have. And he takes care of the problems, with swift jus-tice.

"Ukumhearik zealously guards the dignity of his position and brooks no lack of respect. I know of an instance when seven people were killed because someone spoke harshly to him. Then there was the time when some young bucks from the enemies in the hills, look-ing for excitement, came down one night and stole a pig from a man in Ukumhearik's territory. Ukumhearik stepped right into the affair, not only to get recompense for the pig but to punish the peo-ple who would dare pull such a trick in *his* area. It was to him a per-sonal affront. With some of his warriors, he went to the village of the men who had stolen the pig. Most of the villagers fled, but Ukumhea-rik took a pig and killed one important old man. The old man's wife had just lost her son in a war with the upriver groups, and this was too much for her. She came down from the hills with her three other children — went right past our place — with one baby in her net bag, one under her arm, and the largest tagging along beside her. She found a raft and got on it with her children, pushing out into the river. In the middle she tipped it over — suicide by drowning. So, as a result of this one raid, stealing a pig, five people died."

I asked Rose about the time Ukumhearik almost killed him. The story was famous throughout New Guinea, but I wanted to hear it at first hand.

"Yes, that was strange," Rose told me. "He had been so friendly. But I have learned never to be too surprised when these primitive people change suddenly and drastically. Some say they are unpredictable, but I think it's just that we just don't know what triggers a change. Most of the time it is because they do not understand something, and they are afraid of the unknown. That's what happened in this case.

"These people love to see pictures of themselves," Rose explained, "and Lloyd Van Stone had taken lots of pictures out here. Well, one night we put on a show for a few leaders, projecting pictures against the wall in the house. They were laughing, talking, enjoying themselves immensely. Then suddenly they saw, in full color, the pictures of a young man who had been killed in battle some time before. It takes a long time to send film out, get it processed and returned to us, so three months may have gone by since the picture was taken. And now they saw the figure of that boy, whom they had cremated. The natives screamed, cried, pounded their chests, beat their fists on the floor, then jumped up and ran out of the house like frightened deer, yelling that the white man had the spirits of the living *and* the dead in that box of his.

"Believe me, for three days we didn't know if we'd be alive," Rose continued. "There were swarms of natives around the house day and night — two hundred or more most of the time. They shouted threats, jabbed their spears at the walls and windows. But they were still not sure if they could really kill a white man. They called to our Kapauku couple who had come with us from the Wissel Lakes, and asked them what would happen if they speared a white man. Elisa wisely answered that the white man would go to be with Jesus. His answer threw the natives off, and they still hesitated to make a direct attack.

"We could not stay in the house all the time. Life had to go on. So one afternoon my wife was hanging up some clothes in the back yard and I was standing by to protect her. Suddenly I felt my arms pinned behind my back in an iron grip. Ukumhearik had me fast. He gave an order to some of his warriors to come and put a spear through me. This is about the most sadistic way these people know of taking care of a captured enemy. The arms of the victim are held behind his back and then the sixteen-foot hardwood spear is driven down through him, starting just behind the collar bone, going clear through the body and into the ground, pinning him there until he dies slowly.

"And that is what Ukumhearik ordered his men to do to me. But not a man moved. It was the only time before or since that we know of that Ukumhearik gave a command and his men did not obey."

"Why did they refuse?" I asked.

"I really don't know," Rose said. "All I can say is that divine intervention saved my life. The warriors actually began to move back, looking frightened and acting as if they had seen something I could not see or had heard something I could not hear. So I shook Ukumhearik loose, turned around and said, 'What's going on?' He looked abashed and a bit fearful, very perplexed. And no wonder, since this was the first time his own men had failed to carry out his orders. But for some reason he was not angry with them. The crowd drifted away and did not return. That was the end of the crisis. And within a few days we were getting along with Ukumhearik and his people the way we always had."

Tom Bozeman, who went into the Baliem as a missionary in 1956, has had many close brushes with death. Although he ascribed his safety to divine intervention, I was aware of considerable courage, quick thinking, and determination on his part — and, in similar circumstances, on that of other missionaries there. Perhaps the most deeply disturbing of Bozeman's experiences was his witnessing the eating of human flesh.

"Of course, it is ritualistic cannibalism," he told me. "They do not eat humans for food, although they say the meat tastes good, a lot like pork. They eat only the bodies of slain enemies, that being considered the worst insult one can give to his enemy. They don't eat every enemy by any means, but do it only when they are so angry and aroused that they must be as insulting as possible."

One day he and a fellow missionary saw some Dani warriors on their way past their station, returning from a big battle. They reported that they had won, and that they had killed one of the bravest warriors of the enemy group. They were going to cook him the next day, at the scene of the battle.

"When we got to the scene of the celebration the next day," Bozeman said, "there were hundreds already there, running around, chanting and singing their victory songs. Some women were beating the dead body viciously with their digging sticks, and hurling insults at it. It was very hot that day, so they had put some grass over the body in an effort to keep the sun from spoiling it too fast, but I could see enough to know that the enemy warrior had been speared many times."

The missionaries treated the wounded from the battle, and some others who were sick — and all the time the dancing and chanting went on, growing in force and madness. After about four hours, around noon, one man cut a long pole and laid it across the body. Other men got vines, with which they tied the body to the pole. Then they picked up the pole to carry the body back to the fighting area, about a mile and a half away. To carry out the insult properly, the enemy group had to see them cooking and eating the fallen warrior.

The enemy group was waiting on its side of a deep gulch that served as a boundary, in the hope that the body would be flung into the gulch so they could retrieve it. When they saw the huge crowd with the victors, they set up a tremendous wailing and moaning, calling and pleading for the return of the body. But those with the body called back that they were going to eat the hated enemy in view of his relatives and friends.

"While the fire was being built," Bozeman continued, "there was another hour or so of dancing and chanting which grew wilder and wilder. Women jumped up and down on the body; their hatred of it was something awful to see. And by this time the body was spoiling badly and the smell was terrible. I began to get sick at my stomach, but I had to see. I could not really believe what was happening before my eyes, and I still had to be convinced. I wanted to remonstrate, to stop them, but I knew that they were all so frenzied they would not hear me.

"Finally the men chased the women away and started the business of carving up the body. Some had bamboo knives, some steel knives they'd traded from us. Some had stone axes, a few had steel axes, while a few could find only jagged sharp rocks. First they cut off the toes, then the feet, and then the calves of the legs. Then they stripped the meat away from the bones. It was a reddish-purple color and I saw it plainly, for I was standing only a few feet away. Next some men cut off the hands and went to work on the arms. One man couldn't get an arm off, so he draped it over a sharp rock, took up another rock and banged away at it until he got it free; a long strip of meat was left, clinging to the shoulder.

"A good deal of the meat was roasted there over the fire, cut up into small pieces and distributed through the crowd. No one person ate very much — that was not the point. As many people as possible wanted to participate in the insult to the enemy. Some of the meat was wrapped in leaves, to be taken home and cooked there for the old folks who couldn't travel. Every single bit of meat was used."

Tom Bozeman, Gerry Rose, and other missionaries told me about the position of women in the Baliem, the marriage customs and such, most of which sounded like those in other primitive societies, with minor variations. There is complete sexual freedom for girls until they are married, after which fidelity is expected. While the ordinary native may have only one wife because he cannot afford any more, many have two or three. Some chiefs have five or six, and Ukumhearik has twenty-three or twenty-five — no one can quite agree on the exact number. Some of these are political marriages intended to solidify alliances, and Ukumhearik has wives in many different villages.

Although brides are purchased, at the time the marriage is to take place a woman may say that she does not wish to marry the man she is pledged to. And no one will force her to go through with it. The only strict rule is that she must not marry within her own extended family group, or moiety. If she meets this rule she may choose the man she wants, and if he is agreeable he must make some arrangement with the girl's parents for payment of a bride-price.

Most marriages take place at the big pig feasts, every few years. Many of the couples have waited so long for the big day that they like to make a great drama of it. All the girls from one village who are scheduled to get married leave their village and go down to the river as if to perform certain chores. Meanwhile the intended husbands have gathered in ambush and make a sudden attack. Someone cries out, in mock terror, "The enemy is coming!" and any men of the girls' village who happen to be around run away, leaving the girls unprotected. Each man of the attacking group grabs his woman and carries her off, while the girls weep and scream as if in fear. It all serves to make the ravishing of the bride more exciting, even though she had been "ravished" scores of times before, by numerous men.

Punishment for infidelity varies considerably in the Baliem. Sometimes the "other man," if caught, may pay the husband a pig or two to square things, and the wife gets a severe beating. But sometimes the punishment is more painful. The husband may drive his spear through both legs of his wife and pin her to the ground, leaving her there until he feels she is sufficiently penitent.

I met one young woman who was quite different from all the others I saw in the valley. She was Hennalafu, the attractive twenty-two-year-old daughter of Waganogo the witch doctor. Young as she was, she had had seven husbands. She had lived with some a week or two, with others several months or more. When I met her she had no current husband, but took any man who appealed to her, temporarily. I heard that if she was going down a trail and saw a young fellow she liked, she beckoned to him and took him off in the bush. This sort of thing was all right for unmarried girls — though few were that forward — but not for a woman of her age and who had been married. She got away with it, and with other unconventional activities, because of her independent spirit and the fact that she was the medicine man's daughter. And the men were all quite taken with her, for she was decidedly attractive. At a pig feast, all the young men brought her the choicest bits of pork. As if to contradict her busy sexual activities, she had a kind of tomboy quality about her.

Missionary Tom Bozeman told me about a fire at her village. He had gone there to help put it out and found Hennalafu working hard, right alongside the men; no other women were engaged in what was considered man's work. And she took on many other male duties. Needless to say, the other women didn't like her very much — a fact that bothered Hennalafu not at all.

Tom Bozeman told me, when I was in the Baliem, "A few evenings ago I was down in the village talking to some of the men, and she was standing not far away puffing on a cigarette, the native type. The other women were some distance away, and kept glancing at her. I knew there was something peculiar going on, and finally I noticed what it was. Most women wear net-like string skirts of several thicknesses, but Hennalafu's was of only one thickness — and that very thin. She paid no attention to the disapproving glances of the women because she was concentrating on the men, plainly enticing them in view of everybody."

They had come to know her well at the mission station not just because she was Weepy's daughter, but because she had once been forced to spend some time with them. "One husband she had," Bozeman said, "became involved in an argument over a pig with a subchief.

This chief came to see them, very angry, and she argued back just as vehemently as her husband instead of staying in the background as other women do. The chief hit her over the head with his stone axe and laid it open. Waganogo's witch medicine could do nothing for her, so he brought her to us. Mrs. Bromley, who is an M.D., cleaned the wound and sewed it up, but she held out little hope for the girl's recovery. But Hennalafu got well and is just as wicked as she ever was."

Waganogo is not nearly so powerful as the medicine men in most primitive groups, because Ukumhearik is too important to allow anyone to challenge his authority. But Waganogo is the number two man in that area, because he is a likable and intelligent person. He does not seem to be jealous of the medical activities of the missionaries, as are many witch doctors in other primitive groups. Most of the natives went to him first when I was there, but if his treatments failed they went to the mission, often sent by Waganogo himself.

Perhaps the biggest moment in Waganogo's life came when Gerry and Darlene Rose took him on a plane trip to Hollandia. What impressed him most was that he could travel from the airstrip several miles to the harbor in Hollandia without having to carry weapons and without once meeting an enemy group. The ocean and automobiles and big ships and shops full of goods awed him, but he was really thunderstruck when he went to the government agricultural experiment station and saw an eight-hundred-pound white breeding boar. As Darlene Rose told me, "He viewed it from every angle and then hung on the fence as if stunned and kept saying, 'And it's a pig — a pig!'"

Gerry Rose told me about a funeral he had attended in Ukumhearik's village — Gerry was the first white man ever to be asked to such a ceremony.

"Shortly after we arrived in the valley, I came to know a young fellow named Wagon who often came to visit our camp. He was a likable teenager, interested in everything new and different, and I became quite attached to him. Then one day, I heard that Wagon had been killed in an intertribal battle and that his funeral was about to be held. I went to the village, and found Ukumhearik standing just outside the village enclosure. I did not know if I would be welcomed, but Ukumhearik took me inside the fence and showed me where to sit.

"Inside the village there is a large space shaped like a V, with long houses on both sides and the fence at the open end. There were about three hundred people there, the men were at one end, near the funeral pyre that was being built, women at the other end. Some men were still bringing up wood, others were chopping and splitting logs, and still others were piling them. They were careful about building the pyre, which was about eight feet long, four feet high, and four feet wide; the logs were placed so that the air could circulate freely through them.

"All this time there was a slow, mournful chanting. First the women carried on the rhythmic and lugubrious song and then, without a signal and without a missed beat, the men took it up. Then they both chanted together. After about an hour, the singing suddenly stopped. You could have heard a leaf fall. Not a baby cried, not a pig squealed. I don't know how they did it, but in all that whole crowd there was not a sound. After a few minutes the chanting started again, faster and more frenzied than before. The body was being brought from Wagon's mother's house by the young warrior's closest friends. I could see his many wounds; he had been pierced by thirty or more spears.

"Wagon's friends laid him gently on the wood pyre, on his side with his hands under his head and his knees slightly bent, as if in sleep. They piled more wood around the body and hid it from view. The chanting was going on all this time, increasing in intensity. Then Wagon's bows and arrows, the neckpiece he had worn in battle, his headdress, and all his personal possessions were put on the pyre with him. The fire was started. It was soon blazing and, since I was only about ten feet away, the heat and the stench of burning flesh became almost unbearable. But I just sat there and wept along with all the others, tranced by the never-ending chant.

"Then I saw more people coming into the village. As each person came inside the fence, he stopped to pick up a rock from a cooking pit, then walked with measured tread, in time to the chanting, the length of the village to the pyre. At every step the newcomers hit themselves on the head with the stones, until blood flowed over their faces and bodies. They stood before the pyre for a few minutes, both men and women, then melted back into the crowd to make room for others. Finally more than six hundred people were there.

"It must have taken almost an hour for the pyre to burn out. Then some men took the ashes of the burned bones and buried them in a little circular spot, after which they planted a small tree over it.

"That was the end of the formal part of the ceremony. I got up to leave. I didn't want to stay for the demonstrations of mourning — the cutting off of finger joints, the lopping off of the tops of ears, and so on. As I started to walk away, the older brother of Wagon, dressed in all his finery, called to me. 'Horosee! Horosee!' I turned, and he threw his arms around me, sobbing bitterly and saying over and over again, 'Help me! Help me!' I knew that he was desperately in need of comfort in his great sorrow, and *he* knew that I had a faith that could aid him in his bereavement. He did not yet understand it, but he was searching for the peace and comfort of Jesus. And in time, he will find it."

Since my last trip to New Guinea, I have been in regular communication with many people in the highlands and in the Baliem. And here in the U.S. I've seen Mick Leahy, Gerry and Darlene Rose, Lloyd Van Stone and Tom Bozeman; also two officers of the Christian and Missionary Alliance, Louis King and the late Robert Chrisman, both of whom have made regular trips to New Guinea.

In the Australian New Guinea highlands, all but a few pockets of Stone Age have been brought at least under partial control. And there has been amazing material progress — in roads, plane service, agricultural development. The biggest news, however, has been the election for a parliamentary assembly, about which I've written.

The Baliem Valley and other areas of what was Dutch New Guinea have made worldwide headlines chiefly though two incidents — the tragic mysterious loss of young Michael Rockefeller, son of New York's Governor Nelson Rockefeller, and the transfer of the former Dutch colony to the Indonesians, who call it West Irian.

Michael Rockefeller was a member of an expedition sent to New Guinea, chiefly to the Baliem Valley, by the Peabody Museum of Harvard University. In the fall of 1960, the leader of the expedition, Dr. Robert Gardner, wrote me to ask if he could see the film that had come out of my two expeditions, *Primitive Paradise*. He and Michael Rockefeller and David Putnam came to my apartment for a private showing.

Early in 1961, the expedition set out. Within a few months, however, there were stories of difficulties in the valley. As *Time* magazine summed it up after the end of the expedition,

> For six months in Baliem Valley, the Harvard expedition filmed the natives — and aroused missionaries and Dutch district officers, who complained that the U.S. scientists were stirring the headhunters into tribal warfare to film the battles.

The *New York Times* wrote, on December 6, 1961, "Harvard University's Peabody Museum expedition to the Baliem Valley of Netherlands New Guinea . . . was suspected by both Roman Catholic and Protestant missionaries of stirring up tribesmen to violence."

Most missionaries I have talked to agree with these reports, but one told me that he had no fault to find with the expedition. "They did not need to do any stirring up of the tribes to film warfare. I've watched many a battle myself."

After six months, the Harvard expedition returned home. But within a few weeks Michael Rockefeller went back to New Guinea, in search of art objects for the Rockefeller-sponsored Museum of Primitive Art. This time he went to the southern coast of Dutch New Guinea, a swampy, crocodile and snake-infested region whose natives were known to be cannibals.

After gathering many fine pieces, Michael and a Dutch scientist, with two friendly natives, set out for a village down the coast. They traveled in a double-dugout catamaran powered by an outboard motor, like the one I had used going up the Sepik River. Crossing the mouth of a river, high waves and strong tidal flow swamped the craft and finally tipped it over. Michael and the Dutch scientist clung to the boat while the two natives struck out for shore. After many hours, Michael concluded that they had not made it to land, so decided to swim ashore himself, although by this time they had been swept out to sea. With two empty gasoline cans for buoyancy, he set out, against the advice of his friend. And that was the last that was seen or heard of him.

In the Baliem Valley itself, Ukumhearik still lords it over everyone in his territory, according to my last report, but he limps now and has a hard time climbing hills. And some of the missionaries have decided that, despite his help and friendliness, he is really the villain of the piece in their efforts to convert the natives. It is true that, whereas there have been many conversions in other parts of the valley, there have been almost none in Ukumhearik's domain, where the missionaries have worked hardest. Other missionaries who know the wise chief just as well do not really blame him for this state of affairs.

Most missionaries I have talked with were bitter about the United States's taking such an active role in turning over Netherlands New Guinea first to the United Nations for a short period and then, on May 1, 1963, to Indonesia. There were others, however, who were both surprised and hopeful about the way things were turning out. Among the more optimistic was Robert Chrisman who, until his recent death, was Far Eastern Secretary for the Christian and Missionary Alliance, a man familiar with West Irian.

Chrisman described the place I had visited only five years before, and already it seemed as if I had never been there. The Indonesians, who had caused such apprehension and doubt among the missionaries, were making progress. "They know that the Dutch were held in high regard. They seem to be determined to outdo them," Chrisman said.

To begin with, there was a five-year program to raise standards of living and education of the natives, those of the interior as well as the coast; this meant importing trained teachers from Indonesia, and paying them travel expenses and fairly good salaries. "And government money is helping to supply teachers to mission schools in the highlands," Chrisman went on. "The progress in education in just the first six months was surprising."

The entire cultural tone of West Irian was apparently changing. Children were learning to read and write, learning about current events and important world figures — and they were telling their parents about these amazing things. The trouble was that when the older people clung to their comforting and familiar superstitions, the children lost respect for their elders and family discipline suffered. Chrisman told me that the missions were trying to keep the grown-ups on an educational par with their children. "We're teaching the adults to read as fast as we can," he said. "We've got hundreds of them coming to class every day."

The Indonesians were grappling with public health problems, too.

They have made some big promises, but they've been backing up some promises with deeds: sending in M.D.'s from Indonesia and building a small hospital at Wamena in the Baliem Valley.

But there are new health problems. Originally the interior had no tuberculosis, smallpox, diphtheria, since the Dutch government required physical examinations for everyone. But now with more and more outsiders going in, more of our diseases are showing up. So the government has inaugurated a massive vaccination program, with thousands getting immunity they do not possess naturally. Infant mortality, a long-time problem, is being countered, too, with a far-ranging program for midwives.

Air transportation has been changing the face of the island by bringing the materials of civilization to men who grew up in a Stone Age culture. Chrisman mentioned a bulldozer that was flown into the Baliem in pieces. Assembled there, it helped clear fields for planting. Horses and cattle, once strangers to New Guinea, were ferried in by plane, along with instructions for care and feeding. But the one- and two-motored planes already familiar in the skies over the island are not enough to get a modern society started. Other means of transportation are necessary, and the Indonesians still have a long way to go. A road into the highlands had been planned by the Dutch. Now the Indonesians are pressing forward with this project, costly and difficult as it is.

"Another, and surprising, factor accounting for the progress of the Indonesians," Chrisman told me, "is their language. The Dutch had decided to make their language official, but Dutch is a very difficult tongue. Now Indonesian is to be the official language, although the government also encourages English. It just so happens that Indonesian is one of the easiest languages in the world to learn. And there is available a wealth of literature in that language, and textbooks at all levels. It has made a big difference."

Later reports, however, were not so flattering to the Indonesians. Early in 1966, I learned that they were having serious trouble in the Baliem. Several native groups had attacked government police. Many teachers and technicians were so lonely they left after a year, if they were permitted. Officials of the Christian and Missionary Alliance and other outsiders were no longer allowed into the Baliem Valley, and many missionaries there had suffered arrest and severe restrictions on their activities. It was obvious that the fine Indonesian program had proved too costly to a nation having great economic and political difficulties.

In any event, there would soon be no more Ukumheariks, just as there would be no more Utitiajas; no one so dramatic would come out of that changing world.

As one of the missionaries recently told me, "The old Stone Age world you saw is going. You saw it before the curtain began to descend."

IV
THE HIGH ARCTIC

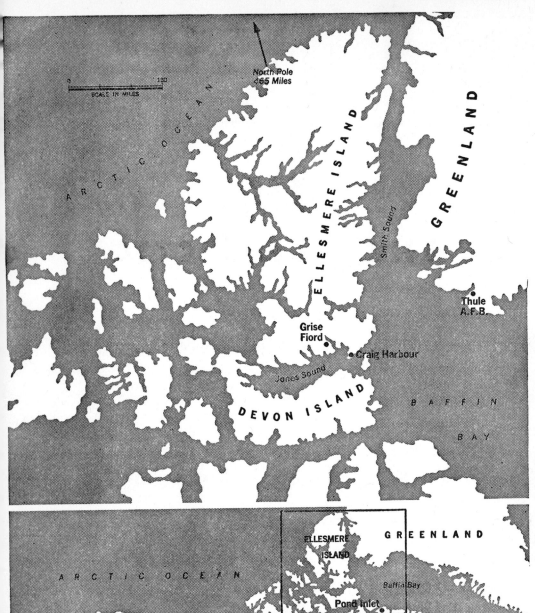

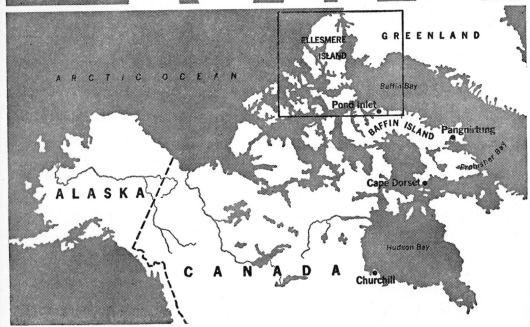

1

The Happiest People in the World

IN THE spring of 1962 I found myself in a small airplane flying over the most desolate country I had ever seen. I had told myself that I would never go to the frozen regions of the earth. I was a man of the tropics — Central Africa, South America, New Guinea. I liked snow, but off in the distance, crowning mountain peaks like Kilimanjaro and Wilhelmina. And here I was flying over nothing but snow and ice, and for some months I would live on and in and under snow and ice. I had hacked my way through miles of tangled jungle; now I was in a land without a single tree: the high Arctic.

As I looked down from the little plane, I could see no "scenery" as such, unless a white iceberg trapped in surrounding sea ice can be considered scenery. And what did this white world offer for my color film? After the blazing bird of paradise plumes of New Guinea, the Arctic was bound to seem dull and lifeless, I thought.

And I was not at all sure what I would film. Seal hunts, obviously, walrus hunts, hopefully polar bears. But I had as yet no unifying concept for the whole film. I had read Rasmussen, Nansen, Sverdrup, Stefansson, Freuchen and other great writers on the high Arctic but I felt as if I were tackling something brand new. Up to this time all my experiences had led naturally from one thing to another; the knowledge I gained from the Pygmies of Africa helped me in my dealings with the Jivaros of South America, and both had prepared me for the primitives of New Guinea. But none of this seemed to pave the way for Eskimos and igloos and temperatures of twenty to thirty below zero. And I wasn't so young any more, I reminded myself. After a quarter of a century of exploring, should I tackle the unknown? Should I keep on pressing my luck?

It all started with the dean of the Dutch diplomatic corps, A. H. J. Lovink, formerly the Netherlands ambassador to Australia, where I had met him on my New Guinea expeditions. He was now ambassador to Canada, a country he loved, and had invited me to Ottawa to attend a dinner and to show my New Guinea film to his guests. One of these guests was Commissioner C. W. Harvison of the Royal Canadian Mounted Police, who took me aside after the screening to ask about my lifelong search for the primitive.

"It seems to me that you've covered the important primitive areas of the world," he said, "except one — the high Arctic. I know you wouldn't be interested in most Eskimo settlements, because they have been influenced by civilization for decades. But I know of one spot where Eskimos still live pretty much as their ancestors did hundreds, perhaps thousands, of years ago."

"Really! I thought there were none left," I said.

"There won't be for long," the commissioner said. "They live on Ellesmere Island, only a few hundred miles from the pole. There are just seventy-two Eskimo men, women, and children, plus two of my constables. No missionary. No Hudson's Bay store. And when you find a settlement without either of these, you'll know you are far from civilization. But in two years the government is going to build a school there, and many changes will follow. I thought you might be interested in filming these Eskimos before they move out of the Paleolithic Age."

"It sounds interesting," I said, "but I've had no experience in . . ."

"Good. Why don't you come to my office tomorrow and I'll tell you more about the last of these unspoiled Eskimos."

The appeal was irresistible. His "Go to the high Arctic before it is too late" was like the challenge of General Smuts that had sent me on my first expedition to Africa. I saw Harvison the next day in his office, where he pointed out on a large mural map the location of the tiny Eskimo settlement. It was at Grise Fiord on Ellesmere Island, well north of the Arctic Circle, three thousand miles north of the United States. Ellesmere itself is large — about six hundred miles long and from two hundred to three hundred miles wide. Grise Fiord, on its south shore, is the only settlement. It is, indeed, the northernmost settlement in the western hemisphere, if not in the world.

"It will not be an easy trip," Commissioner Harvison told me. "Our supply ship, the C. D. Howe, gets there only once a year, when the ice has broken up in late August or early September. And that's no time to see the real life of the Eskimos. So you'll have to fly in on one of our inspection planes, a single-engined Otter. It will leave the next day, and you'll be stuck at Grise Fiord until its next trip. You can stay at the RCMP detachment, but I don't think there's even a cot for you. And, of course, you'll be out with the Eskimos most of the time, eating their food, living pretty much as they live."

"That's the way I like it," I said.

"I know. That's why I want you to go. Another thing — there's nothing official about your film, though we'll help you all we can. You'll be on your own, free to make the kind of picture you want."

By this time I was eager to go, to see and film the last primitive Eskimos. To be able to do that, to have the full cooperation of the RCMP and complete freedom — that was all anyone could ask. There was still a question gnawing at the back of my mind — what was I going to film?

It seemed that late April or early May would be the best time to fly in, for the long night would have ended and there would be good light. The sea ice would still be frozen hard in most places, and I could travel by sled with the Eskimos and live with them in their hunting camps. Then I'd get out before July when the ice begins to break up.

Two air trips to Ottawa were rewarding. I found a competent cameraman who became my assistant producer, Douglas Sinclair. Between us, I felt sure, we could handle most filming problems. To our equipment we added an excellent tape recorder and a small electric generator. This last may sound strange, but I was determined to film inside igloos, which normally have only a weak half-light that filters through the translucent snow of the house. The generator would give us light wherever we wanted it.

Now I was finally flying north with Doug Sinclair and Superintendent Fraser of the RCMP, who was making his rounds of remote posts. Our RCMP pilot had no radio beams or other common navigational equipment to guide him, and his compass was almost useless as we approached and passed beyond the magnetic pole. Even the New Guinea bush pilots, dodging mountains and clouds, were not superior to these amazing fliers.

We set down at Frobisher Bay, Pangnirtung, Cape Christian, and Pond Inlet on Baffin Island, sliding acoss the sea ice on the plane's skis. For much of the flight the sky was overcast, and the weather looked so bad that we sometimes thought we might have to turn back to the last landing — provided it had not been closed in the meantime.

On the last lap to Grise Fiord, the skies cleared and the sunlight glistened on the snow and ice below us. The pilot pointed out Devon Island, separated from Ellesmere by Jones Sound, one of the most turbulent, stormy, and unpredictable bodies of water on earth, swept by gales from the Arctic Ocean and the North Pole. While it is ice-covered most of the year, the side that gets the worst of the winds never completely freezes. That's where we saw, along the edge of the ice floe, a school of white whales frolicking as if imitating porpoises. The plane dipped down so we could get some good footage of them. We left the strip of open water, glided down past a trapped iceberg casting a dark shadow, and landed on the frozen sea at Grise Fiord.

I saw three small wooden buildings and two fur-clad men standing in front of one of them. We taxied close, the plane came to a stop, and the pilot opened the door. I had a hard time getting out because of my heavy fur clothing. The two RCMP constables greeted us warmly. There were only a few planes into Grise Fiord each year, between the annual ship visit.

We all went inside their headquarters building, shed our heavy clothing, and enjoyed cups of hot tea. Occasionally I looked out the window at the bleak motionless landscape.

"Where are the Eskimos?" I asked.

"They're out at their hunting camps," Jenkin said. "This is seal-hunting time, you know."

"How far away?"

"The nearest camp — and the best one for you to see, I think — is about five hours by dogsled. We'll run out there tomorrow."

I knew that the plane was leaving with Superintendent Fraser about noon the next day. I was still not sure enough of this project to like the idea of being stuck there for two months. By the time we would return from our visit to the Eskimo camp, the plane would have gone.

"Is there smooth ice for a plane landing near the camp?" I asked.

"Of course," the pilot said. "There's smooth ice almost everywhere around here at this time of year. Why?"

I turned to Superintendent Fraser and asked if it might be possible for the plane to fly us out to the Eskimo camp in the morning so I could have a look. He agreed that it would be a good idea, and I felt better.

That evening, Sinclair and I talked with the three RCMP men for hours. One thing they kept repeating, in different ways, surprised me: "The Eskimos are the happiest people in the world."

"How can they be," I asked, "when they have to struggle so hard just to survive?"

"I know, it's hard to figure out," Jenkin said. "But you'll see, when you get to know them."

Most of our talk was about hunting, because an Eskimo's life centers around hunting. I asked if I'd have difficulty getting hunting sequences.

Jenkin and Bacchus assured me there would be no trouble at all, that the Eskimos were hunting all the time and would take me along with them. They would cooperate, too, so I could get what I wanted on film. But whatever they did for me would not be allowed to delay or interfere with the hunting, which meant life or death to them.

Obviously, I said, I could get seal-hunting aplenty at this time of year, but what about other animals, walrus, say?

Yes, but we'd probably have to travel about fifty miles to Craig Harbor, where there was open water, which walrus needed.

Caribou?

More difficult, as there were few caribou any more within a few days' travel from the post. But we could try at Tubtuvik, which in Eskimo meant *the place of the caribou*. About thirty miles away.

Polar bear?

Couldn't be sure. There was no special spot to look for them except where the seals were, for bears hunted seal as ardently as Eskimos did. We'd have to trust to luck and hope we'd run into a bear in the course of our other hunting. We'd keep a sharp lookout for their tracks.

What about whale?

Not at this time of year, for whale were hunted from boats during the short weeks of summer, when waterways were open.

Musk-ox?

They have become rare, and even Eskimos were not supposed to hunt them any more. But we might run into one or two small herds.

White fox?

We'd see plenty of beautiful pelts brought to the post for trade, but the peak of the trapping season was over. It didn't matter. There would have been no excitement of a chase, and dead foxes in traps do not make a very interesting or appealing picture.

What about shots of dogs fighting?

All three Canadians smiled. "That will be the easiest of all," Jenkin said. "They're fighting most of the time when they're not pulling or eating, and sometimes even then."

"Do they really sleep out in the worst weather?" I asked. "Half buried in the snow during a storm?"

"Sure, they sleep outside when it's seventy below. When we get a bad storm — and you can be sure we'll get one — you'll see. But you'll have a hard time holding onto your camera with that wind sweeping down on you. Little pups may be brought into the igloo in a storm, of course. And I've seen an Eskimo mother nurse the pup of a bitch that's been killed."

Having encountered this sort of thing in Africa, South America, and New Guinea, I was not surprised.

"How many Eskimos in a hunting camp?" I asked.

Twenty-five or thirty. The Eskimos at Grise Fiord usually went out in three groups. If they stayed together, they would clean out the game in one area too fast, so they separated, sometimes going many miles away. Eskimos liked plenty of room, too; a group of seventy-five or a hundred seemed like Times Square to them.

During our talk I learned that one of the duties of the constables was giving medical aid to the Eskimos, chiefly for respiratory infections: colds, influenza, pneumonia, and occasionally tuberculosis. However, tubercular Eskimos were usually flown out to a hospital "down South," or "outside." Although the men who volunteered for this three-year tour of duty in the north had first-aid and even elementary medical training, there were limitations to the help they could give.

"What do the Eskimos do when one of them is sick?" I asked. "Come here to you?"

"Not often," Bacchus said. "If they felt well enough to travel they wouldn't bother us at all. Half the time it's about their children, anyway, so they usually send someone to fetch us."

Perhaps this medical aid, the visit of a constable to a sick child in an igloo, might give me one sequence for the film. By the time I went to bed, in a sleeping bag on an air mattress on the floor, I had a kind of scenario worked out in my mind. Little did I know how much it would be revised by nature, events, and the magnificent Eskimos themselves.

The next morning we all climbed in the little Otter plane — except for Constable Bacchus, who stayed at the detachment — and flew about fifteen minutes over the frozen water of Jones Sound. Terry Jenkin told me that he was taking me to this particular camp because the settlement's two best hunters were here, and other people I might find interesting.

"They know you are coming, of course," he said. "And they will be glad to work with you, I think. There is almost no employment at which they can earn cash money around Grise Fiord. Further south there is the loading and unloading of supplies, building, and other work once in a while. And some places have formed cooperatives to run fisheries, canneries, art centers, all of which keep some of the people profitably busy. Up here the store, or trading post, is a cooperative, though we assist in managing it. And there's enough game, except in bad years, to support everybody. But they like a chance to earn a little money, to buy a few of the products of civilization. Still, they live just about the way their grandfathers and great-grandfathers did. They're fine people. Just wait and see."

Jenkin pointed out five igloos on the ice as we circled for a landing. I could see people streaming out of igloos and looking up at us, waving. The plane was surrounded the moment it came to a stop, but as we climbed out, the Eskimos stepped back and fell silent.

As Jenkin and Superintendent Fraser talked and shook hands with some of the men in the crowd, Doug Sinclair and I looked them over. Their faces were aglow with life. Some of them gestured and grimaced so expressively that I could sense what they were talking about.

I turned to Doug Sinclair. "We can make a good picture with these people," I said.

"I think so, too." And he was smiling as happily as the Eskimos.

Constable Jenkin came back and led us forward a few steps, making what was obviously a general introduction. Then he turned to me.

"Well, what do you think? Will some of these people do?"

I picked out my cast on the spot. "I want that man there, and that one, and that woman, and that boy, and the smaller boy, and probably that other man over there, and the woman next to him. Maybe more later, but certainly those."

"How did you do it?" Jenkin asked. "You picked the very ones I had in mind. That first man is Akpaliapik, acknowledged leader of the entire settlement and one of the best hunters. The other is Markosie, the finest hunter and a real character. And you picked their wives and one son and a nephew."

I talked through Jenkin with a few of the people I had designated. Markosie, the great hunter, was a man whose smile was infectious and whose eyes danced with life and good humor. Akpaliapik, a few years older, was more serious and dignified; an air of confidence and assurance emanated from him. He was the kind of man who would have been the leader of any group in which he found himself. The Eskimos have no chief in even the vaguest sense, being the most rugged of individualists. But often, through ability and force of personality, one man in a group is asked to make decisions about the hunt, moving camp, and other important matters. He is followed because he is usually right. That was Akpaliapik among the seventy-two Eskimos living near Grise Fiord.

As I looked about and saw children of different sizes and ages, including a baby peeking out from the parka hood of one of the women, I recalled my idea of showing eskimo life from birth to death.

"Do you think it might be possible to film the birth of a baby?" I asked Constable Jenkin.

"I don't know if there are any on the way," he replied. "I'll ask Markosie."

Jenkin translated the Eskimo's answer to his question. "No, there are no babies due now. One was born a few weeks ago, but there will be no more for some time."

Markosie saw my look of disappointment, smiled, and said something quickly to Jenkin. "Markosie says 'Why don't you take my wife and make her pregnant? Then a baby will be born for you.' "

That was my introduction to the cooperative spirit of the Eskimos. While I never took advantage of this offer, I found them willing to go all out in any endeavor during my entire stay.

After an hour at the hunting camp, we flew back to the post, and shortly thereafter the plane went on its way with Superintendent

Fraser. The following two days were overcast, cold, and stormy, so we did not venture out. The weather was beginning to clear when two *komatiks*, or sleds, appeared. The first was driven by the Eskimo special constable, Ningu, who had been on some duty at one of the other hunting camps. He was a soft-spoken, taciturn man of about forty who lived in a small house at the post with his family of five. He had worked for the Mounties for twelve years, and his father had been a special constable on Baffin Island before him. He was a great hunter, an uncanny tracker, and very intelligent.

The second visitor was Okoko, younger brother of Markosie the hunter, who came to tell us that the camp had moved further away and that two of Akpaliapik's children were sick. So events began to decide what I was going to film and when.

"We'll take care of them," Jenkin told Okoko. "Might as well get started now. We can get partway today, anyway."

So there were three sleds on my first trip over the ice — a light one driven by Okoko, one carrying Constable Jenkin and me, and a third driven by Special Constable Ningu, with Doug Sinclair as passenger. Doug and I helped load the komatiks, since much of what they were carrying belonged to us — cameras, generator, lights and sound equipment. Things had to be packed carefully, for a sled takes incredible jouncing about. On top of everything went bear and caribou skins, then all was lashed down with sealskin ropes to the heavy frames. Meanwhile the dogs — there were more than thirty of them — were howling (they never really bark), running back and forth, sometimes snarling at each other. They would hardly stand still to have their harnesses attached, and it was obvious they were impatient to get going. I had been told that there was nothing huskies loved so much as pulling sleds hour after hour, and they acted as if that were true every time we traveled. Of course, they loved to eat, to fight and to copulate (and in that order, I think), but from puppyhood they like nothing quite so much as pulling a sled over the ice and snow. We filmed a shot of husky pups, most of them about half adult size, trotting along beside and in front of the team. They were not hitched. No whip was lashed at them. But they paced along mile after mile, and seemed to be just as indefatigable as their elders.

The true origin of husky dogs is unknown. They would appear to be part dog and part wolf, but at any rate a distinct breed of dog has developed. Archeological findings give no evidence that the earliest Eskimos, who migrated from northeast Asia, had dogs. Evidence indicates that the huskies were first used about one thousand years ago. The average dog on a team weighs about ninety pounds, though some go as high as a hundred twenty pounds. When they are busy, they eat four to six pounds of meat a day, so more than half of an Eskimo's hunting is done for his dogs. The Eskimo, on the other hand, could not hunt without them, so the interdependence of dog and man in the high Arctic is complete. Neither could live without the other.

The ice and snow were smooth when we started out that first day. And the skins on top of the sled made riding very comfortable indeed. At first there was a good deal of noise, what with the dogs howling and the drivers shouting and cracking their thirty- to forty-foot sealskin whips; the whips serve both to get the dogs moving and to give them direction. As each sled got under way, the driver ran alongside and deftly leapt sideways onto the front of the sled. In time I learned to do this myself, for when the ice became really rough I had to jump off and run alongside once in a while until the komatik got on an even keel again.

The dogs spread out in front of us as we glided over the snow. They were attached to the komatik with a fan hitch, quite different from the Nome hitch used in western Canada and Alaska. There are forests in many parts of the west so dogs are hitched to follow narrow trails in double file, each dog on a short leash to a center line. In the east, however, it is better for dogs to fan out, and each one is attached individually to the komatik, with the center of lead dog having a line about ten feet long. Thus the dogs rarely get bunched together in defiles between crags or pack ice. Each dog can more or less pick his own route around ice hummocks and crevices.

While this system works well most of the time, there are disadvantages. A dog on the extreme right, for example, may skirt an upthrusting chunk of ice, which snags his line. He may break it, or the driver may free it in time, or he may be pulled around the ice chunk backwards as the sled goes past it. I saw this last happen, and the dog was thrown right under the big sled. I thought he was dead, but he jumped up after the sled passed over him, howling loudly. He had been bumped and bruised, but he rushed back to his place in the team and ran along for the rest of the way without even being hitched.

One of the dogs on the RCMP team frequently seemed about to entangle himself in rough ice. I thought that he would get his line snagged but he never did. Jenkin told me later what this dog, known as Skookie, was up to. He wanted to lift his leg at almost every chunk of ice he came to, just as a city dog wants to pause at every fire hydrant. Skookie was quick about it, and always managed to race back to his place before the sled caught up with him.

"Skookie's coming to the end of his working life," Jenkin told me when we stopped for some hot tea and a bite. "He has been on this team seven years, which is already a couple of years more than most dogs. You'll notice, too, that he's smaller than any of the others, even the bitches — weighs only about seventy pounds. But he still is one of the best pullers on the team. He must have traveled seven or eight thousand miles in his time; I know of one long patrol that took him more than a thousand.

"Skookie is a terrible fighter," Jenkin went on. "He'll pick a fight with any dog at any time. I can't understand it, because he always gets the worst of it, especially now that half of his teeth are gone. Maybe it's because, being a fighter, he can lord it over the dogs that *aren't* fighters; a few of them are like that. Take Blackie there — biggest dog on the team, almost a hundred and twenty pounds. Blackie just doesn't like to fight, for some reason, and Skookie pushes him around all the time, makes his life miserable when we aren't on the go."

A few weeks later Skookie was killed. He had got in his last fight, over Sheila, a bitch that had just come into heat. Skookie coveted her, but another dog — not Blackie — had different ideas. As a result, one of Skookie's ears was completely torn off, there was a bite clear through one leg, and great chunks were torn out of his hide. He was bleeding to death, too far gone to save, so Constable Bacchus had to shoot him. He and Jenkin were very upset about it, because they had been fond of Skookie.

Generally, Eskimo dogs are not pets in our sense of the word. Some may be fairly friendly at times, but they are completely unpredictable and can turn into snarling wolves in a second, without recognizable cause. In some communities of Eskimos, they have been known to attack and kill small children. They have to be tied down so they can't reach each other while resting on a trip. The dogs are fixed by short leads to a long chain laid out across the top of the snow. Spikes at regular intervals along the chain are driven into the snow to hold it fast, then urinated on so they will freeze tight.

They are freed from the chain for feeding, and then there is a battle royal. When I filmed some of these feeding scenes I was really scared by the dozen or more beasts baring fangs, howling, lunging at the big pile of meat that had been put out for them, attacking each other, tugging at the big pieces. It was all over in a few minutes, and after each feeding there were always a few dogs licking wounds. In the scramble the biggest and most ferocious dogs got the most meat. Markosie explained to me, "The big dogs get the most. They work the hardest."

"But they can be mighty exasperating at times," Jenkin told me. "When they get the idea they want to go one way and you want to go another, they'd get the better of you if you didn't use the whip. But I've got to hand it to them. They can go anywhere. They are absolutely fearless — you'll know it when you see them go after a polar bear. And on a long trip, the men will drop from exhaustion before the dogs do — and the dogs have been doing all the pulling."

I saw plenty of evidence of the dogs' pluck every time we took a trip — and that was often during my stay. Even on that first day out, when we came to a stretch of rough pack ice, I saw the dogs unerringly pick the best route, sliding down between icy crags, with the sled rushing down behind them, tugging up slippery slopes with a komatik that seemed to have a will of its own and a determination to go anywhere but the right direction.

The sled drivers were amazing at these difficult places, too, Eskimos and constables alike. They'd leap off the komatik, push against the front of it to head it past a huge, jagged ice chunk, wrestle it around corners, and help the dogs get it up steep grades. At first I just held on for dear life, gripping the sides of the sled with all my might. But I felt pretty useless doing this, and soon learned to do my share of the pulling and tugging.

When the going is smooth, Eskimo komatiks can make about five miles an hour, but rough ice hummocks, caused by a combination of high winds and tidal action, can cut the speed to about half that. Thus we could often make thirty to thirty-five miles a day without straining ourselves too much. Other times, though, we kept going for twenty-four hours at a stretch, usually because we'd been out and wanted to make home without a single sleep.

Trips were always described as "one sleep," "two sleeps," and so on, depending upon the number of times we made camp for the night. Occasionally, when the weather was fine and we were going to stop only for some food and a few hours' sleep, we did not bother to make igloos or, later in the season, set up a tent. Special Constable Ningu would scan the sky, lift his nose as if inhaling a weather report from the air, and declare that there would be no strong wind or snow for some time. Then we would stop in the lee of an ice ridge or berg, spread our skins on the snowy crust, crawl into our precious sleeping bags, and sleep. And Ningu was always right. He was serious and conscientious, the most solemn of all the Eskimos I came to know.

The komatiks I traveled on were about eighteen feet long. They could carry loads of fifteen hundred pounds plus two men, if pulled to a twelve-dog team. Before the coming of the white man they had been made with runners of whalebone, which was smooth as ice and lasted forever. But big whalebones were hard to come by, so the Eskimos had taken readily to the hardwood planks imported by the Mounties. Each runner is now made of a single oak plank two inches thick and ten inches wide. The two runners are connected by crossbeams, which are lashed with leather thongs. The thongs are strong but allow for some "give" as the sled moves over uneven ice. A few runners on Eskimo komatiks are shed with strips of whalebone left over from the old days before the yearly ship began bringing in lumber.

Whether the runners are of wood or whalebone, however, they have to be "iced" for smooth traveling. This can be done by spreading warm water or snow covered with water, over the runners. The water instantly freezes outdoors. But water is too precious and hard to get in quantity for this to be done often: snow or non-salt ice has to be melted laboriously over small seal-oil or primus stoves. So Eskimos usually use a kind of mud for the basic icing of runners. Mud is not quite the correct term since there is so little earth in the Arctic, even during the brief summer. But they gather, during that comparatively warm spell, a good quanity of mixed dirt and rotted vegetation which they keep over the winter for the sole purpose of forming sled runners. It is molded on the bottoms of the runners about an inch thick, smoothed off, then coated with water, the whole application freezing to a slick surface. As a substitute for mud, the Mounties prefer a thick porridge (cooked without salt) for icing. They carry oats on their trips so they can patch runners that get cracked or broken.

One aspect of travel by komatik that never failed to amaze me was the unerring navigational instinct of the Eskimos. They could set out from the post over a vast expanse of white that to me offered no distinguishing features; they could be diverted from their desired course by extremely rough ice or by open-water leads; but they always wound up at the tiny dot of a hunting camp fifty or more miles away. Not once did I see them fumble or make tentative passes in one direction or another; they always hit their objective right on the nose. They didn't have compasses in this land north of the magnetic pole. And ridges of snow, ice cracks and hummocks were constantly shifting and were unreliable as guide marks. The tracks of other sleds could be obliterated in a few hours if there was wind and snow — and there were both a good deal of the time. In some areas there were hills and valleys and huge piles of rocks underneath the snow and ice that were relatively permanent, but none of these existed over the long expanses of sea ice over which the Eskimos traveled for eight or nine months of the year.

After a year or two in the Arctic, the RCMP constables developed some of this navigational ability, without being able to explain it. And the airplane pilots certainly had it; they usually managed to get where they were going in snowstorms and with almost no visibility. Perhaps human beings were originally endowed with navigational instincts not unlike those of birds, bees, and other animals. The Eskimos have kept them by using them. The Mounties and pilots reactivated them by using them. But the Mounties, good as they were, always liked to have an Eskimo along on a long journey.

When we came on our first trip, to the hunting camp with its five igloos, we were greeted by the howling of dogs — ours and theirs — and many women and children and a few men who greeted us with the never-failing smiles. Although most of the men were out hunting, Akpaliapik was there. His two youngsters were sick, and he had stayed behind, knowing that Jenkin was coming.

The constable followed Akpaliapik to his igloo at once, motioning to me to follow him. We crawled through the small door, and I found myself inside an igloo for the first time. There was more light than I had anticipated, a kind of twilight glow made by sunlight filtering through six-inch-thick walls of snow. After my eyes had adjusted, the translucence seemed stronger, and I could make out all details easily.

There was a strong center of light from the seal-oil stove that Eskimos call a *kudlik*. And another more luminous glow through a window of clear ice.

I pushed myself back beside the door to be out of the way, but Akpaliapik and his wife Ikhaluk, smiling their welcomes, insisted on installing me at one end of the sleeping platform that occupied about two-thirds of the interior of the igloo. Only when they were sure that I was comfortable did they turn their attention to Constable Jenkin and their sick children, who lay under their sleeping furs on the platform, which was made of hard-packed snow, covered with two or three layers of skins, polar bear and caribou.

Jenkin looked first at eight-year-old Jamisie, peering into throat, nose, ears, and taking temperature. The young fellow did not seem very apprehensive, perhaps because he was so busy trying to look at me, the unknown newcomer. When the thermometer was in his mouth, Jenkin turned his attentions to Ouisa, a most attractive girl — no, woman, even though she was only seventeen. Jamisie looked at me and grinned. I pointed to my mouth, shut it tight, trying to tell him to keep his lips closed around the thermometer. He thought this was very funny and laughed. Jenkin turned and spoke to him. Jamisies' mouth closed tight, but his eyes kept sparkling at me. We were sharing some kind of secret joke. When I turned to look at Ouisa, I found her eyes boring into me, but they were cast down at once and a slow blush came over her face. She did not look at me again during that first visit, and every time I saw her after that her eyes sought the ground at her feet. Most Eskimo women are quite shy; she was the shyest I met.

The two children had flu, for which Jenkin gave injections. He said they would be fine within a few days. And when that time came I said I would like to film a reenactment of that first visit to an igloo. Akpaliapik and his family agreed, so we set up the generator outside, fed the wires to lights inside the snow house, and took our pictures. It was crowded inside, even though the igloo was a fairly big one, about twelve feet in diameter. All the action took place on the sleeping platform, and we managed to get some good shots. I had been worried that my "actors" would freeze up during a reenactment, but I should have remembered what good performers most primitive people are. They wanted to go too far, really. Jamisie winced a little too much as the needle went into him, for instance. But I finally convinced my ham actors to play it cool and natural, and we got a good authentic sequence.

An igloo is in many ways a wonderful home. Certainly it represents the perfect use of available materials. There is no doubt that a wooden house is better, particularly if well insulated, but you cannot set up a wooden house in an hour or less and use it for a day or a week or a month and then abandon it, as you can an igloo. Tents will answer those requirements, of course, and Eskimos use them for about three months in the year when the ice breaks up and the good hard-packed igloo snow is gone. Their tents are made of caribou skins, preferably, and they can be warm and comfortable, but winds can blow them down, no matter how well secured they are. Winds can't blow down igloos. The Eskimos are nonetheless happy when the season makes them turn from igloos to tents, happy again when cold sends them back to igloos. Summer is good because it means tents, whale-hunting, fishing for Arctic char (a delectable fish somewhat like salmon), and the yearly visit of the ship. Winter is good because that is the time for trapping white fox. And spring is the time when there are plenty of seals to catch.

The word *igloo* means *house* to an Eskimo, no matter what it's made of. A shack and a snow house are both igloos. The snow house that we know (and I refer to) as "igloo" is called an *iglooviuk*. These vary considerably in size, depending upon the family occupying them and the duration of the stay. The smallest is about six feet in diameter, the kind that may be made by two or three hunters for a one- or two-night stay. The largest may be twenty-five feet across, although the most common igloo is somewhere in between, say twelve to fifteen feet. Sometimes, at a semi-permanent hunting camp, there may be a main igloo joined to one or two smaller igloos which house supplies, food, puppies, and so on.

You can't build an igloo just anywhere; you must have the right kind of snow, packed to a consistent hardness by the wind. I've been on trips when the Eskimos stopped two or three times to test the snow before they found the right spot. They'd stick their knives down into it, make a cut or two, and decide if it was too icy (too hard to cut) or too soft (the blocks would crumble). The ideal is an area in which the snow is hard-packed to a depth of a few feet, so one can cut out good-sized blocks several layers deep. In such cases — but they are rare — a man can make his entire igloo from the spot in which he stands. He cuts out the first layer of blocks, each block about two feet long, eighteen inches wide, and six inches thick, and then starts his walls, placing the bottom blocks so that they slope slightly inwards and rest against each others' sides. The dimension of this bottom layer determines the size of the igloo, of course. If the snow is hard-packed to a considerable depth, the Eskimo may then cut a second series of blocks from the floor within the walls to make his next layer or two of outer sheathing.

Most of the time, however, the builders must cut their snow blocks from the area around the igloo. Its floor is always below normal snow level, however. The blocks are not strictly rectangular, for each edge is sheered so that it will lean against the sheered edge of the next block. While the men are cutting and putting the blocks in place, the women are busy filling up the chinks between them with snow. Each row of blocks slopes in at a greater angle until there is just one round hole at the top, into which a capstone of snow is fitted. Meanwhile the worker on the inside cuts his snow to allow for the hard-packed sleeping platform occupying the rear two-thirds of the house. Then he cuts his way out through the wall, making the igloo's door.

After the door is cut, anywhere from three-quarters of an hour to an hour from starting time, the sleeping skins and other equipment are carried inside. The kudlik is set up at one end of the platform. It is a flat lamp carved out of soapstone, usually rectangular in shape, from eight by twelve to twelve by eighteen inches. The center area has been partly hollowed out to make a kind of dish, which slopes toward the front. Seal oil and fat are put in the depressed area, and they soak into a series of wicks along the front edge, where a low, quiet flame burns when the stove is lighted. Wicks are made from tufts of "cotton grass," or moss, which grows during the short summer. The kudlik gives off a candle-light light that is very pleasant, and its heat is enough to cook anything — slowly — but not enough to melt the snow roof above it.

There is usually a drying rack above the kudlik where mittens, boots, and other wet clothing are dried out. The other essentials of life are nearby, so that all can be reached from the big sleeping platform — guns, harpoons, and a small shelf full of the products of civilization: tea (Eskimos drink gallons of it), pablum (if there are babies in the family), ammunition (if there are guns) and tobacco (if they smoke, as most Eskimos do).

Within an hour, an igloo is reasonably comfortable. The heat of four of five people brings the temperature up; if it is forty below outside, the inside of an igloo may be forty above within an hour, which is not bad when you wear your winter clothing or crawl under your sleeping skins. Breakfast is always prepared by the wife, who can reach everything from her place and pass along the steaming cups of tea, a few chunks of raw seal meat, and pieces of bannock, a form of bread.

Obviously there is not much privacy in an igloo. Father, mother, and children sleep on the platform, along with perhaps a grand-mother, a cousin, an adopted child, and any traveler who may have come along. The often-told tales of Eskimos offering their wives to their guests are absolutely true. They offer everything they have, and they feel that a man needs a woman or a woman needs a man as much as he or she needs food. In the opinion of the Eskimo, the two needs are pretty much the same. I managed to decline these offers graciously and tactfully enough not to offend my hosts.

A group of five or more families usually lives and hunts together. Fathers may arrange for the "engagement" of their children when they are babies, or even before one of them is born. A man wants his son to get a wife who is a good cook, a good sewer of clothes, and one who is — I heard this over and over again — definitely *not* a gossip, a nag, or troublemaker. So he looks at the mother and concludes that her daughter will turn out to be much like her. If he has a son, who is perhaps not more than a year or two old, he may ask for the hand of his friend's daughter even before she is born — providing she turns out to be a daughter. In any event, boys and girls are usually affianced at an early age. But there is no payment, no bride-price — only an understanding. The children grow up aware of this understanding, but they are not completely bound by it.

I saw the fruition of one such understanding while I was there. Okoko, Markosie's younger brother, about nineteen years old, had been promised to Ouisa, Akpaliapik's daughter, since they were babies. Now they were approaching the time when they should get together. Okoko had, as a matter of fact, gone to Akpaliapik the year before, requesting that the marriage should begin. But Akpaliapik had put him off, saying that he was too young and should wait another year. That time had passed, and Okoko asked again. The fathers talked it over, confirmed their agreement of years before, and the marriage — or rather, trial marriage — began. Akpaliapik invited Okoko to move into his igloo, and Okoko accepted. He felt like a big man at this moment, no matter how embarrassed he was as he entered Akpaliapik's igloo. Ouisa was far worse, blushing and staring at the floor. But the family, with its new member, ate together, Akpaliapik giving Okoko, the guest, the choice morsels of seal. Then they all went to bed together on the sleeping platform. The grown ups ostensibly went to sleep. They would not have moved a muscle for anything.

For some weeks Okoko lived with Akpaliapik's family. He went hunting with the men, and his catch belonged to Akpaliapik. Ouisa acted in all respects as his wife, sewing and mending his clothes and warming his feet against her bare stomach when he came in from the cold. At any time either Okoko or Ouisa could have called the whole thing off if they didn't get along. But since all went well, Okoko finally asked Akpaliapik if he and Ouisa could move into *his* father's igloo. Permission granted. A few weeks' trial there, and everything was fine.

Then came the time when the two were to be recognized as adult man and wife. And this was forever. There is comparatively little divorce in the Eskimo world, perhaps because marriage partners take plenty of time getting to know each other beforehand. When the day comes for them to go off on a komatik together, the bride can still run home to her father's igloo or the groom can just fail to appear. Then everyone knows that the marriage is off. And there are no hard feelings. There may be as many as three or four trial marriages before the real thing comes along.

What if there is a child born of the trial marriage? This presents no problem since most families are eager to adopt children and every child is considered part of the entire group. There is no such thing as an illegitimate child in the Eskimo world. Every family in a camp would happily claim any child as its own. And there are many children who spend as much time at their uncle's or grandmother's as at home with their parents. Thus the death of a parent is much less of a blow than it would be in our society. The Eskimo child has dozens of parents.

Eskimos don't think of adoption in our terms. If one family has many children, another family few, the well-supplied family will give a new baby to the other for adoption. I know of one mother who had two boys and desperately wanted a girl. Her closest friend had two girls and a boy. Woman A said to Woman B, "If your next baby is a girl, give her to me." It was a girl. It was a deal. And from that time on, no one thought of the term "adoption." The girl was Woman A's baby, that's all. I know another family that traveled hundreds of miles to Baffin Island to find a boy to adopt.

And how the children were loved! Although I was used to seeing great affection and understanding given to children in most primitive societies, I was deeply impressed by the feelings of older Eskimos for their young ones. I never saw spankings or threats or anger by any Eskimo toward a child, whether his own or not, only much hugging and nuzzling. The traditional nose-to-nose gesture is common, too, but is not the only way to express affection. One the other hand, I have never seen an Eskimo child of any age be pesky or disobedient or even inconsiderate. Maybe they were behaving themselves in my presence. But I was around too long for them to be on their good behavior all the time. They were good, that's all, but they were not browbeaten or subservient. They were respectful of their elders because they wanted to be and because the grown-ups deserved respect.

In the Eskimo family the father is king. His wife is in charge inside the igloo only, but in many ways she exerts considerable influence — sometimes so subtly that he isn't aware of it — on the lord and master. The father rarely abuses his position, but he maintains it. Even when his son has grown up, has his own wife and igloo and sled and dog team, he will expect that son to ask for permission to go out on a hunt, and to accept instructions. The son acquiesces because Eskimo children always accept their fathers' word. The father — in such a rugged world — has usually been right.

There is, however, in any family or group, that day when the son takes over the leadership from his father. It happens overnight, and everyone in the group recognizes the change. Suddenly the son is a greater hunter than his father, a better guide and adviser than his father. Everyone knows it, and without any proclamation, the father recedes into the background and the son takes charge. But the father is still the most honored member of the community. The son will still ask his advice, but do what he thinks best.

As in all primitive societies, there are strict divisions between the work of men and women, but the Eskimos apportion work more evenly than other groups. Both men and women work very hard. They know they are dependent on each other for survival. The men hunt, trap, fish, to bring home food for family and dogs plus skins to trade at the post for the few products of civilization they now require. This work is exhausting, dangerous, and never-ending. The women make all clothing for the family and keep it in good repair; they cook, take care of children (as she works, a naked baby may be tucked in a woman's *amoutik*, or hooded parka, making her look humpbacked). The women also scrape, clean, and dry the skins of foxes, bears, caribou, and seals, using the "woman's tool," a semi-circular knife called an *ulu*. This is demanding labor, for the value of a skin as clothing or as trade goods depends upon removing every particle of flesh or fat without leaving a pinhole or a thin spot in the skin itself.

One reason for the equitable division of labor is the absence of war — now and for centuries past. The male Jivaro, Pygmy, Dani, *et al* had to sit around with their weapons at hand, in case of attack. They had many hours of leisure, while their women worked and they stood guard. But the Eskimo's only enemy has been nature itself. His struggle to gain sustenance from a barren and frozen ground and the sea is war enough; the Eskimo doesn't have time or energy for a battle with other men.

One of the chief activities of women, young and old, is chewing leather. I spent many evenings in Akpaliapik's igloo listening to tales of the hunt as translated by Constable Jenkin. While there, I very often saw Akpaliapik's wife, Ikhaluk, and his daughter, Ouisa, sit and chew leather. Most important were boot bottoms, which might become stiff and crack after they had dried out on the rack above the kudlik. Chewing restored moisture and pliability to the leather. Mittens often needed the same treatment, and thread — really thin leather sinews — for making and mending clothes. These "threads" swell when wet, closing seams even tighter than when dry. This is essential in the usually frozen north. A man's life may depend upon a good seam, for if snow or water gets inside an outfit it can mean death. Each animal skin has its special qualities. Caribou is best for parkas and trousers, for each hair is hollow, making for insulation against the cold, which can drop to 70° below. For boot soles, the skin of the *ugruk*, a big bearded seal with square flippers, is best; uppers come from the more common small seal. Although the RCMP trading post had some manufactured goods, the Eskimos at Grise Fiord still make more than ninety per cent of their own clothing and footwear. Their brothers further south had come to prefer rubber boots and heavy twill parkas.

I enjoyed my evenings in the igloos of the Eskimos. While a snow house is no place for privacy, it exudes an all-embracing warmth that makes any occupant a member of a happy family. (Incidentally, I found none of the unpleasant greasy smell I had read about, possibly because we were so far north.)

Markosie's was a particularly lively home, for he was a compulsive talker, laugher, jokester, and he had an appreciative family. There was his wife, Pangootoo; his mother, Tetecaga; his father, Keeago, one of the best hunters and carvers at Grise Fiord; his daughter, Alisie; much of the time his nephew, fourteen-year-old Imooshie; and his younger brother, Okoko. There was another baby, too, hidden most of the time in Pangootoo's amoutik. While I was there, the family lost one member when Okoko moved over to Akpaliapik's igloo, as a first step in his marriage to Ouisa.

The Eskimo children captivated me, and as time went on they played a more and more important role in the sequences we were shooting of their everyday life. I had brought along some toys, mainly stuffed animals of various kinds. The big hit of the collection was an ingenious, lifelike, windup polar bear that moved its head; the children were fascinated with it because, I learned, it was about the size of a polar bear cub. Later I got some good shots of boys and girls playing, an activity that consumes most of their waking hours. One boy held caribou antlers to his forehead and became the hunted animal, while the others stalked him with their harpoons. They raced down snowy slopes on their sleds, whooping at the top of their lungs.

In one sequence, while the grownups were constructing igloos for a new camp, some of the boys decided to make an igloo of their own. It was about one-third the regular size, but it was as snug and tight as the snow houses their fathers were making. As in most primitive societies, much of the play of boys and girls serves to train them for adult responsibilities.

By the time a boy reached the age of thirteen, like Markosie's nephew Imooshie, he went in for more serious training. Markosie taught Imooshie to handle the dogs and the sled and the thirty-foot whip, to shoot a rifle with accuracy, to hurl the short, heavy harpoon. During the winter Imooshie had accompanied Markosie on his trips to the traplines, and together they had a successful season. As a matter of fact, all the good hunters at Grise Fiord had done well during the winter before I arrived. Constable Jenkin told me that the whale hunting had been good, and they had brought in several hundred white fox skins. Imooshie had come along far enough in his training as a hunter to join our party when we went looking for seal, walrus and bear.

I was pleased when Imooshie and then some of the other young ones started calling me by a name. I couldn't figure out what it was, but it was obviously spoken with respect and affection. Terry Jenkin was a little reluctant to tell me that the name Atatachuk meant *grandfather*. But knowing the high regard Eskimos have for grandparents, I was really flattered. When Markosie, Akpaliapik, and some of the other adults began to use the same name, however, I wondered. Did I look *that* old? Then I realized that many Eskimos are grandfathers when they are forty, and I was glad they had not called me "great-grandfather."

So I shrugged my shoulders and muttered, *Iyonamut*. This word expresses the philosophy of the Eskimo, his patient courage in the face of long, long odds against him. It means something like, "It can't be helped," or "That's life for you," or "I've done my damnedest and now Fate takes over." It is not so much defeatism as acceptance of the inevitable.

I've encountered this attitude, or something like it, in most primitive groups. But it was usually a negative fatalism, a giving-up of the battle, even the will to live. A Jivaro Indian who was convinced that an enemy medicine man had called upon evil spirits to kill him usually gave up all hope. His very hopelessness often led to his death.

One story illustrating the Eskimo's battle with the elements came to me from a government administrator at Cape Dorset, on southern Baffin Island. He told me the experience of two brothers, Navani and Harkuk, who lived and hunted on Baffin Island, real nomads who roamed with their families over hundreds of square miles in search of game, coming in to the post for trading only once or twice a year. One winter the hunting was bad, and the two men used up most of their rifle shells but got little food. Some of their dogs died of starvation; others were eaten by the humans. But then Navani and Harkuk decided that they must reach the post, for only one shell was left and it was still early winter.

They set off on the forty-mile trip with a small sled pulled by their last two dogs. Halfway there, they spotted three polar bears, a mother and two two-year-old cubs almost as big as she was. Here were food and valuable skins, and the Eskimos made up their minds to get those bears — but not at the cost of using their last shell. Navani said he would get the bear with his harpoon, not by hurling it, but by making the bear impale herself on it. The hunter ran up close to the mother bear, braced the butt of his harpoon against the ice, and taunted the bear. A mother protecting her cubs does not need much taunting. She rushed at Navani and ran right onto the point of the harpoon, but did not strike a vital spot. A polar bear takes a lot of killing.

With one swipe of her huge paw, the bear ripped open the side of Navani's head. With another she tore most of the flesh from the hip to one knee. Navani was knocked out, and the bear stood over him, ready to deal the coup de grace. She was concentrating so hard on Navani that she did not see Harkuk running up close. Harkuk poked the barrel of the rifle in the bear's ear and fired — he was taking no chances with his last shot. Harkuk then went after the big cubs and got them both with his harpoon. The two dogs had been killed in the first attack on the bear, and the sled was useless without them. So he skinned the three bears, piled the skins on top of each other on the ground, and put his wounded brother in the middle. Then he started to drag the whole load twenty miles to the post.

As they neared the post, the two Eskimos were singing and laughing. The wounded man was patched and sewed up, and the brothers received a good store of trade goods in exchange for three polar bear skins. Happy ending.

2

Ootook and Nanook

DURING most of my stay on Ellesmere Island we were out accompanying hunters, but there were many days spent "at home," around the Mountie post at Grise Fiord and at different Eskimo camps. We took shots of Markosie bringing in for trade a collection of white fox pelts that almost covered him. They were the last batch from his winter trapping, cleaned and stretched in the sun to dry by his wife, Pangootoo. Another time we filmed Akpaliapik with a huge polar bear skin which was being examined closely by Constable Jenkin to determine its probable value. Some shots inside the small post store showed what products of civilization the Eskimos wanted most — tobacco, tea, flour, sugar, dried fruits, kerosene, pablum, ammunition. When the furs were actually sold in the cities "outside," the amount, less shipping expenses, was credited to the Eskimos' accounts at the post. Polar bear skins were fairly stable in price, but fox pelts fluctuated with the styles of the fashion world.

At the Eskimo hunting camps, Doug Sinclair and I filmed some blinding snowstorms that stopped all hunting. Every few minutes we had to put both hands and cameras inside our fur parkas to keep them from freezing. Later, during a sudden premature two-day warm spell when water on top of the sea ice made traveling by sled difficult, we were delighted to get a fine sequence of Akeeago and Akpaliapik sitting side by side and carving. The Eskimos use soapstone, a soft but heavy stone, gray, and usually nicely grained. It is amazing to watch an Eskimo examine an irregular block of soapstone while he decides what to carve from it. Akeeago said to me once, "I look to see what's inside the stone. Then I can carve it."

Of all the primitive art I have brought back from my expeditions, only the carvings of the Bakuba tribe in Central Africa rival Eskimo sculpture. It is simple, almost stark, but there is a grace and beauty that gives life to the stone. Although the preliminary work is done with a hammer, it is shaped and finished with files. Good Eskimo carving is in growing demand in the museums and among the collectors of the world. In some settlements, such as Cape Dorset on Baffin Island, it is an important source of income, as is also the making of prints, an art that was introduced there by James Houston, for some years the government administrator at Cape Dorset, on southern Baffin Island. Many settlements have formed cooperatives for the sale of animal products as well as art objects. Under the sponsorship of the Canadian government, the cooperatives have recently banded together to help each other.

For the Eskimos at Grise Fiord, carving was only an occasional activity, engaged in when hunting was impossible. During most of the time I was there, hunting was possible, if not always productive. The animal most frequently hunted, most needed by the Eskimo, is the seal. This is not the seal of the circus or zoo, which is usually a sea lion. It is a smaller animal, averaging about eighty pounds in weight, although specimens up to a hundred twenty pounds and more are caught. And it is not the "bearded" or "square-flippered" seal, although the Eskimos prize this rarer beast also; the ugruk, as they call the big fellow, weighs up to eight hundred pounds and supplies wonderfully tough thongs, lines for dogs, and bootsoles.

When the temperature rises a little, and the snow begins to melt, seals enlarge their breathing holes and come up on the ice occasionally. At the same time, the thick layer of sea ice begins to crack in places, through tidal action, forming long "leads" of open water, from a few inches to many feet wide. Along these leads, too, seals come to the surface, clamber onto the ice, and bask in the sun. At this time of year, an Eskimo hunts seals behind a *teliwak*, a square of white cloth fitted on a light wooden frame; inching his way along on his belly, the Eskimo peeps through a slit in the cloth, with his rifle poked through another, lower slit.

A seal on the ice calls for a special word in Eskimo, *ootook*. An ootook sleeps only fitfully, putting its head down and dozing for twenty or thirty seconds, then lifting its nose into the air and peering around for its enemies — polar bear and, near settlements, man. The Eskimo hunter creeps forward during these short snoozes, freezing into immobility when the seal's head goes up for a look. To the seal, a teliwak must look like an ice hummock. But if the hunter is not patient and cautious, that ice hummock will move when the seal looks up, and the animal will slither to its hole in a flash.

Markosie and Akpaliapik usually got within fifty yards of the seal before shooting. But they could get that close only if all conditions were favorable. They had to be upwind of the animal, which might mean a circuit of a mile or more to get in position to start the stalk. The sun had to be hazy or, if strong, high in the sky, so the man and his teliwak would cast no telltale shadow. It doesn't matter too much if a warm spell has melted a little water on top of the ice; I know, for I've wriggled about fifty yards on my belly through a layer of cold water without making a sound that would disturb a seal. On the other hand, if the warm spell has been followed by a freeze, stalking is almost impossible, for the new, thin layer of ice crackles as one moves over it. The seal may hear the crackle after you have spent an hour and a half stalking him — and down he goes into the sea. You stand up and stretch your aching bones and shiver away the small rivulet that got inside your parka, and you want to go home and open a can of food. But your Eskimo friend just shrugs and looks for another seal.

Before white cotton cloth came to the high Arctic with the white man, the Eskimo had no teliwak. He stalked the seal without hiding behind a make-believe ice hummock. This put him at a great disadvantage compared to the seal's other great enemy, the polar bear. The polar bear is, after all, his own teliwak, being almost all white, and thus looking a great deal like an ice hummock when he stays still. Even his sharp claws are set well back on his paws so they do not click as he creeps over the ice. Still there is one emphatic giveaway on a polar bear — his big black snout. He has been seen to creep toward an ootook slowly and quietly, on his belly, just like an Eskimo, but holding one white paw over his nose!

In the old days, Eskimos stalked seals in somewhat the same way, but they had to be more devious, for their clothes were dark, made of animal skins. How could they get within a few yards of a wary seal?

Special Constable Ningu showed me one day, when we were returning from a fruitless walrus hunt. In the distance we saw an ootook.
The wind was right, the sun was right, but we had no teliwak. Ningu
walked to an iceberg between him and the seal; beyond it there was
nothing but smooth, flat ice, covered with a couple of inches of snow.
Ningu came out from behind the berg on his belly, about two hundred yards from the seal. The seal woke up, raised its head, and looked
around. I thought that Ningu would be motionless at this time, but I
realized later that he would have been an unknown and disturbing
dark blob on the landscape to the seal, if he had not moved. Ningu
lifted his head high, pushed himself up on his elbows, turned his head
around, wriggled his buttocks slightly, and waggled his feet. Then he
put his head down between his hands. The seal put its head down for
another quick nap, and Ningu scurried forward on his belly for about
three yards. Ningu told me later, "I think like a seal. I feel like a seal. I
am a seal."

Ningu got closer and closer. The three-hour wait proved to me
once more what endless patience the Eskimos have. Near the end,
when Ningu was only thirty yards away, the seal took fright and
scrambled into its hole. Ningu stood up and trudged back to the sleds.

"My feet are too big," he said. "If your feet are too big, they do not
look like a seal's rear flippers." And, supposedly, the seal knows this.

A few weeks after my arrival, the seal hunting reached its peak.
There were a number of "leads" in Jones Sound, long cracks of open
water caused by the strong currents. Sometimes you could see forty
or fifty or more seals lying on both sides of a lead in the ice, heads
going up, heads going down, flippers wiggling.

But when we got to the cracks in the ice, I forgot about hunting.
How did you get across? That's what Markosie and Akpaliapik
wanted to do, for there was more game on the other side. A four-foot
crack of open water barely slowed them down, for the dogs leaped
over without hesitating. A six-foot crack was enough to make the
dogs hesitate, so Akpaliapik and Markosie just picked the animals up,
one by one, and threw them across. The sleds were long enough to
bridge the crack safely.

Another time we came to a crack too wide to cross, so Akpaliapik
turned to travel along the edge of it. In half an hour he found what he
was looking for, a natural ice bridge in the fissure. The bridge was

strong enough but narrow. Akpaliapik's komatik got across all right, and Markosie followed, with Doug Sinclair shooting the action from one side and I from the other. Two of Markosie's dogs, scrambling for a footing on the narrow piece of ice, slipped and fell into the water. The other dogs pulled the sled across as Markosie lunged toward the water, grabbed the dogs' lines, and pulled them up on the ice. Luckily it was not terribly cold that day, so the dogs were all right. They had been in the icy water less than a minute, and they warmed themselves by pulling the sled at a good clip. If dogs are in the water for more than a few minutes they are done for, and their owner knows it. They come down with a lung infection that kills them in a day or two.

Our party got eight seals that day. But the most exciting find was the baby seal that Imooshie located. The boy was with Markosie beside a breathing hole. The hunter watched the small circle of open water carefully, for it heaved up just before the seal rose to breathe. The harpoon was in the animal before it had a chance to take half a breath, and in a few more minutes Markosie had it up on the ice. As he hauled it away from the hole, Imooshie threw himself down on the ice. He seemed to be sticking his arm down into the hole as far as he could reach.

Then I realized that this was not an ordinary breathing hole, but an *aglo*, leading to a cavern or two in the hard-packed snow where the mother seal bears and cares for its young. This was just about the right time to look for baby seal, for they would be about six weeks old. In another week or two the mother would be teaching the baby to swim and get along on its own.

With a whoop of joy, Imooshie dragged a baby seal from the hole by its flippers. It wriggled and squirmed in his arms and finally flopped to the snow. Imooshie scooped it up again, and everyone near by came up to congratulate him. The seal was a bit under two feet long and weighed about twenty pounds. Since its mother had been killed by Markosie, it would have died in its *aglo*, if some beast of prey had not found it first. So we were all happy at the thought of bringing home a new pet to the Eskimo hunting camp.

The baby seal, however, had other ideas. When it was put down on the snow at the camp, surrounded by delighted children and grown-ups, it had just one idea — to get away. It humped itself along in an awkward seal crawl with such determination that it was funny. But only at first. When faced by a line of friendly children, it turned and raced where it saw an open space. When picked up and petted, it wriggled. When fed, it would not eat.

"Never mind," I said. "It will feel more at home in a few days. And it might as well be here, where people will look out for it." And everyone agreed except the baby seal, who by this time had the name of Tootoo.

So we had a problem on our hands that we had never anticipated. I had two good brief sequences involving the baby seal, but then what could we do with the creature that so determinedly resisted all offers of friendship? There was no place to leave it at the Eskimo camp, so we took it back to the RCMP post at Grise Fiord, where we had to keep it safe from the dogs and from its own desire to go back to its mother's breathing hole. Why didn't we just let it go? It would have died; it did not even know how to swim. A baby seal has to be taught, and this one's mother had not got around to it.

We had planned a trip to Tubtuvik, the place of the caribou, hoping to get some films of this important deer that had in recent years seemed to avoid Ellesmere Island. It was a simple trip for Eskimos, but the baby seal presented problems. Constable Bacchus, Markosie, Akpaliapik, Imooshie, Doug Sinclair, and I were going off together. Constable Jenkin and Special Constable Ningu were scheduled for a few days of travel to Eskimo camps to take care of several cases of influenza and possibly pneumonia that had broken out, leaving no one to take care of Tootoo.

We decided to put together a small crate and bring Tootoo along with us to Tubtuvik, letting him take up valuable space on a komatik. He didn't enjoy the trip at all, but crouched in one corner of the crate and whimpered like a baby the whole time.

The thirty-mile trip to Tubtuvik was uneventful, although I would not have thought so a few weeks before, when I first arrived at Ellesmere. We had stretches of bad hummocky ice, lovely stretches of "smooth sailing," two leads to cross, luckily quite narrow, and we killed four seals along the way. The wind began to whip up vigorously toward the end of the journey and we had trouble setting up the tents we had brought along. We were rushing the season a bit with tents, which usually didn't come into use for another month, but they served. We fed the dogs and chained them down, and drank scalding strong tea and ate bannock, seal liver and heart. And then to bed. By this time I was beginning to learn the Eskimo technique of stripping before climbing into my sleeping bag. At first, I couldn't do it, with the temperature around zero or below. I learned though, because it gave my regular clothes a chance to air and my skin a chance to breathe.

We were peaceful and happy, even though the strong winds tugged at our tents. I had not learned the Eskimo art of falling asleep within a few minutes of lying down. I heard a noise that no one else heard. It was Tootoo, flipping and flapping against the sides of his crate, whimpering and crying. He was not cold. He should not have been hungry. He was just trying to get back to the one spot that he knew as home.

I remember lying there, exhausted and wanting to go to sleep, and thinking of a leopard I had seen in Africa. It had been trapped and put in a strong cage of hardwood with a wire-mesh lining and would have no part of our affection or care. It threw itself against the sides of its cage until its face was a bloody mask, then fell into one corner, half-conscious. If you came back a half hour later, it would have recovered and would throw itself at the cage again, trying to get at you and kill you.

The baby seal did not want to kill. It couldn't. It was not mean, as leopards can be mean and vindictive and bloodthirsty. The baby seal just wanted to go back home, and except for the leopard, I have rarely seen such determination. I crawled out of my sleeping bag, put on my clothes and walked outside. The baby seal's crate was still on one of the sleds, so I pulled it out of hearing range. I slept the rest of the daylight night.

After three rough days of overcast skies, high winds, and no filming we headed for Craig Harbor on the southeastern end of Ellesmere. Craig was the first RCMP post on the island, established in 1923. It proved a most unfortunate choice, for the winds swept down from the North Pole and then were funneled, by two outlying islands, directly at Craig Harbor. Not only that, but the anchorage was not very good for the yearly visit of the ship. Meanwhile, however, everyone put up with it and explored the rest of the island. By 1956, they had found the best possible spot, at Grise Fiord, about forty miles west of Craig Harbor.

There was still a shack at Craig, however, and we intended to stay there, with some of us going into a small tool shop that had managed to withstand the winds. The meeting at Craig was prearranged, since Constable Jenkin and Special Constable Ningu planned to have their medical chores completed in three days, after which they'd bring their boats to Craig so we could look for walrus.

Each boat was loaded on a komatik. One was a twenty-foot Peterhead canoe, wide of beam and as seaworthy as a canoe can be, with a ten-horsepower motor; the other was a sixteen-foot rowboat, with a ten-horsepower motor. The men made the trip to Craig Harbor without incident, except that they wound up with ten seal they had shot on the way. We would have no worries about food for us or the dogs — sixty dogs eat about two hundred and fifty pounds of meat a day. Then we spent three more days while the wind howled and tore at the old shack, and the dogs howled to match the wind, and little Tootoo whimpered and cried and pressed himself against his crate, trying to get out. Meanwhile we ate and drank tea and rested and listened to stories told by Akpaliapik and Markosie, translated into a tape recorder by Constable Bob Bacchus. Once in a while we looked at the two-foot waves that churned up Jones Sound.

Then came a glorious morning, with the sun shining, the fog lifted, the wind low and the sea calm. We sledded the boats into the water — always open at Craig Harbor — and headed north among the ice floes. Ahead of us we could see dozens of seals slipping off the ice into the water. We did not try to catch them because we had plenty of seal for our immediate needs.

In a short time, maybe half an hour, we saw a lone walrus sleeping on a good-sized ice floe that was drifting slowly with the tide. Although it was unusual to find a single walrus apart from its family, we decided that this might make a good hunt for the cameras. Since the wind was wrong, we had to circle around in the open water. We were only a few yards away when the walrus woke up and looked startled. It slid into the water just as Akpaliapik's harpoon went into it. Meanwhile, Markosie had blown up the *avatuk*, a large bladder made of a sealskin sewn up at all apertures. This large float is attached by a fifty-foot line to the harpoon head. The walrus dives for the bottom, but the avatuk keeps him from going too far. He tries to swim away, and the avatuk follows him. Eventually the hunter can get in the final blow. Doug Sinclair and I filmed the kill from the second boat, and watched the Eskimos drag the walrus ashore. Although it had looked huge to me, it was a relatively small walrus, a female weighing no more than fifteen hundred pounds. The old males are more than two thousand pounds.

The next day we saw a huge ugruk, or bearded seal, in the distance, but he slipped off into the water before we got close enough to use even a telescopic lens. We went on, even though the winds were blowing more strongly, and finally sighted a herd of walrus floating on a large ice pan. They were singularly unconcerned as we approached a neighboring ice pan and boarded it with our boats so that we could float along beside them on the tide, not more than forty yards away.

We floated along side by side, taking pictures as fast as we could because we thought that the herd would get frightened and break up any moment. But they were not nearly as worried as we were. There were about twenty of them asleep, lying half on, half off each other. One huge fellow at the northern end of the floe, with his left forequarters draped over one of his females, eyed us casually. He was certainly not frightened, as he had probably never seen humans before. The big fellow yawned, and scratched his ear with one flipper. This annoyed his underlying wife, who shifted petulantly. He slapped her with a flipper and looked around.

I wanted some footage of several tons of walrus sliding off an ice floe into the water, but they were not about to move. I spoke to Constable Jenkins, who asked the hunters to fire a round or two over their heads. With the blast of gunfire, the old boy looked up, and two others turned their heads. Then they settled down again. We waited. And I remember thinking, during this period, that I was not very bright to be standing on a drifting ice floe hundreds of miles north of the Arctic Circle waiting for some walrus to move so I could film them.

We used up a box of valuable cartridges before we got those sedate walrus to move. First they sent a scout to see what we were. He oozed off into the water, swam toward our floe, looked us over, and went back with his report. It was unfavorable, although it made no one panic. They slithered into the water slowly, and we managed to get the whole operation in our cameras. If they had been annoyed, they could have turned around and punctured holes in our boats, which we had launched back into the water. The king walrus has tusks about eighteen inches long.

We headed back to Craig Harbor, a little concerned about the increasingly high winds and choppy water. Jenkin told me later that if we had been out in Jones Sound another half hour we probably would have been swamped, for those big waves were back again.

The winds increased during the night, and the boards in the shack whined, Tootoo whimpered, and the Eskimos slept the sleep of the dead. When the dawn looked even more threatening, we decided we had done all the filming we could. We headed back by dogsled for Grise Fiord. And in a hurry, for the constables and the Eskimos were fearful that sudden high winds might break up the sea ice at the end of Jones Sound.

"If we can get past the headland," Jenkin told me, "we'll be all right, for it breaks the wind." But we were all tense and worried.

For an hour we raced, with the dogs pulling for all they were worth, the men cracking the whips and urging on the dogs. The ice groaned beneath us and I thought it might crack at any moment, but we got around the headland, the winds died, and we were safe. I was riding in the canoe lashed on one of the sleds. Akpaliapik tucked me in with the heavy sleeping furs, and we were on our way. I tried to doze, but was not really sleepy, so I took out a book I had with me, something of Peter Freuchen's. Jenkin later told me that he had never seen anyone travel in such comfortable, kingly luxury in the Arctic.

My reading was interrupted by a detour to a nearby iceberg, where Constable Jenkin had spotted fresh bear tracks. I was out of the boat in a flash, readying my camera and calling to Doug Singlair. But the dogs were not excited, as they would have been if the bear had been within a mile of them. We followed the tracks a short distance, but lost them in an area swept bare by the wind. I was terribly disappointed, but Markosie and Akpaliapik assured me that we would encounter a bear some other time during our hunts.

When we went on, I got on top of a sled covered with gear and skins, rather than into the boat. It was smooth going and the dogs knew they were headed for home.

We were about five minutes from Grise Fiord, and the dogs had started to howl, when I felt a sudden drop in temperature. I had been wearing heavy woolen mittens, but my hands got cold, so I put on a pair of heavy fur-lined leather gauntlets over the wool, as I always did when it was unusually cold. As the dogs got closer to home they ran faster, and the ice got more broken and hummocky. At one point the komatik slid sideways down a slope and crashed into a big hummock. My right hand, gripping the side of the sled, was between it and the ice. I thought my fingers were completely smashed. The pain was excruciating.

Jenkin examined my hand on the spot, and found that the inner woolen mitten was in shreds, whereas the outer leather glove was not damaged. I can't figure it out, and I don't need to, since I suffered only from swollen and purple fingers for a week, a good deal of pain, and the loss of a woolen glove. My luck was still holding.

Special Constable Ningu had to make one short hunt that saddened us all. Tootoo, the baby seal, would not allow himself to be tamed no matter how much we fed and petted him. One day he finally got away from the post. Ningu grabbed his rifle and followed his tracks. In half an hour he was back, with news that he had shot Tootoo. "No point in letting him suffer," he said.

We had another premature spell of warmer weather, with a film of water covering most of the ice. The big ice floes were beginning to break up, but we could still travel for miles on the sleds. A cold snap followed the warm spell, and the surface water froze into sharp-edged slivers that cut the dogs' paws. So Akpaliapik and Markosie got out shoes for their huskies. They were small flaps of sealskin that fitted over the paws and were tied with thongs around the dogs' legs. Each shoe had slits for the claws to stick through, so the huskies could get traction on the ice. The animals didn't seem to mind wearing their boots.

The cold snap was followed by another warm spell, and the time for departure was drawing near.

The plane had to come while there was still enough safe ice to land on. Otherwise it would have to wait more than a month, until August, when it could use pontoons to land on the open water. So it came to take Doug Sinclair and me back to civilization.

Doug and I hated to leave. Not only had we become attached to our Eskimo friends, but we felt that although we had results beyond our expectations, we had not yet exhausted the possibilities of filming the Eskimo way of life.

This was confirmed when we edited the film in New York. In Ottawa again, I showed this first version to Commissioner Harvison and some of the members of his staff. He did not hesitate in granting my request to return to Ellesmere the following year, and he assured me of continued cooperation.

We took off in the Otter in early spring. My excitement grew when we approached Grise Fiord and I spotted the post buildings and saw a crowd gathered on the sea ice where we were to land. As I stepped from the plane I heard someone call. And there, standing about twenty feet from me, was Markosie — taking a picture of me with a small box camera which Jenkin had taught him how to handle, laughing so hard that he could hardly hold the camera still. He thought it was one of the best jokes in the world to be taking a picture of the man who was always so busy taking pictures of others.

We completed filming family life within the igloo during the next few weeks. Last year we had taken good sequences of the Eskimo hunting seal as he basked in the sun on the ice alongside of his aglu or along the edge of a lead in the ice. Under these conditions the Eskimo could use his gun, but now, at this time of the year, when the effect of the Arctic winter had still clamped an ice barrier on the surface of the sea, the seals must be hunted with the harpoon. Seals are mammals and they have to breathe so they manage to keep open a number of small holes for breathing, breaking the ice with their snouts. Sometimes snow banks up over the hole; not enough to cut off the air — just enough to make it hard to locate. If the dogs go anywhere near such a naturally camouflaged hole, they smell the seal and set up a mighty howling. With the breathing hole located, the Eskimo gets the dogs out of the way and takes up his post beside the hole, waiting for the seal to come up and breathe.

Akpaliapik would stand beside such a hole for more than two hours, right arm upraised, harpoon poised. I don't know if anyone has discovered how long a seal can go without breathing, but it is a long time. And a seal has a number of breathing holes. So while Akpaliapik might stand over one, the creature could be taking in air at another hole several yards away.

The harpoon of the Eskimos is stocky and heavy, about five feet long, with a detachable point to which a long line is attached. In the old days the point was made of stone, but is now iron, and it flattens out under the hide when the line is pulled, giving a solid anchor in the hunted animal. The line — supplied by the skin of the ugruk — allows for a run of forty or fifty feet before the tugging match begins. The Eskimo usually wins.

One day luck was with us. We were out on a hunt and had found several breathing holes of seals. Young Imooshie was along and took up his post beside one hole, arm raised, harpoon ready. Markosie and the others were waiting beside other holes. I thought that the picture of a boy hoping to be a hunter would make a good shot, so the camera was going when Imooshie's arm flashed down and he began tugging on the line attached to the harpoon point. I yelled, because the seal was dragging Imooshie toward the breathing hole, and I knew the young man would never let go of his first kill. He called, *"Atak! Atak!"* meaning *uncle,* and Markosie came running. Together they pulled the seal out of the hole. It was a great occasion, so Markosie cut open the seal and we all had lunch. I remember that Markosie and I sat on the seal's carcass while we ate steaming hot liver — you put a chunk in your mouth and cut it off with a knife close to your nose — and heart, and flippers. Those are the delicacies.

Most of the time, however, we brought the seals back to the hunting camp and everyone had his share. And that holds true whether hunting is good or hunting is bad. Even the cleverest Eskimos are faced with possible starvation every few years. The caribou change their migration pattern. The narwhals do not appear in the summer. But the seals are usually there. A hunter who has been lucky brings back his catch and dumps it in the center of the camp. Everyone helps himself to his proportionate share.

One day, the sixty dogs in our camp needing more food, Sinclair, Jenkin and I accompanied Markosie and Akpaliapik on another seal hunt. We were less than an hour away from camp when we came upon the fresh tracks of a big polar bear on the surface snow of the frozen sea. We followed his tracks for about three hours when Akpaliapik spotted him and shouted, *"Nanook! Nanook!"* He was about a half a mile away among some hummocks. Fortunately the bear was downwind so the dogs did not get his scent and become excited. Taking advantage of this fact, we turned the two sleds over, anchoring them so the dogs could not follow us.

We started out, Akpaliapik and Markosie at a good clip, Doug Sinclair, Constable Jenkin and I behind, loaded down with still and movie cameras. It was easy going at first, for the snow was only a few inches deep and hard-packed. But as we went on, the snow got deeper and deeper and so soft that it could not support our weight. As we ploughed through the stuff up to our knees, I realized that I had not fastened the snug tops of my fur-lined boots, which would have kept out the snow. Snow filtered in, and a numbing cold began to creep around my ankles. But I couldn't stop now. Sinclair was in the same fix, and we both swore at ourselves for being so foolhardy. Luckily it was not a terribly cold day, so were not in danger of freezing our feet. It was just mighty uncomfortable. Jenkin wore mukluks and did not have our problem.

I was amazed to see that the Eskimos did not sink deep in the snow as Sinclair and I did. They ran in a kind of crouch, their bodies leaning forward so that the thrust of each step was back rather than down. I tried to do it, but only floundered. In time, however, we slogged our way to the end of the deep soft snow and entered a miniature Alps of ice crags and crevices. We could just barely make out the heads of Markosie and Akpaliapik in front of us, and we hurried after them as fast as we could.

After half an hour of turning and twisting among the big hummocks, we suddenly saw the hunters only a short distance ahead of us. Akpaliapik and Markosie, harpoons ready, were cautiously reconnoitering. They had apparently lost the bear in the maze of ice hills, but knew he was close. Sinclair and I came up beside Jenkin, who told us where he thought the bear was, about fifty yards ahead. We walked up closer to Markosie and Akpaliapik, getting ourselves set for pictures should the bear suddenly appear.

And suddenly it *did* appear, rearing up from behind a hummock that Markosie had pointed out. Nanook surveyed the situation carefully. He looked at each man in turn, then glanced behind and to each side. Then down he went again, out of sight. But within a minute he appeared much closer, walking along majestically, without question the king of the Arctic. He stopped, turned, and climbed up on a hummock, giving us a magnificent close-up. But he was obviously confused and did not know where to go.

Markosie and Akpaliapik moved further apart, so that they could spear the bear from either side if he should make an attack. I shifted my position so I could cover Markosie with my camera, while Sinclair concentrated on Akpaliapik. The bear went back down the hummock and suddenly slid down the ice into a water hole that we had not noticed. Water splashed up around him, but he was only about half submerged.

The hole was a crack made by the tide, and the bear had probably been hunting seal there. His instinct to head for water when in danger sent him to the only water around. But it was anything but a safe place, for he was almost within a spear's throw of both hunters and, being in the hole, he could not make a quick charge.

Akpaliapik took two steps forward and launched his harpoon, attached to a fifty-foot line, with great force. It cut a gash in the bear's chest, and blood streamed down over his white fur. As Akpaliapik pulled in his harpoon for another shot, Markosie sent his weapon flying. The harpoon struck the bear in the head.

The big animal was infuriated, took the spear in his mouth and, using one paw, bent the shaft double.

The bear decided to emerge from the hole; he might have attacked any one of us. The blood was drumming in my head. I was hardly skilled at moving about in deep snow. For once I began to feel my years, tied like weights to my legs. If the animal had gone for me I might have dropped in my tracks.

It seemed to me that the bear epitomized everything the Eskimo had to struggle against in the open wilderness: hardship and uncertainty, an often pitiless nature that was for each member of the community a personal and implacable threat. It was that threat which made these people the most tightly knit, yet most individualized human beings I had ever seen. It made them ready at any moment to give up possession or comfort to a stranger. Not because of some abstract ideal: for them it was the only way of life that made sense. So each man threw into the communal lot his strength, wisdom and skill, as if nature had decreed, *Cooperate or die!*

Perhaps from a distance, or viewed on the screen, the bear would have seemed a thing of beauty; but like the crystal-white landscape, the beauty could best be grasped from a vantage point of safety and warmth. Its determination to make a final charge seemed almost personal — as if it had chosen to settle its score upon me. I waited for the stroke that would end the drama.

It was Akpaliapik who stopped the beast. He lunged with his spear; it struck home. The bear took two steps, then slowly, almost gracefully, it sank down upon the ice.

Soon we were scudding homeward on our sleds, driving like the wind, with the clean, icy air whipping our faces. The sense of danger was vanishing; I was feeling young again.

Yet for a moment I had once more understood something you might call the primitive experience, understood it in the best possible way: by living in it. I had found it before among the Ituri Pygmies, the Jivaros, the Colorados, only by joining them in their most basic life activities: their hunting and fishing trips, their ceremonies, their preparations for war, even their family problems.

What is the meaning of primitive experience? I have tried many times to sum it up, at least for myself, as I did that day on the sled. It means, I think, man confronted by raw nature and answering the challenge with all the incalculable resources of his physical skill, wits, and imagination. The result is anything you want to call it — good or bad — but it surely amounts to the widest range of behavior that any living thing on this planet is capable of. There is no single primitive way.

The Eskimos were in many ways unlike any other primitive people I had known. They had no wars and no life of superstitious fears, like the Stone Age men of New Guinea. They didn't go in for painful initiation rites. They believed in a variety of spirits and taboos, but these were not the controlling, all-pervasive factors in their lives. What better illustration of their freedom from complicated rite or ceremony than Akpaliapik? He was medicine man, or *angakok*, of the Grise Fiord group, and while he was someone to be admired, he was certainly not to be feared.

I couldn't help thinking, as we raced along the snow, that the Eskimo way of life would be changing soon. The radio had brought the welcome news that *C. D. Howe*, the supply ship, was ahead of schedule. In a few weeks it would steam up Jones Sound to Grise Fiord, carrying doctors, nurses, dentists, and X-ray technicians and, perhaps most important, a schoolteacher. On board the ship was lumber for the construction of a schoolhouse. Education would bring the Eskimos swiftly into the modern world.

We were nearing the settlement full of our exciting news about nanook. The dogs hurried their pace, barked loudly, jostled and churned up the snow. We glided over an ice field, careened off hummocks. I knew that in a few weeks people would be asking me how it was that anyone could live in a place like this. Then I thought of Markosie and Akpaliapik, and I knew once more that of all the people I'd seen, the Eskimos were the happiest. They were all convinced that there was no place on earth like the vast, cold expanse where they lived and hunted. And despite the chill wind already turning angry, something inside me agreed.

INDEX